Reading Improvement
in the
Secondary School

Reading Improvement
in the
Secondary School

EMERALD DECHANT
Marymount College of Kansas

Prentice-Hall, Inc., *Englewood Cliffs, New Jersey*

Library of Congress Cataloging in Publication Data

DECHANT, EMERALD V
    Reading improvement in the secondary school.

    Includes bibliographies.
    1. Reading (Secondary). I. Title.
LB1632.D37   428.4'07'12   72-8845
ISBN 0-13-755017-0

PRINTED IN THE UNITED STATES OF AMERICA

10 9 8 7 6 5 4 3

PRENTICE-HALL INTERNATIONAL, INC., London
PRENTICE-HALL OF AUSTRALIA, PTY. LTD., Sydney
PRENTICE-HALL OF CANADA, LTD., Toronto
PRENTICE-HALL OF INDIA PRIVATE LIMITED, New Delhi
PRENTICE-HALL OF JAPAN, INC., Toyko

*To my wife, Deloris,
and to our children,
Randy, Lori, and Pami*

Contents

6   Teaching Word-Recognition Skills: The Decoding Process   *135*

Introduction   Terminology   *Phonics and Phonic Analysis*
Phonetics   Phonemics   The Alphabet   Word Analysis
Phonic, or Phonetic, Method   Linguist   Linguistic Phonics
Teaching the Beginning Consonant   *The Letters* K *and* Q
The Sounds Represented by C *and* G   *The Sounds Represented by* D
The Sounds Represented by N   *The Sounds Represented by* S
The Sounds Represented by T   *The Sounds Represented by* X
The Sounds Represented by Y   *The Sounds Represented by* Z
Teaching the Short Vowel   Teaching the End Consonant
Teaching the Beginning Consonant Blends
Teaching the Ending Consonant Blends   The Speech Consonants
The Diagraph Ch   *The Diagraphs* Sh *and* Th
The Diagraphs Wh, Gh, Ph, *and* Ng   The Long Vowels
The Principle of Variability   The Principle of Position
The Principle of Silentness   The Principle of Context
The Diphthongs   Teaching the Long Vowels
The Effect of *R* on a Preceding Vowel
Teaching Structural Analysis Skills   *Teaching the Compounds*
Teaching -ing   *The Past Tense with* ed   *Contractions*
Syllabication   Accentuation   Silent Letters
Multisyllabic Words   Common Sight Words   Summary
Questions for Discussion   Bibliography

7   Developing a Meaningful Vocabulary   *204*

Introduction   Techniques for Teaching Meaning
Study and Analysis of the Context   Synonyms and Antonyms
Qualifying Words   Overworked Words and Phrases   Homonyms
Roots, Prefixes, and Suffixes   Compound Words
Figurative and Idiomatic Expressions
Developing Skill in Using Punctuation Marks as Clues to Meaning
Study of the Dictionary, Text Glossaries, and Word Lists
Study of Technical Vocabularies   A Chart for the Classroom
Summary   Questions for Discussion   Bibliography

8   Advancing the Student's Comprehension Skills   *242*

Introduction   Comprehension Skills   Developing Comprehension Skills
Word Meaning   Phrase Meaning   Sentence Meaning
Paragraph Meaning   Reading for the Main Idea   Reading for Details
Reading for Organization   Reading for Evaluation (Critical Reading)

Reading Improvement
in the
Secondary School

SECONDARY READING:
AN OVERVIEW

It is important that the teacher and the reader of this book acquire some understanding of how reading in the secondary school fits into the total picture of reading education. Every teacher should understand the total process.

We begin our exploration of the reading process by taking a look at definitions of reading.

The Latins had a phrase, *tot capita, tot sententiae,* that perhaps best describes our predicament when we seek to define reading. There are just about as many descriptions or definitions of reading as there are "reading experts." Let us then reserve our definition of reading until later and list here eight characteristics of reading:

1. *Reading is a sensory process.*

    Reading requires the use of the senses, especially vision. The reader must react visually to the graphic symbols. Reading is the successful response to the visual or graphic forms of language. The symbols themselves must be legible, the eyes must see clearly and singly, and the light must be adequate. The good reader must also *hear* the sounds in words. The student needs to be able to make proper associations between the spoken sound and the graphic symbol.

2. *Reading is a perceptual process.*

    Reading occurs when meaning is brought to graphic stimuli. It is ultimately an intellectual act. It is a progressive apprehension of the meanings and ideas represented by a sequence of words. It includes seeing the word, recognizing the word, being aware of the word's meaning, and relating the word to its context. This is perception in its fullest sense.

3. *Reading is a response.*

Reading is a system of responses made to some graphic stimuli. These include the vocal or subvocal muscular responses made at the sight of the word, eye movements during reading, physical adaptations to the reading act such as postural changes, critical and evaluative responses to what is being read, emotional involvement of the reader, and meaningful reactions to the words.

4. *Reading is a learned response.*

Reading is a response that must be learned by the student and is under control of the mechanisms of motivation and reinforcement. Reading is a perceptual process, but it is also an associative process. It involves the *learned* association of the spoken with the written word. The same laws of learning that govern all other learned processes govern the student's learning to read.

5. *Reading is a developmental task.*

Development tasks have one basic characteristic: The student's readiness for them depends on the student's general development. There is a most teachable moment for each of the specific skills in reading. The student's level of achievement in reading depends on his overall growth and development.

6. *Reading can be an interest and a motive.*

Reading may become an interest or a goal in its own right. It may then motivate other activity.

7. *Reading is a learning process.*

Reading may become one of the chief media for learning. The student can use reading to acquire knowledge and to change his own attitudes, ideals, and aspirations. Genuine reading involves integration and promotes the development of the reader. As Aldous Huxley points out, "Every man who knows how to read has it in his power to magnify himself, to multiply the ways in which he exists, to make his life full, significant and interesting."

8. *Reading is a language process.*

Reading is a process of putting the reader in contact and communication with ideas. It is the culminating act of the communicative and language process, initiated by the thoughts of the writer and expressed through the symbols on the printed page. Communication from writer to reader occurs only if the reader can take meaning to the printed page. Without the reader, communication via the printed page is impossible. Reading might be described as the recognition and perception of language structures as

wholes, leading to the comprehension of both the surface and deep meanings which these structures communicate.*

Part I consists of two chapters: Chapter 1, "Introduction," and Chapter 2, "The Nature of the Reading Process." Chapter 1 identifies the general goals of reading instruction on the secondary level and the specific
goals of this book. It deals with such topics as the need for reading
instruction on the secondary level, the reading competency of the secondary school student, the goals of a secondary developmental program,
and the specific deficiencies in reading that need to be corrected.

* Marilyn Birkley, "Effective Reading Improvement in the Classroom through
Teacher Self-Improvement Programs," *Journal of Reading,* 14 (November 1970),
94–100.

Introduction

IN THIS INTRODUCTION WE SHOULD LIKE to identify the general goals of reading instruction on the secondary level and the particular goals of this book. Goals of teaching reading on the secondary level have been gradually developed through the years, and being able to identify them seems to be a first essential for an effective reading program.

Educators have come to accept that reading instruction and learning to read are lifelong, sequential, and developmental processes, extending from kindergarten through high school, college, and adult life. We expect gradual refinement of all skills (19). We look for both horizontal and vertical growth in word knowledge, comprehension, study skills, rate skills, content-area reading skills, and overall reading habits and interests. We have come to accept that direct teaching of reading skills must proceed in an unbroken line from first grade through twelfth, buttressed by the application of skills in every subject where reading is a significant means of learning (9).

We now realize that not even the brightest youngster in the best of schools can learn all he needs to know about reading by the end of six or eight years of schooling (8). The reasons for this are readily apparent. First of all, as Einstein noted, "reading is the most complex task that man has ever devised for himself." Reading involves the interpreting of printed symbols and the making of discriminative reactions to the ideas expressed by them. Second, it is the experience of teacher after teacher that reading processes can be taught and learned only in the context of the ideas and the content of the reading materials themselves (8). Third, with the tremendous variety of knowledge that is being discovered and

5

accumulated each day, we are literally "burning up" reading skills faster than we can develop them (17). It is rather preposterous to assume that by the time the pupil reaches sixth grade he has developed all the skills needed to assimilate the vast amount of knowledge taught at the high school level. Fourth, and perhaps of greatest significance, many students come to the secondary school with a definite lag in the development of their reading skills.

And yet, there exists today a noticeable void in the teaching of reading, after the elementary years. Squire (17), surveying 158 high schools, found that in the tenth grade less than 5 percent of the instructional time was devoted to the teaching of reading and in the twelfth grade it was less than 3 percent. There is still far too little provision for developmental reading programs in the junior and senior high schools. We are still not helping enough students meet the more complex demands of the curriculum that they are being asked to master. Society requires adolescents to read so they may come to know and to learn, but we are not doing our best in helping them to master the developmental tasks necessary for such learning.

It is not enough for the subject-matter teacher to complain, "But he can't read." What is usually meant by such a statement is that the student cannot read *this* or *that* textbook with adequate understanding. The word *read* should always be used as a transitive verb. The student is not just reading; he is reading in a given area. As a little boy said, "You can't read readin', you gotta read sumpin' " (13).

CHANGES IN THE 1970s

One of the major characteristics of reading education in the 1970s may well be the witnessing of an organized extension of the developmental reading program into the secondary grades. More and more junior high and high school teachers are looking upon themselves not only as teachers of history or science but also as teachers of reading.

In the past the science teacher, the mathematics teacher, the social studies teacher, and the English teacher perceived themselves as untrained for a role in reading instruction. Consequently they felt that reading was the domain of the reading specialist, and they were unwilling to accept personal responsibility for reading instruction. This conception is gradually changing.

The high school teacher today accepts that he has something to contribute to the total reading program, but he is the first to admit that he also needs the help of the specialist.

Making a dual program work, in which one aspect involves the setting up of a special reading improvement program with a specialist in charge and another aspect involves the provision of functional teaching of reading by instructors in the various subject-matter areas, means that there must be both expert teachers of reading and subject-matter specialists who understand and respect each other's goals (9). It may well be that each expects too much from the other (9). The subject specialist wants every student to be reading up to grade level. When this does not occur, the reading program is perceived as a failure. The reading teacher, on the other hand, may want the subject-matter teacher to use easier textbooks than do in fact exist.

The content teacher's first concern is the teaching of *content,* the specific body of knowledge that includes extensive information and specific concepts. He may not see the need to teach *process* or the procedures by which students acquire information and generate concepts (11). He rarely selects resource materials merely because they require the use of certain reading skills and can serve as the vehicle for their development (11). The reading teacher on the other hand is principally concerned about skills. He teaches reading directly and for its own sake. The content teacher teaches reading fundamentally as a process to aid students' acquisition of course content.

Even assuming that he has a co-responsibility with the reading specialist, the high school teacher still asks: "How can I cover the course content assigned by the curriculum makers and at the same time teach reading?" Davis (8) answers this question in this way:

1. Give attention to student's readiness for reading the assigned material.
2. Give attention to the readability of assigned textbooks and supplementary reading material.
3. Show students how to preview reading material.
4. Help students realize the importance of varying style of reading to fit the materials and the purpose for reading.
5. Help students locate supplementary reading material on the subject.
6. Help students improve their knowledge of the vocabulary of the subject.

Doing one of these, however, or even all of them, does not seem to be sufficient. *This book is at least partially being written because new and specific instructional techniques are required for teaching reading on the junior high and high school levels.*

The content-area teacher and even more so the reading specialist will readily see the significant role of each when both realize that the best materials for teaching comprehension skills on the high school level are the textbooks used in the regular classroom. The content of the material determines to a great extent the process by which we read. The application of reading skills to the learning of content in literature, history, mathematics, science, and other subjects is just as important in the secondary school reading program as is direct teaching of the basic reading skills.

THE READING COMPETENCY OF THE STUDENT

We have already intimated that many secondary students cannot read up to grade level, but more importantly perhaps, many cannot read on their ability level.

Witty (22) in 1938 already noted that all high school teachers face the responsibility of adapting assignments to, of utilizing to a maximum, and of further developing the reading abilities of students who differ as much as six or eight grades in reading competence.

An analysis by a national advisory committee on dyslexia, entitled *Reading Disorders in the United States,* August 1969, published by the Department of Health, Education, and Welfare, gives the following statistics: (1) The National Center for Health Statistics reports in a study of seven thousand children between the ages of six and eleven that 25 percent of the eleven-year-olds read at levels two or more years below their grade level; (2) the norms on the *Metropolitan Achievement Test* indicate that the number of children who have not advanced beyond the primary level is 15 percent by the end of the fifth grade even among those who have never repeated a grade; and (3) a study in 1968 in Montgomery County, Maryland, a prosperous area with a well-supported school system, indicated that 13.3 percent of the children were underachievers in reading.

In the city of New York, 4,000 seventh graders were retained in 1958 because they were reading at or below fourth-grade level (16, p. 5). Foster (10) reports that in the Phoenix, Arizona, high schools, out of 1,106 entering freshmen tested, 21.4 percent had a reading ability of fifth grade or lower and 34 percent could not read at the seventh-grade level.

Furthermore, even among those who are reading at their level of ability, there are too many whose reading ability is not adequate for reading the textbook and the reference materials used on their grade level. It is said that at least three million young people in grades seven to twelve in America today are being given American literature, English literature, and World literature textbooks that they cannot read (2).

Unfortunately, we have not come close to approximating the improvability of the study habits (and, we might add, reading habits) of American high school students (23). A wide discrepancy still exists between what is actually being done and *what could be done*. The high school's obligation to work with retarded readers is no less so than on the elementary level. A society committed to universal public education must make every effort to permit each student to develop to his fullest.

The reading problems on the high school level, however, are not the sole or even the primary fault of poor teaching, lack of teaching, or even our lack of commitment to high school youth. Through our efforts at mass education, we have enticed more and more students to continue their education through and beyond the high school years. The results, while generally good, are not without some problems:

1. The overall intellectual level, capacity, or potential of the average student in the average high school classroom as measured by scholastic aptitude tests is somewhat less than it was forty years ago.

2. Because of our policies of promoting students on the basis of social and chronological growth and because of the concentrated efforts by professional educators and dedicated citizens which have increased the holding power of our schools, a greater percentage of students are staying in school and graduating, but also more are reading below grade level.

3. The range of individual differences is much greater in today's classroom. There are more slow learners, reluctant learners, disadvantaged readers, *and* retarded readers in the average classroom.

4. For some strange reason we expect all students to be able to read the same text, even though for some it is far too difficult and for others far too easy.

It is a safe estimate (see Figure 1-1) that at the ninth-grade level, in a classroom where IQs range from 85 to 145 and where the average age is 14, there will be roughly eight grade levels represented in that class. There will be some student who is capable of functioning mentally like the average youngster of 11.9, and there will be another who will function like the average youngster of 20 (college sophomore). About two-thirds of the group will have mental ages ranging from 11.9 to 16.1.

It is a well-known fact that the more effective the instruction on the elementary level, the greater will be the range of differences on the high school level. Thus, a chief reason for some of our problems on the high school level is the very fine education that many elementary school children are receiving.

The high school teacher is faced with the task of individualizing education for these youngsters without the benefit of multiple-level texts, often in overcrowded classrooms, in a school setting that does not have an organized reading program or a specific time set aside for the teaching

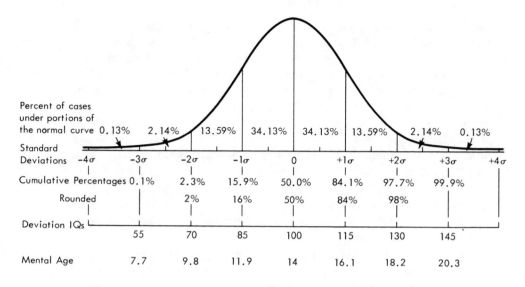

Percent of cases under portions of the normal curve	0.13%	2.14%	13.59%	34.13%	34.13%	13.59%	2.14%	0.13%
Standard Deviations	-4σ	-3σ	-2σ	-1σ	0	$+1\sigma$	$+2\sigma$	$+3\sigma$	$+4\sigma$
Cumulative Percentages	0.1%	2.3%	15.9%	50.0%	84.1%	97.7%	99.9%
Rounded		2%	16%	50%	84%	98%	
Deviation IQs	55	70	85	100	115	130	145
Mental Age	7.7	9.8	11.9	14	16.1	18.2	20.3

FIGURE 1-1

of reading, with a student who often does not want to improve his reading, and more importantly without adequate preparation in reading. Crowded classrooms and inadequate materials are no less causes of educational inadequacies than is teacher ineffectiveness, and yet teachers and teaching methods have to bear the brunt of public attack.

Teachers have always had to bear the brunt of criticism for inadequacies in instruction, especially reading instruction. Although some few teachers may indeed take off in September, cover a predetermined amount of material, and land in June only to find that one by one students have been lost, most teachers are doing an excellent job.

STUMBLING BLOCKS TO GOOD READING PROGRAMS

If elementary teachers are not solely or even primarily to blame for the inadequate reading performance of many high school students, who or what is to blame? Perhaps the greatest stumbling blocks to expanded and improved reading programs on the secondary level and to improved performance on the part of the student are the following (3):

1. There is no set pattern or adequate blueprint to follow in organizing a comprehensive high school developmental reading program, or for that matter, a corrective or remedial program.

2. There is often an unwillingness to budget adequately for a high school reading program.

3. There is a dearth of professionally trained and qualified reading personnel to teach secondary reading.

Let us first address ourselves to the last of these. Probably the most immediate and most urgent problem in meeting the reading needs of secondary students is staffing schools with teachers who have the necessary training to provide adequate instruction in reading in their content subjects (19). Unfortunately, only Indiana and Pennsylvania require junior high–high school teachers to have a course in reading as part of their professional education sequence.

The dearth of reading programs at the secondary level is another obvious block to good reading education. A study (4) in 1969 of the status of reading services in New Mexico secondary schools found that there were reading programs in only 79 of 217 secondary schools. Furthermore, the study reported that 76 percent of the personnel serving the secondary reading programs would not qualify for certification; 22 percent of the teachers had not had a single course in reading methodology.

Burnett (5) asked why there had been so little progress in making the teaching of reading an integral part of the high school curriculum and concluded that the fault lay with the teacher's preservice education. University faculty emphasize content and textbook learning while generally playing down the importance of materials and methods. The methods course teacher is pitied or despised by his academic colleagues. The content-area teacher does not consider reading to be a part of his subject area, and the result is that the secondary teacher trainee's orientation in reading is either nonexistent or at the best very general and superficial.

The task of the secondary teacher is aggravated even more by the lack of agreement on an organized sequence in teaching reading skills and the frequent and often unwarranted switching from one pedagogical procedure to another. With these conditions, it is exceedingly difficult to think of oneself as qualified and as knowing what needs to be taught and how to teach it.

Another of the problems on the high school level has been that of placing responsibility for meeting the needs of various readers. A special committee of the Kansas Association for Supervision and Curriculum Development divided the responsibilities as follows (12):

1. An extension of the developmental reading program which was begun in the elementary school is the responsibility chiefly of the English teachers.

2. Instruction in the reading skills peculiar to each subject-matter field is the responsibility of the teachers of each subject-matter field, including, of course, English.

3. Rapid progress reading instruction for pupils who, because of some misfortune or irresponsibility in the past, are not reading up to their capacity can best be carried on by specialized reading teachers.

4. Developmental reading for severely retarded or disabled readers, which may or may not involve remediation in reading as much as the removal of handicaps or blocks to the learning of reading, can best be carried on by specialized reading teachers.

5. Improvement in reading for academically talented pupils, who, although they are already reading well above their grade level, can read still better, can probably be directed by an interested and capable teacher or by a specialized reading teacher.

Even when the school employs a reading consultant, and this is becoming more common, we may not always be accomplishing what we thought we would. It is certainly true that when a consultant alerts a school to special reading needs, all teachers, not just the remedial teacher, can work to upgrade reading (21), but too often the rest of the faculty may feel that employment of a specialist frees it from major responsibility in reading. This is not desirable and will only stifle a program.

THE GENERAL GOALS OF A DEVELOPMENTAL PROGRAM

Before considering the specific goals of the secondary reading program and the specific deficiencies of the secondary learner, let us look at the more general goals of a developmental reading program on the secondary level.

1. The developmental program coordinates reading with the student's other communicative experiences.

2. The developmental program is a continuous program extending through the elementary and secondary grades and college. It provides instruction and guidance in basic reading skills, both silent and oral, in content-area reading, in study skills, and in recreational reading.

3. The developmental program is a flexible program that is adjusted at each level of advancement to the wide variations in student characteristics, abilities, and reading needs. Readiness for reading as a concept is applied at all age and grade levels.

4. The developmental program has a stimulating classroom setting in which attitudes and interests favorable to the development of habitual reading are developed effectively.

5. The developmental program provides plentiful reading materials that cover a wide range of difficulty and interest.

6. The developmental program provides for continuous measurement and evaluation of the effectiveness of the program as a whole and of its more specific aspects.

7. The developmental program provides for continuous identification and immediate remediation of deficiencies and difficulties encountered by any student.

8. The developmental program includes differentiated instruction to meet the needs of each student, but it does not ignore the commonality of needs, interests, and abilities among students.

9. The developmental program looks upon reading as a perceptual process rather than as a subject. Reading is taught on all levels in all subject areas by all teachers.

10. The developmental program emphasizes reading for understanding, thinking, and learning and aims to develop critical skills and flexibility in comprehension and rate in accordance with the student's abilities and purposes and the difficulty levels of the materials.

11. The developmental program allows each student to progress at his own success rate to his maximum capacity.

12. The developmental program seeks to develop reading maturity. A mature reader reads all kinds of materials. He perceives words quickly and accurately and reacts with correct meaning. He reads both for information and for recreation. He gets personal satisfaction from reading. He is a skillful, self-reliant reader who enriches his understandings and satisfactions throughout his life by reading.

13. The developmental program, based on sequential instruction in the basic skills and upon the need for differentiated instruction, gives appropriate emphasis to the sight and phonic methods and to group and individualized instruction.

Certainly, these goals are formidable. How to achieve these goals and how best to proceed so as to help us come closer to their attainment is difficult to outline.

Instruction in reading on the secondary level may be developmental, corrective, and remedial. It must be developmental because not even the brightest youngster can learn in the elementary school years all he needs to know about reading. It must be corrective and remedial because some students are not reading as well as they should.

The developmental aspect includes (1) basic instruction in fundamentals of learning to read, (2) organized instruction in each content area, and (3) encouragement of personal and recreational reading (16).

In many secondary schools, developmental instruction is still voluntary. Both corrective and remedial programs are more common and are often required courses.

In summary, a program of high school reading should *extend* and *develop* (16). It should extend those skills introduced in the elementary school and should develop those demanded by the more complex materials and learning tasks in high school. There is just not enough time in the elementary school to develop all the skills that the student will need in high school. The reading problem in the high school is often not so much a case of a breakdown as it is a failure to achieve a "buildup."

THE SPECIFIC GOALS OF THE SECONDARY READING PROGRAM

The specific goals of the secondary reading program are perhaps best identified by an analysis of the problems that students experience in reading.

McDonald (15), Crane (7), and Karlin (14), summarize, each in his own way, the deficiencies or needs of the high school reader. These include:

1. Deficiencies in vocabulary skills, particularly in the content areas
2. Lack of basic sight vocabulary
3. Deficiency in word-attack and structural analysis skills
4. Deficiency in sentence and paragraph comprehension
5. Inability to locate information, to get at the facts, to organize and remember ideas
6. Inability to read for study purposes
7. Need for deeper levels of interpretation and critical reading
8. Lack of fluency in reading
9. Narrow reading interests
10. Inability to outline or summarize a selection
11. Poor spelling ability
12. Inability to adjust reading habits to different reading situations and purposes

Karlin (14) summarizes the six major areas for which a secondary school reading program must make provision: *comprehension* (literal and interpretive understanding, critical evaluation, and individual word meanings); *study skills* (the location, selection, organization, and retention of information, following directions, and reading graphic aids); *appreciation* (style, form, ideas, and imagery); *rate of understanding* (varied speeds for reading narrative and expository writing, skimming, and scanning); *interests* (the development and extension of reading for leisure); and *word recognition* (structural analysis, phonics, and the dictionary).

It is practically impossible to discuss in detail within a few hundred pages all the phases of a complete reading program, and this book does not propose to do so. Rather, we have concentrated on the answers to a few basic questions: *What is reading?* (Chapter 2); *Who is the learner?* or *Whom must we teach?* (Chapters 3 and 4); *What is to be learned?* or *What must we teach?* and *How does the student learn the more advanced reading skills?* (Chapters 5, 6, 7, 8, 9, and 10); *What can the teacher do when the student is severely retarded in reading?* (Chapter 11); and *What are appropriate materials for the secondary level?* (Chapter 12).

In attempting to answer these questions we have divided the book into three parts:

Part I—Secondary Reading: An Overview
    Chapter 1—Introduction
    Chapter 2—The Nature of the Reading Process
Part II—The Nature of the Learner
    Chapter 3—The Secondary Learner
    Chapter 4—The Secondary Learner *(Continued)*
Part III—Introducing the Secondary Reading Program
    Chapter 5—Characteristics of Good High School Reading Programs
    Chapter 6—Teaching Word-Recognition Skills
    Chapter 7—Developing a Meaningful Vocabulary
    Chapter 8—Advancing the Student's Comprehension Skills
    Chapter 9—Teaching Content-Area Reading Skills
    Chapter 10—Teaching Rate of Comprehension
    Chapter 11—Corrective and Remedial Reading in the Secondary School
    Chapter 12—Materials for the Teaching of Reading

RATIONALE FOR THE BOOK

Why another book? Another book will not remedy all deficiencies, and yet concerned secondary teachers want information on how to organize a reading program, how to conduct a school reading survey, how to conduct a remedial reading program for seriously disabled readers, and how to provide demonstration teaching and laboratory training programs for content-area teachers, and they ask what is the place of reading machines, television, programmed learning, autoinstructional devices, and paperback books in the high school? We hope the book will provide some of this information and knowledge.

This book is concerned with reading method and the actual teaching of reading. Thus, the book is written mainly for the practitioner or the *teacher-in-service*. Our first concern has been the problems of the teacher *in the classroom*. Nevertheless, we hope that the book will be of genuine value to the remedial teacher, the reading specialist, and the reading supervisor. We hope that it meets the needs of those students preparing to become teachers and the needs of teacher aides, technical assistants, and paraprofessionals; and we also hope that administrators will find it helpful in obtaining a better understanding of the reading process.

The weakest link in many reading programs is often an untrained or a disinterested administrator. It is the administrator who must have primary responsibility for inaugurating and implementing a successful reading program. The reading program will be no better than the kind of leadership provided. Artley (1) notes that the efficiency of a secondary school reading program depends on the quality of the staff, but also on the dynamic leadership of the principal. He adds that if the principal is convinced that learning to read is a lifetime activity, if he understands the nature of the reading process, the developments in reading, and the goals of reading instruction, and if he has imbued his staff with these convictions, then every teacher will tend to be a reading teacher in his own area.

The good administrator establishes a systematic program of professional stimulation, study, and teacher growth within the school (6). He works behind the scenes and through the reading committee to stimulate, guide, and direct a program of professional growth. We thus hope that the book will be carefully read by all secondary school administrators and will be used in schools for the in-service growth of teachers.

BIBLIOGRAPHY

1. ARTLEY, A. STERL, "Implementing a Developmental Reading Program on the Secondary Level," *Reading Instruction in Secondary Schools,* Perspectives in Reading, No. 2, p. 1. International Reading Association, 1964.
2. AUKERMAN, ROBERT, "Readability of Secondary School Literature Textbooks: A First Report," *English Journal,* 54 (September 1965), 533–40.
3. BAMMAN, HENRY A., "Organizing the Remedial Program in the Secondary School," *Journal of Reading,* 8 (November 1964), 103–8.
4. BOWREN, FAY F., "The Status of Reading Services in New Mexico Secondary Schools," *Journal of Reading,* 13 (April 1970), 513–18.

5. BURNETT, RICHARD W., "Reading in the Secondary School: Issues and Innovations," *Journal of Reading,* 9 (April 1966), 322–28.

6. CLELAND, DONALD L., "Reading and the High School Principal," *Journal of Reading,* 9 (January 1966), 157–62.

7. CRANE, AUGUST, "Actions and Reactions to Reading in the Public and Parochial Secondary Schools," *The Training School Bulletin,* American Institute for Mental Studies, 64 (August 1967), 62–65.

8. DAVIS, STANLEY E., "High School and College Instructors Can't Teach Reading? Nonsense." *North Central Association Quarterly,* 34 (April 1960), 295–99.

9. EARLY, MARGARET J., "The Meaning of Reading Instruction in Secondary Schools," *Journal of Reading,* 8 (October 1964), 25–29.

10. FOSTER, GUY L., "Freshman Problem: 44% Couldn't Read Their Texts," *The Clearing House,* 29 (March 1955), 414–17.

11. HERBER, HAROLD L., "Reading Instruction in Content Areas: An Overview," *Research in Reading in the Content Areas,* Syracuse University, 1969, pp. 1–12.

12. HOBSON, CLOY S., "Teaching Reading in the High School: Part I: Introduction," *Kansas Studies in Education,* p. 3. Lawrence: University of Kansas Publications, February 1960.

13. JONES, DAISY M., "Teaching Reading Skills in the Content Areas," *Claremont Reading Conference Yearbook,* pp. 159–69. Calif.: Claremont Graduate School, 1966.

14. KARLIN, ROBERT, "Teaching Reading in High Schools," *Education,* 84 (February 1964), 334–38.

15. MCDONALD, ARTHUR S., "What Research Says about Poor Readers in High School and College," *Journal of Developmental Reading* (Spring 1961), 184–96.

16. SIMMONS, JOHN S., "The Scope of the Reading Program of Secondary Schools," *The Reading Teacher* (September 1963), 31–35.

17. SQUIRE, JAMES, "Reading in the American High Schools Today," *Reading and Inquiry,* pp. 468–72. International Reading Association, 1965.

18. STANCHFIELD, JO M., "The Reading Specialist in the Junior High School," *Journal of Reading,* 8 (April 1965), 301–6.

19. SUMMERS, EDWARD G., "A Suggested Integrated Reading Outline for Teacher Education Courses in Secondary Reading," *Journal of Reading,* 9 (November 1965), 93–105.

20. TAYLOR, EARL A., *Eyes, Visual Anomalies and the Fundamental Reading Skill.* New York: Reading and Study Skills Center, Inc., 1959.

21. THOMAS, ELLEN LAMAR, "A Reading Consultant at the Secondary Level," *The Reading Teacher* (March 1967), 509–19.

22. WITTY, PAUL A., *Reading in High School and College,* Forty-seventh Yearbook, National Society for the Study of Education, Part II, pp. 18–19. Chicago: University of Chicago Press, 1938.

23. YOUNG, ROSS N., *Reading in the Junior and Senior High School,* p. 2. Minneapolis: Educational Test Bureau, 1927.

The Nature
of the Reading Process

CHAPTER **2**

IN THE INTRODUCTION TO PART I OF THIS BOOK, we viewed eight different aspects of reading. We also mentioned that there are about as many definitions of reading as there are reading experts. Nevertheless, it is possible to categorize reading definitions into two types: (1) those that equate reading with interpretation of experience generally and (2) those that equate reading with interpretation of graphic symbols.

In type 1 we might speak of reading *pictures,* reading *faces,* and reading *the weather.* The golfer reads *putting greens,* the meteorologist reads *weather,* the detective reads *clues,* the geologist reads *rocks,* the astronomer reads *stars,* and the doctor reads *symptoms of illness.* Benjamin Franklin in *Poor Richard's Almanac* had such a definition in mind when he wrote: "Read much, but not too many books."

Most definitions of reading given in professional textbooks, however, are of the second type. Reading in this sense involves the comprehension and interpretation of ideas symbolized by the printed page (9).

A team of experts, under the sponsorship of the United States Office of Education, tentatively defined reading as "a term used to refer to an interaction by which meaning encoded in visual stimuli by an author becomes meaning in the mind of the reader."

Let us address ourselves in more detail to reading as the interpretation of graphic symbols.

**READING AS INTERPRETATION OF
GRAPHIC SYMBOLS**

When reading is defined as the interpretation of graphic symbols, we imply that the reader must be able to identify the word and be able to associate appropriate meaning with it. Reading requires identification *and* comprehension.

Reading is far more than recognition of the graphic symbols. It is much more than the mere ability to pronounce the words on the printed page; it is more than simply matching the spoken code with the written code. Decoding is complete only when *meaning* is associated with the symbol. Reading is even more than the gaining of meaning from printed materials. The reader is stimulated by the writer's words, but he in turn vests these words with his own meaning. "Reading typically is the bringing of meaning *to* rather than the gaining of meaning *from* the printed page (22, p. 22).*

And yet, it is not enough to put our own stamp of meaning on the words. Langman (16, p. 19) notes that to read is to comprehend the meaning of visually presented word sequences; the reader must follow the thought of the *writer* (16, p. 23). Thus, the reader may and even must gain meaning from the printed page. This occurs when the writer's symbols stimulate the reader to combine or reconstruct his own experiences in a novel way. The reader must be able to appreciate the particular nuances of meaning if he is to interpret the message correctly.

Gray (12), discussing the dimensions of the reading process, stated that these include recognition, understanding, reaction, and integration. Shaw (20) noted that reading is the process of seeing or perceiving independent items, of observing and assimilating their interrelationships, and of integrating or grouping them into main ideas.

Obviously, reading of graphic symbols consists of two processes: the mechanical processes involved in bringing the stimuli to the brain and the mental processes involved in interpreting the stimuli after they get to the brain. When the light rays from the printed page hit the retinal cells of the eyes, signals are sent along the optic nerve to the visual centers of the brain. This is not yet reading. The mind must function in the process, the signals must be interpreted, and the reader must give significance to what he reads. He must bring *meaning* to the graphic symbol. Meaning depends to a great degree upon the reader's ability to recreate those experiences for which the symbol stands. The critical element in

---

* Henry P. Smith and Emerald V. Dechant, *Psychology in Teaching Reading* (Englewood Cliffs, N.J.: Prentice-Hall, Inc., 1961), p. 22. Reprinted by permission.

reading often is not what is on the page, but, rather, what the graphic symbol signifies to the reader (22). *Reading thus is the process of giving the significance intended by the writer to the graphic symbols by relating them to one's own fund of experience.*

READING—A SENSORY PROCESS

Reading begins as a sensory process. Reading is a visual process and a word-identification process. Sensation is the first occurrence in all perception. The reader reacts visually (in the case of Braille, kinesthetically) to the graphic symbols. He must visually identify and recognize upon subsequent occasions the language symbol.

The Eye Movements in Reading

In reading, the eyes do not make a continuous sweep across the page. They move in quick, short, staccato movements with pauses interspersed. Eye movements are characterized by fixations, interfixation movements, regressions or refixations, and return sweeps. The time elements in reading are two: fixation time and movement time.

A *fixation* is the stop that the eye makes so that it can react to the graphic stimuli. It is the pause for reading. During fixations the intake process is suspended and the inner process of reading occurs. The length (in terms of words) and frequency of the fixation vary with the difficulty of the reading material, and the reader's facility in word recognition, with his vocabulary level, with his familiarity with the content, with his purpose, with his ability to assimilate ideas, and with the format of the printed page. For example, the more difficult the reading matter, the longer and more frequent the fixations tend to be. The length may vary from as much as .22 seconds for reading easy material to .32 seconds for reading objective test items (27).

The length of the pause includes both seeing and thinking time. The reader must have time to see and to process the visual stimuli. Fixation time accounts for about 92 to 94 percent of the reading time; *interfixation eye movements* take from .01 to about .023 second (27) and account for about only 6 to 8 percent of the reading time.

Buswell (5, p. 26) found that the average child in grade one made between 15.5 and 18.6 fixations per 3½-inch (21-pica) line. The average college student made only 5.9 fixations on a line of similar length. Other studies (23, 30, p. 133) indicate that the average college student makes about 8 fixations per 4-inch (24-pica) line. And Taylor (25) reports that the average first grader makes about 224 fixations per hundred words; the average ninth grader, about 105; the average twelfth grader, about 94; and the average college student, about 90.

Thought-unit reading sometimes is wrongly identified with the concept of phrase seeing or with the suggestion that it is possible or even common to read three or four words per fixation (25, p. 17). Even though a child reads in thought units, he rarely comprehends more than one word per fixation. Thought units, then, must consist of a series of fixations (25, p. 17).

A *regression* is a reverse movement. It is a return to a previously fixed letter, syllable, word, or phrase for a refixation. It is a fixation in a right-to-left direction on the eye-movement photograph (10, p. 17). Eye deficiencies that have prevented accurate sensation, inadequate directional attack, and improper coordination between vergence (permitting single vision) and focus (permitting clear vision) are frequent causes of regression (10, p. 17). Sometimes the reader regresses out of habit. Such a student lacks confidence and feels the need for constant rereading.

Regressions are not necessarily bad. Most of them may well be means by which the student corrects himself and learns (11). Regressions occur when the flow of thought is interrupted or when perceptions are recognized as inaccurate (3). Eye movements frequently overreach or underreach the limits of the reader's recognition span. Regressions for verification, for phrase analysis, and for reexamination of a previous sentence seem especially useful. The flow of thought may be broken in numerous ways, such as by failing to comprehend the basic meaning of a word, by failing to comprehend the meaning suggested by the context, or by failing to interrelate the meanings of all the words.

The number of regressions made per hundred words varies from reader to reader. The average first grader makes about fifty-two; the average ninth grader about twenty; and the average college student about fifteen.

Upon completing a line the reader makes a *return sweep* to the beginning of the next line. The return sweep takes from forty to fifty-four milliseconds (27). If the next line is missed entirely or if the eye lands on a point before or after the first word of the new line, the reader must locate the proper place and a refixation is required.

Developmental Aspects of Eye Movement

Eye-movement skills develop rapidly during the first four grades, but after this relatively little improvement occurs. A slight improvement may occur between grades six and ten, after which a leveling process occurs (1, pp. 105–6).

Oculomotor behavior has come to be regarded primarily as a symptom of the underlying perceptual assimilative processes. There is an interaction and an interdependence between the oculomotor activity and the central processes (26). Eye movements do not cause but merely reflect efficient or poor reading performance. Faulty eye movements as judged by frequent regressions are primarily the result of poor understanding of subject matter, not of uncoordinated eye muscles. Generally, as the difficulty of the material increases and as the reader takes greater pains to read well, the pauses become more frequent and grow longer (28). The difficulty of the material rather than the nature of the subject matter is the crucial element.

The immature reader generally does not vary his eye movements with the difficulty of the reading matter or with a change of purpose. The good reader, on the other hand, is distinguished from the poor reader by his better word recognition, word analysis, and comprehension, and these are frequently reflected in more efficient eye movements. Thus, eye-movement patterns reflect the efficiency of the central processes of comprehension (27) and are generally symptomatic of the level of reading maturity the student has achieved. The poor reader makes extra fixations and regressions because he does not understand, and he needs training to improve word recognition and comprehension rather than eye movement.

Under certain conditions both good and poor readers show irregularities in their eye movement. And, although eye-movement surveys indicate that many students have not developed the habit of perceiving materials in a left-to-right progression while making a minimum number of fixations and regressions (24, p. 32), one must always remember that most of these surveys involve situations that are somewhat atypical. The student's eye movements might be different in normal reading.

The Eye-memory and Eye-voice Spans

Thought-unit reading, as noted previously, is not the same as interpreting an eyeful of print at a time. Because of this distinction, we speak of the eye-memory span in silent reading and the eye-voice span in oral reading.

The eye-memory span is the distance the eyes have traveled ahead of the point at which interpretation occurs. The eye-voice span is the distance the eyes have moved ahead of the point at which the pronunciation occurs. The mature reader has a wide eye-memory span and a wide eye-voice span. He does not commit himself to an interpretation until he has read a sufficient amount of material. He delays his interpretation of the visual intake until he has perceived enough material to grasp a thought unit (14, p. 75). He keeps in mind a sufficient amount of context so as to make the best interpretation. We find a similar span in listening. The good listener listens for meaning and for thought units rather than for one word at a time.

Generally, in silent reading the mature reader has a span of from fifteen to twenty letters. In oral reading it is slightly less. Rate improvement depends, to a great extent, on the shortening of the fixation pauses and on the lengthening of the eye-memory and eye-voice spans (14, p. 81).

Auditory Readiness

Auditory factors are also significant for reading achievement. The good reader can discriminate between the many sounds that form words. Unless he can do this, he will not be able to make the proper associations between the spoken sound and the graphic symbol.

The most natural way of teaching reading is still to go through the spoken word. Thus we say to the child: "Look at this word. This word says (spells) cat." The spoken word is the familiar stimulus; the written word is the novel stimulus. Gradually, with repeated associations between the written and the spoken word, the child brings to the written word the same meanings that he previously attached to the spoken word.

Some students experience difficulty in associating with the written word the meaning that has been associated with the spoken word. Much of this difficulty stems from failure to identify the written word properly. Some may not see the word distinctly and correctly. Some may even fail to look at the word. They do not really identify the word. Thus reading should always be a look-while-you-say activity.

Other students are handicapped because they are not able to discriminate between the various phonetic elements of words, do not hear and do not speak the sound correctly, and thus will confuse words. No student learns to pronounce distinctions that he does not hear. The resultant confusion leads to an inability to associate the sound with the appropriate printed symbol.

READING—A PERCEPTUAL PROCESS

Reading, however, is more than a sensory process. It is more than a skill to be learned through practice; it also is a conceptual and thinking process. Conceptual thought is required to react with meaning to the word, the sentence, and the paragraph. Reading and thinking are inseparable processes when the printed word provides the stimulus for thought (21).

Perception refers to the interpretation of everything that we sense. We give meaning to what we see, hear, taste, smell, and touch. At a very elemental level, such as when the perceiver sees a black dot on a white background, sensation may dominate perception and the percept may have few characteristics not found in the stimulus. At a more complex level, the sensation is clothed with the perceiver's wealth of past experience and values, and the percept reflects the biological and environmental characteristics of the perceiver.

Thus, although reading begins with sensation and the subsequent recognition of the printed symbol, the critical element in the reading act is the response with meaning rather than the recognition of the symbol. Perception must include the arousal of meaning. To understand the meaning of a word, the reader needs to have some awareness of the experiences that the word stands for. Readers sometimes become so engrossed with the mechanical aspects of reading, with word identification and pronunciation, that they fail to understand the need for comprehension.

Reading, which requires interpretation of what is read, occurs only when the reader understands what he is reading (6). Korzybski notes that reading is the reconstruction of the events behind the symbols. And Semelmeyer (19) points out that reading should bear the same relationship to experiences or events that a map bears to the territory it is supposed to represent.

Since the symbol has no meaning of its own, perception must go beyond the sensory data. It must, and does, involve information that is not present to the senses. The reader does not see the object, person, or experience of which the author writes. His eyes are in contact with a word, in fact with the light rays that are reflected by the word, and so it is impossible for him to see meaning. And yet, the student takes meaning to the word. He has learned the meaning of the word with the same mental operations that he used to learn the meaning of a squeaking door, a clap of thunder, a barking dog, or a square room (18). His reactions to the printed word are determined by the experiences that he has had with those objects or events for which the symbol stands. This is what we mean by perception. Perception is a consciousness or awareness of the experiences evoked by a symbol.

Specific and Generic Meaning

Individuals differ in their ability to react to symbols, and their interpretations have varying degrees of accuracy. They think of words in their general or specific sense (8, p. 120). Aphasics, individuals who have lost the ability to react to and handle abstract symbols, do not react with a general meaning. A "bear" indicates not a class of bears but one specific bear in their experience. Frequently, poor readers are like aphasics in their reactions to symbols.

Jan-Tausch (15), studying 170 children in the fourth to the seventh grade, found that good readers were characterized by abstract thinking and that poor readers demonstrated concreteness in behavior. The relationship is more significant in the upper grades, suggesting perhaps that reading comprehension at the upper-grade levels is more abstract. Other studies show that intelligence is more closely related to reading comprehension at the *upper-grade* levels than at the lower levels. Thus intelligence may become a more important determinant of reading success as the abstractness of the materials read increases.

Specific reactions to symbols are also observable with older children. They find abstract words especially difficult and identify them with specific experiences: "Beauty is when you comb your hair neatly." "Sportsmanship is when you do not kick somebody." Children easily give meaning to *a book, a building, a car,* but not to the more complex concepts represented by the words *beauty, democracy,* and *truth.*

Another example may be taken from reading itself. Students frequently make substitutions when they read. The good reader tends to substitute words that harmonize with the context. The poor reader, on the other hand, substitutes words that do not fit the context. He may not have had sufficient experience to bring the appropriate meaning to the printed page, and communication between writer and reader does not occur. He cannot see the relationships between the various words and the various ideas communicated.

Generally, the writer and the reader communicate only if they are capable of assigning some common meaning to a symbol. This means that they must have had some commonality of experience. And usually they must be able to make a generic response to their experience.

With experience the person makes the word generic in meaning. He abstracts, forms concepts, learns to associate these concepts with printed symbols, and identifies the word with a category or a class of objects. When perception is on an abstract level, when the reader associates a concept with a word, then, indeed, perception is a kind of summing up of the meanings of numerous sensory impingements (18). The reader then is capable of bringing sufficient meaning to the printed page to permit him to obtain from the page an approximation of the experience that the writer is trying to convey. The reader attains an understanding of the writer's experience and hence his perceptions. Only then is communication via reading taking place.

And yet, the perception of a word is rarely completely congruent with the meaning intended by the writer. Furthermore, concept-environment concordance is rarely completely present. Verbal symbols at best are inadequate substitutes for direct experience. There is no direct connection between symbol and referend, the datum, object, or event.

The Development of Meaning

Since the good reader may well be differentiated from the poor reader by his ability to take the appropriate meaning to the page, the reading teacher is concerned about the development of meaning and concepts. We know that students can learn to conceptualize. Depth and variety of experience perhaps are most significant. And the broader the concept, the more abstract it is, the greater is the amount of experience needed for its formation.

Pupils go through stages as they learn to interpret words. Concrete and specific concepts are probably developed first. Gradually, pupils engage in more complex thinking. The concept of time in sequence and the concepts of latitude, sphericity, date line, zone, altitude, or longitude, for example, generally do not develop before grades six or seven. Cause-and-effect relationships are rarely understood before the age of nine, and many social concepts escape learners until they are twelve or thirteen.

Even though experience is a major determinant of meaning, other elements are important. The culture in which one lives surely is an important determinant of what a word will mean. We also know that each perceptual experience has its emotional matrix. In this sense reading involves feeling. The affective state of the reader may distort, color, or alter meaning to such an extent that communication becomes impossible. Some things forever escape our comprehension because we cannot accept them emotionally. Reading is decoding; it is a cognitive response involving perception and cognition; but it is also an affective response (2).

These elements—culture, experience, affective factors, and our own perception of them—combine to make our interpretations of a word a very personalistic experience. Because our reactions are organismic and involve our whole being, it is almost impossible to communicate perfectly. Our interpretations and our meanings are truly our own.

ORAL READING

Even though the major emphasis in reading today is on silent reading, students need to become good oral readers. Students benefit educationally by reading aloud prose, poetry, or drama.

Oral reading has diagnostic values. It is helpful in testing for fluency and accuracy in reading. Since reading requires the association of a printed form with an oral equivalent, it would seem only logical that oral reading would be used to emphasize this relationship.

But most important perhaps is that oral reading teaches the youngster that writing is a record of the oral language, although an incomplete record to be sure (4). The intonation pattern cannot be fully represented by writing. The tone of voice (the paralanguage) and the gestured bodily movements (the kinesics) are only crudely represented by underlined words, exclamation points, or word choice (sauntered, gesticulated). The pupil right from the beginning should read aloud the whole sentence. This develops an awareness of the intonation pattern and is probably the best preventer of word-by-word reading.

Oral reading requires all the sensory and perceptual skills required in silent reading, such as visual discrimination, rhythmic progression along a line of print, and the ability to take to the word those experiences that the writer, by his peculiar choice and arrangement of words, hoped to call to the reader's attention. Oral reading also requires skills beyond those needed in silent reading.

Habits of oral reading usually are quite different from those in silent reading. The pupil who exercises great care in his oral reading may pass over the difficult words in silent reading. In oral reading there are generally more fixations, more regressions, and longer pauses. Oral reading is generally slower than silent reading. In oral reading, reading rate is limited by pronunciation; in silent reading, it is limited only by the ability to grasp meaning. Oral reading calls for interpreting to others; silent reading only to oneself. Oral reading demands skills in voice, tempo, and gesture and in sensing the mood and feeling intended by the author. And, there are some differences in neural pathways in oral and silent reading.

Oral reading, like silent reading, consists of a complex of skills. The good oral reader:

1. Interprets the author's meaning accurately
2. Transmits correctly the author's meaning to the listener
3. Makes a proper interpretation of the author's feelings and moods
4. Reads in meaningful thought units
5. Is accurate and clear in articulation, enunciation, and pronunciation
6. Gives an accurate translation of the writer's punctuation marks into pauses, stops, etc.
7. Is fluent and smooth in reading, keeping the eye well ahead of the voice
8. Has suitable quality and volume of voice
9. Has suitable pitch
10. Has unlabored speech
11. Avoids labored precision in reading aloud
12. Has appropriate rate
13. Has proper posture

14. Looks at the audience at frequent intervals
15. Holds the attention of the audience

The good oral reader must get the author's meaning, must sense his moods, and must be able to convey the author's meaning and mood to others. He must recognize words instantly, using good phrasing, pronunciation, and proper voice inflection. He needs to adapt his voice to the room and must have auditory and visual contact with the audience. He should be poised and confident, and must assume the proper posture. He must keep his eyes well ahead of his voice, must enunciate clearly, must pronounce correctly, and must hold the attention of the audience. The good oral reader cannot be many other things. He cannot, for example, be a word caller, jerkily attacking one word at a time in a high-pitched monotone and giving little consideration to meaning (7).

Thus, oral reading should rarely be done without previous silent reading. From the beginning, stress should be on naturalness of tone. The teacher should encourage this by asking the student to read the sentence in the manner that he would speak it, since the best model for oral reading is speech. Passages should frequently be read to the student to give him a feeling of conversational tone.

The teacher also needs to pay particular attention to the student's articulation, enunciation, and pronunciation. Pronunciation should be corrected tactfully, without embarrassing the student. Mispronounced words should be practiced as parts of a sentence.

The student must also learn appropriate pitch, quality, and volume of voice. Voice factors are important for the listener. Listening is more or less difficult depending on the voice qualities of the reader. The student needs to be given the opportunity to read to one student, to read to a group, and to engage in choral reading.

The most essential vocal skills are phrasing and smoothness. The reader must be able to keep his eyes well ahead of his voice so he can organize and group the words, giving them the proper inflections. This means that the student should read simple materials without too many new words. Generally, materials written by the student himself which are based on the vocabulary that he knows are most effective. Many errors of communication are the result of faulty phrasing or grouping of words. Generally, phrasing will be appropriate if the student understands what he is reading. Sentences should be broken into phrases and clauses. Only if the reader understands what he reads can he convey a significant message.

The teacher can check up on the student's proficiency here by asking him to read two or three lines aloud and then stopping him. The student then is asked to say aloud additional words that he read silently, but that he has not yet read aloud. A narrow eye-voice span indicates that the student needs help in looking ahead.

The oral reader must also learn to emphasize words properly. He does this by giving the word more stress, by elongating the pronunciation, or by saying it with a higher pitch.

A technique with a lot of possibilities in developing oral reading skills has been described by Wilson (31). His students' oral reading was taped, and the students then listened to their own reading in the language laboratory. Each lesson concentrated on a specific oral reading skill. The student analyzed his reading, reread the story orally, and then compared the two readings. Testing seemed to indicate that significant improvement occurred as a result of the program.

Botel (4) suggests additional techniques:

1. Make sure that written-down speech is a record of clear, complete sentences.
2. Record student speech and teach students to read the materials as they were spoken in the first place.
3. Provide choral speaking and reading opportunities.
4. Encourage dramatizations.
5. Make sure that silent reading precedes oral reading and that oral reading is fluent.
6. Let pupils see how a shift of stress in a sentence alters the meaning of the sentence.

SUMMARY

In this chapter we have looked at two different types of definitions of reading and have concluded that a student does not become a good reader of graphic symbols without becoming a reader of experience.

Reading thus requires three things: The student must identify the symbol; he must associate meaning with the symbol; and to do the latter, he must have acquired the necessary experiences.

THE READING PROCESS

```
                      Reading
         ┌──────────────┴──────────────┐
   Identification              Association
      of the                      of
     Symbol (s)                 Meaning          Experiences
                                  with      ◄──── Provide the
                              the Symbol (s)      Bases for
                                                  Meaning
```

In addition, we examined reading as a sensory and as a perceptual process. As a *sensory* process, reading is dependent on certain *visual* skills. The eyes must have matured to the point where they can react to printed symbols. They must be able to distinguish one printed form from another. They must focus on minute stimuli, and they must progress from left to right and from one line to the next. Reading is dependent also on certain *auditory* skills. The reader must be able to discriminate between the many sounds that form words.

Reading is also a *perceptual* process. The reading act is complete only after the reader has interpreted the printed symbol by bringing meaning to it. Meaning itself is dependent on experience, culture, the emotional state of the reader, and the reader's ability to reconstruct his experiences. Meaning is complete only when the reader has developed the ability to pick out the key words and to relate words and sentences to one another.

Finally, the importance of oral reading was outlined. Oral reading has educational, social, and diagnostic values. Since fluency in oral reading seems to be just as much of a basic reading skill as is silent reading, the reading program must make provision for the development of those skills required for successful oral reading.

QUESTIONS FOR DISCUSSION

1. Discuss the implications of Gray's description of the reading process on the teaching of reading.
2. Is it desirable to develop the eye movements of the reader? In your answer discuss the relationship between eye movements and the central processes of comprehension.
3. Reading is said to be a thinking process. Find four reading passages that illustrate the thinking processes of analysis-synthesis, problem solving, inference, and organization.
4. Why in the definition of reading is it necessary to include the words: "giving the significance *intended by the writer* to the graphic symbols"?
5. Reading in this chapter is described as "the bringing of meaning to the printed page." What are the implications of this for the slow learner or reader, for rate improvement training, and for reading in the content areas?
6. What is the relationship between degrees of comprehension and experiential background?
7. Discuss the following statements:
   a. Reading should bear the same relationship to experiences or events that a map bears to the territory it is supposed to represent.

b. Perception is a kind of summing up of the meanings of numerous sensory impingements.

c. Reading is the development or creative construction of meaning in response to external stimuli, usually written words.

d. The greater the number of concepts that the reader has fixed through words, the better will be his understanding of what he reads. Comprehension, or the apprehension of meaning, is a direct function of (*1*) the number of words the person knows and (*2*) the number of meanings that he associates with each word.

BIBLIOGRAPHY

1. BALLANTINE, F. A., "Age Changes in Measures of Eye Movements in Silent Reading," *Studies in the Psychology of Reading,* Monographs in Education, No. 4, pp. 67–108. Ann Arbor: University of Michigan Press, 1951.

2. BARRETT, THOMAS C., "Goals of the Reading Program: The Basis for Evaluation," *Evaluation of Children's Reading Achievement,* Perspectives 8, 1967, pp. 13–26. International Reading Association.

3. BAYLE, EVALYN, "The Nature and Causes of Regressive Movements in Reading," *Journal of Experimental Education,* 11 (September 1942), 16–36.

4. BOTEL, MORTON, "What Linguistics Says to the Teacher of Reading and Spelling," *The Reading Teacher,* 18 (December 1964), 188–93.

5. BUSWELL, G. T., *Fundamental Reading Habits: A Study of Their Development,* Supplementary Educational Monographs, No. 21. Chicago: University of Chicago Press, 1922.

6. DALLMANN, MARTHA, "Reading for Meaning," *Grade Teacher,* 74 (February 1957), 34, 97.

7. DAWSON, MILDRED A., "The Role of Oral Reading in School and Life Activities," *Elementary English,* 35 (January 1958), 30–37.

8. ———, and HENRY A. BAMMAN, *Fundamentals of Reading Instruction.* New York: Longmans, Green and Company, 1959.

9. DEBOER, J. J., and MARTHA DALLMANN, *The Teaching of Reading,* p. 19. New York: Henry Holt and Co., 1960.

10. *The Evolution and Growth of Controlled Reading Techniques.* Huntington, N.Y.: Educational Developmental Laboratories, Inc., 1958.

11. GOODMAN, KENNETH S., "A Linguistic Study of Cues and Miscues in Reading," *Elementary English,* 42 (October 1965), 639–43.

12. GRAY, W. S., "Growth in Understanding of Reading and Its Development among Youth," *Keeping Reading Programs Abreast of the Times,* Supplementary Educational Monographs, No. 72, pp. 8–13. Chicago: University of Chicago Press, 1950.

13. HEBB, D. O., *A Textbook of Psychology.* Philadelphia: W. B. Saunders Co., 1958.

14. HILDRETH, GERTRUDE, *Teaching Reading.* New York: Holt, Rinehart & Winston, Inc., 1958.

15. JAN-TAUSCH, JAMES, "Concrete Thinking as a Factor in Reading Comprehension," *Challenge and Experiment in Reading.* International Reading Association Conference Proceedings, 7 (1962), 161–64.

16. LANGMAN, MURIEL POTTER, "The Reading Process: A Descriptive, Interdisciplinary Approach," *Genetic Psychology Monographs,* 62 (August 1960), 1–40.

17. LEVERETT, HOLLIS M., "Vision Test Performance of School Children," *American Journal of Ophthalmology,* 44 (October 1957), 508–19.

18. NORBERG, KENNETH, "Perception Research and Audio-Visual Education," *Readings for Educational Psychology,* ed. W. A. Fullagar, H. G. Lewis, and C. F. Cumbee, pp. 26–36. New York: Thomas Y. Crowell Company, 1956.

19. SEMELMEYER, MADELINE, "Can Johnny Read?" *Education,* 77 (April 1957), 505–12.

20. SHAW, PHILIP, "Rhetorical Guides to Reading Comprehension," *The Reading Teacher,* 11 (April 1958), 239–43.

21. SHORES, J. HARLAN, "Dimensions of Reading Speed and Comprehension," *Elementary English,* 45 (January 1968), 23–28, 43.

22. SMITH, HENRY P., and EMERALD V. DECHANT, *Psychology in Teaching Reading.* Englewood Cliffs, N.J.: Prentice-Hall, Inc., 1961.

23. STROUD, JAMES B., *Psychology in Education.* New York: Longmans, Green and Company, 1956.

24. TAYLOR, E. A., *Eyes, Visual Anomalies and the Fundamental Reading Skill.* New York: Reading and Study Skills Center, 1959.

25. TAYLOR, S. E., H. FRACKENPOHL, and J. L. PETTEE, *Grade Level Norms for the Components of the Fundamental Reading Skill,* Bulletin No. 3. Huntington, N.Y.: Educational Developmental Laboratories, Inc., 1960.

26. TAYLOR, STANFORD E., "Eye Movements in Reading: Facts and Fallacies," *American Educational Research Journal,* 2 (November 1965), 187–202.

27. TINKER, M. A., "Recent Studies of Eye Movements in Reading," *Psychological Bulletin,* 55 (July 1958), 215–31.

28. ———, "Time Relations for Eye-Movement Measures in Reading," *Journal of Educational Psychology,* 38 (January 1947), 1–10.

29. ———, "The Use and Limitations of Eye-Movement Measures in Reading," *Psychological Review,* 40 (July 1933), 381–87.

30. WALKER, R. Y., "The Eye Movements of Good Readers," *Studies in Experimental and Theoretical Psychology: Psychological Monographs,* 44 (1933), 95–117.

31. WILSON, ROBERT M., "Oral Reading is Fun," *The Reading Teacher,* 19 (October 1965), 41–43.

THE NATURE
OF THE LEARNER

PART TWO

In Part I we emphasized the sensory and the perceptual nature of the reading process. The emphasis was on the *nature* of the reading process. In Part II our emphasis is upon the *learner*. Reading is a response made by a *learner*. Reading must be learned by a *learner*. It is interrelated with the learner's total growth and development. Students show vast differences in physical, intellectual, social, and emotional development. They have different backgrounds, experiences, and interests, and they have received different instruction.

Chapters 3 and 4 attempt to identify the student who learns to read well and the student who frequently ends in failure. They are designed to help the teacher to become a better interpreter of the symptoms and causes of reading disability, to study the correlates of reading achievement and proficiency, to study the student to discover any inhibitory factors to making the response for successful reading, and to remedy deficiencies that exist. They are designed to help the teacher to understand students in general, students on the level on which he is teaching, and the individual student in the classroom. We are interested in answering *why* certain students have more difficulty than do others.

The causes of behavior are multiple, complex, and interrelated. The student is a product of both heredity and environment, and generally it is impossible to differentiate the particular role of each. Development in reading closely parallels and is an expression of the forces of human development generally. Indeed, if teachers could truly divorce achievement in reading from other aspects of growing up, they might be able to produce a standardized product.

Unfortunately, this is not possible. The student reads with his biology and his geography, with his nature and his nurture. He is a product of the interaction of heredity and environment, and these forces are accountable for the vast differences between students. No two students develop to the same point at the same time in any given characteristic. Growth and development are variable, and so is achievement in reading.

Four differing assumptions are today adduced to account for reading difficulty (48): Reading difficulty is attributed to *some malfunction,* preventing the student from benefiting from experience (damage to left cerebral hemisphere); to the *absence of some function,* which needs to be added (lack of phonic skills); to *something that is present but must be removed* (dislike for reading); or to *mismatches between student and task* (improper material, mode of instruction). Nevertheless, there is for each learner a most teachable moment for learning to read and for the learning of every subsequent reading skill. This teachable moment depends on many factors. Thus, the following two chapters attempt to identify those aspects about students that have a major bearing on their teachable moment in reading. Chapter 3 will emphasize the experiential, intellectual, and physical aspects.

The Secondary Learner

VIII.   *AUDITORY ADEQUACY*

    A. Types of Auditory Deficiency

    B. Causes and Symptoms of Hearing Deficiencies

    C. Tests of Hearing

    D. Educational Implications

IX.   *NEURAL ADEQUACY AND READING*

    A. Projection and Association Areas

    B. Wordblindness

    C. Cerebral Dominance

X.   *SUMMARY*

READING IS A DEVELOPMENT TASK. It is a task that the student must perform to satisfy his own needs, so that he may satisfy the demands made upon him by society and so that he may be better prepared to handle subsequent developmental tasks. As with other developmental tasks, suceess in reading is determined by the learner's state of progress in other areas of development, and in turn this success affects the student's development in these areas.

There are both biological and environmental determinants of readiness for and achievement in reading. Among the more important ones are the student's intellectual, physical, social, and emotional development, his general proficiency in language, and his sensory equipment. Success in reading also depends on the student's proficiency in auditory and visual discrimination. It is assured by a wide background of personal experience, by a genuine interest in reading, *and by an adequate instructional program.* The student, if he is to learn, must perceive the learning situation as meeting his needs. He must also have had adequate preparation so he can profit from the present learning experience.

These determinants of learning and achievement are inextricably interrelated. Obviously, no one single factor determines a learner's success. It is rarely a single variable that accounts for reading disability. It is the pattern, the complex of correlates, with which we must be concerned. The student must have a certain degree of readiness in each of the areas because each in its own way may contribute to reading disability or prevent future growth. It is illogical to expect to produce a successful reader by promoting growth and development in a few specifics while ignoring others. The teacher must examine the composite of interacting elements, and on the basis of them must identify each student's *overall* readiness for reading and learning.

Nevertheless, some factors contribute more to achievement than do others. They are relatively more important than others; they have a higher weight value in the correlate pattern. A student might be ready for reading in all areas except motivation. The absence of motivation alone may keep the student from learning. If the student does not want to read, no reading will occur.

The teacher must thus ascertain the student's readiness in each of the specifics. If some one element interferes with learning to read, it needs to be identified. The effect of inhibitory factors is multiplicative rather than additive.

Too often we look for the reason for reading success or failure in the wrong place. It is so easy to overplay the role of some of the correlates of reading disability that sometimes we may overlook the significant. Too often we look for and find a single cause in *all* reading disability cases. It is far too easy to assume that something is a cause when it may not be so. The measurable and the observable simply are not identical at times with the significant, and Pascal notes that "we should not judge the truth of things by our capacity to conceive them." A cause may well be shared in common by reading disability and by its correlates.

The causes of reading disability are so varied that the poor reader becomes the object of inquiry of many people, not always to his own advantage. The optometrist may discover an instance of exophoria and immediately conclude that this is the chief cause. The psychiatrist notices the pupil's anxiety and may conclude that this is the chief problem. Daddy and Mamma simply notice the boy's laziness.

And yet, proceeding as though correlation meant causation is not entirely without its heuristic values. Perhaps this is why it is so easy to equate the two. Correcting the visual problem, removing the anxiety, or motivating the student may be the best that we can do, and it is often better than nothing.

As we examine possible causal factors in reading achievement and disability, it is necessary to remember that sometimes the same behavioral characteristic may be both symptom and cause. A poor reader generally develops anxiety and perhaps even a dislike for reading. In this instance, anxiety and dislike for reading are symptoms. Anxiety may also initiate the reading disability by prohibiting the use of the student's intellectual energies. In the latter instance, anxiety may be the cause.

In evaluating causal factors in reading disability, the teacher needs to remember that when significant adults in a student's life believe the pupil can learn and achieve, he tends to do so (30); and in their diagnostic efforts teachers must come to see that all mistakes in reading are significant. There simply is no such thing as a meaningless mistake(30). Each mistake assists the teacher in planning correction and remediation.

The premises of this and the subsequent chapter are simply the following:

1. Reading is a response made by a learner and must be learned by a learner. The major element in any learning process is the learner. We must understand him.
2. Reading achievement is interrelated with the learner's total growth and development.
3. Growth and development of the learner are variable, and so is achievement in reading.
4. It is imperative that the teacher understand the *causes* for this variability in achievement.
5. Those variables (adequate experience, etc.) that are associated with good achievement in reading, if absent (lack of experience), may become causes of reading deficiency.
6. There is for each student a teachable moment for learning each of the reading skills. This teachable moment depends on those elements with which this chapter deals.

Let us now examine more closely each of the factors that make for achievement or lack of achievement in reading.

EXPERIMENTAL BACKGROUND

Experience is the basis for all educational development. Concepts develop from experience, and their richness and scope are in direct proportion to the richness and scope of the individual's experience. One of the more naive beliefs is that a student's academic performance is a simple function of innate ability. The most important reason for the difference between the adult's concepts and the child's concepts is the differential in experience and knowledge. And, frequently, the significant reason for differences in reading achievement is the differential in experience, and opportunity for experience often depends on whether or not one is favored by socioeconomic status. Vilscek (46), for example, found a functional relationship between socioeconomic class and mental age. The lower the mental age of the pupil, the higher the socioeconomic level had to be for initial learning to read; and conversely, the lower the socioeconomic level, the higher the mental age had to be.

Socioeconomic status is an individual's position in a given society, as determined by wealth, occupation, and social class. Social class in turn is a grouping or division of a society, made up of persons having certain common social characteristics and usually formed on a combination of criteria: similarities in education, vocation, value systems, custom, family, and wealth. It is an aggregate of individuals who occupy broadly similar positions on the scale of prestige.

There are basically five factors that contribute to or are the product of social class differences. The first of these is personal prestige. In each community certain persons hold prestige positions, and the children of these persons are favored in many ways. The daughter or the son of a prominent lawyer, physician, professor, or athlete falls into this category. Another determinant of social class is one's possessions. High income and a large and expensive home go along with high social status. Generally the home will be in a "favored" neighborhood, and the people who inhabit it will associate with people of note. Persons also differ in their interaction with people. Persons high on the socioeconomic ladder tend to have more significant interactions, and generally with people of similar status. Class consciousness is another determinant or result of social class differences. Children in our society are aware of class differences and develop attitudes toward one another that encompass these differences. Finally, the various classes are differentiated by the values, standards, and beliefs that their individual members hold.

Warner found, using the *Warner Index of Status Characteristics,* that approximately 3 percent of the population belongs to the upper socioeconomic group, 38 percent to the middle group, and 59 percent to the lower group.* The criteria for classification were occupation, source of income, house type, and dwelling area. The following divisions occurred:

Upper-Upper—1.4%	Upper-Middle—10%	Upper-Lower—34%
Lower-Upper—1.6%	Lower-Middle—28%	Lower-Lower—25%
3.0%	38%	59%

Social class provides certain economic advantages for the student, but it also determines what goals the student will seek, what attitudes he will hold, how motivated toward school he will be, his interest in school and its curricular offerings, and the friends he will choose, and it is positively related to intelligence, adjustment, achievement, educational level attained, church activity, interests, age of marriage, work adjustment, educational aspiration, and language experience and skills. Social class is

* W. Lloyd Warner, *Social Class in America* (New York: Harper and Brothers, 1960).

one of the chief factors that helps to account for the individual differences among students and as such is a determinant of individual differences in behavior, learning, and achievement.

Most studies show that pupils from upper-socioeconomic homes come to school more ready than those from lower-socioeconomic homes to learn the tasks needed for success. The middle-class home contains "a hidden curriculum" (24) which permits the pupil to deal appropriately with school experiences. Even the amount and kinds of reading are different in different sections of the country, among various occupational groups, and among individuals of various socioeconomic groups. Barton (5) found in a survey of twelve hundred teachers that the most important single determinant of success in reading in school is socioeconomic class. When he divided classrooms according to the socioeconomic status of the pupil's parents (using a combination of income and occupation), he found that reading retardation rose steadily through the first six grades for working-class children and especially for the lower skilled. The evidence shows that black children do not read as well as white children on an average, not because of an absence of symbolic activity, but because the black student, especially from lower socioeconomic groups, has a different cultural base in which the language is different from that of the middle-class white person. It may also well be that students from lower-socioeconomic homes are at a distinct disadvantage in learning to read because they have spoken and heard language patterns that interfere with the comprehension of both oral and written materials. It is important to point out that the socially deprived do not lack the capacity to develop the cerebral functions upon which advanced learning is based. They simply have not had the opportunity to do so.

The attitudes of the middle-class home are especially significant. The middle-class home encourages care of and pride in property, renunciation and sacrifice for the sake of future rewards, seeking of education, and achievement in government, business, industry, or education. Its emphasis is upon respectability, morality, money, organizational ties, group goals, self-improvement through education, and community improvement.

The student from the middle-class home has been taught that education is power. He has learned that education is a chief means for moving up the social status ladder. The middle-class child is more likely to have attended nursery school and kindergarten, and his parents have probably been more conscientious in teaching him communication skills, the use of the pencil, and the fundamentals of the alphabet. His parents tend to have positive attitudes toward scholastic achievement, and they will reward him for success in this area. His parents have emphasized the need for finishing high school and going to college. They have encouraged him to enter a profession. They emphasize grades, they go to PTA meetings, and they visit the school.

Schools themselves are geared to middle-class values and goals. Most teachers are middle class oriented. Students are expected to conform, to be successful in academic subjects, to react to reward, praise, and good grades, to stay in school, to value education, and to seek the approval of others.

The teacher is generally committed to cleanliness, punctuality, regular attendance, effort, enthusiasm, and neatness in personal appearance. He values thrift, ownership, and financial security. He extols honesty. He stresses the importance of reason and intellect, and he encourages continuous control of one's emotions. He uses proper and correct language and operates on the premise that hard work and self-discipline will be rewarded. He has a strong sense of duty and responsibility and proposes that learning and education are the chief means of improving one's social position.

Unfortunately, the child from the lower-class home has no such motivations. More of the lower-class youth drop out of high school, and fewer of them go on to college. Many of the reasons for this are motivational. Many lower-class children do not feel free to approach teachers with their problems. They do not see the practical value of school learnings. They feel socially inferior in school. Their parents do not really care whether they continue in school or not. And many feel that teachers are unsympathetic to their needs. For these students school does not lead to self-realization.

The school is a social system. In essence, it is a three-position system involving administrator, teacher, and student. The student is a member also of other social systems within the school, such as his friends, his teammates, or his clique. And, the student's behavior is often influenced more by some of these other systems, the clique to which he belongs or a friend whom he admires, than by what the teacher wants.

The student from the less-privileged class is usually not as interested in being a high achiever in academic areas. A girl might rather be homecoming queen than a straight *A* student. A boy might rather be the top athlete.

A student's social status in the school, then, does not depend only on how well he achieves in academic work. It depends also on the activities he participates in and the status that the school population accords these.

The student seeks to satisfy his needs, and he will use the various social systems in the school to satisfy these needs. If the group to which the student belongs satisfies his "basic" needs, but if this same group does not value achievement, the student may be a poor achiever. One group may emphasize popularity and participation in the extracurricular life of the school. Another group may emphasize academic achievement.

Teachers should also note that

1. Socioeconomic status is related to language proficiency. Black children from middle-class homes have a better command of language in terms of its classificatory and problem-solving functions than those from lower-class homes.

2. Studies (6) show that youngsters from lower-socioeconomic groups tend to believe that they have little control over what happens to them and that their actions are influenced chiefly by fate, chance, or other powerful people. They feel that their own behavior cannot determine the outcomes they desire. Liddle and Rockwell (31) note that deprived children are more accident prone because they do not see the world as governed by cause-and-effect relationships. The world simply acts on them. They live for today and profit relatively little from experience. There is a tendency to ascribe everything to "bad luck." There is little foresight which might prevent accidents or other unwanted situations. The children have a tendency to grow up feeling that they are not very important and become careless with their own safety.

3. Davis (17) found that the goals of the lower-socioeconomic groups are different from those of the middle and upper groups and that the lower-class pupil's excitement to learn is crippled by the lack of available rewards.

4. Perhaps the chief drawback of the disadvantaged youth in school is that he lacks recognition and understanding from teachers.

5. Although high socioeconomic status is not a completely accurate indicator of reading achievement, it generally goes hand in hand with broadness of experience and with language facility (51). This broadness of experience and the added language facility result in superior achievement in reading by equipping the student with the tools for meaningful reaction to the printed page. The symbols on the page are empty unless the reader endows them with meaning. For this the student needs the appropriate experience.

The following statements summarize the importance of experience and, indirectly, of socioeconomic status for reading achievement:

1. Experience is one factor that accounts for differences in reading achievement, and lack of experience may be a cause of reading disability.

2. Experience and maturation are the basis of all educational development. To predict behavior both the person and the environment must be considered as a constellation of interdependent factors.

3. Differences in learning ability of students are related to their biological

potentials, but also to the environmental opportunities. Some students become reading disability cases because the environment does not call forth their potential.

4. It is impossible to predict the learning of the student without knowing the structure of his social environment, the types of behavior that are rewarded, and the types of rewards that are provided.

5. The student from the middle-class home has an advantage because his home contains "a hidden curriculum" (24) which permits him to deal appropriately with school experiences.

MATURATIONAL DEVELOPMENT

Even though we began this chapter by emphasizing experience, the student's achievement depends as much on maturation or genetically determined growth as on experience, learning, or environmentally induced growth. Baller and Charles (2, p. 22) note that maturation is an unfolding or a "ripening" of an individual's potentials which he possesses by virtue of being a member of a given species or more specifically by virtue of his biological inheritance.

We generally assume that the student receives his biological inheritance through maturation, while he acquires his social inheritance through learning. Maturation, however, is a prerequisite to much learning, and environment and experience are prerequisites to maturation.

The student's achievement is certainly affected by inadequacies and delays in maturation or in development of the physical-physiological functions. There is a difference between maturational delays and developmental delays (8). Developmental delays are delays in progress in which the experiential aspects play a predominant role; in maturational delays, physical-physiological determinants are of primary importance.

Belmont (8) notes that the stage as well as the rate of physical maturation influences and is probably influenced by the nature of the pupil's experience. And Harris (23, p. 3) notes that without maturation the pupil cannot learn, and without experience he has nothing to learn.

Belmont adds that just as it is very difficult for a seven-month-old child to establish voluntary control over bowel function for biological reasons (the nerve pathways necessary for this function are not yet completely myelinated and, hence, are not voluntarily operational), so there are varying degrees of biological maturational preparedness to undertake learning.

Maturational changes usually are orderly and sequential. Wide variations of environmental conditions seem to have little effect on maturation. The nervous system develops regularly according to its own intrinsic pattern. There thus seems to be very little benefit in rushing the maturation process.

Teaching and other environmental stimulations, however, are not useless. Students need appropriate environmental stimulation if maturational development is to progress at an appropriate rate. In many instances the student has inadequacies in his experiential background. The teacher cannot overemphasize either maturation learning or experience learning. Too much emphasis on maturation may lead to useless postponing of what can be learned; too much emphasis on learning or experience may lead to futile attempts at teaching that for which the student is not ready. Nevertheless, instruction must march slightly ahead of development. Instruction must be aimed not so much at the ripe as at the ripening function (47, p. 104).

In summary:

1. Students generally become ready for specific learning tasks at different ages.
2. Students develop reading skills most readily if they are built upon the natural foundation of maturational development. They put most effort into tasks that are neither too difficult nor too easy, that are within their "range of challenge"—that are possible for them but not necessarily easy.
3. Students should not be forced into readiness for either beginning reading or for any subsequent reading skill before maturational development is adequate. Such premature training may lead to no improvement, to only temporary improvement, or to actual harm. Premature training may destroy the student's natural enthusiasm for a given activity, and it is doubtful that drill and exercises will ever be a substitute for maturation.
4. Generally, the more mature the student is, the less training is needed to develop a given proficiency.
5. The teacher can promote the student's readiness for a given learning task by filling the gaps in his experience.
6. Readiness may refer to an intrinsic state of the organism, but also to the extrinsic acculturation of the organism (7). The latter is often referred to as *building readiness*, but some note that readiness comes with age, not with special drills or practice. It may be that both concepts have meaning in that a student is more or less ready dependent upon the method and materials used in teaching and that building readiness comes to mean such things as removing blocks to learning and filling gaps of experience.

Readiness may depend more on our ability to translate ideas into the language and concepts of the age level we are teaching than on maturation (12).

Pestalozzi in 1802 said it very beautifully when he wrote:

"To instruct man is nothing more than to help nature develop in its own way, and the art of instruction depends primarily on harmonizing our messages, and the demands we make upon the child, with his powers at the moment."

Thoreau, in *Walden,* noted: "If a man does not keep pace with his companions, perhaps it is because he hears a different drummer. Let him step to the music which he hears, however measured or far away."

7. The student whose difficulty is basically maturational, who is a slow developer, may *best* be helped by being given the opportunity to catch up (8). Some students are far advanced in one modality, but quite slow in another. Often the method of teaching must be adapted to the student's differential maturation in the various modalities. Many of the correlates of reading difficulty, such as reversals, poor auditory discrimination, figure-ground difficulties, and poor speech, are instances of inadequate maturation or perhaps immaturity of Gestalt functioning (26).

INTELLECTUAL DEVELOPMENT

Experience and maturation alone do not guarantee success in reading. The student needs certain intellectual skills. He must perceive likenesses and differences, must be able to remember word forms, and must possess certain thinking skills. He must have developed an appropriate memory and attention span. He must be able to associate symbols or language with objects and facts, to anticipate what may happen in a story or a poem, to express his thoughts in his own words, and to think on an abstract level. He must be able to give identity and meaning to objects, events, and symbols. He must be able to categorize or to associate the particular object or experience with the appropriate class or category.

Intellectual development is a function of both biology and environment. Biology sets the limits to the student's mental development, and how close the student comes to attaining his potential depends upon the environment and the use that he makes of that environment. It depends also upon other factors, among which are opportunity, challenge, desire, nutrition, rest, self-discipline, aggressiveness, and the need to achieve. Thus, biology provides the potential and the environment converts it into abilities. "Native ability" actually is the potential to become able; achievement is realized potential.

Intelligence has always been difficult to define. Surely one of the reasons for this is the removal of intelligence from the realm of time. An individual's potential for intellectual activity at the moment of conception may not be the same as his potential at birth or indeed at any given moment of life.

At conception the child possesses what might be described as native intellectual endowment. Biology has set a limit at that time to the child's intellectual capacity. In a later portion of this chapter we discuss the human brain. The brain is biologically determined, and the "mind," "intellect," "cognition," or "perception" must operate through this brain. In a very real sense, man's potential for intellectual behavior is completely dependent upon the proper functioning of the brain.

Aphasia is an instance of improper brain functioning. As a result of cerebral injury, the aphasic is unable to deal with symbols. He can think only on a concrete or specific level. He cannot think abstractly, he cannot categorize, and he is unable to think of the individual object as a member of a class. He cannot, for example, see that a polar bear and a brown bear are bears. These have an individuality for him that does not allow for categorization.

If brain injury can so limit human thought, biology can do likewise. Inadequacy in the genes is a very real cause of inadequate brain development. Nervoid idiocy, amaurotic idiocy, gargoylism (grotesque bone structure), phenylpyruvic idiocy, and primary microcephaly, to mention a few, are caused by gene disturbances.

Intelligence can be viewed in another way. At the moment of birth the child has an intellectual potential that has been limited and defined by biology but now is also conditioned by environment. The child's intra-uterine existence may have been favorable, or it may have been unfavorable for the realization of the child's full intellectual potential at the moment of conception.

Experience has shown repeatedly that the brain, and hence the intellectual functioning of the child, may be damaged by infection, by birth trauma, by toxic agents, or by endocrine disorders. It may be damaged by pressure upon the fetus, by faulty position of the fetus, by temperature changes, by overexposure to X rays, by premature separation from the placenta, by umbilical cord complications, by an overdosage of the mother with drugs, by delayed breathing of the infant, or by forceps delivery. Barbiturates may produce asphyxiation in the fetus. The mother can also pass on to the child certain diseases that interfere with normal brain development, such as smallpox, German measles, scarlet fever, syphilis, and tuberculosis.

Finally, intelligence may be viewed as the student's present functioning level. This is essentially what scholastic aptitude tests measure. If the student's environment or experience is defective, however, it frequently happens that a measure of the student's present functioning level is not a good indicator of his true potential. It is not uncommon to have a student obtain scores like the following on a group intelligence test: linguistic IQ—85, quantitative IQ—115, and total IQ—100. The linguistic score and the total score probably are the best predictors of the student's present scholastic functioning level. Scholastic functioning depends most on the learner's ability to deal with symbols, and the linguistic score measures this ability. The quantitative score may be closer to the student's true potential. The chances are that a student with such discrepancies between linguistic and quantitative scores is from a poor cultural environment, has a reading problem, or is bilingual. If the causative factor is removed, it is not uncommon to find that the IQ score of such a student will rise from fifteen to twenty points.

The teacher is essentially an environmentalist. Even though he cannot add to the student's basic capacity, he can do much to encourage the student to develop his potential. The student commonly has a much greater mental capacity than he is willing to use. As teachers, our task is to challenge the existent capacity of the student rather than to try to add increments to his native endowment.

In the light of this discussion the biological-environmental controversy seems to be a pseudoconflict. The relative contribution of biology, for example, depends upon the trait under consideration, upon the individual possessing the trait, and upon the environment. Thus, in some environments, the principal cause of reading inadequacy may be biological in origin; in others, where there is inadequate teaching, it may be environmental. Most hereditary-or-environment discussions are actually concerned with structural or functional factors. Teachers are more concerned with the following: Is reading failure caused by structural or functional conditions? For a more complete discussion, see the section on "Wordblindness" in this chapter.

Mental Age

For years intelligence was thought to be a unitary factor. Today, few adhere to this point of view. Some persons are spatially or artistically intelligent; others are numerically or verbally intelligent. Some are better able to discover underlying principles; others have a remarkable memory. As educators, we are most interested perhaps in the student's scholastic aptitude. This is essentially a combination of verbal and numerical intelligence and is usually expressed as a mental age or an intelligence quotient.

Mental age (MA) refers to the *level of mental development* that the person has attained. It is the student's score on an intelligence test expressed in age units, or put another way, it is the average age of the individuals who attained that score in the standardization process (43, pp. 216–17).

Thus the average five-year-old child has a mental age of five; the average child of ten, a mental age of ten; and the average youth of fifteen, a mental age of fifteen. But because it has generally been accepted that beyond the age of fifteen or sixteen the mean scores on intelligence tests no longer increase significantly, the average youth of eighteen or twenty will still have a mental age of but fifteen or sixteen.*

The Intelligence Quotient

Another term, the intelligence quotient (IQ) refers to the *rate of mental development*. We all remember the simple formula: Distance equals Rate multiplied by Time ($D = R \times T$).

We may use an analogous formula in thinking about mental age and IQ: thus, $MA = IQ \times CA$. In the formula the MA refers to the distance that the student has traveled mentally; the IQ refers to the rate at which he has been going; and the CA refers to the length of time that he has been at it.

If we think of an IQ of 120 as meaning that the person has advanced at the rate of 1.2 years mentally for each year of chronological life (up to the age of fifteen or sixteen), and of an IQ of 80 as meaning that he has advanced 0.8 of a year mentally for each year of chronological life, the formula ($MA = IQ \times CA$) is easy to understand and to use. A ten-year-old boy with an IQ of 120 has a mental age of twelve ($MA = IQ \times CA$—1.2×10). Another ten-year-old with an IQ of 80 has a mental age of eight ($MA = IQ \times CA$—0.8×10). The first boy attained the mental level of the average twelve-year-old; the second, the mental level of the average eight-year-old.

The following four statements summarize the IQ:

1. IQ is the rate of mental development.
2. $IQ = \dfrac{MA}{CA} \times 100$.
3. An IQ of 120 means that the individual has developed 1.2 years mentally for each year of chronological life.
4. An IQ of a given magnitude also describes the percentage of persons in the general population that possess that IQ.

Let us give some consideration to this last point. IQ also may be defined in terms of a relative position among a defined group of persons.

---

* Actually, the scores cease to increase at the average of fifteen or sixteen years, and thus for some they do not increase at an earlier age and for others they increase at a later age.

An IQ tells how much above or below the average an individual is when comparing himself with persons of his own age. It measures the person's ability relative to persons of his own age group.

Educational Implications

The IQ is not an adequate criterion for reading achievement. It is significant, however, in that it puts a ceiling upon individual achievement. Individuals with an IQ below 25 have little chance of learning to read; those with an IQ below 50 will experience difficulty with abstract materials; and those with IQs between 50 and 70 will rarely be able to read above a fourth-grade level.

The IQ is also an important long-range predictor of the youngster's performance. The child with a 150 IQ who is only six years old may not be as efficient a reader as the child with a 100 IQ who is ten years old. With time, however, the chances are that he will reach a higher level of reading proficiency.

Mental age, generally, is a much better indicator of reading readiness and achievement than is IQ, especially at the early levels. To be able to read, many skills are necessary that come only with age.

Correlations between intelligence and reading ability generally vary from about .35 in the first grade to about .65 in the sixth grade. Cohen and Glass (16) found no significant relationship between IQ scores and reading ability in the first grade; in the fourth grade, IQ and reading ability were significantly related. These findings are important. They imply that intelligence is a greater determinant of reading success in the later grades than in the earlier grades. In the later grades, reading scores are an expression of proficiency in content-area reading. Content-area reading generally requires greater use of those skills that we associate with intellectual activity.

Even though the correlations between intelligence and reading achievement are high, they are not perfect. Intelligence is not the sole, or necessarily the best, indicator of reading readiness or achievement. High intelligence does not guarantee success in reading. Research indicates that the great majority of poor readers have IQs between 80 and 110 (50, p. 228) and that frequently the most severely retarded readers in relation to their mental age have IQs of 130 or more.

PHYSICAL DEVELOPMENT

We have discussed three determinants of the student's achievement in reading. Let us look at another group of related conditions which, for want of a better term, we shall refer to as *physical factors*.

The student is both physical and physiological. Functions such as vision, hearing, and thought are possible only through certain organs of the body—the eye, the ear, or the brain. If the organ is defective, the function is likely to be impaired. This may, especially in vision, hearing, and thought, lead to serious reading difficulties. In general, good health is conducive to good reading, and poor health is often associated with reading deficiency.

PHYSICAL HEALTH

Reading is an act, a performance, or a response that the reader makes to the printed page. Unfortunately, certain factors may prohibit making the response. Glandular dysfunction (18), hemoglobin variation, vitamin deficiencies, nerve disorders, nutritional and circulatory problems, heart conditions, infected tonsils, poor teeth, rickets, asthma, allergies, tuberculosis, rheumatic fever, or prolonged illness can lower reading achievement.

Eames (19) points out that tumefaction of the pituitary gland may lead to a reduction in eye span and consequently to an increase in the number of fixations. Hypothyroid conditions may prevent normal fixation and thus lead to daydreaming, poor attention, slow word recognition, and general fatigue. Diabetes mellitus is associated with visual defects, confusions, excessive regressions, and loss of place.

Schiffman (36), however, states that there is no known relationship between errors of biochemical functioning and any specific reading syndrome.

Eating habits are related to a student's overall functioning and may also be a direct cause of poor learning. Far too often the student either does not eat at all or gulps down a few bites to satisfy his mother.

The teacher must be cautious in interpreting the relationship that physical factors seemingly have to reading deficiency. Generally, physical inadequacies contribute to, rather than cause, reading problems. Illness keeps the student from school and makes him miss important phases of instruction. Any physical inadequacy makes it difficult to become enthusiastic about learning and may result in lowered vitality, in depletion of energy, in slower physical development, and hence in mental retardation. Physical inadequacies cause the student to center attention on them and away from learning. The student with a smashed finger, a broken hand, a headache, or poor eyesight may be unable to concentrate on a learning task. The malnourished youth does not have the energy to be an effective learner.

Sometimes a lowering of the student's basic vitality is closely related to the functions required for successful reading. The basal metabolic rate, BMR, for example, affects the convergence of the eyes. If the rate is low, the student may not be able to aim his eyes properly in binocular vision and thus may frequently regress, omit words, lose his place, and become fatigued. Fatigue makes it difficult to become interested in a reading task. Attention suffers and comprehension is usually lowered. As nervous tension builds up, the student becomes disinterested and disgusted and may even turn from reading completely.

VISUAL ADEQUACY

We already have spoken of the student's need for visual proficiency. For efficient reading the student must learn to focus and to coordinate the eyes, to move them along a line of print, and to make appropriate return sweeps. He must see clearly and distinctly both near and far, must be able to change focus and to fuse the impressions of each eye into a single image, and must have visual memory for what he has seen. He must be able to sustain visual concentration, must have good hand-eye coordination, and must be able to perceive size and distance relationships accurately.

It is difficult to evaluate the specific effect of the various disturbances. The eyes can make amazing accommodations so that words may be seen clearly. With the proper motivation the student may learn despite visual handicaps. He can ignore a distortion from one eye if he sees clearly with the other or if he adjusts his reading position to compensate. He may suppress the vision in one eye or alternate from one eye to another. The result is monocular vision. Generally, however, for effective vision the student must be able to use his eyes in unison.

Visual Acuity

Visual acuity does not seem to have the significance for reading achievement that some other visual conditions have. First: Reading is a near-point task. One could fail the visual acuity test at twenty feet but possess good visual acuity at sixteen inches. Second: To read the average book, one needs only 20/60 visual acuity.* Nevertheless, acuity is important. Each student should probably have at least 20/30 acuity at far point.

The emmetropic, or normal, eye sees with 100 percent of acuity only a very small portion of the visual field, perhaps no more than four or five letters.

* Snellen's formula is $V = d/D$. V represents visual acuity; d is the distance at which the person is reading the letters; and D is the distance at which the person should be reading. Thus 20/60 means that the person sees at twenty feet what he should see at sixty feet. A 20/20 notation means that the student has 100 percent visual efficiency at far point.

Refractive Errors

Refractive errors are due to damage to, disease of, or weakness in the lens or other portion of one or both eyes. Refractive errors can generally be corrected by glasses. Glasses, however, do not increase the sensitivity of the eyes. They help the eye to focus and lower eye strain but frequently fail to provide normal vision.

Myopia, or nearsightedness, is perhaps the most common among the refractive errors. The myopic eye is too long, with the result that the light rays come into focus in front of the retina instead of on the retina. This forces the student to hold the book closer than the normal sixteen inches or so. Distant vision is generally blurred. Concave lenses are usually prescribed for myopic conditions. Among honor students in college, who do significantly more reading than the average college population, the incidence of myopia is 66 percent.

Hyperopia, or hypermetropia, is generally known as farsightedness. Where the myopic eye is too long, the hyperopic eye is too short. In this case, the image falls behind the retina. To remedy this condition, convex lenses are prescribed. In school testing for farsightedness, if the student reads the 20/20 test line with + 2.00 diopter lenses, he should be referred to an eye specialist.

Another type of refractive error, *astigmatism,* is the inability to bring light rays to a single focal point. Vision is blurred and distorted. The underlying cause is an uneven curvature of the cornea of the eye. The cornea is spoon shaped rather than spherical. Unless the distorted image is corrected by the use of cylindrical lenses, the student fatigues easily and usually dislikes close work or prolonged distant vision. Astigmatism is a major cause of ocular asthenopia, or eyestrain. Headaches are common, similar letters and words are confused, and the student experiences difficulty in sustained reading.

Binocular Errors

The binocular errors have the commonality of giving the student a double image. Either the two eyes do not aim correctly or they give conflicting reports. When the ocular maladjustments are minor, the individual may compensate for them. If the maladjustments are major, the student may see two of everything or the two images may be so badly blurred that he sees neither image clearly. Somehow he needs to suppress one stimulus. When he can suppress it only partially or only temporarily, he is likely to lose his place, to omit words, or to regress.

Strabismus, or muscular imbalance, stems from an incoordination of the muscles that move the eyeball. The eyes are actually aiming in different directions. One eye aims too far outward, too far inward, or in a different vertical plane from the other eye. A severe case of strabismus may result in double vision; a less severe case, in a general blurring of the image.

There are three types of strabismus, or heterophoria. When the deviation is outward, it is called *exophoria* (walleyes); when it is inward, *esophoria* (cross-eyes); and when one eye focuses higher than the other, *hyperphoria*. Hyperphoria may lead to jumping of lines or misplacement of a word to a line above or below.

Even a moderate amount of heterophoria, or tendency of the eye to deviate, results in fatigue. As the reader tires, his eyes tend to deviate even farther. Attempts to counteract this increase fatigue. A vicious circle is set up. The student becomes inattentive and irritable, loses his place, omits, and regresses. This incoordination is sometimes corrected by cutting some of the eye muscles.

Some research indicates that myopic children with phoric conditions read about as well as do children without phoria, but that children with phorias at far point have poorer reading skills.

Two additional binocular defects are *lack of fusion* and *aniseikonia*. To see clearly, the lenses of the two eyes must be in focus. The images must fuse correctly, thus giving one mental picture.

An inability to fuse correctly is manifested by mixing of letters and words, inability to follow lines across a page, loss of place, and slowness in reading.

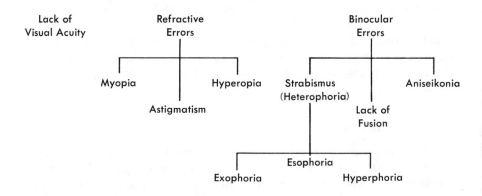

FIGURE 3-1   VISUAL DEFICIENCIES

Aniseikonia occurs whenever there is a difference in size or shape between the two ocular images. As a result fusion is difficult, and the reader may become tense, experience fatigue, and have headaches.

Figure 3-1 illustrates the various visual defects that are present among school youth. Although other visual defects exist, the incidence of these is not as great.

Symptoms of Eye Disturbances

The teacher of reading cannot be satisfied with a general knowledge of eye defects. He needs to know the individual student's eye condition well enough to answer a number of specific questions (42, p. 163): Does the student need special reading materials? When should he wear his glasses? Does he require special lighting? Can he read for prolonged periods of time?

The teacher must frequently seek help from a specialist. Perhaps the teacher's chief responsibility here is to be familiar with the symptoms of eye defects.* A knowledge of these will help him to detect visual problems before they have become visual defects. He should be able to identify functional problems before they have become structural problems.

Teachers are often appalled by the poor concentration of some of their students. Unfortunately, in this instance "poor concentration" is not a good term. The student can usually concentrate, but it is on only one idea at a time. His attempt to maintain single vision or to clear blurred vision may prevent concentration on the mental task at hand. His cortical powers are entirely directed to the maintenance of basic visual skills. This same need for conscious control of the ocular factors could keep the student from reading as rapidly as he might.

Educational Implications

Eye defects of one sort or another are rather common. These defects increase throughout the grades and may play an important role in reading inadequacy. Good readers in the elementary grades generally have fewer visual defects than have poor readers. In high school and college—possibly because by high school many of those with poor vision have left school, and those who remain have adapted their scholastic approach to their reading deficiencies—there are few indications of visual differences between good and poor readers.

Generally, the incidence of myopia does not distinguish the good reader from the poor reader. Myopia may even be associated with better than normal progress. Although hyperopia seems to occur somewhat more frequently among poor readers (20, p. 7), the evidence is not definitive. There also is a lack of agreement concerning the effect that

---

* See Gertrude E. Knox, "Classroom Symptoms of Visual Difficulty," *Clinical Studies in Reading,* II, Supplementary Educational Monographs, No. 77 (Chicago: The University of Chicago Press, 1937); and Samuel M. Diskan, "Eye Problems in Children," *Postgraduate Medicine,* 34 (August 1963), 168–78.

astigmatism has on reading. It may be a handicap to successful reading when the learner has a severe case.

Failure of the eyes to coordinate, as in strabismus and in lack of fusion, and failure of the eyes to give images of the same size seem to have more serious impact on reading development. When the deviations are vertical, as when one eye focuses higher (hyperphoria), the reader frequently loses his place and fixates at a point either below or above the line on which he should be reading. He frequently complains of not understanding what he is reading. This condition seems to occur with equal frequency among both good and poor readers. When the deviations are lateral, the convergence may be insufficient as in exophoria, or excessive as in cross-eyes (esophoria). The former condition seems to occur more frequently among poor readers than does any other heterophoric condition. It leads to omissions, regressions, and loss of place.

Difficulties with fusion and aniseikonia also seem to be more common among poor readers than among good readers. Taylor (44) reports that a survey of some two thousand children with academic difficulties showed that 95 percent of these lacked sufficient coordination and had difficulties with fusion. They failed to show the thirteen to nineteen diopters of convergence required to direct the eyes toward a single fixation point at thirteen inches of reading distance while maintaining appropriate divergence or eye balance.

Taylor adds that deficiencies in binocular control lead to inadequate word perception and consumption of an excessive amount of energy in maintaining single vision. The student will fatigue easily and will experience distraction, poor comprehension, constant moving of the head, and difficulties in concentration.

Any interpretation of the relationship between visual defects and reading must consider the likelihood of multiple causation. Some students are more sensitive to visual problems than are others. Some are able to perform well in short test periods and thus escape detection through the usual methods. Perhaps some eye defects have not yet been identified. We know far too little about the syndromes or patterns of reading defects generally. Eye defects may be but one of a number of factors contributing to a reading deficiency. Some students with defective vision become good readers, and others without any visual difficulty do not learn to read. This does not indicate, however, that good vision is unimportant to reading. Eye defects are a handicap to both good and poor readers.

Visual Screening Tests

Two simple tests that the teacher can use are the *Point of Convergence Test* and the *Muscle Balance and Suppression Test* (13). The *Point of Convergence Test* is administered by holding a penlight or a pencil in front of the student. The examiner gradually moves the pencil horizontally toward the student's nose until the student sees two pencils. The near point of convergence is the distance in inches from that point on to the eye. Normal near-point convergence is from one to three inches. In the *Muscle Balance and Suppression Test,* a two- or three-foot string is held by the student. One end of the string is held against the bridge of the nose by the index finger, with care being taken so as not to block the line of sight of either eye. A knot is tied in the string sixteen inches away from the eyes. The student is instructed to look at the knot. Normally, he will see the two strings touching each other at the knot, making a V shape. If the two strings seem to cross in front of the knot, the condition is esophoria; if they cross behind the knot, it is exophoria. Orthophoria, or normal muscular balance, is present if the strings cross at the knot. If only one string is seen, the student is suppressing one eye. If one string is higher than the other, the condition is hyperphoria (13).*

AUDITORY ADEQUACY

Auditory adequacy includes hearing, listening, and comprehension; it encompasses auditory acuity, auditory discrimination, auditory blending, and auditory comprehension.

Hearing is the process by which sound waves are received, modified, and relayed along the nervous system by the ear (27). It is our prime concern in this section.

Auditory acuity is the recognition of discrete units of sound (49). Auditory discrimination is the ability to discriminate between the sounds, or phonemes, or a language. Auditory blending is the ability to reproduce a word by synthesizing its component parts (14, p. 113). Finally, hearing is not complete until the hearer can comprehend and interpret what he has heard.

Normal acuity is variously defined. Some believe that a hearing loss of as little as six decibels puts one in the hard-of-hearing group; others would put the cutoff point at fifteen or more decibels. Because of this difference in definition, writers have reported percentages of hearing deficiencies ranging from 3 to 20 percent. Generally, it is estimated to be about 5 percent.

Types of Auditory Deafness

There are two kinds of auditory deficiency: *intensity deafness* and *tone deafness.* A tone-deaf person cannot discriminate between pitches.

* For a discussion and description of commercial visual screening tests see Emerald Dechant, *Improving the Teaching of Reading* (Englewood Cliffs, N.J.: Prentice-Hall, Inc., 1970), pp. 64–66.

Intensity deafness is of three types: (1) *Central deafness* is caused by damage to the auditory areas of the brain or by a neurotic conversion reaction (hysteria). (2) A *conductive loss* stems from an impairment in the conductive process in the middle ear. Either the eardrum is punctured or there is a malfunction of the ossicles, the three small bones in the middle ear. This reduces the person's hearing ability, affecting the loudness with which he hears speech, but if the loudness of the sound is increased, he hears and understands. A person with a conductive loss can hear his own voice through bone conduction. Thus, the voices of others sound much softer than his own. To compensate, he frequently speaks softly so his voice will seem to conform to the voices of others around him. (3) *Nerve loss* stems from an impairment of the auditory nerve and affects clarity and intelligibility of speech. A person with such a loss hears the speech of others but may not understand what he hears. The high-tone nerve loss prevents him from hearing and distinguishing certain speech sounds, especially such sounds as *f, v, s, z, sh, zh, th, t, d, b, p, k,* and *g.* Articulation is generally affected. The student may speak too loudly or may develop monotony in his voice. He frequently shows signs of misunderstanding the teacher. The student may be thought of as mentally retarded. Figure 3-2 categorizes the various types of auditory deafness.

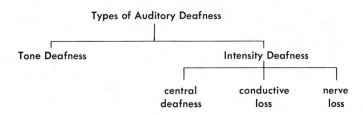

FIGURE 3-2

Causes and Symptoms of Hearing Deficiencies

In more than 75 percent of the cases of deafness, German measles, erythroblastosis fetalis, meningitis, bilateral ear infection, fluid in the middle ear, obstructions in the ear canal, or a family history of deafness can be identified. In the remaining cases, the chief symptom is the inability to speak at the customary age.

The following behaviors may be indicative of hearing problems:

1. The student is inattentive during lectures in the classroom.
2. The student turns the head toward the speaker, cups the hands behind the ears, or tends to favor one ear.

3. The student complains of ringing or buzzing in the ears.

4. The student listens with a tense facial or blank expression.

5. The student confuses words with similar sounds.

6. The student hears the speech of others but may not understand what he hears.

7. The student has special difficulty with the sounds *f, v, s, z, sh, zh, th, t, d, b, k, g.*

8. The student speaks in a monotone or the pitch is unnatural.

9. The student fails to respond to phonic instruction.

10. The student's pronunciation is faulty.

11. The student breathes through the mouth.

Tests of Hearing

The hearing of every student showing any of the above symptoms should be tested. Bond and Tinker (10, p. 113) suggest a number of methods for doing this. A loud-ticking watch may be used as a simple test. Normally a person can hear the ticking up to a distance of about forty-eight inches. Anything less than twenty inches probably indicates hearing deficiency. For a more accurate test, an audiometer may be used. Audiometers produce sounds of different frequency and intensity levels for the purpose of measuring auditory sensitivity. They permit the audiologist to obtain an audiogram of an individual's hearing in terms of frequency and intensity.

Educational Implications

O'Connor and Streng (34) divide the hard of hearing into four groups. Those with an average loss of twenty decibels or less in the better ear require no special treatment, although it would be wise to seat them advantageously in the classroom. Students in the twenty-five to fifty-five decibel loss group may need speech training, and those with a loss of thirty-five decibels may need a hearing aid. A third group with losses ranging from fifty-five to seventy-five decibels usually cannot learn to speak without aid. The individuals in this group are considered educationally deaf. A fourth group consists of those who are suffering more than a seventy-five-decibel loss. Members of this group cannot learn speech through sounds, and ordinarily the public school is unable to meet their needs. They require special treatment. Persons with a forty-decibel loss across the speech range will have particular difficulty with *ch, f, k, s, sh, th,* and *z.*

Loss of hearing can aggravate a reading deficiency. Studies have generally indicated that the ability to discriminate speech sounds is important for speech and reading development. Without it, students cannot isolate the separate sounds in words and thus find phonics training incomprehensible. In seeking to understand the relationship between auditory deficiencies and reading disability, however, we must again remember that causes often are complex rather than simple, multiple rather than single. Auditory factors may be especially important when there is a severe hearing loss, when the specific hearing loss involves high-tone deafness, or when instruction puts a premium on auditory factors. The exclusive use of the phonic method with a student who has suffered a hearing loss may prevent achievement in reading.

The student will be at a disadvantage if the teacher fails to distinguish between mistakes in reading and differences in pronunciation. The student who reads "I write wif a pin" has read correctly but may not have spoken the way the teacher would speak. Admonishing this student for poor reading may only hurt him. In fact, the student may not be able to hear the difference between *with* and *wif,* or *pen* and *pin,* even under the most favorable of instructional procedures.

Retardation occurs much more frequently among students with defective hearing than among students with normal hearing. When the hearing defect is unilateral, achievement is not so adversely affected as when the hearing defect is bilateral. Deaf students are educationally handicapped much more than are the hard of hearing. Even low-level perception of sounds allows for most of those experiences that are essential to normal development in speech and language. Generally, as hearing loss increases, reading achievement becomes poorer.

The teacher cannot be satisfied, however, with the mere detection of auditory deficiencies. He cannot do much about improving the student's auditory acuity. A hearing aid is much simpler. The teacher can do much in developing the student's auditory discrimination skills. He must train the student in the awareness of sound, in making discriminations among simple speech patterns, such as differences between vowels, and in the finer discriminations necessary for speech. The latter involves the ability to distinguish the phonetic elements within words.

NEURAL ADEQUACY AND READING

The brain controls the rest of the body by sending commands, as it were, through a network of eighty-six major nerves that expand into thousands of smaller nerves. The nerves spread from the brain through the brain stem down the spinal cord. The nerves may be likened to miles of telephone wire; the brain, to a central switchboard. The impulses travel through the neural network, transmitting sensory data and messages.

Obviously, brain activity is much more complex than a telephone switchboard connection. In the neurons, through a combination of glucose and oxygen, an electrical charge builds up. At a certain level of buildup it discharges, becoming the nerve impulse that moves from neuron to neuron. It is a combination of these nerve impulses, or tiny bursts of electrical energy, that we record on electroencephalographs and that result in thoughts and actions. The transmission of the impulse from one neuron to another is chemically controlled. It is not the impulse itself but a resulting chemical, acetylcholine, that stimulates a muscle and makes it move.

The mysteries of brain activity are many. The reticular formation in the brain stem seems to make it possible for us to pay attention or to ignore the multitude of stimuli that bombard us. The thalamus plays a role in the perception of pain. Rage and fear are produced when the amygdala is stimulated. Destruction of the amygdala leads to extreme nymphomania in the female cat and to satyrism in the male. Electrical stimulation at the proper spot can cause a cat to purr contentedly when hurt or to become panicky at the sight of a mouse. The usually fierce rhesus monkey will permit itself to be petted when stimulated at the caudate nucleus.

Projection and Association Areas

Research by Gall, Dax, Broca, Jackson, Head, Wernicke, Goldstein, Halstead, Sherrington, and the Penfields and recent experiments with electrical stimulations of the brain have given us much information concerning the projection areas of the brain. Figure 3-3 shows the auditory, visual, motor, and sensory areas. Two fissures, the fissure of Rolando and the fissure of Sylvius, separate the brain into lobes. That part lying in front of the Sylvian fissure is known as the frontal lobe. The sense organs are connected with their special projection areas in the cortex, and essential sensory processes occur there. An injury to the visual projection area, for example, may cause blindness.

The functions of the brain, however, are not restricted to the projection areas. More than three-fourths of the brain consists of association areas. The associations between the various sensory and motor areas are the result of learning.

When the child touches a burning match, a sharp signal of pain is received in the projection area. He avoids a burning match later, not because of the pain, but because he associates the pain with the sight of fire. To be meaningful, the experience of the present must be related to the experiences of the past. This occurs in the association areas. There the sensory and motor areas are united into the countless hookups, and the "memory" of the past is preserved.

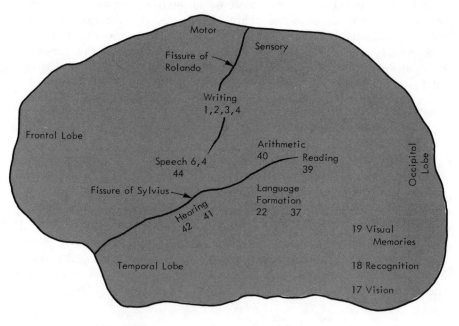

FIGURE 3.3   THE BRAIN

(Thomas H. Eames, "Visual Handicaps to Reading," Journal of Education, 141 (February 1959), 35. Reproduced by permission of the Journal of Education, Boston University Press.)

The impulses that travel through the neural network may be blocked by injuries along the neural path or by damage to the brain itself. Eames (19) notes that interferences with the frontal-occipital fasciculus affect auditory memory and create difficulties in the learning of phonics. Other interferences in the association areas affect eye movement and eye span.

The visual projection area is surrounded by an association area known as the parastriate cortex. A second association area, known as the peristriate cortex, surrounds the parastriate cortex. If the parastriate cortex is injured, the person cannot recognize or identify what he sees. If the peristriate cortex is injured, the person may be able to recognize what he sees, but he cannot recall the appearance of objects when they are not in view.

The nerve impulse travels from the retina along the optic nerve to visual area 17 (Figure 3-3) in the occipital lobe. This area is concerned with seeing without recognition. In areas 18 and 19 recognition and visual memory occur. There the words are recognized as words. In area 39, the angular gyrus, the meaning of the word is comprehended. Eames (20, p. 4) notes that interpretation of symbols (letters, words, syllables) and recognition and visual memory for word forms occur here. A lesion in this area will interfere with the ability to read (20, p. 4). In the part of the brain lying between the hearing and reading areas, roughly areas 22 and 37, the association of sounds and visual symbols occurs. Thus, since reading is commonly an association of a visual symbol with an auditory symbol, this part is of major importance in reading and is called the language-formation area. Injury in this area results in the inability to name one's concepts.

Wordblindness

The term *wordblindness* has traditionally meant inability to remember word forms. We use it here to mean any condition, whether permanent or temporary, that makes it impossible for the student to read. The condition may be either structural or functional.

FIGURE 3-4   WORDBLINDNESS

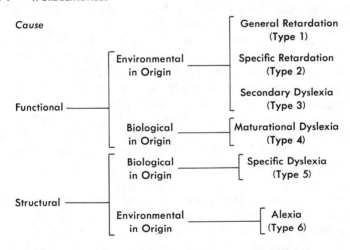

Hinshelwood (25, p. 53) points out that any condition that reduces the number of cortical cells within the angular (area 39) and supramarginal (area 40) gyri of the left side of the cortex or that interferes with the supply of blood to that area lowers the functional activity of that part of the brain and will be accompanied by a diminished retention of the visual images of letters and words. He (25, p. 102) felt that treatment for structural wordblindness consists in developing (1) a visual memory for the letters of the alphabet, (2) an auditory memory for words by having the student spell aloud the word letter by letter, and (3) a visual memory for words.

Severely handicapped readers, however, need not always have suffered structural defects. For example, such conditions as inadequate instruction, emotional disturbances, lack of interest, or social incompetency may terminate in a reading problem.

Cerebral Dominance

A condition thought to be dependent on the development of the brain is *cerebral dominance*. This term implies that one cerebral hemisphere is more important in behavior or functionally more efficient than the other. The left hemisphere commonly is the language hemisphere, and for most individuals, since most of us are right-handed, it also is the dominant hemisphere.

There are, however, exceptions to this general rule. Some persons are left-handed (right dominance), some are ambidextrous with neither hemisphere being dominant (lack of dominance), and in others the dominance changes from activity to activity. The latter is termed *crossed dominance* and is seen in individuals exhibiting left-eyedness and right-handedness. Do these conditions hinder reading proficiency?

Orton (35) suggested that in learning to read the pupil develops memory traces for words both in the dominant (left for the average individual) and in the nondominant (right) hemisphere, but that those in the nondominant hemisphere normally are mirror images of the former and thus are suppressed. He adds that if cerebral dominance is well developed by the time reading begins, reading proficiency is not affected. If, however, no special dominance is developed or if the engrams, or memory traces, in the right hemisphere (left dominance) become active, reading difficulties occur, and the pupil will read once with a left and then with a right orientation.

In cases of lack of dominance (as in the ambidextrous person), the engrams of each hemisphere are equally dominant, and the reader may become confused and indecisive in his reading. He sometimes reads in a left-to-right direction and at other times reverses the direction. Letters and words are reversed because the pupil sometimes uses the mirror images developed in the nondominant hemisphere.

Although Orton did not concern himself with the left-handed individual, similar difficulties may arise. The left-handed person has a natural tendency to move from right to left in attacking words. And if he follows this natural tendency in reading, he will see little difference between the printed words and their mirror images. This results in reversals of words and word forms.

Unfortunately, it is not at all clear that reversals, confusion in orientation, and reading disability are related to lack of or left cerebral dominance.

Ketchum (29) states that Orton's views are no longer tenable. He suggests that difficulties in directional stability may arise from inefficiencies within the nonverbal hemisphere itself.

Dominance is not an either-or proposition; rather it is a matter of degree. To some degree everyone is two-handed, the embryo is completely symmetrical, and the development of a dominant hand is a gradual process. Ananiev (39, p. 31), in an investigation of the dominant eye, dominant ear, and dominant hand, also found that a different member may be preferred for a different function.

Poor readers, however, especially those showing up in reading clinics, generally show a greater frequency of undeveloped dominance. Harris (21, p. 254), for example, reports that a high proportion of reading disability cases develop preference for one hand later than the age of nine. In a later study (22) he suggests that if tests are sufficiently discriminative, genuine relationships between reading disability and laterality are found.

Silver and Hagin (38), in an intensive study of eighteen subjects over a period of years, concluded that the persistence of anomalies of laterality, even when maturation in perceptual areas has occurred, suggests that for some children "reading disability may be a basic biologic defect resulting from the failure to establish clear-cut cerebral dominance."

Alexander and Money (1) believe that defective direction sense and defective space-form perception may explain some cases of reading retardation, but the presence of these defects alone is not sufficient to cause retardation. The defect may be explained in some pupils by a maturation lag or developmental defect in direction sense and in space-form perception (32). The authors developed the *Road Map Test,* which is an outline map of several city blocks, to measure direction sense. The pupil is required to follow a route and to report whether he turns to the left or to the right at each corner. It was found that right-left spatial orientation normally becomes established between eleven and fourteen years of age, but dyslexic boys between eleven and fourteen made significantly more errors than did the standardization group.

Muehl (33) found that left lateral subjects made more left and right recognition errors than consistent right lateral subjects, suggesting that left laterality might be associated with unique patterns of visual or perceptual behavior.

The research data are far from being definitive. Cohen and Glass (16) found significant relationships between knowledge of left- and right-hand dominance and reading ability in the first grade, but not so in the fourth grade. Those first-grade pupils who knew the difference between left and right and who had a dominant hand tended to be the better readers. Crossed dominance (right-handed left-eyed or vice versa) was found not to be related to reading ability. The data indicated that it might be better to be left-handed than to be mixed. The authors suggest that in the first grade it may be worthwhile to develop techniques for firmly establishing hand dominance and directional certainty.

Stephens and others (41) found no relationship between crossed eye-hand preferences and reading readiness; Balow (3, 4) reported that hand preference and eye preference, either singly or interactionally, or knowledge of right or left were not significantly associated with readiness or with reading achievement; Belmont and Brick (9) reported that retarded readers were not differentiated from normal readers by mixed dominance; and Tinker (45) concluded from her study that laterality is not a factor in reading disability. Most studies, like that of Cohen and Glass, show that hand preference becomes better established with age.

In summary:

1. Learning occurs in an organism, and whatever affects the nervous system of the organism may affect learning. Lack of neurological organization may be a key factor in reading difficulty.
2. The more we know about nerve excitation and brain functioning, the better we will understand the student's ease or difficulty of learning.
3. We may have two types of learners: those who have had appropriate neural development for learning and those who have not.
4. Since nerve impulses are tiny bursts of electrical energy brought about by chemical changes, it may well be that some learning deficiencies reflect subtle chemical changes (40).

SUMMARY

This chapter has examined four broad conditions that account for some of the differences in reading achievement: experiential background, maturational development, intellectual development, and physical development. A knowledge of these factors alone is not enough to provide adequately for the student's reading needs. Few of us, however, would deny their importance.

This chapter should have cautioned us in the interpretation of reading failures. Not all students can learn to read with ease. Some students want to learn but attain little success. They are motivated; they are not lazy or indifferent. For some of these achievement in reading is difficult because they are handicapped intellectually, experientially, physically, or physiologically.

Teaching reading would be rather simple if the teacher knew exactly how to bring forth the desired responses from the student. Unfortunately, the same stimulus or teaching will elicit different reactions from different students and even from the same student at different times. Some explanations for variability in behavior have been stated in this chapter. In the following chapter we shall examine additional reasons why students are different and why they will behave differently in the classroom.

QUESTIONS FOR DISCUSSION

1. State five basic principles of growth and development and point out how they apply in the teaching of reading.
2. Is it possible to raise all children's reading proficiency to the same level? Why?
3. What is the advantage of a broad experiential background in reading?
4. Discuss the reasons for identifying, at least in a general way, the student's intellectual capacity, and discuss the implications of this for the student's reading achievement.
5. Discuss visual adequacy and its implications for the developmental reading program.
6. Discuss the relationship between neural functioning and achievement in reading.
7. Elaborate on the statement: "Not all students can read with ease."
8. Discuss the following:
   a. Development in reading closely parallels and is an expression of the forces of human development generally.
   b. Intelligence test scores are not as significant for determining readiness for learning to read as for predicting achievement in reading in later grades.
   c. Mental age is not as significant for determining readiness for beginning reading as is ability in visual and auditory discrimination, but achievement in reading is a more direct function of intelligence than of auditory or visual discrimination.
   d. The poor reader is distinguished from the good reader by (1) his inability to perceive the relationship to one another of the details within the total word shape or (2) his inability to perceive parts and details, in which case he perceives unanalyzable wholes. He is weak in the ability to analyze the visual and auditory structures of words and in the ability to synthesize phonetic units to form whole words.
   e. The greater the amount of energy the reader must expend in reading (because of physical inadequacies, for example), the less he tends to read.

    f. The mind (perceptual and cognitive processes), not sight, is the limiting factor in rate of recognition.

BIBLIOGRAPHY

1. ALEXANDER, DUANE, and JOHN MONEY, "Reading Disability and the Problem of Direction Sense," *The Reading Teacher,* 20 (February 1967), 404–9.
2. BALLER, WARREN R., and DON C. CHARLES, *The Psychology of Human Growth and Development.* New York: Holt, Rinehart, & Winston, Inc., 1961.
3. BALOW, I. H., "Lateral Dominance Characteristics and Reading Achievement in the First Grade," *Journal of Psychology,* 55 (1962), 323–28.
4. ———, and B. BALOW, "Lateral Dominance and Reading Achievement in the Second Grade," *American Educational Research Journal,* 1 (1964), 139–43.
5. BARTON, ALLEN, "Social Class and Instructional Procedures in the Process of Learning to Read," in *Twelfth Yearbook of the National Reading Conference,* ed. Y. Melton Culberth, and Ralph C. Staiger, Milwaukee, 1962.
6. BATTLE, ESTHER S., and JULIAN B. ROTTER, "Children's Feelings of Personal Control as Related to Social Class and Ethnic Group," *Journal of Personality,* 31 (1963), 482–90.
7. BECKETT, DOROTHY B., "Philosophical Differences in Reading Concepts," *The Reading Teacher,* 18 (October 1964), 27–32.
8. BELMONT, HERMAN S., "Psychological Influences on Learning," *Sociological and Psychological Factors in Reading,* pp. 15–26. Proceedings of the 21st Annual Reading Institute, Temple University, Philadelphia, 1964.
9. BELMONT, LILLIAN, and H. G. BRICK, "Lateral Dominance, Lateral Awareness, and Reading Disability," *Child Development,* 36 (March 1965), 57–71.
10. BOND, GUY L., and MILES A. TINKER, *Reading Difficulties: Their Diagnosis and Correction.* New York: Appleton-Century-Crofts, 1967.
11. BOTHWELL, HAZEL, "The Child with Impaired Hearing," *NEA Journal,* 56 (November 1967), 44–46.
12. BRUNER, JEROME S., *On Knowing,* p. 108. Cambridge: Harvard University Press, 1962.
13. BRUNGARDT, JOE B., and MIKE J. BRUNGARDT, "Let's Stop the Prevailing Injustices to Children," *Kansas Teacher,* 73 (January 1965), 14–15, 50.
14. CHALL, JEANNE, FLORENCE G. ROSWELL, and SUSAN H. BLUMENTHAL, "Auditory Blending Ability: A Factor in Success in Beginning Reading," *The Reading Teacher,* 17 (1963), 113–18.
15. CLARK, W. W., "Boys and Girls—Are There Significant Ability and Achievement Differences?" *Phi Delta Kappan,* 41 (November 1959), 73–76.

16. COHEN, ALICE, and GERALD G. GLASS, "Lateral Dominance and Reading Ability," *The Reading Teacher,* 21 (January 1968), 343–48.

17. DAVIS, A., *Child Training and Social Class in Child Behavior and Development.* New York: McGraw-Hill Book Company, 1943.

18. EAMES, THOMAS H., "The Effect of Endocrine Disorders on Reading," *The Reading Teacher,* 12 (April 1959), 263–65.

19. ———, "Physical Factors in Reading," *The Reading Teacher,* 15 (May 1962), 427–32.

20. ———, "Visual Handicaps to Reading," *Journal of Education,* 141 (February 1959), 1–36.

21. HARRIS, A. J., *How to Increase Ability* (3rd ed.). New York: Longmans, Green and Company, 1956.

22. ———, "Lateral Dominance, Directional Confusion, and Reading Disability," *Journal of Psychology,* 44 (October 1957), 283–94.

23. ———, *Effective Teaching of Reading.* New York: David McKay Co., Inc., 1962.

24. HENRY, JULES, *Culture against Man.* New York: Random House, Inc., 1963.

25. HINSHELWOOD, JAMES, *Congenital Word-Blindness.* London: H. K. Lewis and Company, Ltd., 1917.

26. HIRSH, KATRINA DE, "Psychological Correlates of the Reading Process," *Challenge and Experiment in Reading,* 7 (1962), 218–26. International Reading Association.

27. HORWORTH, GLORIA L., "Listening: A Facet of Oral Language," *Elementary English,* 43 (December 1966), 856–64, 868.

28. JENSEN, M. B., "Reading Deficiency as Related to Cerebral Injury and to Neurotic Behavior," *Journal of Applied Psychology,* 27 (December 1943), 535–45.

29. KETCHUM, E. GILLET, "Neurological and Psychological Trends in Reading Diagnosis," *The Reading Teacher,* 17 (May 1964), 589–93.

30. LADD, ELEANOR M., "Individualizing Instruction in Classroom Corrective Situations," *Vistas in Reading,* II, Part I, 254–56. International Reading Association, Newark, N.J., 1967.

31. LIDDLE, GORDON P., and ROBERT E. ROCKWELL, "The Kid with Two Strikes against Him," *Safety Education,* 43 (December 1963), 2–5.

32. MONEY, J., D. ALEXANDER, and H. T. WALKER, JR., A *Standardized Road-Map Test to Direction Sense.* Baltimore: Johns Hopkins Press, 1965.

33. MUEHL, S., "Relation between Word Recognition Errors and Hand-Eye Preference in Preschool Children," *Journal of Educational Psychology,* 54 (1963), 316–21.

34. O'CONNOR, CLARENCE D., and ALICE STRENG, "Teaching the Acoustically Handicapped," *The Education of Exceptional Children,* Forty-ninth Yearbook, National Society for the Study of Education, Part II, pp. 152–76. Chicago: University of Chicago Press, 1950.

35. ORTON, S. T., "An Impediment to Learning to Read—A Neurological Explanation of the Reading Disability," *School and Society,* 28 (September 1928), 286–90.

36. SCHIFFMAN, GILBERT B., "An Interdisciplinary Approach to the Identification and Remediation of Severe Reading Disabilities," *Junior College and Adult Reading Programs,* pp. 14–26. National Reading Conference, Milwaukee, 1967.

37. SCHUBERT, DELWYN G., and HOWARD N. WATSON, "Effects of Induced Astigmatism," *The Reading Teacher,* 21 (March 1968), 547–51.

38. SILVER, ARCHIE A., and ROSA A. HAGIN, "Maturation of Perceptual Functions in Children with Specific Reading Disability, *The Reading Teacher,* 19 (January 1966), 253–59.

39. SMIRNOV, A. A., "Psychological Research, 1953–5," in *Psychology in the Soviet Union,* ed. Brian Simon, pp. 29–45. Stanford: Stanford University Press, 1957.

40. SMITH, D. E. P., and PATRICIA M. CARRIGAN, *The Nature of Reading Disability.* New York: Harcourt, Brace and Co., 1959.

41. STEPHENS, W. E., E. S. CUNNINGHAM, and B. J. STIGLER, "Reading Readiness and Eye Hand Preference Patterns in First Grade Children," *Exceptional Children,* 33 (1967), 481–88.

42. STRANG, R., and D. K. BRACKEN, *Making Better Readers.* Boston: D. C. Heath & Company, 1957.

43. STROUD, JAMES B., *Psychology in Education.* New York: Longmans, Green and Company, 1956.

44. TAYLOR, STANFORD E., *Speed Reading vs. Improved Reading Efficiency.* Huntington, N.Y.: Educational Developmental Laboratories, Inc., April 1962.

45. TINKER, KAREN J., "The Role of Laterality in Reading Disability," in *Reading and Inquiry,* ed. J. A. Figurel, pp. 300–303. Proceedings of the International Reading Association, 1965.

46. VILSCEK, ELAINE C., "An Analysis of the Effect of Mental Age Levels and Socio-Economic Levels on Reading Achievement in First Grade." Unpublished doctoral thesis, University of Pittsburgh, 1964.

47. VYGOTSKY, LEV SEMENOVICH, *Thought and Language,* ed. and trans. Eugenia Hanfmann and Gertrude Vakar, p. 104. New York: John Wiley & Sons, Inc., 1952.

48. WEINER, MORTON, and WARD CROMER, "Reading and Reading Difficulty: A Conceptual Analysis," *Harvard Educational Review,* 37 (Fall 1967), 620–43.

49. WEPMAN, JOSEPH M., "The Interrelationship of Hearing, Speech and Reading," *The Reading Teacher,* 14 (March 1961), 245–47.

50. WITTY, PAUL, and D. KOPEL, *Reading and the Educative Process.* Boston: Ginn and Company, 1939.

51. WORLEY, STINSON E., and WILLIAM E. STORY, "Socio-Economic Status and Language Facility of Beginning First Graders," *The Reading Teacher,* 20 (February 1967), 400–403.

The Secondary Learner (continued)

CHAPTER **4**

READING IS A COMPLEX PROCESS. It is a composite of many skills, habits, and attitudes. The good reader possesses these qualities. To acquire them one needs a certain amount of readiness or proficiency in many related areas.

Chapter 3 emphasized the need for a wide background of experience, for maturational and intellectual growth, for physical health, for visual and auditory adequacy, and for freedom from neurological defects. These are necessary conditions, but they do not assure success in reading. It is illogical to expect to produce a successful reader by promoting growth and development in only certain specifics. The teacher of reading must give consideration to all aspects of development.

Educators frequently overlook the student's wholeness. They have dealt separately with his intelligence, his physique, his emotions, and his social skills. Each expert sees the student in light of his own biases and his own discipline. Each fragments the learner, and each is a piece worker. Someone has suggested that if a student were to appear in the midst of a group of educational psychologists he would be a stranger to them. We sometimes forget that all aspects of the student's development are interrelated and that he usually advances on an even front in all areas. And yet, it is easier to discuss the student's development by dissecting him, as it were. Let us then continue to examine those factors about all students that have a bearing on their achievement in reading.

SOCIAL-EMOTIONAL DEVELOPMENT

To help students both to develop adequate personalities and to become successful readers, the teacher of reading needs to understand the facts, principles, and symptoms of social and emotional development. He must be able to interpret student behavior. He must know how a student's social and emotional reactions influence his reading and how reading failure or success influences his emotional and social development.

Educators have long debated what the goals of the school program are or should be. On one thing all are agreed. The student is the focal point of this program. In essence, educators believe that good education generally (and reading instruction particularly) should enhance the personal and social adjustment of the student.

Emotions are an important aspect of human development. Without emotional behavior, life would be dull and personalities would be flat and uninteresting. Few individuals would achieve, for none could feel the joy of success or long for the esteem of others.

Sometimes, however, emotional development is maladjustive. Thus, studies show that the incidence of maladjustment among poor readers is greater than among good readers. It is not always easy to establish whether personality maladjustment is the cause, the effect, or a concomitant circumstance. Frequently it is impossible to tell whether emotional maladjustment or social maladjustment causes reading failure, or whether reading failure causes maladjustment. Some studies have failed to find a positive correlation between reading failure and personality maladjustment. Not all emotionally disturbed students are poor readers, nor are all poor readers emotionally disturbed.

All students have physiological needs. They need water, food, sleep, and warmth to maintain their physical well-being. They also have psychological needs. They need to feel secure. They long for affection and for friendship. They want the respect of others and go to extremes to win the esteem of their peers.

The self-image, or self-concept, of the learner is so obviously a significant determinant of learning that sometimes it does not receive the attention that it deserves. Kinch (24, p. 481) defines the self-concept as "that organization of qualities that the individual attributes to himself." Self-esteem is the degree of similarity between the self you are and the self you would like to be. Kinch believes that the individual's self-concept guides or influences the behavior of that individual. He proposes that the actual responses of others to the individual are important in determining how the individual will perceive himself and that this perception will influence his self-concept which, in turn, will guide his behavior.

Brookover and others (5) studied the significance of the self-concept on achievement. They defined self-concept in a learning situation as one's own conception of one's ability to learn. They found, using seventh-grade pupils, a significant relationship between self-concept and performance in the academic role (GPA), even when IQ was held constant.

Holmes (20) studied the variables that were most clearly related to high school students' reading speed and comprehension. He found that most closely related to reading power were verbal analogies, vocabulary in isolation, vocabulary in context, and listening comprehension, each accounting for 16 percent of the variance. Other factors exerted less influence, and even when all of them were added together, still 25 percent of the variance was unexplained. This led Strang (44) to comment that such imponderables as the individual's value system, his self-concept, or his purpose or set may be among the substrata determinants of reading achievement.

The Early Years

By the age of six the average child has already become a rather well-structured individual. He has learned to walk, can control his bowels and bladder, can dress and undress, and can feed himself. He ties his shoes, bathes, and brushes his teeth. He lives an orderly life, eating three times a day and sleeping a desirable number of hours.

He has become a member of his family. He identifies with his brothers and sisters and with his father and mother.

He is curious. He wants to know. He has developed his senses and communicates in sentences. He discriminates, generalizes, and makes judgments. He generally accepts society's rules and can discriminate between right and wrong.

He wants things for himself, is egocentric, and has unbounded faith in rules. "It's not fair" are common words for the six-year-old. He tags along with the "gang" and by seven or eight would rather be with them than with his family, but he is still somewhat of an outsider looking in.

Preadolescence

The preadolescent, who is from nine to thirteen years of age, is another person altogether and because of this is perhaps the most difficult to understand. He is neither child nor adolescent. Generally no visible sex change has as yet taken place. The voice is shrill and penetrating. The "other" sex is still something that he cannot deal with if left alone for any length of time.

The preadolescent is difficult to live with. He does not want to be loved and he does not appreciate what he gets. He is extremely restless, especially physically. He is easily bored and does not know what to do to occupy his time. He enjoys the wild fantastic story and is fascinated by gory detail. He is easily offended and is constantly accusing the adult of not understanding him or of mistreating him. The concept of gratitude seems to be stricken from the inventory of his emotions. The worst meal at the neighbors' is described more glowingly than the best-planned feast his mother arranged for his birthday (35).

The preadolescent does not want to submit to parent-accepted manners. He often reverts to infantile habits, antics, or irritating behavior. A cleavage develops between *you* and *us,* between the parents and the child. The preadolescent consequently develops a deep need for the peer clique or gang. He would rather side with his pal than with his parent, despite deep love for the parent. Peer codes and values take precedence over adult values.

Adolescence

The teacher of reading in the high school should understand the nature of the period of transition known as adolescence—the needs and developmental tasks of the adolescent, the influence that the peer group exerts over his behavior, the effects that body and biological changes have on his behavior, and the problems that he encounters. The teacher should also take a close look at his own attitude toward adolescents. A principal is said to have commented thus: "My most difficult problem is due not to the pubescence of the pupil, but to the menopause of the teacher."

A few observations might profitably lead us into our discussion:

1. There is an increasing tendency to accept adolescence as the social process through which a clear and stable self-identification is established. The key question for the adolescent seems to be, Who am I? The central developmental task of this period is self-definition.
2. This self-identification occurs through interaction with one's peers rather than with one's parents. The adolescent looks to his peers for social reward and recognition. This is so because:
   a. The values, skills, and knowledges of the parents are considered obsolete. Parents are perceived as old-fashioned and out of touch.
   b. Economic specialization has brought about an alienation of father and son. The son must seek his own occupation.

    c. The adolescent contributes little economically to the family. He is a school-goer and a spender of family funds.

3. Although physiological maturity is obtained quite automatically, social, emotional, and psychological maturity are acquired only with self-discovery. Adolescent conflict may thus be perceived as the means by which a person learns to know himself. No opportunity for conflict may mean no adolescence and consequently no opportunity to develop the sense of individuality. It has been shown that in lower social classes, where less conflict exists, adolescence is less of a distinct social phenomenon.

4. The extent to which adolescence becomes a period of stress and strain depends on:

    a. Social conditions—In a society where the child's world and the adult's world are similar, the adolescent will have less difficulty in making the transition from childhood to adulthood. If the society is in a period of rapid change, however, the transition will be more difficult. The adolescent has to adjust to society's problems as well as his own.

    b. Personal commitment—The transition is more difficult or less difficult depending upon the adolescent's willpower, self-education, and self-determination.

    Muss (30, p. 4) notes that sociologically, adolescence is the transition period between childhood and adulthood; psychologically, it is a period requiring special behavioral adjustments; chronologically, it is a period between twelve or thirteen and twenty or twenty-one, occurring somewhat earlier in girls than in boys.

    During the preadolescent growth spurt and puberty, adolescence may predominantly be a biological fact. Adolescence, however, is not synonymous with puberty. Puberty is the point in adolescence at which sexual maturity has been attained; pubescence is the period of about two years preceding puberty, during which the physiological changes that lead to sexual maturity occur. Pubescence is the period of the appearance of secondary sex characteristics and the maturation of the primary sex organs. For girls, the period may last for only six months; for boys, it may last two years. Adolescence, on the other hand, lasts for about eight years, involving numerous changes other than pubertal.

    In some societies there is no adolescence, only pubescence. Puberty moves the person from childhood to adulthood. Adolescence thus for the most part might be a social invention, whose limits are set by social institutions and mores. The end of adolescence is marked largely by social changes, social autonomy, emancipation from family social control, successful employment, and marriage. When the adolescent leaves home, gets a job, or can vote, it is generally an indication that he has left childhood and moved into adulthood.

Unfortunately, the transition from childhood to adulthood is not as easy in the United States as it is in many primitive societies. In our country, especially in middle-class families, a boy or a girl may spend ten years making the transition from childhood to adulthood. On the one hand, we infantilize the youngster, keeping him parasitic and dependent on adults; on the other hand, as soon as he graduates from high school, he is suddenly expected to be a man. In lower-class families the transition is somewhat smoother. Many children from these homes leave school early, get married, and assume adult roles.

The adolescent is often treated in an ambiguous manner by his parents, teachers, and other members in his society. He is not permitted certain childhood behaviors, nor is he permitted certain adult behaviors. He may not be allowed to drive a car, to buy liquor, or to marry. These are goals in his life space but are inaccessible because of parental restrictions, the moral code, or legal limitations. The adolescent finds himself without a clear understanding of his status and his obligations. He does not know whether his behavior will lead him toward or away from his goals. This lack of cognitive structure explains his great uncertainty. It may also explain why adolescence is often referred to as a period of storm and stress, of *Sturm und Drang*.

Lewin described the adolescent as being in a sort of "no-man's land." He is neither adult nor child; he is a marginal man standing on the boundaries of adulthood and childhood, but yet he is both child and adult, being influenced at times by childlike modes of behavior and at times by adult modes. Though anxious for psychological weaning, he still yearns for the warm milk of mother love (41, p. 69).

A child is a child; an adult is an adult; but an adolescent is a bit of each. The adolescent frequently is too young to do some things and too old to do others. That adolescence is an important period in a person's development is readily apparent, and we realize it is not without its problems. As we look at the adolescent of today, fully recognizing that our perception is distorted by "psychological presbyopia of old age" or by paramnesia, especially the psychological amnesia brought about by our unwillingness to recall our own adolescence as it really was, we nonetheless are faced with a few hard facts. The adolescent today tends to be more disturbed, less tranquil, and less sure of his values and goals. The adolescent is often in conflict with parents, with the values they hold dear, and with the traditions, mores, and customs of his culture. And, there are more delinquents. Delinquency, suicide, and drug and alcohol addiction are problems of adolescence. During adolescence there is an increasing separation of teen-agers from adult society. Youngsters seek more and more peer approval for their behavior.

The adolescent is in a constant conflict over group belongingness.

For this reason his behavior is like that of a person in minority groups. The marginal man is an "eternal adolescent." Like the marginal man the adolescent is in conflict with the attitudes and values of parents and thus finds anchorage only in the peer group. He has a tendency to assume radical positions, to be negative, rebellious, indifferent, lethargic, and melancholic, and to seek recognition, independence, and self-determination.

In recent years, we have witnessed an increasing cleavage between parents and their adolescent children, and yet the rebellion against parents is not nearly as great as some would like to suggest. A study of three thousand Minnesota adolescents and preadolescents found that both boys and girls express more favorable than unfavorable attitudes toward their parents (17).

In another study (7) students in ten midwestern high schools were asked which would be the hardest to take if, in joining a club, their parents were against it, their teachers were negative, or it meant breaking with a close friend. About 53 percent of boys and girls gave parental disapproval as being the hardest to take.

Parents and adolescents do disagree, especially as to the time when the adolescent should be considered to have attained maturity. The adolescent frequently wishes to engage in activities that symbolize adulthood, and parents often consider him too young for these activities. Rather than a rejection of parental norms, this disagreement reflects the adolescent's eagerness to be considered an adult.

Sawrey and Telford (39, p. 66) note that the social development for the adolescent includes developing one's own individuality, accepting responsibility for self-direction, crystallizing one's sex role, being accepted by the opposite sex, finding a preliminary vocational direction, and participating in a formally organized adolescent society.

Schneiders (41) points out that the adolescent needs to grow up and mature; to develop independence of thought, action, feeling, and emotion; to develop a deep sense of responsibility; to achieve self-discipline; to develop worthwhile goals; and to develop self-identity, sex identity, normal psychosexual development, and heterosexual orientation.

Adolescence is also a period of physical and biological change—a period of physical effervescence. During adolescence the child becomes a mature, physical being. The bones of the body grow in length, width, and thickness. The wisdom teeth appear, and the face becomes an adult face. Boys become relatively stronger than girls. Sexual maturity is attained. In boys it is often a period of sheer force, of athletic prowess, and of physical work. In girls, it is a period of intense and sustained activity and of movement, as in dance. Adolescence is, for both sexes, a period of general physicosexual tension and excitability. Sattler (38, p. 43) notes that the chief emotional discovery of youth is the discovery of lovableness. Every boy wants to know whether his affection, and hence his being, is acceptable, and every girl wants to know whether she is caressable and kissable.

During infancy and babyhood the boy and the girl are usually interested only in themselves. In early childhood children seek the companionship of others regardless of sex. At about eight or nine, play groups begin to divide on a sex basis. Boys and girls prefer to play with members of their own sex. Between ten and twelve, a certain degree of antagonism is prevalent between sex groups. At thirteen, girls lead the way in establishing friendships with the opposite sex; boys may still act aloof. Between fourteen and sixteen, boys start to show interest in girls. Individual boys and girls begin pairing off. After sixteen, dating becomes common.

Stafford (42, p. 11) notes that adolescence is a period of "Wanderlust." It is a time for love for life in all its exuberant vitality. German psychologists speak of *Wandertrieb* and *Wanderlust.* This refers to the adolescent's restlessness, to his desire to get away, and to a need to be on his own. In Germany there often is *Wandertag,* a special day set aside in school once a month in which the students go on a hike to a forest, lake, or castle.

The adolescent wants to feel important, to be considered as somebody of worth, and to achieve adult status, but perhaps more than anything to have status in his peer group.

Status is a social relationship, involving the mutual interaction of two or more human beings (10, p. 7). In a social relationship the behaviors and emotions of all members are influenced by the behaviors and emotions of the other members. Status is based on social rank of members within the group. The adolescent is constantly striving for a position of high status within the peer group.

Status always implies rank and privilege. The status of individual members is anything but equal (10, p. 11). An adolescent has a specific rank in the social family. He is ranked above the child, but below the adult. The role that he is expected to play is determined by the culture in which he lives, by the family, church, school, his peers, or other less significant groups.

It is difficult for the adolescent to achieve status. He lives with his parents and is dependent upon them for his food, clothing, schooling, shelter, and medical care. He may not be allowed by law to become part of the labor market. He may be treated like a child, being subjected to the same types of discipline as are elementary school children.

The adolescent thus finds it extremely difficult to become emotionally independent of his parents and to become self-directing. He finds it even more difficult to achieve economic independence. The adolescent wants his own room and telephone. He feels ashamed of anything that in any way suggests that he is tied to his mother's apron strings. He is resentful of a teacher who treats him like a small child. Longer periods of schooling, child-labor laws, unavailability of jobs, restrictive ages for marriage and voting all help to keep the adolescent dependent upon the adult.

The peer group is one of the major social and educational institutions in adolescent culture. The peer group is a primary and highly cohesive face-to-face group of adolescent age mates (28, p. 57). It is initially a unisexual, but may become a heterosexual, group and arises generally in response to the need to deal with the challenges of maturation. The peer culture is the sum total of the social interactions among similar age mates. The adolescent who cannot fit into a constructive peer group is indeed unfortunate.

The peer group permits deviation only within a limited degree. It has a very useful function. It gives the individual status, group affiliation, and a frame of reference. It provides the individual with acceptance, approval, recognition, prestige, security, and feelings of identification and belongingness, and it helps the adolescent to achieve emancipation from the home and parents. It gives the adolescent an opportunity to develop his conversational powers, experience in getting along with others, and practice in social skills and in judging people, and it develops loyalty toward others. Perhaps most significant, it permits the adolescent to develop a self-concept.

Personal Adjustment and Reading Achievement

Students vary in their behavior for many reasons, and to adjust the school program to meet the needs of each student is practically an impossible task. There seems to be no ready solution to reading difficulties. Reading failure will perhaps always be with us. Failure of any kind makes the satisfaction of the student's needs rather difficult. It prohibits the actualization of his potentialities. It threatens especially self-esteem and the student's esteem in the eyes of others, thus thwarting both emotional and social adjustment. Failure in reading is a continuing block to normal development. For the poor reader, self-esteem and self-actualization rarely become a reality.

Reading is a developmental task. It is a task that the student must perform to satisfy his own needs so that he may satisfy the demands made upon him by society. There is no adequate compensation for success in reading. In the academic work of today's school a learner cannot succeed partially. He either succeeds or he does not, and without success in reading, success in almost any other area becomes an improbability, if not an impossibility.

Poor reading ability threatens social acceptance and thus leads to feelings of inadequacy. The student is subjected to bad publicity, as it were. The poor reader is a student who has compared unfavorably with his peers. He has competed but has failed to meet competition. Such a student is humiliated and hurt. He becomes a social reject in his own mind and in the minds of others. He feels ashamed. He may become shy and withdrawn. He is thought to be "stupid," and even his parents may show discouragement and dissatisfaction with him, for their egos have suffered. Their youngster has not measured up to their expectations.

It is not difficult to see why the poor reader, rejected by others and lacking the self-confidence that comes with success, should be tense, antagonistic, self-conscious, nervous, inattentive, defensive, discouraged, irritable, fearful, frustrated, defiant, indifferent, restless and hypercritical. Unable to achieve recognition through success in reading, he may stutter, be truant, join gangs, and engage in destructive activity. He may show evidence of a psychological tic or of psychosomatic conditions; he may bite his nails.

Bettelheim (3, p. 392) notes that the poor student who fears failure, even if he does his best, will frequently protect himself by *deciding not to learn*. He convinces himself that he wants to fail rather than that he cannot succeed. He begins to feel that he could do rather well if he wished. Bettelheim adds that this is an insidious process. The more the pupil falls behind academically, the more his pretense of adequacy is threatened and the more pronounced becomes his deviant behavior. The fourth grader might defy the teacher; by the eighth grade he defies police and society.

Schiffman (40) believes that many retarded readers, especially on the *secondary* level, have such a negative level of aspiration and such a low self-estimation that they cannot succeed. This lack of achievement motivation is often encouraged by parents and teachers. In a study of eighty-four functional junior high slow learners, Schiffman found that 78 percent had average intelligence scores on either the Verbal or the Performance scales of the WISC and 39 percent had average scores on both, but teachers felt that only 7 percent and the pupils themselves and their parents felt that only 14 percent had average ability.

Adolescents learn to behave in ways that they consider appropriate to themselves. What is considered appropriate often depends upon the expectations of the significant people about them. It is in his interaction with significant others that the student develops an image of himself as a learner. In the classroom, the student often learns only that which he believes the significant others in his life expect him to learn. If others think him to be a poor reader or a poor learner, he tends to be one.

Research indicates that most learners come to school with rather well-adjusted personalities. Personal maladjustment seems more frequently to be an effect of rather than a cause of reading failure. In some cases, however, personal maladjustment seems to precipitate problems with reading. Educational malfunctions, most commonly those of reading, frequently signify emotional problems.

Harris (16) suggests that painful emotional events during early efforts at reading may turn the young learner against reading. The young reader may also at times transfer feelings of resistance from his mother to the teacher, or from his eating to his reading. A pupil may seek gang approval by not learning to read. Finally, he may exert so much energy in repressing hostile impulses that he has little left for intellectual effort.

Numerous other emotional conditions may hinder success in learning generally. Difficulties in adjusting to a new environment make it impossible for the student to expend the energies needed for learning. Poor parent-child relationships, sibling rivalry, unfair comparisons with a neighborhood prodigy, lack of encouragement from the home, and negative attitudes of parents to learning in general may lead to failure. A frontal attack on the reading problem of a student who is emotionally disturbed may have little effect.

Great care, however, must be taken that the emotional symptoms that result from reading failure are not immediately advanced as the cause of the reading problem. The first assumption that should be made is that the emotional disturbances are the result rather than the cause of the reading failure. Most emotional reactions in reading disabilities can be explained as the learner's frustrated reactions to a task that is incompatible. One of the really great rationalizations in the classroom for doing nothing or giving up is that the student is emotionally disturbed.

In cases of severe emotional disturbance, a thorough study of the student's physical, mental, social, and emotional development is needed, an investigation that is not usually possible by one person alone. Psychiatrist, psychologist, teacher, social worker, pediatrician, neurologist, and others need to cooperate in resolving the emotionally disturbed student's learning and emotional disorders.

The teacher must be slow in attributing the reading difficulties of even one student to emotional or social problems. Poor readers do not have an identifiable personality. Poor readers may be well adjusted or poorly adjusted; they may run the gamut of personal deviation. There is no one-to-one relationship between type of adjustment difficulty and type of reading retardation.

The relationship between reading disability and emotional and social maladjustment and personal maladjustment in turn prevents further growth in reading. It is quite conceivable that in certain cases reading failure and personal maladjustment have their own distinct causes. Generally, if the reading failure is an emotional problem, the pupil will have difficulties in other academic areas also. If the emotional problem was caused by failure in reading, it will be reduced when the pupil learns to read.

Holmes (19) points out that in discussing reading and personality difficulties with students and their parents, phrases such as "reading diagnosis and treatment" are often more acceptable than phrases such as "personality maladjustment and therapy."

In dealing with the severely emotionally disturbed student who is also a reading disability case, therapy and remedial reading must often be combined. The greater the intensity of the emotional problem, the greater tends to be the need for both therapy and individual instruction. Various therapeutic techniques—play therapy, group interview therapy, and individual interview therapy—have been used successfully.

Therapy removes pressures and tension and clears the way for attentive concentration on the reading material. In most cases it removes a fear of reading and allows the student to develop attitudes favorable to reading.

In summary:

1. Emotions are reactions to environmental stimuli that also motivate behavior.
2. Some types of emotion facilitate learning, and some hinder or prevent learning.
3. The relationship between maladjustment and learning to read might be any of the following:
   a. Maladjustment causes reading failure.
   b. Reading failure causes maladjustment.
   c. Maladjustment and reading failure have a common cause.
   d. Maladjustment and reading failure each have their own distinct cause.
   e. The relationship often is circular: Maladjustment causes reading failure, and reading failure in turn increases maladjustment; or reading failure causes maladjustment, which in turn increases reading failure.

MOTIVATIONAL READINESS

Achievement in reading is dependent also on the student's motivational readiness. Lack of interest is an important cause of poor reading. To achieve in reading, the student must want to learn.

The Nature of Interest

Interests are defined as positive attitudes toward objects or classes of objects to which we are attracted (14, p. 213). Ryans (37, p. 312) says that interests are learned responses which predispose the organism to certain lines of activity and facilitate attention. Getzels (15) defines interest as a disposition which impels an individual to seek out particular objects, activities, understanding, skills, or goals for attention. Cummins and Fagin (9) suggest that interest is an emotional involvement of like or dislike which is associated with attention to some object. Interest is the set of attending, the tendency to give selective attention to something.

Interests are the active forces that direct our attention to activities or objects. They determine whether the student will read, how much he will read, and in what area he will read. Interests arise through the inter-action of our basic needs and the means we use to satisfy them. The student who is interested in reading is usually the student for whom read-ing satisfies the basic needs of self-esteem, esteem of others, curiosity, and success and personal adequacy.

As teachers, we are concerned with two phases of interest. First, the interest of the student must somehow be captured if he is to read; and second, we must help the student to make reading a habitual activity. Indeed, it is at the point when reading becomes a permanent mode of behavior that reading acquires a motivational force of its own (49, pp. 57, 58).

Our prime concern is that students do read. A reader is not a student who can read; he is a student who does read. The kindergarten teacher, especially, is more interested in fostering interest in reading than in de-veloping specific reading skills, but even the secondary teacher should not be so busy teaching reading skills that he neglects to develop readers.

Adolescents' Reading Interests

Generally, young people prefer fictional materials to informational materials, and prose to poetry. Their preferences for reading content show great variations and are influenced most by their age, sex, and intelligence. Girls read more than boys, and interest in reading reaches a peak during the junior high years and then declines sharply.

In the junior high years boys prefer comic books, animal stories, western stories, adventure, fiction, humor, and biography; girls prefer fiction, comic books, animal stories, biography, and western stories.

On the high school level girls prefer romance, society, and fashion, but they also read adventure, science, and mystery stories; boys like sports, adventure, mystery, action, exploration, travel, science, mechan-ics, and politics. Humorous books and books on hobby pursuits also are popular during this period.

We have already mentioned that intelligence plays a major part in determining what students will read. Generally, the areas of interest of more-intelligent students are on a slightly higher level than are those of less-intelligent students. Students with high IQs read books that are more difficult and more adult. Boys who score high on intelligence or aptitude tests (IQ 130 or more) read mystery stories, biographies, history, historical fiction, comics, scientific materials, sports, humor, and westerns; girls of above-average intelligence read historical fiction, modern novels, biographies, mystery stories, teen-age books, sports, animal stories, science, history, and books treating social problems (1).

Walberg (46), in a study of the reading habits of students "who elect to take physics in high school," found that almost a quarter indicated that they had not read much nonfiction. These students seem to have more interest in science fiction than in literature. Girls expressed more interest in historical novels, mystery stories, literary classics, biographies, and autobiographies. Boys more often enjoyed technical and professional books. Both boys and girls ranked mystery stories as first in interest, and roughly half indicated that they did not enjoy technical-professional books.

Emans and Patyk (13) note that interests are influenced by (1) the nature of the topic and (2) the motive of the reader; usually the more closely the topic and the reader's motives are interrelated, the more intense will be the interest of the reader. Waples (47) and Getzels (15) list various motives for reading: informative, identificational, aesthetic, and recreational. Emans and Patyk (13) found that high school students read chiefly for recreation. Boys ranked seeking information considerably higher than did girls. Students above the median in intelligence ranked reading for aesthetics higher than those below the median. The poor reader tended to seek identification in his reading.

Developing Interests

It is often said that "appreciation should be caught, not taught," but, as Duffy (12) notes, the evidence seems to indicate that students cannot catch it by themselves. They need help, especially from teachers.

The development of interests is a lure and a ladder activity (8). The student must be lured to new interests through the ladder of suitable materials. The teacher must introduce the student to the appropriate reading materials in a way that motivates him to action.

Few deny the importance of a lifetime interest in reading. Norvell noted that the reading habit is the most important academic aim of the school (31).

This interest in reading is not self-perpetuating. The seventh grader probably reads more than he ever did before; by the time he is through high school his reading has decreased tremendously. Few high school graduates habitually read books. An impressive proportion of young people recall that they virtually stopped reading (or at least stopped enjoying reading) in high school (4).

The root of the reading difficulties of a given student is often his mental attitude. He may not like school, and he may like reading less. In such a case, there may be no genuine disability. The student is disinterested and therefore has not developed competency.

Motivation flows from interest. Without interest there is usually no will to do, no drive to learn. Without motivation the student will not develop into a mature reader.

The solution to the reluctant reader's problem begins with a change of attitude. The student will not be an adequate reader until he wants to read. How do you get him to read? The teacher can promote interest in reading in numerous ways:

1. Help students find delight, pathos, and enjoyment in reading. This can be done only if the student is taught to read well.
2. Provide a wide selection of easy reading materials—materials that students *may* read, not *must* read. When we say to children, "You must read this," we may be creating nonreaders. The student should not feel depraved because he does not like *As You Like It*.
3. Guide each student to books he can read independently. While interest in a book is a powerful motivational factor, interest alone is not enough to make a difficult book easy to read (12).
4. Help each student to find materials of appropriate content and difficulty. Do not emphasize literary content only. Become familiar with the interests of adolescents. Generally, the content should provide adventure, action, humor, romance (for girls), biography, surprise, or mystery. The stories should be about people and heroes and about people with whom the reader can identify. The teacher should take special interest in the student's independent reading.
5. Use book exhibits, book fairs, book advertisements, periodicals, and bulletins to stimulate interest in reading. Provide books to fit students' immediate interests.
6. Give students an opportunity to share their reading experiences through book reports, panels, or round-table discussions. Permit them to discuss the author, plot, theme, setting, and style.
7. Develop a book club or a hobby club. Choose a "Book of the Week." Devote an assembly to a particular author or invite a favorite author to school.
8. Introduce students to the reading topic by illustrating the content with TV, films, recordings, and other audiovisual aids. Give an introduction to the book to create interest. Whet their curiosity.
9. Provide class time for library reading.
10. Let students read more than one version of a biography.

11. Stay in the background. The student's recommendation of a book carries more weight than the recommendations of ten teachers.

12. Recommend the sports page, magazines, or even the comics to students who do not read.

13. Let the student keep a record of his own progress, of the books that he has read, of the books that he would like to read, and of the movies he has seen that are based on books. Nothing is so discouraging as a teacher who is concerned more with errors than with successes. The teacher should be an exciter rather than an examiner or a tester.

14. Help the student to look upon himself as a reader. Self-concept is closely related to reading success, and a student who does not see himself as a reader will rarely possess the reading habit (12, p. 255).

15. Have reading materials parallel the student's interests. This means that the teacher needs to know the field of adolescent literature. The teacher needs to identify the student's interest and to introduce the student to books dealing with topics of special interest to him. Anita E. Dunn, Mabel E. Jackman, and J. Roy Newton in *Fare for the Reluctant Reader* (Albany: Argus-Greenwood, Inc., 1964) provide an annotated bibliography for students in grades seven through twelve. The books are listed alphabetically by author under categories that represent these teen-age interests: adventure, sports, love, careers, tips for teens, and mystery. Other book lists are the following:

    a. Adams, Ruth, *Books to Encourage the Reluctant Reader*. Englewood Cliffs, N.J.: Scholastic Book Services.

    b. *Books for Reluctant Readers*. Garden City, N.Y.: Doubleday and Company, Inc. This annotated book samples English classics, poetry, music, science, social studies, teen-age interests, and novels. Each book is accompanied by a designation of interest level and of reading level.

    c. Bush, Bernice, *Fare for the Reluctant Reader: Books, Magazines, and Audio-Visual Aids for the Slow Learner in Grades 7–10*. Albany: New York State University.

    d. Martin, Marvin, "Fifty Books They Can't Resist," *Elementary English*, 39 (May 1962), 415–16. For sixth graders.

The teacher cannot ignore the interests of students, nor can he always feed the student only what he likes. He must stimulate the student to acquire taste and to increase the variety of his interests.

Developing Reading Tastes

It is frequently an observation that many students do not read, that the quality of what some read is inadequate, and that schools are not developing a permanent interest in reading in many youngsters.

The teacher can remedy this situation. First: He must use his understanding to help the student choose books that will lead him to a higher level of appreciation. It is not enough to know that the book does not positively "harm" the student. The teacher must encourage him to read books that make a positive contribution to his cultural, social, and ethical development. Second: He must be well acquainted with the books that he recommends. When he recommends a book to a student, he must have the conviction that the content and the style will motivate him to read it. Third: He must know the specific interests of each student. If he is to help develop reading tastes, he must consider the student's interest patterns, his voluntary reading, the availability of materials, and the time that he has for leisure reading. He must also know the level of the student's reading abilities. He cannot nurture interest with books too difficult to be read easily.

Painter (32) adds that the key to the building of lifetime reading habits lies with an interested teacher who will help students in basic reading skills, who has read so extensively that he is able to guide young people to books congruent with their interests, who can present poetry effectively, who helps with materials and background to build an understanding of literature, and who uses various methods of teaching literature.

SEX AND READINESS

Teachers have always been concerned with differences in achievement between boys and girls. One of the more obvious differences is in achievement in reading. Girls as a group achieve better than boys in reading. They learn to read earlier, and fewer of them are significantly retarded in reading. They generally seem to perform better than boys in English usage, spelling, and handwriting.

Girls and boys exhibit differences also in other areas. For example, the incidence of stuttering, defects in color vision, and brain damage is substantially greater among boys. Boys also tend to lisp more. Girls tend to be better than boys in auditory and visual discrimination. The incidence of left-handedness, ambidexterity, and high-frequency hearing loss is greater among boys.

Numerous attempts have been made to explain the differences in reading achievement. In general, the explanations have emphasized either heredity or environment. It has been suggested that girls have an inherited language advantage or that they reach maturity about a year and a half earlier than boys. Bentzen (2) advances the hypothesis that the boy's problems stem from the stresses put on his immature organism by a society that fails to make appropriate provisions for the biological age differential between boys and girls. Since attainment of a skill or neuromuscular maturation seems to depend upon the myelination of the motor and association tracts, myelination may be completed earlier in girls than in boys.

Some writers suggest that today's schools are more fitted to the needs of girls. Most of the teachers, especially on the elementary level, are women, and they may adjust more easily to girls than to boys. Studies also indicate that girls are promoted on lower standards and that both men and women teachers tend to overrate the achievement of girls and to underrate the achievement of boys. A study by Davis and Slobodian (11), however, indicated that teachers showed no differences in verbal behavior toward boys and girls. They report that teachers did not call on girls with greater frequency, did not direct more negative comments toward boys, and did not treat boy responses differently during reading instruction. Apparently, on the basis of this study, differential teacher behavior is not a significant cause of sex differences in reading achievement.

The expectations of society require boys and girls to play distinctly different roles. Girls are supposed to be good, to be feminine, and to achieve in school. On the other hand, boys are expected to be active and to excel in sports rather than in books. Most of us tend to shape our life in the direction in which we consider ourselves most appreciated. Girls, in addition, use reading more frequently for recreation than do boys. Reading materials generally are more in accordance with the interests of girls.

Not all reading disability cases are referred to the reading clinic. And of those who are referred, not all of them may be referred for reading disability alone. It is quite possible that boys more frequently than girls tend to manifest their reading problems through aggressive tendencies, and as a result more of them are referred to the clinic. The reading problems of well-behaved girls may go undetected or may be taken care of in the classroom (45, p. 114).

Studies have generally found that intelligence is more variable among boys than among girls. It may be that the reading ability of boys is also more variable, giving rise to a larger number of boys who are poor readers (45, p. 112).

A comparative study (34) of reading in Germany and the United States reveals that the mean reading scores of fourth- and sixth-grade German boys exceed those of German girls and that the variability of scores is greater among the girls than among the boys. These findings are just the reverse of those in this country and suggest that sex differences may best be explained by cultural and environmental factors. It is interesting to note that the teaching staffs in Germany, even in elementary school, are predominantly male.

That there are sex differences in reading achievement in favor of the girls in this country can hardly be questioned. Vast differences also exist among the boys themselves. What educational implications do these differences have? Two educational recommendations have been based on these differences: Boys should begin first grade later than girls; separate mental age norms should be devised for girls and boys.

In an attempt to evaluate these recommendations, Clark (6) investigated sex differences in mental ability and achievement. His study is particularly significant because (1) eight measures of mental ability and six measures of achievement were used; (2) the study involved third, fifth, and eighth grades; (3) he used a nationwide sample; (4) he used statistical controls in his analysis of differences in mental ability between boys and girls, so that the effects of variations in age were eliminated; and (5) in his analysis of achievement differences between girls and boys, the effects of variations in both age and mental ability were controlled.

The data indicated that intelligence as measured by the *California Test of Mental Maturity* is independent of sex. No significant differences were found between the sexes in reading vocabulary, reading comprehension, and arithmetic reasoning. In mechanics of English, however, the fifth- and eighth-grade girls did better than the boys. In spelling, the girls had better scores at all three grade levels. Thus, even when differences that are attributable to age and mental age are held constant, the girls still excelled in spelling and English mechanics.

Clark concludes that (1) sex differences in intelligence are nonexistent; (2) since there were no differences in arithmetic and reading, the differences that are so noticeable in actual classroom conditions are attributable to environmental factors such as interest; (3) girls have a definite advantage in English and spelling; and (4) since a great variability in ability and achievement exists at all grade levels, educational decisions must give first consideration to the individuality of each pupil.

Educational provisions must ultimately be for the individual pupil. It is not enough to know what is best for the group. It is not enough to know what type of reading program will benefit most boys or girls. The teacher must prescribe for the individual boys and girls, and as soon as he attempts this, he realizes that differences between boys and girls and between one boy and another—differences other than sex—play a significant role in reading achievement.

INSTRUCTIONAL INADEQUACIES

The instructional inadequacies sometimes evident in the teaching of reading are variables of achievement that need to be evaluated. The student's level of achievement that he will attain in reading depends on his background of experience, his intellectual, physical, emotional, and social development, and the instructional program he receives.

Poor teaching may be a cause of reading disability or of lack of achievement in reading. Poor teaching is no less a handicap than is poor vision. It may even be true that reading disability cases are sometimes not understood because we have not looked in the right place. It is considerably easier to suggest multiple causality than to admit that our instruction has been inadequate. It is easier to seek the cause of reading disability in lack of experience or emotional upset than to take a hard look at the instructional program.

We do not solve all educational ills through more money, outmoded in-service programs, gadgets, mechanical devices, proposal writing, and new materials and approaches. Heilman (18) notes that "outstanding instructional programs in reading will be achieved only through outstanding instruction."

Instruction may be inadequate because the teacher does not know how to teach reading, because instruction is not adapted to the individual student, because it is unsystematic, because the teacher does not emphasize the basic skills, because the teacher uses a single method exclusively, or because the teacher does not understand the student.

Reading disability is also related to numerous other factors that can be grouped under the general heading of institutional variables. The school environment is an important determinant of learning. Is the school achievement oriented? Is the school environment unnatural?

The type of control exercised in the classroom, the kinds of instructional materials, the library facilities, the expectations that the administration and staff have of the student, the teacher-student ratios, the grading practices, the grouping practices, the type of classroom organization, and the types of measurement and evaluation have a direct bearing on the rate of reading disability in a given school. It is obvious that the student must normally have reached a more advanced developmental stage to succeed in reading in a class of thirty-six students than in a class of twelve or thirteen students (26, p. 27).

In 1964, 17.4 percent of all children from five to seventeen moved from one residence to another, and one-third of these moved from one county or state to another. The literature tends to indicate that moving from place to place can result in impairment of family life, social development, and emotional adjustment. Moore (29) evaluated the effects of this moving on performance in high school, using 2,566 seniors as his population for study. He found that a wide range of moving is followed by no consistent differences in high school performance (achievement test scores and grade-point averages), except that there is a slight tendency for the highly mobile to become less involved in school activities. The researcher concluded that some students are hurt by moving, while others are helped.

READING—A LANGUAGE EXPERIENCE

A common cause of poor reading is inadequate language development. It is strange, but true nonetheless, that reading theory and teaching have concerned themselves largely with psychological, sociological, physical, and neurological matters but have not concerned themselves rigorously enough with language. Reading must be regarded as a language-related process; it must be studied in relation to language.

Teachers must be concerned then with the significance of language and communication for the reading process. The general assumption underlying this section is this: The first step in introducing the youngster to reading and in assuring success in reading is to provide him with an adequate development in listening and speaking.

The teacher of reading needs to understand communication and language for the following reasons:

1. The pupil's proficiency in the communication and language skills, both speaking and listening, is the best indicator of his readiness for reading. In fact, intelligence test scores may basically represent past opportunities for language experience.
2. The teacher himself cannot understand the reading process without understanding communication and oral language development.
3. The more alike the patterns of language structure in the reading material are to the patterns of language structure used in speaking, the better the student's comprehension tends to be.

Communication is the heart of the language arts. Without communication, listening or reading cannot occur. Reading takes place only when the youngster shares the ideas that the communicator intends to convey. In every sense of the word, reading is the culminating act of the communicative process, initiated by the thoughts and the signs or symbols put on the printed page by the writer.

If reading is communication and if indeed it is a linguistic process, this has certain implications for the teaching of reading:

1. Language training should accompany reading instruction every step of the way. A linguistic background for reading lessons should be continuously built at each stage of growth.

2. Reading success depends upon the student's aural-oral experience with words. Development in reading closely parallels development in listening and speech. Reading involves the same language, the same message, and the same code as hearing of spoken words. The only difference is that in reading the contact is made on the central nervous system by light vibrations through the eyes; in hearing, it is by sound vibrations through the ears.

3. Every reading lesson should be an extension of language and a means of developing the student's linguistic skill.

4. If the student cannot sound the individual phoneme, he probably will not be a good oral reader. He will have difficulty with phonics. He may also have more difficulty in transmitting meaning.

5. Genuine reading proficiency may mean the ability to read language structure. The best reader may be one mentally aware of the stresses, elongations of words, changes of pitch and intonation, and rhythms of the sentences that he reads. If he reads the way the writer would like it to have been said, true communication of meaning may be possible.

6. The student's comprehension of speech and his oral use of language should be checked frequently. Appraisal of the linguistic competency of all slow learners and language-handicapped youth should be a part of the diagnostic and remedial program.

7. Some of the effort expended in teaching slow learners and particularly disadvantaged students by dint of drills and devices might better be expended in working on development in oral language and comprehension. Instruction should begin with familiar materials, *materials that represent the student's speech**

THE SLOW LEARNER

The last sentence in the list above leads us into the special problems of the slow learner, the gifted learner, and the disadvantaged learner. Those very elements that have concerned us in Chapter 3 and in this chapter are the factors that identify these learners and that determine the difficulty or ease with which they attack the printed page. Let us begin with the slow learner.

The slow learner may or may not be retarded in terms of his ability level, but he is almost always retarded as to grade level. He generally has an IQ between 70 and 90, and thus *his major deficiency may be in the*

---

* For a complete discussion of language and its implications in the teaching of reading, see Emerald Dechant, *Improving the Teaching of Reading* (Englewood Cliffs, N.J.: Prentice-Hall, Inc., 1970), pp. 137–161.

area of intellectual development. This pupil begins to read at age seven or later, will read slowly and haltingly, and achieves below grade level in areas other than reading, such as spelling or arithmetic. He generally does not need a remedial program. Pushing him may only hurt him. He may interpret it as dissatisfaction with his wholehearted efforts. By the time he reaches ninth grade, he may be reading three or four grade levels below his actual grade placement.

The classroom teacher can help the slow learner by applying one or a combination of the following techniques in his content-area teaching.

1. By providing a friendly, accepting, and encouraging relationship. Teacher attitudes substantially affect the performance of the slow learner. The teacher must believe in the improvableness of the learner.

2. By creating a learning environment where simple reading is important. Each learning experience should grow out of a need. Teach him to read road signs, city directories, a letter from a friend, want ads, newspapers, an application blank, a menu. The slow learner needs to learn the working vocabulary required to function effectively as an American citizen.

3. By pacing the learning according to the student's ability.

    a. Introduce only a few materials at any given time.

    b. Review daily.

    c. Introduce materials in varied contexts.

    d. Simplify materials, explanations, and techniques.

    e. Use short periods of instruction.

    The basic vocabulary needs to be carefully controlled. Build many reading situations which require him to use his limited vocabulary over and over again. These students need aural-oral experience with words. The use of workbooks is especially recommended.

4. By coordinating all the language arts. Let the student do oral reading. Sometimes he needs to hear himself say the word to understand what he is reading. A multisensory approach makes learning a concrete process for him.

5. By not underestimating the slow learner's ability to learn. Don't simply let him do busy work.

6. By having the student see his progress in each lesson through individual and objective evidence. Nothing succeeds like observed and tangible success.

    a. Have him keep a card file of words that he has learned to spell or read.

    b. Have him construct a picture dictionary, perhaps of shop tools. The teacher needs to provide opportunities for the student to "shine" in some area.

    c. Have him graph his progress each day.

7. By providing drill on new words:
   a. Let the student write, pronounce, and read the word.
   b. Use all the sense avenues.

8. By providing ample opportunity for review, repetition, and overlearning. The slow learner has difficulty with both immediate and delayed memory. The slow learner profits greatly from repetition. He needs this to retain the information and to reinforce learning. He may get the gist of a story only in spurts. Each rereading adds more to his understanding. The teacher needs to spend a great deal of time in developing new concepts. The slow learner has a great need for a systematic and developmental reading program. He needs step-by-step instruction. He must be permitted to use his knowledge in various contexts.

9. By individualizing instruction. The teacher needs to give as much individual help as possible.

10. By not putting him into a remedial program simply because he is reading below grade level. Far too many slow learners fill Title I classes.

11. By using concrete illustrations to develop concepts and generalizations. The slow learner has difficulty with abstract reasoning. He is slow to perceive relationships, to make inferences, to draw conclusions, or to generalize. He needs to be helped to reason through discussion periods, dramatization, etc.

12. By providing short-range goals. Projects should not be too long, and rewards should be frequent.

13. By emphasizing the visual and auditory characteristics of words. Word analysis is very helpful. The teacher may encourage lip movements, vocalization, and pointing to a word. The teacher needs to emphasize phonogram-phoneme relationships.

14. By breaking complex learning tasks into small steps. The use of programmed materials and teaching machines is especially recommended for slow learners. They divide the task into small steps and use frequent repetition and other supportive cues to make the correct response dominant.

15. By employing a variety of teaching techniques.

16. By emphasizing far more the quality of the student's learning experiences than their quantity. Going too fast produces nothing but confusion. The slow learner appears to have little need for rapid reading skills. The student needs repetitive practice but also varied practice.

17. By seeing to it that all directions are definite, specific, and detailed.

18. By familiarizing himself with methods of teaching specifically designed for the slow learner. Among these are the following:

a. Bruechner, Leo J., and Guy L. Bond, *Diagnosis and Treatment of Learning Difficulties.* New York: Appleton-Century-Crofts.

b. Featherstone, Joseph, *Teaching the Slow Learner.* New York: Columbia University Press.

c. Kephart, N.C., *The Slow Learner in the Classroom.* Columbus, Ohio: Charles E. Merrill Books, Inc.

d. Kirk, Samuel A., *Teaching Reading to Slow-Learning Children.* Boston: Houghton Mifflin Company.

19. By familiarizing himself with and by using materials designed for the slow learner. Chapter 12 lists many such materials.

THE DISADVANTAGED LEARNER

The disadvantaged learners are the ill housed, ill fed, ill clothed, and ill educated. They are white, black, Indian, Chicano, Puerto Rican. The disadvantaged learner is of no single race or color. Poverty and failure to achieve the goals established by the mainstream of society are shared by people of all colors and national origins. The culturally deprived student is a learner who simply lacks enough of the opportunities and advantages available to most American youth. The disadvantaged families are not deprived because they are black or Puerto Rican, but because they have been deprived of adequate employment and income.

In general, students of lower-socioeconomic groups lack proper self-image, feel alienated from the larger social structures and the school, have little academic drive, do not use the school language, read substantially below their ability level, and have poorer achievement and more frustration, and as a consequence of these more of them fail, become behavior problem cases, or drop out of school. Frequently, ability grouping, which groups the poor student with other poor students, has only tended to increase the educational disadvantage of the student from the lower-socioeconomic home.

We need to differentiate between the student who is retarded because of a verbally impoverished environment and the student who is retarded because of deficient brain matter. It is also obvious that we need to present different stimuli, and we need to present them in a different way for the learner who is deficient because of lack of previous learnings. An inadequacy that has resulted from inadequate prior learning is easier to assess than one that is the result of inadequate capacity.

The need to improve the language and reading skills of the disadvantaged student is apparent. The following techniques might prove helpful:

1. Make every effort to obtain a true estimate of the student's potential. Do not use tests that only hammer home the point that he is stupid.

2. Teach disadvantaged students to "learn how to learn." They do not know what it means to be taught. They need to learn the reading-study skills: skills in locating information, in organizing information, in retaining information, and in adjusting rate to purpose and difficulty of the reading selection.

3. Build on oral language as a prerequisite to dealing with printed language. This student will not know a word like *steeple*, although a dozen steeples may be visible from the classroom window. He often does not have a word to designate his concepts. He has no oral referent for the printed word. Develop experiential and oral meanings for words.

4. Develop speaking-reading-writing relationships through the use of audio-visual devices and concrete illustrations. Discuss or have them read about a popular movie or a sporting event. Many visual stimuli should be presented together with the verbal stimuli. Make tapes of the student's oral reading.

5. Teach reading as a life-related process. Use how-to-do-it books and books about minority groups, sports, or science fiction to stimulate and interest them. Experientially deprived students, perhaps more so than any other group, learn by doing. In the middle and upper grades the youngster needs to develop an awareness that reading is important. Too often, his inability to read causes him little concern.

6. Reading assignments should be brief and concrete.

7. Display books strategically and attractively for personal and group examination. Show a filmstrip about a book; read from a book. Make available materials that present his own ethnic group in a good light. Instead of trying to get him to adopt a new culture, help him to improve within the framework of his own culture.

8. Give special attention to readiness for reading in the content areas and for learning. Be reasonably certain that students have a chance of understanding the materials. Develop semantic sensitivity to the idea that words have more than one meaning.

9. Do not limit the approach in reading to any one method.

10. Teach phonics and structural analysis as a means of figuring out the pronunciation of words. Few disadvantaged students know either the alphabet of letters or the alphabet of sounds. Emphasize visual and auditory discrimination, but especially auditory discrimination. The disadvantaged student profits from auditory and visual perception activities. He has more perceptual difficulties. He recognizes fewer objects than other youth. He is deficient in auditory attention and interpretation of skills,

and he experiences great difficulty in blending sounds. He learns less from what he hears than does the middle-class learner.

11. Provide an atmosphere of trust where the student can learn self-assurance and self-direction, raise his aspirational level, and develop pride in himself. For example, choral reading may be used to great advantage. This permits the student to respond, and yet it does not single him out if he makes an error. Programmed materials give him all the time he wants or needs without pressuring him for an answer. They permit him to check on his own answer without subjecting him to embarrassment because the teacher or another student saw his error or deficiency. The teacher must proceed on the assumption that the student can improve.

12. Make use of materials that are specifically designed for culturally deprived learners. Students should have a reasonable chance of understanding the materials. They should be slightly below their instructional level. A program on junior high–senior high school level for disadvantaged learners is *Reading in High Gear* by Science Research Associates. Other materials available are:

   a. *Holt's Impact,* Holt, Rinehart & Winston, Inc.

   b. *Macmillan Gateway English Program,* The Macmillan Company

   c. *Project ACE,* Scott, Foresman, & Company.

   d. *Turner-Livingston Reading Series,* Follett Publishing Company.

   e. *The Way It Is,* Xerox Company.

   A brochure, *A Reading List for Disadvantaged Youth,* is available through the American Library Association. Another source is Allan C. Ornstein, "101 Books for Teaching the Disadvantaged," *Journal of Reading,* 10 (May 1967), 546–51. The teacher of experientially deprived students will also want to become familiar with:

   a. Ansara, Alice, *A Guide to the Teaching of Reading.* Cambridge, Mass.: Educators Publishing Service.

   b. Bloom, B. S., Allison Davis, and Robert Hess, *Compensatory Education for Cultural Deprivation.* New York: Holt, Rinehart & Winston, Inc., 1965.

   c. Frost, Joe L., and Glenn R. Hawkes, *The Disadvantaged Child: Issues and Innovations.* Boston: Houghton Mifflin Company, 1966.

   d. Gowan, John C., and George D. Demos, eds., *The Disadvantaged and Potential Dropout.* Springfield, Ill.: Charles C Thomas, Publisher, 1966.

   e. Hellmuth, Jerome, *Disadvantaged Child,* two volumes. New York: Bruner/Mazel, 1970.

   f. Horn, Thomas D., ed., *Reading for the Disadvantaged: Problems of Linguistically Different Learners.* New York: Harcourt, Brace & World, Inc., 1970.

g. Rosen, Carl L., and Philip D. Ortego, "Resources: Teaching Spanish-Speaking Children," *The Reading Teacher*, 25 (October 1971), 11–13.

h. Strom, Robert D., *Teaching in the Slum School*. Columbus, Ohio: Charles E. Merrill Books, Inc., 1965.

i. Taba, Hilda, and Deborah Elkins, *Teaching Strategies for the Culturally Disadvantaged*. Skokie, Ill.: Rand McNally & Co., 1966.

j. Webster, S. W., ed., *The Disadvantaged Learner: Knowing, Understanding, Educating*. San Francisco: Chandler Publishing Company, 1966.

13. Greatly expand the amount of time that is devoted to reading instruction. On the upper-grade levels put special emphasis on study skills.

14. Structure the reading program in such a way that the student thinks of reading as the process of bringing meaning to the page. Don't ask the student, "What does this word mean?" His answer will probably be wrong. Rather, ask him, "What does this word make you think of?" Such a question preserves his self-concept and allows the teacher to develop new or additional meanings.

15. Take an attitude of "positive expectancy" toward the student, focusing on his assets rather than his weaknesses. As Niemeyer, president of Bank Street College, notes: "A major reason for low achievement among children in poor neighborhoods is the low expectation as to their learning capacity held by teachers."

The disadvantaged learner often manifests considerable ingenuity in expression, but teachers do not appreciate the language through which it is voiced. Mark Twain once remarked: "Nothing so needs reforming as other people's habits." This is about the way teachers proceed in dealing with the speech problems of the disadvantaged.

It may well be that many reading failures among minority children are explained by the teacher's ignorance of nonstandard English rules. It cannot be emphasized enough that the use of nonstandard English is not caused by cognitive defects (48). Labov (25) has analyzed the idiosyncrasies of black English and notes its *r-lessness*. This makes homonyms of such words are guard-God, court-caught, carrot-Cat, Paris-pass. The *l* is also consistently dropped, producing homonyms out of such words as toll-toe, help-hep, fault-fought. Frequently, such double consonant sounds as /st/, /ft/, /nt/, /nd/, /ld/, /zd/, and /md/ are reduced to one: rift-rif, mend-men, wind-win. Labov suggests that these language idiosyncrasies may cause difficulty for black children in recognizing many words in their standard spelling. Stewart (43) notes, however, that if the differences are regular and consistent enough, the black child may develop his own sound-spelling correspondences which will permit him to deal effectively with word-identification problems. Recent analyses certainly indicate that black

English is a highly structured system that is not inferior to any other system in a linguistic sense. Some authors, who do not accept this, proceed as though black children had no language at all. This does not mean that standard speech should not be taught, but it raises questions as to how to introduce reading to these children. Some readers are now available through the Education Study Center, Washington, D.C., where the same story is written both ways: one in black English and one in standard speech.

Because differences in grammar are often considered more significant than differences in pronunciation, oral language training should probably focus on them. There is also a need to develop listening skills (48).

McDavid (27) notes that a reading program is effective in proportion to its use of the language habits that the student has acquired in speaking. The disadvantaged youth is disadvantaged precisely because he brings to school language habits that are not used in the reading program, are not recognized as legitimate by the school, and all too often are either overtly or covertly punished by the school. This learner suffers as long as the school is not willing to use the language that he brings to school (43).

Teachers need to realize that differences in language do not mean inferiority (22). And yet, this is exactly what is conveyed when there is a pedagogical attack on the student's language in school. Book after book describes the minority youngster as nonverbal, but he is nonverbal only in the classroom. The black child, through his word games and bantering, amply demonstrates his verbal ability. Instead of being nonverbal, he is actually verbally different.

It is an error to assume that the minority pupil has lazy lips and a lazy tongue or that his language is sloppy and he is a verbal cripple. He shows amazing consistency in his language production. Black students always pronounce the final voiceless /th/ as /f/ in words like mouth, bath, both, south; they do not generally pronounce the final /b/, /d/, /g/, /k/, /p/, and /t/.

Johnson (22), after making the above observations, concludes that instead of teaching standard English to black youth as a replacement dialect, we should teach it as an alternate dialect; we should teach it as an additional linguistic tool to be used in appropriate situations.

The disadvantaged learner is essentially inexperienced in language. He knows too few words and too few meanings. The teacher must accept his manner of expression but also must guide the learner toward using complete sentences. This learner's language, while quite adequate away from school, is not adequate for success in school. Engaging the learner in conversation, fostering language development through role playing and dramatic representation, and reading aloud to him each day are all good procedures to use in developing language competency.

THE GIFTED LEARNER

Too often in a discussion of reading, the needs of the gifted learner are overlooked. Whereas most gifted students are probably reading substantially above grade level, there are many whose reading achievement is substantially below their ability level. In fact, many of them are seriously retarded. Many of them are deficient in study approaches to chapter-length materials or demonstrate inflexibility in reading rate. Helping these students to achieve appropriate educational growth requires that the teacher know how to identify the gifted, know their characteristics as learners, and know how to make educational adjustments to meet their needs.

To identify the gifted learner, we must reach some agreement as to what we mean by *gifted*. In the case of the slow learner, our criterion was low IQ. The IQ as the criterion of giftedness, however, is not completely satisfactory for at least two reasons: (1) Although low IQ generally guarantees low accomplishment, high IQ does not guarantee high accomplishment, and (2) although the gifted learner generally learns anything quite easily, frequently the gifted are highly successful in one area and less successful in others. Thus some would consider a pupil gifted if his performance were consistently remarkable in any valuable line of human activity.

Generally, however, standardized intelligence test results have been used as criteria both to identify the gifted and to define giftedness even though tests are never completely reliable or valid and some types of gifted learners do not express their full capabilities on intelligence tests. Even when we use high IQ as our criterion, we still must decide the specific range of IQ levels that is to mark giftedness. A person is generally considered gifted if he has an IQ of 130 or above, although some programs use a higher cutoff point.

As a group, students with superior IQs are less neurotic, less selfish, more self-sufficient, more mature socially, more self-confident, taller, heavier, and healthier than average learners. Their major strength, however, is their academic prowess. They tend to learn through association rather than through rote memory. They perceive relationships and like to deal with abstractions. They are curious, creative, and imaginative. They tend to work individually, but they enjoy preparing and giving oral and written reports, organizing and cataloging materials and information, and sharing their experiences with their classmates. They tend to write both prose and poetry creatively and effectively. Frequently, what they choose to read and learn is on an adult level, and they are attracted to school subjects that require abstraction. Also, their social consciousness and responses indicate a higher degree of maturity than do those of average students.

The tremendous potential of the gifted students for academic achievement and social leadership carries with it a high challenge and responsibility for educational guidance. This calls for creative teaching. The following points summarize some of the problems that will emerge in teaching the gifted learner.

1. Gifted learners are likely to become irritated by the repetition that slow learners need to reinforce their learning.
2. The student usually prefers to read to learn.
3. Materials are often too simple.
4. The student should be exposed early to critical reading, rate improvement, use of the dictionary, and content-area reading. He needs guidance in appreciation, in detecting mood and tone, and in recognizing literary devices. He needs to question and evaluate the authority of the source material. He must learn to identify the author's purpose, to understand inferences, to anticipate outcomes, and to analyze the author's style.
5. In teaching the gifted learner, the teacher should emphasize such things as abstracting principles and significant interrelationships, synthesizing facts and drawing conclusions, tracing themes and analyzing their importance to the selection as a whole, and criticizing on the basis of all the various forces involved.
6. The intellectual qualities of the gifted often render superfluous traditional patterns of classroom instruction. The student needs problem-centered teaching and student-teacher planning.
7. The teacher must know when to guide, when to direct, and when to get out of the way.
8. The teacher must help the student to develop intrinsic rather than extrinsic motivations.
9. The gifted are not impressed by tight scheduling, close supervision, rigid administration, authoritative teaching, and traditional forms of evaluation.
10. The student needs to be provided broad exposure to and immersion in content. He needs to be taught to see interdisciplinary relationships and to reorganize knowledge. He needs active encounters with academic knowledge.
11. Basic changes in the curriculum rather than simply "patchwork adjustments" are necessary.

Various procedures have been suggested for adjusting instruction to the needs of the gifted learner. Generally, the adjustments have taken one of the following forms:

1. Honors courses.
2. Seminars, especially on the high school level. These are often for non-credit.
3. Special course work.
4. Noncurricular groupings. These bring students together in drama, crafts, language, music, etc.
5. Regular classroom grouping.
6. Credit by examination.
7. Telescoped curriculum. This provides a two-year program in one year.
8. Early admissions, especially on the high school and college levels.
9. Extra courses for credit.
10. Sectioning. Students of all levels of ability are together in the morning, but in the afternoon the more able participate in a special program.
11. Acceleration.
12. Enrichment in the regular classroom. The best form of adjustment may still be a diversification of instruction by a competent teacher.

SUMMARY

In Chapters 3 and 4 we have examined numerous factors that have a bearing on the student's achievement in reading. The teacher cannot ignore them. To help the student most he must have a clear understanding of each factor.

The teacher of reading must know his subject matter. The task variables, the things to be taught, are important determinants of reading success.

This is not enough, however. He must also understand the individual variables. He must understand the nature of the learner. This has been the import of Chapters 3 and 4. The student's development in reading is dependent upon all the other interrelated aspects of his total development. Each student's development is different and so is his achievement in reading. Only by knowing each student can the teacher base his educational decisions on a psychology of individual differences.

The student's "wholeness" is very significant. A learner is not really like a jigsaw puzzle that we can put together, piece by piece. The resultant mosaic may differ appreciably from the original youngster (40).

And yet, we need to remind ourselves once in a while that we still have vast areas of ignorance as to just what are the causes of reading disorders in certain children (23). We have perhaps focused too much on the differences between individuals (the interindividual differences) and not enough on the differences within individuals (the intraindividual differences). Traits and abilities covary: A student's word perception skills normally develop in a close relationship to his comprehension skills. Powell (33), however, notes that when normally covarying abilities become discrepant, difficulty arises. In such cases a differential diagnosis is necessary.

Finally, the chapter examined the special problems of the slow learner, the disadvantaged learner, and the gifted learner.

QUESTIONS FOR DISCUSSION

1. What is the teacher's role in socializing the student?
2. Discuss five significant activities through which the teacher can develop an interest in reading.
3. Explain the interrelationship of motives, needs, meaning, interest, habit, and concentration.
4. Explain the concept *wholeness* or the meaning of the following: "The whole learner goes to school," or "The whole learner reads."
5. In two parallel columns list conditions under which reading failure leads to personal maladjustment, and personal maladjustment leads to reading failure.
6. Discuss the following statements:
    a. The tendency to read is a function of habit strength, of drive (motivation), of the stimulus, and of incentive motivation (reinforcement).
    b. The more reading the student does, the greater is the tendency to engage in additional reading. Genuine interest in reading is developed through actual reading.
    c. The more reading satisfies personal motives, the greater is the tendency to read.
    d. The more interesting reading becomes and thus the closer it comes to being a motive in its own right, the greater is the tendency to read.
    e. The effective tendency to read is equal to the total tendency to read minus the inhibitory factors that tend to block performance. Among the inhibitory factors are health, fatigue, amount of energy needed for reading, and number of unreinforced reading experiences.
    f. The greater the amount of energy the reader must expend in reading, the less he tends to read. (The more difficult the materials, the quicker the student becomes fatigued.)
    g. The more frequently reading is unrewarded, the less the student tends to read. (The student who reads but does not understand tends to lose his interest in reading.)
    h. There is variability in a student's tendency to respond through reading.

    i. Motivation is a decreasing function of massed practice. (Massed practice tends to lead to fatigue.)

7. Assuming that the reading of the slow learner is functional, identify the reading activities that might be included in a junior high reading program for slow learners.

8. What reading methods might best be used with slow learners?

9. Discuss:

    a. The disadvantaged reader is retarded because of a verbally impoverished environment. How is he different from the slow learner?

    b. The disadvantaged reader needs to learn how to learn. What is meant by "learning how to learn"?

10. Identify the special adjustments that you would make for the gifted reader and defend your choice.

BIBLIOGRAPHY

1. BARBE, WALTER B., "A Study of the Reading of Gifted High-School Students," *Educational Administration and Supervision,* 38 (March 1952), 148–54.

2. BENTZEN, FRANCIS, "Sex Ratios in Learning and Behavior Disorders," *American Journal of Orthopsychiatry,* 33 (January 1963), 92–98.

3. BETTELHEIM, BRUNO, "The Decision to Fail," *The School Review,* 69 (Winter 1961), 377–412.

4. BROENING, ANGELA M., "Development of Taste in Literature in the Senior High School," *English Journal,* 52 (April 1963), 273–87.

5. BROOKOVER, W. B., T. SHAILER, and A. PATERSON, "Self Concept of Ability and School Achievement," *Sociology of Education,* 37 (Spring 1964), 271–78.

6. CLARK, W. W., "Boys and Girls—Are There Significant Ability and Achievement Differences?" *Phi Delta Kappan,* 41 (November 1959), 73–76.

7. COLEMAN, JAMES S., *The Adolescent Society.* New York: The Free Press of Glencoe, 1961.

8. COMMITTEE OF THE UPPER GRADES STUDY COUNCIL, "Developing the Reading Interests of Children," *Elementary English Review,* 20 (November 1943), 279–86.

9. CUMMINS, W. D., and BARRY FAGIN, *Principles of Educational Psychology.* New York: Ronald Press, 1954.

10. DAVIS, ALLISON, *Psychology of the Child in the Middle Class.* Pittsburgh: University of Pittsburgh Press, 1960.

11. DAVIS, O. L., and JUNE JENKINSON SLOBODIAN, "Teaching Behavior toward Boys and Girls during First Grade Reading Instruction," *American Educational Research Journal,* 4 (May 1967), 261–69.

12. DUFFY, GERALD G., "Developing the Reading Habit," *The Reading Teacher*, 21 (December 1967), 253–56.

13. EMANS, ROBERT, and JOHN PATYK, "Why Do High School Students Read?" *Journal of Reading*, 10 (February 1967), 300–304.

14. EYSENCK, H. J., *The Structure of Human Personality*. London: Methuen & Co. Ltd., 1953.

15. GETZELS, JACOB W., "The Nature of Reading Interests: Psychological Aspects," *Developing Permanent Interest in Reading*, Supplementary Educational Monographs, No. 84, pp. 5–9. Chicago: University of Chicago Press, 1956.

16. HARRIS, A. J., "Unsolved Problems in Reading: A Symposium II," *Elementary English*, 31 (November 1954), 416–30.

17. HARRIS, DALE B., and SING CHU TSENG, "Children's Attitudes toward Peers and Parents as Revealed by Sentence Completions," *Child Development*, December 1957.

18. HEILMAN, ARTHUR W., "Moving Faster toward Outstanding Instructional Programs," *Vistas in Reading*, II, Part I, 273–76. Eleventh Annual Convention, International Reading Association Conference Proceedings, Newark, N.J., 1967.

19. HOLMES, J. A., "Emotional Factors and Reading Disabilities," *The Reading Teacher*, 9 (October 1955), 11–17.

20. HOLMES, JACK A., and HARRY SINGER, "Theoretical Models and Trends toward More Basic Research in Reading," *Review of Educational Research*, 34 (April 1964), 131–33.

21. HORWORTH, GLORIA L., "Listening: A Facet of Oral Language," *Elementary English*, 43 (December 1966), 856–64, 868.

22. JOHNSON, KENNETH R., "Teacher's Attitude toward the Nonstandard Negro Dialect—Let's Change It," *Elementary English*, 48 (February 1971), 176–84.

23. KETCHUM, E. GILLET, "Neurological and Psychological Trends in Reading Diagnosis," *The Reading Teacher*, 17 (May 1964), 589–93.

24. KINCH, JOHN W., "A Formalized Theory of the Self-Concept," *American Journal of Sociology*, 68 (January 1963), 481–86.

25. LABOV, W., et al., *A Study of the Nonstandard English of Negro and Puerto Rican Speakers in New York City*, Columbia University Cooperative Research Project: Phonological and Grammatical Analysis, I (1968), *Use of Langue in the Speech Community*, 2 (1968).

26. MALMQUIST, EVE, "Organizing Instruction to Prevent Reading Disabilities," *Reading as an Intellectual Activity*, International Reading Association Conference Proceedings, pp. 36–39. New York: Scholastic Magazines, 1963.

27. McDAVID, RAVEN, "Dialectology and the Teaching of Reading," *The Reading Teacher*, 18 (December 1964), 206–13.

28. McGOVERN, JOSEPH D., "Group Dynamics in Adolescence," *Psychological Counseling of Adolescents*, ed. Raymond J. Steimel, pp. 51–67. Washington: Catholic University of America Press, 1962.

29. MOORE, HARRY R., "Geographic Mobility and Performance in High School: Part I and Part II," *Journal of Secondary Education,* 41 (November 1966), 326–31; also 41 (December 1966), 350–52.

30. MUUSS, ROLF E., *Theories of Adolescence.* New York: Random House, Inc., 1962.

31. NORVELL, GEORGE W., *What Boys and Girls Like to Read,* p. 182. Morristown, N.J.: Silver Burdett Company, 1958.

32. PAINTER, HELEN W., "The Teacher's Role in the Development of Lifetime Reading Habits of Secondary School Students," *Journal of Reading,* 8 (March 1965), 240–44.

33. POWELL, WILLIAM R., "The Nature of Individual Differences," *Organizing for Individual Differences,* Perspectives 9 (1967), 1–17.

34. PRESTON, RALPH C., "A Comparative Study of the Reading Achievement of German and American Children," *Changing Concepts of Reading Instruction,* International Reading Association, VI 109–12. New York: Scholastic Magazines, 1961.

35. REDL, FRITZ, "Pre-Adolescents—What Makes Them Tick?" *Child Study,* 21 (1944), 44–48, 58–59.

36. RUDDELL, ROBERT B., "The Effect of the Similarity of Oral and Written Patterns of Language Structure on Reading Comprehension," *Elementary English,* 42 (April 1965), 403–10.

37. RYANS, DAVID G., "Motivation in Learning," *Psychology of Learning,* Forty-first Yearbook of the National Society for the Study of Education, Part II. Chicago: University of Chicago Press, 1942.

38. SATTLER, HENRY V., "A Realistic Approach to Sexual Maturation," *Psychological Counseling of Adolescents,* pp. 34–50. Washington: Catholic University of America Press, 1962.

39. SAWYER, JAMES M., and CHARLES W. TELFORD, *Educational Psychology.* Boston: Allyn & Bacon, Inc., 1964.

40. SCHIFFMAN, GILBERT B., "An Interdisciplinary Approach to the Identification and Remediation of Severe Reading Disabilities," *Junior College and Adult Reading Programs,* pp. 14–26. National Reading Conference, Milwaukee, 1967.

41. SCHNEIDERS, ALEXANDER A., "The Dynamics of Child-Parent Relationships in Adolescents," *Psychological Counseling of Adolescents,* ed. Raymond J. Steimel, pp. 68–80. Washington: Catholic University of America Press, 1962.

42. STAFFORD, JOHN W., "Adolescence, The Prelude to Maturity," *Psychological Counseling of Adolescents,* ed. Raymond J. Steimel, pp. 3–14. Washington: Catholic University of America Press, 1962.

43. STEWART, W. A., "On the Use of Negro Dialect in the Teaching of Reading," in *Teaching Black Children to Read,* ed. Joan C. Baratz and Roger W. Shuy, pp. 156–219. Washington, D.C.: Center for Applied Statistics, 1969.

44. STRANG, RUTH, "The Reading Process and Its Ramifications," *Invitational Addresses,* pp. 49–73. International Reading Association, 1965.

45. VERNON, M. D., *Backwardness in Reading.* London: Cambridge University Press, 1957.

46. WALBERG, HERBERT J., "Reading and Study Habits of High School Physics Students," *Journal of Reading,* 11 (February 1968), 327–32, 383–89.

47. WAPLES, DOUGLAS, BERNARD BERELSON, and FRANKLYN R. BRADSHAW, *What Reading Does to People,* pp. 74–80, 123. Chicago: University of Chicago Press, 1940.

48. WELTY, STELLA L., "Reading and Black English," *Language, Reading, and the Communication Process,* pp. 71–93. International Reading Association, Newark, N.J., 1971.

49. WHEAT, H. G., *Foundations of School Learning.* New York: Alfred A. Knopf, Inc., 1955.

INTRODUCING
THE SECONDARY
READING PROGRAM

PART THREE

The junior high–high school program continues the primary-intermediate reading program. It is a program of extension and development. Reading development must be one of continuing growth, endless refinement. The reader's critical powers are constantly challenged by the weight of concepts, the density of ideas, and the abstract symbolism of his everyday reading (7). The secondary program should thus extend those skills introduced in the elementary school and develop those demanded by the more complex materials and sophisticated tasks in high school. There is just not enough time in the elementary school to develop all the skills that the student will need in high school. All teachers in the secondary school should be familiar with the *total* reading program. Each teacher should appreciate its continuity.

Part III begins with Chapter 5, "Characteristics of Good High School Reading Programs," which focuses on developmental instruction and ends with Chapter 11, "Corrective and Remedial Reading in the Secondary School," which focuses on corrective and remedial instruction. In between these two chapters are those that emphasize the specific skills that need to be developed and extended on the high school level.

The teacher of reading must know the basic skills and abilities essential to learning to read, and he must know how to teach them. This is especially true on the high school level. There the teacher must know the optimum sequence of skills to be learned so that he can fuse simpler skills into more complex skills. It is only by identifying the hierarchy of skills that it is possible to pinpoint the place where the retarded reader falls behind and to provide the proper remediation.*

Part III consists of the following chapters:

Chapter   5—Characteristics of Good High School Reading Programs
Chapter   6—Teaching Word-Recognition Skills
Chapter   7—Developing a Meaningful Vocabulary
Chapter   8—Advancing the Student's Comprehension Skills
Chapter   9—Teaching Content-Area Reading Skills
Chapter 10—Teaching Rate of Comprehension
Chapter 11—Corrective and Remedial Reading in the Secondary School
Chapter 12—Materials for the Teaching of Reading

These chapters form the heart of the book. They deal specifically with the skills that need to be taught.

* Helen M. Robinson, "Significant Unsolved Problems in Reading," *Journal of Reading,* 14 (November 1970), 77–82, 134.

Characteristics of Good High School Reading Programs

CHAPTER **5**

READING PROGRAMS ON THE SECONDARY LEVEL are about "as different as the colors in Joseph's coat" (19). It would be desirable if we could say: "This is the way to organize the secondary program," or "Here is the blueprint for an ideal program," but we are not that fortunate or that omniscient. Nevertheless, there must be a *master* plan (5, pp. 28–29). Without it, the special programs for developmental teaching are liable to be nothing more than a conglomerate of bits and pieces.

Today there are various innovative practices such as performance contracts by private industries, use of tutors, teacher aides, or other para-professionals, individualized instruction, programmed materials, and use of multimedia approaches and computers, but a good reading program cannot be lifted from a book or purchased from a commercial source (24, p. 33). It must be developed locally by a fully committed staff. Flashy hardware, shelves of material, and indeed specialized **personnel** do not make a good reading program. It is the product of the coordinated efforts of many people working over a long period of time (24, p. 119).

After surveying and evaluating high school reading programs, Court-ney (7) noted that 50 percent or less have reading programs and that most of these are essentially remedial or feebly developmental, usually voluntary, and unfortunately too often without strong administrative fiat, and yet there seems to be little doubt that the junior and senior high have need for both developmental and remedial programs. In this chapter our concern will be the developmental program. It reaches all students at each level of accomplishment. Its basic assumption is that reading improvement is a lifelong process.

THE DEVELOPMENTAL PROGRAM

Otto and Smith (24, pp. 28–29) have schematically described the developmental program. We concur with them that there is a single overall reading program consisting of several specialized forms of instruction.

FIGURE 5-1   THE DEVELOPMENTAL PROGRAM

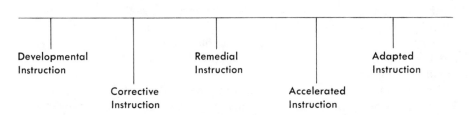

Teachers need a clear understanding of the word *developmental*. Too often, developmental comes to mean a program essentially different from the remedial program. We do not like the term *remedial reading program*. Remediation along with diagnosis is an integral phase of the developmental program. Diagnosis and remediation must accompany all effective teaching. The developmental program is responsible for systematic reading instruction at all school levels. It includes developmental, corrective, and remedial instruction. We use the term *corrective instruction of reading* to refer to situations in which remedial activities are carried on in the regular classroom. When the remediation occurs outside the regular classroom, we term it *remedial teaching*. It seems clear that in an ideal situation or some sort of educational utopia, where there would be no retardation, the concept of and need for remedial teaching might disappear.

Corrective instruction usually occurs in the regular classroom. If a special teacher is available, the student might be assigned to him several times a week for forty-five to sixty minutes.

Corrective instruction stresses sequential development in word attack and comprehension skills but uses special techniques and materials and concentrates on a particular reading deficiency. The corrective program is in addition to regular reading instruction.

Remedial teaching, because of its expensiveness, is necessarily limited. It is a slow process, on a one-to-one basis or at most on the basis of one teacher to three to eight students. Because of the expenses involved, even when a special remedial teacher is available, it is probable that instruction will be individualized rather than strictly individual.

The school thus needs to limit the number of students that will find themselves in a remedial classroom. As we have already noted, some poor readers, and in this group belong slow learners reading up to their ability, reluctant readers, and disadvantaged readers, for the most part should be kept in the regular classroom. Some retarded readers need corrective reading but can still stay in the regular classroom. Only the severely retarded readers need to be taken out for full-time special instruction.

Remedial teaching or corrective teaching is not justified if it is not different from regular reading instruction. The instruction needs to be on a broader basis. *The corrective or remedial teacher needs to be completely familiar with the skills to be taught at all levels. He must be able to telescope, as it were, the total reading program into a relatively brief period of instruction. He must appreciate and understand the continuity of the total reading program.*

Accelerated instruction provides for the needs of the bright and well-motivated learner. *Adapted* instruction is an adaption of pace and expectations to the limitations of the slow learner.

The ultimate aim of the reading program is achievement by each learner up to the limit of his abilities.

The focus of the reading program is upon each individual learner, not upon groups of learners or upon grade-level performance (5, pp. 28–29). It is not what the group does that is important, nor even whether an individual measures up to grade level. The chief concern is that the individual learner do as well as he can.

Otto and Smith (24, pp. 35–36) provide guidelines for assigning students to the various instructional levels. Placement is based on intelligence and achievement and is schematically portrayed in Figure 5–2.

FIGURE 5-2   READING ACHIEVEMENT

INTELLIGENCE	Below Grade Level	Grade Level	Above Grade Level
Above Average	Remedial	Corrective	Accelerated
Average	Corrective Remedial	Developmental	
Below Average	Adapted Corrective Remedial		

UNDERLYING PRINCIPLES

Assuming then that a need exists for high school programs, let us describe the principles that should permeate a good program.

1. As we already mentioned, the most significant prerequisites seem to be administrative conviction, direction, and provision. The administrator alone possesses the prestige and persuasion to carry through a sound high school reading program (7). He must encourage and insure that the reading philosophy is implemented in logical and innovative ways (27). He needs to provide the impetus for defining the reading program's philosophy and must be the facilitator of that philosophy by extending it to the entire school. On the other hand, the administrator cannot turn on the reading program by a mere flick of a switch. The administrator does not accord reading the respect it deserves when he assumes that anyone can teach reading and assigns reading classes to whatever teacher has a free period.

2. It must be clear why the program exists, and its purpose, goals, and objectives must be closely identified and stated behaviorally. There is only one goal of the reading program, and that is that each student read up to his ability level. The objectives must be explicitly defined in terms of student needs. The program must help each student to read as well as his abilities permit; his progress should not be gauged to the grade level in which he is.

3. The program should reflect the cooperation and involvement of the entire staff. Only in this way will teachers come to accept that "every teacher is a reading teacher." In the more successful programs a reading committee, composed of representatives of all areas of the curriculum, usually functions in the determination of the definition of reading, the philosophy of the program, and its implementation.

4. The program must be tailor-made for the school in which it is housed.

5. It should be clear whether the program will be a separate entity or perhaps have subdepartmental status within the English or counseling departments.

6. The staff needs to exhibit competency in reading. The staff must be well trained. They must be able to teach reading skills in a logical, structured fashion. It is unfair to assign "the English teacher" to teach reading, whether it be developmental, corrective, or remedial.

7. Facilities, materials, and equipment must be adequate. They should vary in type, in interest, and in range of ability.

8. There should be careful and continuous appraisal of each student's reading proficiency together with diagnosis of special difficulties as well as continuous appraisal of the effectiveness of the program as a whole. The diagnosis determines the level at which instruction is to begin and the specific reading needs of each student. Goal setting and diagnosis go hand in hand. The *Teacher Informal Reading Package* (17) can be used to do this.

9. An effective program touches every student and utilizes the talents of every teacher (18). The content-area teachers must assume major responsibility for teaching the reading/study skills needed in the content areas. But this is not enough. Special reading teachers must work with the content teacher by developing units of instruction, by team teaching in subject areas, and by diagnosing students' disabilities in the content areas. In addition there must be an ongoing evaluation and in-service education and a well-staffed clinic to which students with special problems can be referred.

10. The procedures for reinforcing the objectives and skills must be clearly identified.

11. The program should emphasize reading as a lifelong, mature habit, and the aim should be to produce a mature reader.

12. The program needs to have the support of the parents.

13. While we generally look unfavorably at in-service programs that encroach on teachers' time, in-service teachers can help classroom teachers in many ways (22). They can distribute journal articles on reading instruction, discuss and evaluate standardized test results, have teachers investigate new and effective reading programs, or get teachers to try out new materials and practices. The classroom teacher needs *practical* help (22). He benefits most when the idea is demonstrated in the classroom, when he is shown how to use materials, and when he himself is given the time to formulate a plan for implementation of new ideas.

SYSTEMATIC INSTRUCTION IN THE BASIC SKILLS

It has been our experience that even when a program in the secondary school seems to grow out of sound principles, there still is concern as to *what to teach* and *how to teach* whatever needs to be taught.

In the summary of Chapter 2 we noted that there are two basic reading skills: identification of the symbol and association of meaning with the printed symbol. (In *Improving the Teaching of Reading,* pp. 204–42, we have discussed these processes at great length.)

Unlike the elementary teacher, the secondary teacher is rarely called upon to introduce reading to the learner. He more commonly intervenes in a corrective or remedial way. Nevertheless, let us make a few summary observations about reading methodology.

A good reading program gives due consideration to both identification and meaning. It teaches students to be proficient in attacking words and in reading with understanding. Most "methods" of teaching reading (word-configuration approach, linguistic approach, Words in Color, Initial Teaching Alphabet, Language-Experience, phonic approaches, etc.) focus on the aspect of word identification. They are designed to teach the student to identify the printed word, to differentiate it from every other word, and to recognize it upon seeing it again in a different context.

Today most teachers probably use a combination, or eclectic, approach. Some begin with the total word and then *more or less* simultaneously break it down into its phonemic elements (Analytic-Synthetic Method). Others begin with the phonemes and then combine these to form meaningful words (Synthetic-Analytic Method). The pupil must be able to synthesize the parts into a whole and to analyze the whole into its parts.

We do not feel there is great value at this point to elaborate profusely on the theory of methodology. Rather, we hope that in Chapters 6, 7, and 8 we have detailed how the pupil can be taught to recognize words *and* to read with meaning.

A few statements might serve to summarize our thinking on methodology.

1. Most children learn to read regardless of the method. Many different methods can and do eventually lead to reading proficiency. One type of program does not seem to be clearly superior to all others or best for all learners.

2. Certain methods or specific teaching approaches make a world of difference for the individual learner.

3. The method that works best for a given student depends on the individual learner. Not all learners profit to the same extent from a given method. What is good for slow learners may not work with gifted learners.

4. No one program seems to provide for all learners' reading requirements.

5. The "best" method for *most* learners has both an analytic *and* a synthetic emphasis. There are few pure-configuration methods, and few programs ignore phonics completely.

6. Some teachers do not make use of the best that is available, but if the teacher is a good teacher, other factors can often be attributed to teacher effectiveness.

7. A given method may well produce excellent results under one set of conditions but may result in failure under a different set of circumstances.

It is not enough to know how to teach; one must also know *what* to teach. What are the specific skills that the student must learn?

Because of the nature of the reading process and the individuality of youngsters, it seems illogical to suggest that certain learnings are peculiar to seventh grade or to senior high school. *Skill development does not come in capsule form.* One cannot dish out to seventh graders the seventh-grade capsule and to twelfth graders the twelfth-grade capsule.

It is also for these reasons that all teachers should be familiar with the *total* reading program. Each teacher needs to appreciate its continuity. He needs to know at what level the student is working, what he has learned, and what he probably needs to learn. Introduction of reading skills is useless unless the student's subsequent reading experiences serve to maintain those skills.

The student must gradually pass from learning to read to reading for learning. There are differences here among students as in almost any other area of human accomplishment. There are differences among students in *rate* of learning, but also in *capacity* of learning. Some students will never master all the skills. This again reinforces the need for individualization of each student's reading program. The teacher must start each student at the point of success that he has attained and must permit him to advance as far as he can as rapidly as he can.

In general, reading skills can be divided into the following seven broad areas:

1. Perceptual skills
2. Literal-comprehension skills
3. Word-recognition skills
4. Interpretative and appreciative skills
5. Reading-study skills
6. Rate-of-comprehension skills
7. Oral-reading skills

These skills, which we have detailed in Chapters 6–10, encompass all those that the mature reader acquires in the course of his successful progress through the developmental program. It is only when he fails to do so that we need to provide corrective and remedial instruction, which is the concern of Chapter 11.

SAMPLE PROGRAMS

There is no way to prescribe a program that will meet the needs of all schools. No two schools will have the same degree of success with the same program. The effectiveness of a program is dependent upon school size, philosophy, administrative leadership, range of student ability, teacher competency and preparation, and facilities and materials.

It is impossible to detail the great variety of programs that does exist, but here in outline form are some variations, some of which overlap, that these programs take:

1. Reading is taught to all freshmen who score below a certain point on entrance tests. Other students receive regular English instruction. In such a program it might be best to team the reading teacher with the English teachers.

2. All freshmen receive six to eight weeks of instruction in developmental reading as part of the English course or perhaps the social studies class. The developmental reading program is a required course. Reading teachers do the teaching. They may or may not be assigned to the English department. Sometimes an orientation class provides planned study-skills lessons.

3. When students return to the English class they may still be required to spend at least one hour per week in supervised classroom reading.

4. All subject-matter teachers instruct students in those reading skills that are specifically relevant to their context. A reading specialist works more or less in an advisory capacity to the classroom teacher, provides in-service training, and may work with special cases.

5. In smaller schools (five hundred or fewer students) a reading teacher provides basic developmental instruction for all students, gives special attention to the retarded, offers an enrichment program or an accelerated reading program for the gifted and college bound, and during one period of the day is available for consultation with the subject-matter teachers about individuals and about textbooks and assignments. Sometimes an honors seminar is offered in the evening.

6. In a program where the major aim is to bring expert corrective instruction to the students in particular need, there is a special reading teacher whose load is substantially lighter than that of other teachers. There may be individual and small-group tutoring.

7. The larger school system, which includes perhaps four high schools with a total enrollment of five thousand or more, generally has both reading teachers and reading consultants. There may be a reading coordinator

who is responsible for setting up the program, developing the course of study, selecting and ordering materials and equipment, setting up the laboratories, training new teachers, and providing overall supervision.

8. In some situations a reading specialist or consultant functions as a reading teacher in the classroom.

9. Many systems have a special reading laboratory or reading center equipped with the best mechanical devices and reading materials. The class comes to the reading center and is taught by the reading specialist or by the regular teacher in a specific area, with the assistance and direction of the reading specialist.

10. Some schools focus attention on the reading needs of their students, especially those who are retarded, by means of summer reading improvement programs.

11. Some schools make special provision for corrective and remedial programs for disadvantaged youth, delinquents, or the emotionally disturbed.

More schools obviously need programs, whether it be one of the above or a program making multiple provisions. An even greater need exists for a thorough evaluation of existent programs.

The following suggestions might prove helpful in planning within-classroom modifications:

1. Use team teaching, permitting the grouping of students into very small units when needed. Disadvantaged students might be assigned to small classrooms or subgrouped for specific teaching.

2. Reduce the teacher-student ratio.

3. Use "reserve teachers" or "supplemental teachers" to work with groups of eight to twelve for one hour each day to help the lowest reading groups.

4. Assign "master teachers" on the basis of one master teacher to six to ten less-experienced teachers to help them and to work with small groups.

5. Use "remedial reading teachers" to give demonstrations for classroom teachers and to secure needed materials for teaching reading.

6. Use parents in the classroom as aides to help students listen to tapes and to use the library and to help the teacher with record keeping.

A program that includes paraprofessionals might use them in one of the following ways (26):

1. Have them listen to a student read.

2. Have them assist students in selecting books.

3. Have them help the slow learner in carrying out directions as he does an assignment.

4. Have them correct workbook or other specific assignments.
5. Have them supervise seatwork or makeup assignments.
6. Have them supervise committee activities.
7. Have them help students who missed instruction through illness, etc.
8. Have them direct remedial drill work.
9. Have them operate audiovisual equipment.
10. Have them distribute and collect materials.

GROUPING IN THE SECONDARY SCHOOL

The secondary teacher today is faced with larger classes and a greater spread of individual differences. Homogeneity is nonexistent when we consider the interpersonal and the intrapersonal differences among students (2). There is obviously no economy in trying to teach students what they are not ready to learn or for that matter in making students who have already learned a skill mark time until all others in the class will have learned the same skill (30). The teacher therefore needs to make curricular changes and class organizational changes to provide for these differences. We have seen the emergence of dual track systems, such as college preparatory and vocational; sometimes acceleration is practiced. In many schools various forms of intraclass grouping occur (11).

Mills (19) notes that corrective and remedial programs often take the form of:

1. Semihomogeneous grouping in the regular classroom
2. Provision for special instruction in small groups
3. Team teaching, involving instruction in basic skills as well as reading in content areas
4. In-service training for regular classroom teachers
5. The reading laboratory

Reading method always functions in the context of a specific type of classroom organization, but "a plan of organization is not a method of teaching. It is a facilitator of method, perhaps, but no more." Either the classroom is organized on a group basis with some attempt at individualization, or individualized instruction is emphasized and groups are formed as needed.

Historically classrooms have been organized into groups, and the emphasis has been upon the development of a group organization that would permit the greatest amount of individual growth.

Unfortunately, the search for a happy balance between grouping and individualization is still in progress.

In the 1880s educators were already complaining about the lockstep in reading education. The complaint was that all students were forced to advance along a common front at the same rate of speed. Each student had the same book, was asked to learn the same material, and was judged by the same academic standards.

Four characteristics typically affect the differences between and within individuals: normality, variation, covariation, and velocity (25). Most traits show the characteristic of normality, or normal distribution. Variation refers to the deviations among the members of any species. Normal distribution of traits necessarily implies variation.

Grouping is an attempt to reduce variation, but because of intraindividual differences as well as interindividual variation, homogeneous grouping results in only about a 20 percent reduction of the variation (1). Variations in student ability thus remain about 80 percent as great in so-called homogeneous groupings as in the heterogeneous or unselected classroom.

Traits and abilities also covary. A student's word perception skills normally develop in close relationship to his comprehension skills. It is when selected reading skills do not covary in the usual way that difficulties occur and that a differential diagnosis beomes necessary (25).

Students also grow, develop, mature, and learn at an *individual* rate or velocity.

The chief concern in reading has unfortunately been how one child differs from another. Perhaps we should focus on the way an individual reader differs within himself. We need to be concerned whether the learner is reading up to his expectancy level or up to his capacity. Many important instructional decisions can and must be based on an analysis of this differential (25).

Ability Grouping

With the increased emphasis on individual differences in the 1920s and with the publication of the twenty-fourth yearbook of the National Society for the Study of Education, *Adapting the School to Individual Differences,* came a new classroom organization. It was termed *ability grouping* and for some time was thought to be the answer to the problem. In this approach pupils of the same ability used the same basic reader, and it was assumed that their individual needs were being met.

Unfortunately, pupils were commonly divided into three groups, average, above average, and below average. The pupil was rarely able to move from one level to another.

Individualized Reading

In an attempt to overcome some of the inadequacies of ability grouping, there arose in the early 1960s an interest in individualized reading.

This approach suggested that the student *seeks* for what he is physiologically and psychologically ready and that he shows his readiness through the spontaneous *selection* of the materials that he wants to read.

Self-selection is considered to be a necessary aspect of individualized reading. Teachers have always encouraged youngsters to explore reading materials apart from those used in the classroom. Perhaps, in individualized reading, the pupil is encouraged to take a more active part in the selection of the materials.

The advantages claimed for individualized reading are many. Perhaps the most significant is the attitudinal change in the learner (6). Students seem to be more interested in reading. They read more at home. They show more interest in improvement and develop more favorable attitudes toward school in general. They often show improvement in work habits, self-motivation, and self-confidence. They seem to engage in more independent thinking and show better self-management.

In individualized reading, the purposes for reading are primarily individual and only secondarily group. The group serves as a sounding board for the individual to test the accuracy of the ideas acquired and to permit him the luxury of sharing the knowledge and insight that he has acquired.

The teacher thus works with the individual, detecting his needs and providing for these needs as the student's work reveals them. He keeps an accurate record of the student's accomplishments and inadequacies and helps him to pace his activities in accordance with his interests, aptitudes, and previous achievements. The teacher is not the prime director of the learning process and indeed never has been. Teaching may be a group process, but learning has always been an individual process.

Individualized reading does not seem suitable for students who cannot work independently or who cannot select or pace themselves wisely, and it is not economical when instruction can be provided more simply and in less time in a group situation than in a one-to-one teacher-student conference. And skills are not learned simply by reading. The poor reader does not become a good reader by selecting and reading materials that he enjoys. Practice of itself is not enough.

THE NEED FOR ECLECTICISM IN
CLASSROOM ORGANIZATION

In *Psychology in Teaching Reading* (28, pp. 383–89) the principles that should guide classroom groupings were outlined. It was pointed out that total homogeneous groups are never possible and that when formed, groupings should be related to the specific learning task. Groups are occasioned when students show a commonality of achievement, interest, or need. Students may be grouped to help each other in a learning activity. Such groups may be labeled *team groups*. Students may be grouped when they show the need for the same skill development. The teacher may form intraclass groups for the purpose of reinforcement, reteaching, or independent work (9).

Groups should be changed (10) when students give evidence of growth or when their reading needs can be better met in another group. More specifically, a learner may be moved from one group to another because of excessive absence, because he does not understand words, because he has not learned certain basic skills, because the book is too difficult, or because he is falling too far behind others in the group. He may move because he has shown rapid improvements in an area or because he might profit from the exposure to a faster moving group. At times, the teacher may simply want to know what a trial in a new group can do.

Obviously, class organization is only one phase of the total reading program. To group heterogeneously, homogeneously, or individually is not the total answer.

The good educational program has always had some aspect of the individualized program, and the individualized program does not eliminate all group aspects. If indeed we do believe in the individuality of the learner, then it is difficult to ignore either approach, for one student may learn better in group situations, another in independent study. And even the same student may learn better when shifting from one approach to another as the occasion and his own needs demand.

Total individualization of instruction thus may *not* be individualizing the reading program. For some students it may be an inappropriate organization. Individualization really means that the teacher accommodates the situation to the learner and not the learner to the situation. He does not force him entirely either into a group structure or into an individualized, one-to-one, student-teacher structure. We now realize that some types of learning may best be obtained through individualized instruction; others, through group instruction. Groups of five may be best for discussion purposes; groups of two or three may be best for practice exercises (20); and the teacher may be best for testing the student's comprehension of what he read individually.

Thus, the teacher's role is ultimately determined by the situation in which he finds himself. Sometimes he must become quite directive and sometimes he functions best in a permissive, laissez-faire role. He moves between the two extremes, neither advocating a just-let-them-read point of view nor limiting all the student's reading to the textbook. He avoids both the turn-them-loose, permissive approach and the stick-strictly-to-the-textbook approach (3).

The instructional procedures must be altered to accommodate individuals within the group. "Taking the student where he is" does not simply mean selecting materials on his grade level. Emphasis must be placed on his specific needs.

Individualized reading and grouping are not incompatible. A teacher-student conference is a group. Sometimes the teacher will have three, five, or as many as eight youngsters about him. All the group may need help in the same reading skills, may want to discuss the same story, or may want to read aloud to each other. Students may be grouped on an interest basis, on a need basis, or for social reasons. It is even possible to subgroup within ability groupings and to individualize instruction in each of them. Some students learn better with a friend. A study by Bradley (5) indicates that children worked better in pairs than under the direction of a teacher or when working alone.

When students work on a unit activity, they may work in groups. Education cannot become so individual that socialization is ignored. The student is by nature individual; with learning he becomes a social animal.

There are even occasions when the entire class can and should work together. There *never* is and never has been justification for "total class teaching of reading" (29, p. 97).

Mobile groups based on constantly changing objectives and the needs of the learners imply a constant awareness of the individuality of the learner. The groups should be based on the achievement of students in a particular skill rather than on their overall achievement. It is possible that the best and the poorest reader will be in the same group. Both may need help in a specific reading skill such as vocabulary, speed, or comprehension. Flexible groups thus are ever changing and make the attainment of immediate objectives that are consistent with immediate needs possible (14).

Recent studies have not resolved the issues of organization. Lambert (15), in a study involving over six hundred pupils in grades one and six, reported significant gains in reading and study skills for pupils who were grouped regularly, but not so for those grouped on a pupil team basis; in the second year, the team groups showed greater gains. Newport (21), evaluating the Joplin interclass ability grouping plan where fourth- through sixth-grade pupils are grouped homogeneously without regard to grade level, reported on nine studies of the plan and concluded that the results of most studies have not favored the plan, but interclass grouping seemed as effective as ability grouping within the self-contained classroom. In general, parental, teacher, and pupil acceptance of the plan was good, but pupils in the lower group expressed dissatisfaction and preferred to be transferred to higher groups (13). Goldberg and others (8) reported that the findings concerning ability groupings were inconclusive.

Borg and Prpich (4), in a two-year study comparing the performance of slow-learning tenth-grade students assigned to ability-grouped English classes with students of comparable ability and past achievement who were members of regular heterogeneous English classes, found:

1. No significant differences in English achievement for both replications of the study. Ability-grouped students made significantly greater gains on the *STEP Essay Test* during the year.
2. No significant differences in study methods or attitudes.
3. No significant differences on the *STEP Listening Test*.
4. Some evidence that the ability-grouping treatment was associated with better self-concept, better class participation, and more positive attitudes.

The Developmental Reading Program has little quarrel with attempts to individualize the reading program. It does insist that principles of student development should guide the methods and procedures used. With this in mind, let us make a few observations:

1. At times it is desirable to teach a class as a whole.
2. Grouping may reduce or narrow, but it will not completely eliminate the range of differences in a class.
3. Combinations of group and individual instruction seem to be indicated at present.
4. No organizational plan of itself insures reading success.
5. The reading program should make provision for the progressive development of skills.
6. The effectiveness of the program depends on the number and quality of reading materials.
7. The search for a happy balance between grouping and individualization is still in progress. It is our feeling that heterogeneous grouping with mobile

flexible subgrouping, rather than homogeneous grouping, has the most to offer in the regular classroom. Flexible subgrouping seems especially helpful in dealing with the problems of the student who needs corrective reading instruction. It permits the organization of clusters or subgroups of students with common reading needs.

ORGANIZING FOR CORRECTIVE AND REMEDIAL READING

As we have stated previously, corrective reading instruction should be reserved for the regular classroom. A few cautions are in order. Corrective instruction cannot be so organized as to embarrass the student and should certainly not be substituted for such pleasurable activities as recess or physical education. Nor should it give the appearance of simply being squeezed into the school day.

Even with a reduction of the teacher-student ratio and with subgrouping, there is no easy solution to students' reading problems. The teacher may need outside help. One pattern of organization for corrective instruction may include the use of additional teachers or aides. The use of team teaching or of reserve or supplemental teachers to work with small groups has been found beneficial. Some schools assign a master teacher to work directly with the teacher during the regular reading period. The special reading teacher may help the classroom teacher by giving classroom demonstrations in the use of specific methods or materials. The teacher may initiate team learning, in which students subgroup as a team and work together in the learning of new concepts, in applying skills, or in reviewing. Tutoring, a situation in which one student works with one or more students who need help, has been used by many teachers.

Staggered scheduling is another organizational device useful in planning developmental and corrective reading instruction. In the developmental setting staggered scheduling is sometimes labeled divided-day, split-day, extended-day, or staggered-day organization. It provides a reading period in the morning with one-half of the class, which arrives early, and another period in the afternoon with the other half of the class, which stays late. Warner's study (31) indicates that this form of organization is advantageous to both teacher and student and results in superior reading achievement.

In a corrective setting, those youngsters who are to be kept in the regular classroom but who need special help in reading may be asked to report to school an hour early or leave an hour late. Lunch periods could be staggered for similar effect.

Pupils who are seriously retarded may have to be taken out of the regular classroom and put into a special room where a remedial reading teacher or a special teacher will work with them. Sometimes no classroom space is available, and the school may have to use mobile equipment. In another school the remedial teacher may function out of the reading materials center.

Organizing for remedial instruction requires that students be dismissed from the regular classroom at scheduled times during the regular school day so that they can go to the remedial classroom for special instruction. The student reports to the remedial class for perhaps one lesson per day and then returns to his own classroom.

Remedial instruction may be given during a regular study period or during a subject-matter class. Sometimes the student is given remedial instruction before school begins or after school ends. In some schools remedial instruction is provided during the homeroom or the activity period. In other schools remedial instruction becomes a part of the English class.

The remedial room should be equipped with audiovisual materials of various types, filmstrip projector, tachistoscopes, accelerating devices, record players, tape recorder, and listening stations. It should contain books of all types, supplementary readers, programmed reading materials, multilevel reading laboratories, testing and diagnostic materials, magazines, and all kinds of word-recognition and comprehension development materials.

SUMMARY

This chapter has focused on various aspects of a good high school reading program. We examined the developmental nature of this program, including the underlying principles of such a program and the instruction that is needed in the basic skills. The remainder of the chapter dealt with such aspects as sample programs, grouping in the secondary school, and organizing for corrective and remedial organization.

BIBLIOGRAPHY

1. ANASTASI, ANNE, *Differential Psychology*, p. 320. New York: The Macmillan Company, 1958.
2. BAMMAN, HENRY A., "Organizing the Remedial Program in the Secondary School," *Journal of Reading*, 8 (November 1964), 103–8.

3. BETTS, EMMETT ALBERT, "Issues in Teaching Reading," *Controversial Issues in Reading,* Tenth Annual Reading Conference, Lehigh University, 1 (April 1961), 33–41.

4. BORG, WALTER R., and TONY PRPICH, "Grouping of Slow Learning High School Pupils," *Journal of Secondary Education,* 41 (May 1966), 231–38.

5. BRADLEY, MARY A., "The Construction and Evaluation of Exercises for Providing Meaningful Practice in Second Grade Reading." Unpublished doctoral dissertation, Boston University, School of Education, 1957.

6. CALDER, CLARENCE, R., JR., "Self-directed Reading Materials," *The Reading Teacher,* 21 (December 1967), 248–52.

7. COURTNEY, BROTHER LEONARD, "Characteristics of a Good High School Reading Program." North Central Association Annual Meeting, March 29, 1966.

8. GOLDBERG, MIRIAM, et al., *The Effects of Ability Grouping.* New York: Teachers College Press, 1966.

9. HAMM, RUSSELL L., and VICTORIA JACOBSON, "In-Class Grouping in Reading at the Secondary Level," *Reading Improvement,* 5 (Fall 1968), 36–38.

10. HAWKINS, MICHAEL, "Changes in Reading Groups," *The Reading Teacher,* 21 (October 1967), 48–51.

11. HOOVER, KENNETH H., and HELENE M. HOOVER, "A Plan for Grouping in the Secondary Classroom," *Education,* 88 (February-March, 1968), 208–12.

12. JOHNSON, MARJORIE S., and ROY A. KRESS, eds., *Corrective Reading in the Elementary Classroom.* International Reading Association, Newark, N.J., 1967.

13. KIERSTEAD, R., "A Comparison and Evaluation of Two Methods of Organization for the Teaching of Reading," *Journal of Educational Research,* 56 (1963), 317–21.

14. KNIGHT, ELVA E., "Mobility Grouping," *Reading Bulletin 224.* Chicago: Educational Service Department, Lyons and Carnahan.

15. LAMBERT, P., et al., "A Comparison of Pupil Achievement in Team and Self-contained Organizations," *Journal of Experimental Education,* 33 (1965), 217–24.

16. LICHTMAN, MARILYN, "Keys to a Successful Reading Program," *The Reading Teacher,* 24 (April 1971), 652–58.

17. ———, *Teacher Informal Reading Package,* Washington, D.C.: Catholic University of America, June 1970.

18. MCDONALD, THOMAS F., "An All-School Secondary Reading Program," *Journal of Reading,* 14 (May 1971), 553–58.

19. MILLS, DONNA M., "Corrective and Remedial Reading Instruction in the Secondary School," *Reading as an Intellectual Activity,* 8 (1963), 56–59.

20. MURPHY, HELEN A., "Mutual Aid in Learning in the Primary Grades," *Changing Concepts of Reading Instruction,* ed. J. Allen Figurel. International Reading Association Conference Proceedings, Vol. 6, pp. 81–84. New York: Scholastic Magazines, 1961.

21. NEWPORT, JOHN F., "The Joplin Plan: The Score," *The Reading Teacher,* 21 (November 1967), 158–62.

22. OLSON, ARTHUR V., "Organizing the Secondary Reading Program," *Reading Improvement,* 3 (Winter 1966), 33–38.
23. OTTO, WAYNE, and RICHARD A. MCMENEMY, *Corrective and Remedial Teaching of Reading.* Boston: Houghton Mifflin Company, 1966.
24. ———, and RICHARD J. SMITH, *Administering the School Reading Program.* Boston: Houghton, Mifflin Company, 1970.
25. POWELL, WILLIAM R., "The Nature of Individual Differences," *Organizing for Individual Differences,* Perspectives 9, 1967, 1–17, International Reading Association.
26. RAUCH, SIDNEY J., "Using Paraprofessionals as Reading Aides," *Reading Methods and Teacher Improvement,* pp. 184–95. International Reading Association, Newark, N.J., 1971.
27. SANDERS, PETER L., "Impetus, Participant, Facilitator—A Definition of the Administrator's Role," *Journal of Reading,* 14 (May 1971), 547–52.
28. SMITH, HENRY P., and EMERALD V. DECHANT, *Psychology in Teaching Reading.* Englewood Cliffs, N.J.: Prentice-Hall, Inc., 1961.
29. VITE, IRENE W., "Grouping Practices in Individualized Reading," *Elementary English,* 38 (February 1961), 91–98.
30. WALKER, JERRY L., "Conducting an Individualized Reading Program in High School," *Journal of Reading,* 8 (April 1965), 291–95.
31. WARNER, DOLORES, "The Divided-Day Plan for Reading Organization," *The Reading Teacher,* 20 (February 1967), 397–99.

Teaching Word-Recognition Skills: The Decoding Process

CHAPTER **6**

G.   The Sounds Represented by *X*
H.   The Sounds Represented by *Y*
I.   The Sounds Represented by *Z*

IV.   *TEACHING THE SHORT VOWEL*

V.   *TEACHING THE END CONSONANT*

VI.   *TEACHING THE BEGINNING CONSONANT BLENDS*

VII.   *TEACHING THE ENDING CONSONANT BLENDS*

VIII.   *THE SPEECH CONSONANTS*

A.   The Digraph *Ch*
B.   The Digraphs *Sh* and *Th*
C.   The Digraphs *Wh, Gh, Ph,* and *Ng*

IX.   *THE LONG VOWELS*

A.   The Principle of Variability
B.   The Principle of Position
C.   The Principle of Silentness
D.   The Principle of Context
   1.   The combination *Oo*
   2.   The combination *Ei (Ey)*
   3.   The combination *Ie*
   4.   The combination *Ou*
   5.   The combination *Ow*
   6.   The combinations *Au* and *Aw*
   7.   The combinations *Ew, Ue, Ui,* and *Eu*

X.   *THE DIPHTHONGS*

XI.   *TEACHING THE LONG VOWELS*

XII.   *THE EFFECT OF R ON A PRECEDING VOWEL*

XIII.   *TEACHING STRUCTURAL ANALYSIS SKILLS*

MANY STUDENTS HAVE LEARNED to apply most of the word-recognition skills by the time they reach junior high, but many have serious gaps or deficiencies. These deficiencies must be eliminated through developmental or corrective reading programs at the high school level. Every high school student, especially the one who has not progressed as much as he might, can benefit from instruction when the basic skills are developed in a logical and sequential manner.

The focus of this chapter is on the decoding process.* It explores the skills needed by the reader if he is to decode the written language with ease and accuracy. It must be clearly understood, however, that decoding is complete only when meaning is associated with the printed symbols.

Some would define reading as "the act of turning the stimulus of the graphic shapes on a surface back into speech" (17), and Bloomfield differentiated between the *act of reading* (recognition of grapheme-phoneme correspondences) and the *goal of reading* (comprehension), but reading always involves comprehension. Reading is not simply the recognition of the symbol-sound correspondences to the point where the reader responds to the marks with appropriate speech.

This chapter emphasizes the development of an understanding of the correspondences between the English spelling system and the English

* For a more complete discussion see Emerald Dechant, *Linguistics, Phonics, and the Teaching of Reading,* (Springfield, Ill.: Charles C Thomas, Publisher, 1969).

sound system, in other words, the grapheme-phoneme correspondence. It is based on the assumption that if the student is ever to become a mature reader, he must be adept in the use of the graphic, or written, code of language. And it is based on the further assumption that unless the teacher has a formal knowledge of the nature and structure of language, he cannot teach a student to decode the written language.

TERMINOLOGY

Before getting into the specifics of linguistic phonics instruction, let us clarify a few terms.

1. *Phonics* is the study of the speech equivalents of printed symbols and the use of this knowledge in identifying and pronouncing printed words (9, p. 324). It is learning that involves the association of the appearance of a letter or letter combinations with a given sound (9, p. 330). It is the study of sound-letter relationships in reading and spelling. It represents the various teaching practices that aim to develop the student's ability to sound out a word by matching individual letters by which a word is spelled with the specific sounds that these letters say. *Phonic analysis* is the actual process of sounding out letters or letter combinations to arrive at the pronunciation of the word.

2. *Phonetics* is the study of speech production; it is the study of the sounds used in speech, including their pronunciations, the symbolization of the sounds, and the action of the larynx, tongue, and lips in sound production. Phonetics does not concern itself with the ways words are spelled by the traditional alphabet. It seeks to develop phonetic alphabets which represent graphically the actual pronunciations of linguistic forms. Dictionaries contain phonetic transliterations.

3. *Phonemics* is the study of how sounds function to convey differences of meaning; it is the study of the speech sounds used in a language. It is thus a study of phonemes. Phonemic analysis deals only with those sounds that are significant in the language (the phonemes) and ignores the nonsignificant differences (the allophones). The p sound in *pet, spot, suppose*, and *top* is slightly different in each instance, but the difference is considered to be nonsignificant. The phonemes are the smallest sound units in a language. Phonemes combine to form morphemes which are the smallest units of language that can bear meaning. The written phoneme is a grapheme, and the writing of graphemes in proper order to form morphemes is *orthography*, or spelling.

4. The *alphabet* is a set of graphic shapes that represent the phonemes of the language.

5. *Word analysis* is an inclusive term which subsumes all methods of attacking words. Phonics is one form of word analysis.

6. *Phonic, or phonetic, method*—There are various methods of identifying a word. The phonic method is often considered to be a synthetic method because it begins with the word element or the sound of the letter and gradually advances to the total word. This designation is actually in error. There are some phonic methods that are termed *whole word phonics* which begin with the total word.

7. A *linguist* is a scientist who studies a language in terms of its basic structure, including sound patterns, stress, intonation, and syntactic structure.

8. *Linguistic phonics*—We use this description because we recommend that the letter be sounded only in the context of the total word. This approach is sometimes referred to as the *phonemic-word approach* because the structure of the language is studied through symbol-sound relationships in whole words (13). It is our view that comparing and contrasting basic spelling patterns with the appropriate or correlative sound patterns leads to independence in attacking new words. Thus, the individual letter is generally not sounded; it is only named. The sounds represented by *b, c, d* exist only in the context of a word or a syllable. The *o* combination with *y*, as in *boy*, has a distinct sound; its sound depends on the pattern in which it occurs. Blending, which is a common problem in phonics, ought not to be a problem in a linguistic approach.

TEACHING THE BEGINNING CONSONANT

Table 6-1 summarizes the consonant sounds of the English language. Consonant sounds are either *voiced* or *unvoiced*. They are voiced if they are accompanied by vibration of the vocal cords; they are unvoiced if there is no vibration of the vocal cords. Knowledge of voiced and unvoiced consonant sounds is important because it helps in making the sounds and in pronouncing words.

TABLE 6-1   THE CONSONANT SOUNDS OF THE LANGUAGE

| Plosives | | Fricatives | | Nasals | Semivowels | |
Voiced	Unvoiced	Voiced	Unvoiced	Voiced	Voiced	Unvoiced
/b/	/p/	/th/	/th/	/m/	/r/	/h/hw/
/d/	/t/	/v/	/f/	/n/	/l/	
/g/	/k/	/z/	/s/	/ng/	/y/	
		/zh/	/sh/		/w/	
		/j/	/ch/			

The voiced consonant can only be vocalized in connection with a vowel sound (for example, /be/). The sound represented by *f*, on the other hand, can be made with the upper teeth and the lower lip without using the chords, and it is therefore termed an unvoiced sound and the consonant *f* is an unvoiced consonant.

The consonant letters *b, f, h, j, k, l, m, p, q, r, v,* and *w* represent only one sound. The only exception is the /v/ sound of *f* in the word /of/. The consonant letters *c, d, g, n, s, t, x, y,* and *z* represent more than one sound. Nevertheless, some of the consistent letters still present problems for the learner. At the end of this chapter, under the heading "Silent Letters," we have summarized instances in which the consonant letter is not sounded.

The Letters K and Q

In the letters *k* and *q*, the consonant blends *nk* and *sk*, and the speech consonant *ck*, the student meets special problems. The student needs to learn that certain sounds can be written in two ways. The much more common hard *c* and the *k* represent the same sound. If the student remembers that *k* sounds like the *c* sound he has heard in the word /cat/, he should have little difficulty pronouncing the words correctly.

The letter *k* does not occur too frequently at the beginning of the word. In this position the letter *c* is more common. The *k*, however, is much more frequent than the *c* at the end of the word. This knowledge should be especially helpful in spelling.

The letter *q* occurs only in the combination *qu* and usually has the sound of /kw/. It may also be simply a /k/ as in *liquor.* Occasionally, the /kw/ sound is separated as in *liquid* /lik'wid/. *Que* at the end of a word is simply a /k/ sound: *unique, clique, critique.**

The following additional observations are in order:

1. The speech consonant *ck*, at the end of the word, preceded by a short vowel, is simply /k/ as in *back.*
2. *Ank* is /angk/ as in *bank, blank, drank, flank.*
3. *Ink* is /ingk/ as in *kink, blink, brink.*
4. *Unk* is /əngk/ as in *bunk, dunk, flunk, junk, plunk.*
5. *Onk* is /ängk/ as in *honk* or /əngk/ as in *monk.*
6. *Kn* is simply an /n/ as in *knack, knell, knit, knock, knob, knoll, knot.* Gn is simply /n/ as in *gnash, gnat, gnaw.*

* It may be desirable to introduce the student to the *gu* combination along with the *qu* combination. Examples are *guard, guess, guest, guide, guilt, guardhouse, guilty, guitar, intrigue, safeguard.* The *gu* in *penguin* is pronounced /gw/.

The junior high–senior high student should have little difficulty in reading words like those in Table 6-2. They illustrate the various *k* and *q* sounds.

TABLE 6-2   MONOSYLLABIC WORDS FORMED WITH *K* AND Q

ark	crock	hock	knell	park	rock	speck
ask		honk	knit	peck		spunk
	dark	hulk	knob	pick	sack	stack
back	deck	husk	knock	plank	sank	stalk*
balk*	Dick		knoll*	pluck	sick	stark
bank	disk	ilk	knot	plunk	silk	stick
bark	drank	ink		prank	skid	stink
bask	drink		lack	prick	skiff	stock
beck	duck	junk	lark	punk	skill	stuck
black	dunk		lock		skim	stunk
blank	dusk	keg	luck	quack	skin	sulk
blink		kept		quaff	skip	swank
brink	elk	kick	mark	quart*	skit	
brisk		kid	mask	quell	skulk	tack
buck	flank	kill	milk	quest	skull	talk*
bulk	flask	kiln*	mink	quick	skunk	tank
	flunk	kilt	monk	quill	slack	task
calk*	folk*	kin	muck	quilt	slick	tick
cask	frank	king	musk	quit	slink	trek
click	Frank	kink			smock	trick
clink	frisk	kiss	nick	rack	snack	
cluck		kit	Nick	rink	sock	walk*
crick	hack	knack		risk	spank	wick
						wink

* Balk (bȯk); calk (kȯk); folk (fōk); kiln (kil, kiln), knoll (nōl); stalk (stȯk); talk (tȯk); walk (wȯk); quart (kwȯrt).

The Sounds Represented by C and G

c represents   /k/ as in *cat*—unvoiced
/s/ as in *cent*—unvoiced
/sh/ as in *vicious*—unvoiced

g represents   /g/ as in *go*—voiced
/j/ as in *giant*—voiced
/zh/ as in *garage*—voiced

C and *g* generally represent a soft sound before *e, i,* or *y; c* becomes an /s/ as in *cede* and *g* becomes a /j/ as in *age*. In the exceptions, the *c* is pronounced /sh/. The most common exceptions to the *g* rule are *get, girl, give, tiger,* and *finger*.

The soft sound at the end of a word is usually spelled *ce* (dance), *ge* (age), or *dge* (badge). *Dge* occurs after short vowels; after a consonant, the sound is spelled *ge* (change). In words borrowed from the French (rouge, garage, mirage, corsage, sabotage, menage, camouflage, barrage, espionage), *g* is a /zh/ sound. The letter *c* in combination with *i* or *e* also may have an /sh/sound as in *vicious* or *ocean*.

G is silent before *n* (align, arraign, benign). *C* is silent after *s* (ascend, ascent, descent), in the combination *ck* (back), and in such words as *czar, indict, victuals*.

Here are some common words containing the soft *c* sound:

bicycle	fierce	pounce
bounce	fleece	prance
brace	flounce	price
cancel	force	prince
cease	glance	quince
cede	grace	race
ceiling	hence	scarce
cell	ice	since
cent	juice	slice
chance	lace	sluice
choice	lance	source
cinch	mice	space
circle	mince	splice
cite	nice	spruce
cyclone	niece	stance
cymbal	once	thence
cyst	ounce	thrice
dance	pace	trace
deuce	peace	trance
dice	pence	trice
dunce	piece	twice
face	pierce	vice
farce	place	whence
fence		wince

Here are words illustrating the soft *g* sound:

age	blunge	change	dingy
badge	bridge	charge	dirge
barge	budge	college	dodge
beige	bulge	cringe	doge
bilge	cage	digest	dredge

edge	ginger	liege	sludge
Egypt	gist	lodge	smudge
engine	gorge	manger	splurge
flange	gouge	merge	sponge
fledge	grange	nudge	stage
forge	grudge	page	stooge
fringe	gurge	pledge	strange
fudge	gym	plunge	surge
gage	gypsy	purge	tinge
gauge	gyrate	rage	trudge
gem	hedge	range	urge
gene	hinge	ridge	verge
gent	hodgepodge	rouge	wage
germ	huge	sage	wedge
gibe	judge	siege	
gin	large	sledge	

Words of one syllable ending with the sound of /j/ are usually spelled with the *dge* ending if the sound is immediately preceded by a short vowel sound (edge, fudge), and with the *ge* ending if the sound is immediately preceded by a long vowel sound or a consonant (cage, change). Other illustrative words are the following: badge, bridge, budge, dodge, dredge, fudge, hedge, lodge, sledge, sludge, smudge, trudge, nudge, pledge, ridge, grudge, judge, edge; age, beige, cage, stage, stooge, wage, page, huge, rage, sage, siege, gage, challenge, arrange, emerge. In only four plurisyllabic words is *dge* pronounced as *j* (knowledge, cartridge, partridge, and porridge).

The following exercises teach the discrimination between the variant sounds of *c* and *g*:

1. The student is asked to make a rule for the sounds represented by *c* or *g* by filling in the blank spaces in a statement like the following: *c* usually represents a soft sound when it is followed by the vowel letters —, —, and —, and it represents a hard sound when followed by the vowel letters —, —, and —.

2. Have students write /k/ or /s/ below each *c* in a list of words to indicate what the *c* represents. The same exercise also can be used to teach the sounds represented by *g*.

a. circulate
  /s/ k/

b. circumstance

c. cylindrical

a. apologetic
  /i/

b. gigantic

c. gorgeous

The Sounds Represented by D

> *d* represents /d/ as in *danger*—voiced
> /j/ as in *soldier*—voiced

The letter *d* usually represents /d/ as in *danger*. It may also represent /j/ as in *soldier* or *individual*. It is silent before *g* (badger, dodger, edge) and in such words as *adjunct, adjust, handkerchief, handsome,* and *Wednesday.*

D in combination with *u* also says *j* as in *gradual, deciduous, schedule, fraudulent, nodule, pendulum, graduate, individual, residual,* and *incredulous. D* in combination with *i* has the *j* sound in only two words: *soldier* and *cordial.*

The Sounds Represented by N

> *n* represents /n/ as in *not*—voiced
> /ng/ as in *finger*—voiced

The letter *n* generally represents the /n/ heard in *not* or *fan.* It represents /ng/ when it occurs before *k* (bank, drink, dunk, or monk); when it comes before a *c* that represents /k/ as in *uncle;* and when it occurs before a *g* pronounced /g/ as in *finger* /fing-ger/. It is silent after *m* as in *autumn, column, condemn, damn, hymn.*

The Sounds Represented by S

> *s* represents /s/ as in *see*—unvoiced
> /z/ as in *his*—voiced
> /sh/ as in *sure*—unvoiced
> /zh/ as in *treasure*—voiced

Table 6–3 illustrates the conditions that control the sound of *s.*

TABLE 6-3

---

1. /s/   a. At the beginning of a word or a syllable: *sell, sunset.*
       b. As the initial letter of a consonant blend: *best, task, spring.* This usage is regular with *sc, sk, sl, sm, sn, sp, st,* and *sw.* The consonant digraph *sh* is an exception.
       c. In conjunction with another *s* at the end of a word: *dress, miss, fuss, recess.*
       d. After *f, k, p, t: maps, cats;* and unvoiced *th: myths.*

2. /z/ a. After *b, d, g, ge, h, l, m, n, ng, q, r, v, w, y,* voiced *th,* and long vowels: *cobs, lids, gags, judges, pills, hams, vans, cars, lives, bellows, lathes, flies.*

   b. At the end of some one-syllable words: *as, has, was, is, his.*

   c. When the *s* occurs between two vowels: *arise, closet, miser;* words ending in *se* may have the sound of /s/ as in *house* or of /z/ as in *arose.*

3. /es/ a. After *j, s, x, z, ch, sh, zh* (after *y,* change the *y* to *i* and add *es,* e.g., *ladies: dresses, boxes, inches, dishes, fizzes, flies.*

   b. The *e* in *es* is silent in the third person singular: *goes, hoes;* and in the plural of words: *stones;* except after sibilants: *horses.*

4. /sh/ or /zh/ as in *sure.*

The consonant letter *s* represents /sh/ or /zh/ when it precedes *ure* (sure, insure, insurance, treasure, measure). It is necessary to call attention to the *ure* in the root word to explain the *sh* sound of *s.* The *s* also represents /sh/ in such words as *sugar, issue, tissue.* The *s* is silent in such words as *aisle, fuchsia, bas-relief, Carlisle, debris, Illinois, island, isle, Louisville, viscount, chamois, corps, rendezvous.*

1. An exercise like the following helps the student to differentiate between the *s* and *z* sounds:

as		his
|s| or |z|	|s| or |z|	|s| or |z|
|s| or |z|	|s| or |z|	|s| or |z|
	(He) bats	
|s| or |z|	|s| or |z|	|s| or |z|
(He) puffs		this
|s| or |z|	|s| or |z|	|s| or |z|

2. Another exercise requires students to write /s/ or /z/ below each *s* in a list of words to indicate the sound that the *s* represents.

a. museum

b. preserve

c. surprise

d. weasel

e. mistaken

f. lasting

The Sounds Represented by T

t represents /t/ as in *top*—unvoiced

/ch/ (tsh) as in *picture*—unvoiced

The consonant letter *t* represents /t/ as in *tent* or *time* or /ch/ when it is immediately followed by *ure* as in *picture* or *pasture*.

The *t* is silent in *bustle, castle, chasten, chestnut, Christmas, fasten, hasten, hustle, listen, mortgage, mustn't, often, soften, thistle, whistle.*

The Sounds Represented by X

x represents /ks/ as in *box*—unvoiced

/gz/ as in *exact*—voiced

/z/ as in *xylophone*—voiced

The consonant letter *x* usually represents /ks/ as in *box, fox, coax, flax, flex, flux, hex, hoax, jinx, pox, pyx, vex.* When it occurs at the beginning of a word (xylophone) or in an unstressed syllable that precedes a vowel sound (exact), it represents /z/ or /gz/.

The Sounds Represented by Y

Y represents /y/ as in *yes*—voiced

/ī/ (vowel) as in *my*—voiced

/i/ (vowel) as in *crypt*—voiced

The letter *y* usually represents /y/ as in *yacht, yearn, yule.* It may also function as a vowel and then represents either /ī/ or /i/. Illustrative words of *y* as /y/ are the following: yacht, yak, yams, yank, yap, yard, yarn, yawn, yea, year, yearn, yeast, yegg, yell, yelp, yen, yes, yet, yield, yip, yoke, yolk, yond, you, young, your, youth, yowl, yule.

The Sounds Represented by Z

z represents /z/ as in *zoo*—voiced

/s/ as in *waltz*—unvoiced

/zh/ as in *azure*—voiced

The consonant letter *z* usually represents /z/ as in *blaze, zip,* or *frieze.* It may also represent /s/ as in *waltz* or /z/ as in *azure.* Illustrative words for the regular /z/ sound are the following: adz, blaze, breeze, bronze, buzz, craze, daze, doze, faze, fez, fizz, freeze, frieze, froze, fuzz, gauze, gaze, glaze, haze, jazz, phiz, prize, quiz, raze, razz, size, sneeze, snooze, squeeze, wheeze, zeal, zest, zinc, zing, zip, zone, zoo, zoom.

Workbook and other teacher-prepared materials may be used to teach the consonant sounds and the technique of consonant substitution. The following exercise is illustrative:

Have the student indicate the sound represented by each underlined letter.

```
c = k, s, sh
g = g, j, zh
d = d, j
n = n, ng
s = s, z, sh, zh
t = t, ch
x = ks, gz, z
z = z, s, zh
```

cascade k,   k,   genes _____
arduous _____   mixture _____
cats _____   judicial _____
station _____   vitiate _____
conscience _____   practice _____
barbecue _____   precipice _____
presidency _____   gauge _____
unicycle _____   flagon _____

TEACHING THE SHORT VOWEL

By the time the student gets to junior high he is well aware of the vowel sounds /ā/, /ē/, /ī/, /ō/, and /ū/ and /ă/ /ĕ/, /ĭ/, /ŏ/, and /ŭ/. He probably knows the effect that adding an *e* has on a syllable containing a short vowel letter in the medial position. But, not all students know these matters. Many students, for example, do not know that the letters *w* and *y* are sometimes used as vowels and often are referred to as *semivowels.* The letter *w* functions as a vowel when it immediately follows another vowel letter in a word of one syllable or in the same syllable, for example, *down, shown, blew,* or *new.* The letter *y* is usually a vowel when it is at the end of a word or a syllable (*rely*), when it is the only vowel letter in a word or a syllable (*by*), when it immediately follows another vowel letter in a word or in the same syllable (key), and when it precedes a consonant letter in one-syllable words ending with *e* (type).

The *o* is frequently pronounced as a short *u* /ə/. The following monosyllabic and plurisyllabic words are illustrative:

come	blossom	gallop	mongrel	salmon
does	boredom	galop	monkey	scaffold
done	bottom	godson	month	season
dove	button	govern	monthly	seldom
glove	cannon	grandson	mormon	sermon
love	carrot	hammock	mother	smother
none	canyon	handsome	mutton	shovel
one	color	havoc	oneself	stomach
shove	comfort	honey	oneway	scallop
some	coming	idol	oven	someone
son	common	income	parrot	sometime
ton	compass	kingdom	patron	sometimes
won	confront	lemon	phantom	someway
abbot	cotton	lesson	pilot	summon
above	cover	lonesome	pivot	symbol
among	crayon	loveless	piston	symptom
apron	donkey	lovely	poison	synod
atom	dragon	loving	prison	tendon
bacon	dozen	mammon	purpose	tiresome
ballot	falcon	mammoth	random	wagon
baron	felon	matron	ransom	welcome
beacon	flagon	melon	reason	wisdom
become	freedom	method	reckon	zealot
bigot	frontal	Monday	ribbon	
bishop	gallon	money	riot	

It is interesting to note that in most instances the *o* is followed by *m, n, p, t,* or *v.*

An exercise such as the following teaches the short *u* sound of *o.* Have the student circle the correct pronounciation.

1. A ton [$\begin{smallmatrix} tun \\ ton \end{smallmatrix}$] of gold.

2. A lot [$\begin{smallmatrix} lot \\ lut \end{smallmatrix}$] of fish.

3. A son [$\begin{smallmatrix} son \\ sun \end{smallmatrix}$] of Jim.

4. He has done [$\begin{smallmatrix} dun \\ don \end{smallmatrix}$] his job.

An analysis of two-syllable words reveals that the letter preceding the final letter in a word is often silent when followed by *n* or *l*. Thus:

bison	garden	lesson	metal	prison
bitten	glisten	lighten	model	redden
button	glutton	listen	mitten	rotten
chosen	gotten	madden	mutton	sadden
christen	hasten	maiden	pardon	sharpen
cotton	hidden	mason	parson	sudden
dozen	kitten	mantel	petal	tassel
frozen	lessen	medal	pistol	tighten
				widen

Workbooks and other teacher-prepared materials may be used to teach the phoneme-grapheme correspondences. The following exercises are illustrative:

1. Put a line through each picture that has a short *a* sound in the middle.

2. Have the student circle the word that rhymes with the name of the picture and let him write the word.

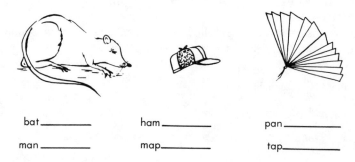

bat_____   ham_____   pan_____

man_____   map_____   tap_____

3. Have the student write the missing vowel letter.

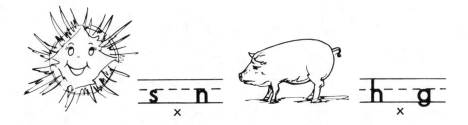

4. Have the student circle the vowel sound that he hears.

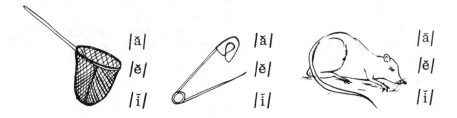

Through exercises like those above, the student should learn the
following:

1. The letters *a, e, i, o,* and *u* are vowel letters.
2. When these letters say their names, they have a long sound.
3. These vowel letters also have a short sound. The short sounds of the five
   vowel letters are best illustrated in words like *apple, egg, ink, ox,* and
   umbrella.
4. The technique of medial-vowel substitution must also be taught. The student
   learns that changing the vowel letters alters both the appearance of the
   word and its meaning. The student must be taught medial-vowel substitution
   inductively. He must see what changing the vowel does to the form of the
   word, to its pronunciation, and to its meaning.
5. When there is only one vowel letter in a word, that word is a one-syllable,
   or monosyllabic word.
6. When there is only one vowel letter in a word (as in words like *at* and
   bat), and when that vowel letter is followed by a single consonant letter
   (*at* or *bat*), then the vowel usually has its short vowel sound.

7. The student learns to apply the rule, principle, or generalization to the accented syllable in plurisyllabic words:

tiptop	bobbin	bandit	bellhop
bonnet	blacktop	bedbug	cabin

TEACHING THE END CONSONANT

One of the basic sound-sense patterns in the language is the *phonogram*. Some even suggest that the phonogram is *the* natural unit of the English language. The phonogram is a closed syllable that begins with a vowel (*eg, eb, ac, in, ill, ate, ing, oat,* etc.) and produces a single speech sound. The phonogram is generally phonetically stable and regular in sounding, its form is consistent, and it has a basic utility in reading.

Joos (11, p. 90) notes that the sounding of vowels is regulated (in most cases) by the letter pattern that follows the vowel and that since the phonogram has the vowel plus its following letter pattern, the reader quickly learns to see the entire pattern as a unit. Joos adds that experience justifies this observation: Pupils taught to analyze words into phonograms quickly read sound-symbol patterns and are safely past letter-by-letter perception.

By the time the student has mastered the beginning and end consonants and short vowels, he should be able to deal with the following phonograms:

ab	eb	ib	ob	ub
ac	ed	ic	od	ud
ad	eg	id	og	uff
aff	ell	if	om	ug
ag	em	iff	on	ull (dull)
am	en	ig	op	um
an	ep	ill	ot	un
as	et	in		us
at	ex	ip		ut
		is		
		iss		
		it		
		ix		

In addition, he will have to learn such common endings as the following:

ack	ead	ich	oast	unk
age	eak	ick	off	ure
aid	ease	igh	oil	ush
ake	eat	ight	oke	uy
alk	ee	ike	old	
all	eech	ile	oll	
and	eek	ilk	ome	
ank	eel	ine	onk	
ar	een	ing	ood	
ark	eep	ink	ook	
arm	eet	int	ool	
arn	ent	ird	oom	
arne	ern	itch	oot	
atch		ith	ore	
ay			orn	
			orse	
			oss	
			ough	
			ought	
			ound	
			our	
			ouse	
			out	
			ove	
			ow	
			own	
			oy	

Doubling of Consonant Letters at End of a Word

Some of the consonant letters are doubled at the end of a word. The letters most frequently doubled are *f, l,* and *s.* Other consonants that may be doubled at the end of a word are *b, d, g, m, n, p, r, t,* and *z.* For example: ebb, add, puff, egg, hill, mumm, Finn, Lapp, err, purr, burr, miss, mitt, fuzz.

The consonants *c, h, j, k, q, v, w, x,* and *y* are never doubled at the end of a word. Note that *cc* and *gg* when followed by *e, i,* or *y* represent two distinct sounds: *success, suggest.*

The student's problem with double consonants tends to be more of a spelling problem than a reading problem. Here is a list of words useful in teaching the doubling of consonants.

Ending in FF	*Ending in RR*		*Ending in SS*
bluff	err (ər)	bass	bliss
buff	burr (bər)	brass	hiss
cliff	purr (pər)	class	miss
cuff		glass	boss (bȯs)
duff		grass	joss
huff		mass	moss (mȯs)
muff		pass	toss (tȯs)
puff		Bess	muss
riffraff		bless	
ruff		dress	
skiff		less	
sniff			

Ending in LL

all (ȯl)	bell	Bill	bull (bůl)
ball	dell	dill	cull
call	dwell	fill	dull
fall	fell	hill	full (fůl)
gall	hell	ill	gull
hall	jell	Jill	hull
pall	mell	mill	lull
tall	Nell	pill	mull
wall	sell	rill	null
	tell	sill	pull (půl)
		till	
		will	

The most common exceptions are *as, bus, clef, gas, has, his, if, is, nil, of, pal, plus, pus, this, thus, us, was, yes, beef, dwarf, golf, half, loaf, meal, mail, roof, self, soil, thief, wheel,* and *wolf.*

In a compound word such as *bookkeeper* or *cattail,* the double consonant letters represent a long consonant sound that has the acoustic effect of a double consonant sound. For example, compare *cattail* and *catty.*

A workbook exercise helpful in teaching the doubling of the final consonant may require the student to underline the correct form in sentences such as the following:

1. The hen got (of, off) the top of the hut.
2. Jeff has a can (of, off) pop.
3. Dad is filling his car with (gas, gass).
4. The cat (hised, hissed) at the dog.

Workbooks and other teacher-prepared materials may be used to teach the end sounds. Teaching of phonograms, of rhyming, and of end consonants are very similar.

The following exercises are illustrative:

1. Have students pick from a series of letters the one that completes a word. Write the end consonant.

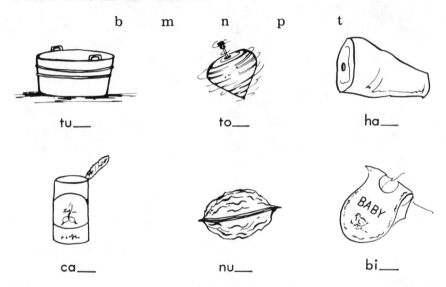

b   m   n   p   t

tu___   to___   ha___

ca___   nu___   bi___

2. Have students write the proper consonant letter in the blank space. In this exercise the letters are not listed as in exercise 1.

do___   to___   bo___

tu___   ho___   fa___

3. Have the student write the beginning and ending letter of the name of a picture. What letters come before and after the vowel letters?

_e_ _e_ _i_ _i_

_o_ _u_ _u_ _u_

TEACHING THE BEGINNING CONSONANT BLENDS

The consonant blends must be distinguished from the speech consonants *ch, sh, th, wh, ck, gh, ph, qu,* and *ng.* These latter are digraphs and thus are two consonants that represent a single speech sound. The consonant blends, on the other hand, consist of two or more letters each having its own distinct sound. The following two-letter beginning consonant blends occur: *bl, br, cl, cr, dr, dw, fl, fr, gl, gr, pl, pr, sc, sk, sl, sm, sn, sp, sq, st, sw, tr,* and *tw.* Of all the double consonants, only *st, sp,* and *sk* occur at the beginning *and* at the end of a word.

The sounds represented by the consonant blends are those exemplified by key words in the following list:

bl /bl/ as in blue
br /br/ as in bring
cl /kl/ as in clean
cr /kr/ as in cream
dr /dr/ as in dress
dw /dw/ as in dwarf
fl /fl/ as in flag
fr /fr/ as in free
gl /gl/ as in glass
gr /gr/as in grass
pl /pl/ as in play

pr /pr/ as in pride
sc /sk/ as in scold
sk /sk/ as in skate, mask
sl /sl/ as in sleep
sm /sm/ as in smoke
sn /sn/ as in snow
sp /sp/ as in spoon, clasp
st /st/ as in stop, nest
sw /sw/ as in swing
tr /tr/ as in tree
tw /tw as in twig

Here is a list of words that we have found helpful in teaching each of the blends. Many of these words can be illustrated pictorially.

bl—blot, blanket, blade, blotter, black, block, blue, blob, blank, blacktop, blame, bless, bliss, bluff, blink, bled, blaze

br—brad, brag, bran, brass, brat, bred, brim, bring, broom, bracelet, branch, bridle, briefcase, bridegroom, bride, bread, bridge, brick, brown, broomstick, bracket, brute, broke, brave, brace

cl—clad, clam, clan, clap, class, clef, cliff, cling, clip, clod, clog, clot, club, clown, cloud, clock, claw, classroom, clamp, clove, click, cluck, clink, close

cr—crayon, cracker, croquet, crowbar, cross, crown, crate, crack, crock, crane, crime, cry, crave, craze

dr—dress, drumstick, drink, drawer, dragon, dresser, dryer, drape, drugstore, druggist, drank, drunk, dry, drive

dw—dwarf, dwell, dwelling

fl—flapjack, flagpole, flashlight, flower, fly, flake, fling, flame, fluke, flank, flask, flunk

fr—freighter, friar, frame, fruit, Frank, frisk, fry, froze

gl—globe, glove, glasses, glare

gr—grapefruit, grandstand, griddle, grave, grape, green, gray, grasshopper, grime, gripe, grade, graze, grace, grass

pl—plate, plume, planter, pliers, plow, plane, plank, plant, pluck, ply, place

pr—pretzel, prune, present, propeller, protractor, priest, prime, probe, prove, prose, prank, pry, prize, price

sc—scooter, scale, scarf, scarecrow, scare, scope

sk—skate, skull, skeleton, skunk, ski, skillet, skirt, sky, skid, skiff, skim, skin, skit

sl—slide, slack, slate, slime, slope, slick, sly, slice

sm—smack, smoke, smock, smile, smite

sn—snake, snowman, snack, snowshoes, snail, snare, snore

sp—spade, spy, spank, spark plug, sparrow, spider, spoon, spool, sparkle, spare, spire, spike, spine, speck, spunk, space

sq—squat, squall, squid, squint

st—stagecoach, starfish, stoplight, steamboat, stop sign, steeple, stove, stick, stool, stairs, stake, stable, stapler, statute, store, stunk, stuck, stock, stink, sty, stack, stale, stare, stoke, stole, stone

sw—swing, sweater, swallow, swan, sweat shirt, switch, sweeper

tr—train, truck, tree, tractor, trick, track, triangle, trunk, tray, trinket, tricycle, trophy, tramp, trailer, tripod, trash, trade, tribe, trike, try, trace

tw—twenty, twelve, tweezers, twinkle, twins, twine, twice

The student also needs to learn to deal with the beginning three-letter blends: *chr, phr, sch, scr, shr, spl, spr, str,* and *thr.* Here are common monosyllabic words beginning with these combinations:

chr—Christ, chrome

phr—phrase

sch—scheme, school

scr—screech, screen, scroll, script, scrunch

shr—shrank, shred, shrewd, shriek, shrill, shrimp, shrine, shrink, shroud, shrub, shrug

spl—splash, spleen, splice, splint, split, splotch, splurge

spr—sprain, sprang, sprawl, spray, spread, spree, spring, sprint, sprite, sprout, spruce, sprung

str—strafe, strain, strait, strand, strap, straw, stray, streak, stream, street, strength, stress, stretch, stride, strife, strike, string, stripe, strive, strode, stroll, strong, strove, stray, struck, strung

thr—thrash, thread, threat, three, thresh, threw, thrice, thrift, thrill, throat, throb, throng, through, throw, thrush, thrust

The consonant trigraphs, such as *chm* (drachm), tch (match), and *ght* (thought), representing a single speech sound, should be taught after the student has mastered the three-letter blends.

TEACHING THE ENDING
CONSONANT BLENDS

After the student has learned to handle some of the beginning consonant blends, he is ready to learn the end consonant blends. Below we list some common two-consonant endings, some of which are not necessarily consonant blends.

The student cannot be expected to learn all of these at one time. How the teacher introduces them will depend on the vocabulary to which the student can react with meaning.

ENDING CONSONANT COMBINATIONS

ck—back, hack, jack, lack, Mack, pack, quack, rack, sack, tack, black, crack, slack, smack, snack, stack, track, deck, heck, neck, peck, Dick, kick, lick, Mick, nick, Nick, pick, quick, sick, brick, click, flick, prick, slick, stick, trick, tick, wick, cock, dock, hock, lock, mock, rock, sock, tock, block, clock, crock, flock, frock, smock, buck, duck, luck, suck, tuck, cluck, pluck, stuck, truck

ct—act, pact, tact, fact, duct, sect, tract, pict, strict

ff—staff, chaff, gaff, quaff, cliff, miff, skiff, sniff, stiff, tiff, whiff, doff, scoff, off, bluff, buff, cuff, fluff, gruff, huff, muff, puff, scuff, snuff, stuff, tuff

ft— raft, draft, craft, graft, shaft, aft, deft, left, cleft, theft, lift, rift, drift, swift, gift, shift, thrift, sift, loft, oft, soft, tuft

lb— bulb, alb

lc— talc

ld— bald, scald, held, meld, weld, bold, cold, fold, gold, hold, mold, old, sold, told

lf— calf, half, elf, self, shelf, golf, wolf

ll— all, ball, call, fall, gall, hall, pall, small, squall, stall, tall, wall, bell, cell, dell, dwell, fell, sell, shell, smell, spell, swell, tell, well, yell, bill, brill, chill, dill, drill, fill, frill, gill, grill, hill, ill, kill, mill, pill, quill, rill, shrill, sill, skill, spill, still, thrill, will, doll, bull, full, pull, cull, dull, gull, hull, skull

lm— balm, calm, psalm, palm, elm, whelm, helm, realm, film

lp— alp, scalp, help, yelp, gulp, pulp

lt— fault, halt, malt, salt, vault, exalt, belt, dealt, dwelt, felt, knelt, melt, pelt, smelt, welt, built, gilt, guilt, hilt, jilt, kilt, lilt, tilt, wilt, silt, stilt, bolt, colt, jolt, cult, adult

mb—climb, lamb, bomb, tomb, comb, dumb, numb, crumb, limb, womb

mp—pump, stamp, tramp, clamp, ramp, blimp, crimp, camp, hump, stump, clump, dump, cramp, damp, lamp, tamp, limp, romp, pomp, stomp, bump, lump, plump, rump, slump, trump, hemp, imp, jump, primp

nd—band, bland, brand, gland, grand, hand, land, sand, stand, wand, bend, end, blend, fend, lend, mend, rend, send, spend, tend, trend, wend, wind, bond, fond, blond, pond, fund

ng—bang, fang, gang, hang, pang, rang, sang, slang, tang, bing, bring, ding, king, wing, ping, ring, sing, sling, sting, swing, ting, bong, dong, gong, long, song, pong, tong, clung, flung, rung, slung, stung, sung, swung

nk—bank, sank, tank, blank, clank, crank, drank, flank, frank, plank, prank, spank, tank, fink, kink, link, mink, pink, sink, wink, blink, brink, drink, slink, stink, honk, bunk, dunk, junk, punk, sunk, drunk, flunk, skunk, spunk, stunk, trunk

nn—Finn, inn

ens—lens

nt—ant, can't, grant, pant, plant, rant, scant, slant, want, bent, dent, lent, sent, spent, tent, went, dint, lint, flint, glint, hint, mint, print, stint, tint, font, front, blunt, brunt, bunt, grunt, hunt, punt, runt, stunt

pt—apt, rapt, kept, slept, swept, wept

rb—garb, barb

rc—arc, marc

rd—lard, bard, card, hard, ward, yard, curd, lord, chord, cord

rf—dwarf, wharf, serf, surf, turf, scarf

rl—snarl, gnarl, Carl, earl, twirl, Burl, churl, curl, furl, girl, hurl, knurl, pearl, swirl, whirl, uncurl, unfurl

rm—arm, farm, harm, warm, alarm, charm, storm, form, worm, squirm, term

rn—barn, darn, warn, earn, learn, yearn, fern, urn, turn, concern

rp—harp, carp, sharp, warp, slurp, burp, chirp

rr—parr

rt—art, Art, cart, dart, part, smart, tart, wart, hurt, curt, dirt, shirt, pert, sort, court

sc—disc

sk—desk, disk, flask, cask, mask, ask, bask, task, tusk, dusk, frisk, brisk, husk, musk, risk

sm—spasm, prism, ism

sp—clasp, asp, gasp, grasp, lisp, crisp, rasp, hasp, wisp

ss—pass, miss, hiss, toss, bass

st—nest, mast, fist, cast, mist, frost, crust, blast, last, dust, lost, test, best, blest, rest, rust, pest, just, twist, bust, crest, gust, hast, jest, west, trust, crust, fast, grist, host, must, past

tt—mitt, putt

Workbook and other teacher-prepared materials may be used to continue the teaching of consonant blends and the technique of consonant substitution. The following exercises are illustrative.

1. Have the students write or circle the proper consonant blend in various types of exercises. Have the student circle the correct beginning consonant blend.

2. Have the student write under each picture the initial consonant blend of the name of each picture.

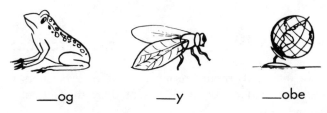

___og   ___y   ___obe

Exercises such as the following will be useful in teaching the end consonant blends:

1. Have students pick from a series of consonant blends the one that completes the name of a picture.

ck,   nk,   ff,   lb,   ll

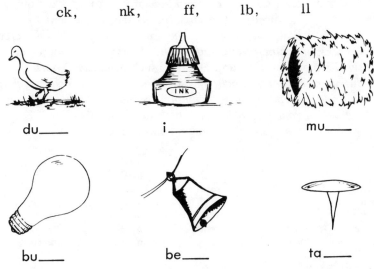

du___   i___   mu___

bu___   be___   ta___

2. Have students complete the spelling of each word by adding *k* or *ck.*

mil___   du___   in___

des___   ta___   so___

THE SPEECH CONSONANTS

Speech consonants or digraphs are not a blend of two letters to represent one sound; the individual sounds represented by the digraph are readily identifiable.

The Digraph Ch

The digraph *ch* may represent four distinct sounds: /ch/, /j/, /sh/, and /k/.* The unvoiced *ch* is a combination of /t/ and /sh/. Sometimes it is pronounced as a voiced /j/, as in *spinach*. It is equivalent to /sh/ in words of French derivation, such as *cache, chagrin, chef, Chicago, creche, gauche, machine, machinery,* and *moustache*. It has a /k/ sound in some words derived from the Greek and Hebrew, such as *chasm, chorus, Christ, chrism, Christmas, chrome, Enoch,* and *scheme,* and also in *ache, backache, chemist, chloride, choral, technic, technique, headache, orchid, school,* and *Czech*. In *drachm, schism, yacht,* and *fuchsia,* the *ch* is silent. Here are common words exemplifying the regular /ch/ sound:

arch	chap	choke	leech	ranch
batch	charge	couch	lunch	reach
beach	charm	crotch	lurch	squelch
beech	chin	crutch	march	stanch
belch	chip	ditch	preach	starch
change	chirp	drench	punch	staunch
chant	choice	leach	quench	stench

The Digraphs Sh and Th

The digraph *sh* presents no special reading difficulties. The following common words exemplify the /sh/ sound:

ash	mesh	share	shop
bash	mush	shark	shorn
brash	plush	sharp	short
brush	rash	shave	should
bush	rush	shawl	shout

The *th,* on the other hand, may be the unvoiced /th/ as in *think, thin, thank* or the voiced /th/ as in *this, that, them*. The final *th* usually is

* This is another way of saying that the /ch/, /j/, /sh/, and /k/ sounds can be spelled as *ch*. For a complete listing of multiple spellings of consonants, see Appendix.

voiceless except in *smooth, booth, mouth, with,* and in *the* endings as in *bathe.* Some *verbs* (mouth, bequeath, and smooth) have dropped the final *e* but still follow the rule. Some nouns with an unvoiced singular (mouth) have a voiced plural. When the final *ths* is preceded by a short vowel sound (deaths) or by a consonant (months), it is generally unvoiced. The words *cloths, truths, youths,* and *wreathes* may have either. *Th* in *Thomas, Esther,* and *Thompson* is simply a /t/.

The following words illustrate the *th* sound in monosyllabic words:

Unvoiced /th/

bath	forth	sooth	thong	thrush
berth	fourth	south	thorn	thrust
birth	froth	strength	thought	thud
booth	growth	teeth	thrash	thump
breadth	hath	thank	thread	thwart
breath	health	thatch	threat	tooth
broth	hearth	thaw	three	truth
cloth	heath	theft	thresh	twelfth
couth	mirth	theme	threw	warmth
dearth	mouth	thick	thrice	wealth
death	myth	thief	thrift	width
depth	ninth	thigh	thrill	worth
doth	north	thin	throat	wraith
earth	oath	thing	throb	wrath
faith	sixth	think	throng	wreath
fifth	sloth	third	through	youth
filth	Smith	thirst	throw	

Voiced /th/

baths	smooth	their	these	though
bathe	soothe	them	they	thus
breathe	that	then	this	thy
clothe	the	thence	those	with
scathe	thee	there	thou	wreathe
scythe				writhe

The Digraphs Wh, Gh, Ph, and Ng

The combination *wh* may be pronounced as /hw/ or simply as /h/. The combination *gh* may be pronounced as a simple /g/; it may be an /f/; or it may be silent. We have seen that in the combination *igh* the *gh* is silent. *Ph* commonly is an /f/ sound. It may also be sounded as /v/

(Stephen) and as /p/ (diphthong, diphtheria, naphtha), or it may be silent (phtalin).

Here are words that illustrate the observations just made:

> Wh sound—whack, whale, wharf, what, wheat, wheel, wheeze, whelm, whelp, when, whence, where, whet, whew, (hwu, hu), which, whiff, whig, while, whilst, whim, whine, whip, whirl, whish, who (hü), whoa, whole (hōl), whom (hüm), whoop (hüp), whose (hüz), why

> Silent gh—aught, bough, bought, brought, caught, dough, drought, eight, freight, height, light, naught, neigh, night, nought, ought, plough, sleigh, sought, straight, though, thought, through, weight, wrought

> Gh as /f/—cough, draught, laugh, rough, slough, tough, trough

> Gh as /g/—ghost, ghoul

> Ph as /f/—phase, phew, phlegm, telephone, photograph, phrase, alphabet, hyphen, phonograph, phone, graph, photo, autograph, nephew, philosophy, typhoon, orphan, physics, asphalt, prophet, phobia, symphony, physical, sphere, saxophone, sophomore, geography, phonics, pamphlet, biography

The digraph *ng* represents /ng/: *sing, rang, long, singer.* The combination *ng* is not always a digraph. In plurisyllables such as *linger, finger,* and *stronger,* the consonant *n* represents /ng/ at the end of the first syllable and *g* represents /g/ at the beginning of the last syllable.

In teaching the discrimination of the various sounds of speech consonants and digraphs, the teacher may ask students to write the correct sound below each underlined letter combination in a series of words:

butcher	chivalry	this
/ch/	/sh/	/th/
chemist	spinach	physical
/k/	/j/	/f/
Stephen	laugh	whom
/v/	/f/	/h/

THE LONG VOWELS

Since the short vowel occurs much more frequently than the long vowel, the student should customarily sound the vowel letter as a short sound. If the word thus formed does not sound like a word that he already knows or if it does not make sense in the context, then another attempt must be made.

Four principles may help more advanced students to arrive at the correct word: the principle of variability, the principle of position, the principle of silentness, and the principle of context.

Before delving into these, a few observations seem in order.

1. The student learns vowel generalizations or rules best by *frequent* experiences with words that exemplify the rule.
2. These experiences should be *consistent.* Thus, any of the exceptions mentioned in this, or for that matter in any other section, should be learned as sight words.
3. Only those rules that have wide applicability are worth teaching.

The Principle of Variability

The principle of variability simply means that the pronunciation of the written vowel may change from one word to another or that the same vowel letter can represent more than one sound. The letter *e* may represent /ĕ/ as in *bed* or /ē/ as in *he.* The student must gradually learn and apply the following variations:

a	e	i
/a/ (hat)	/e/ (bed)	/i/ (bit)
/ā/ (fade)	/ē/ (mete)	/ī/ (bite)
/ä/ (car)		
/e(ə)/ (care)		

o	u	y
/ä/ (lot)	/ə/ (hut)	/y/ (crypt)
/ō/ (so)	/yü/ (use)	/ȳ/ (cry)
/ȯ/ (off)	/ü/ (lute)	
/ȯ/ (orb)	/u̇/ (pull)	

There are numerous spellings for each of the various vowel sounds. Table 6-4 gives such a list.

TABLE 6-4   MULTIPLE SPELLINGS OF VOWEL SOUNDS

short a /a/ or /ă/	long a /ā/
a (bat, chaff)	a (lake)
ai (plaid)	ai (pain)
au (laugh)	au (gauge)
	ay (day)
short e /e/ or /ě/	ea (break)
	ei (veil)
a (any)	ey (obey)
ae (aetna)	eigh (weigh)
ai (said)	a + e (safe)
ay (says)	ee (melee)
e (pet)	

ea (feather)
ei (heifer)
eo (leopard)
ie (friend)
u (bury)

short i /i/ or /ĭ/

e (pretty)
ee (been)
i (sit)
ia (carriage)
ie (sieve)
o (women)
u (busy)
ui (build)
y (hymnal)

short o /ä/ or /ŏ/

a (was)
o (not)
ou (hough)
ow (knowledge)

short u /ə/ or /ŭ/

io (nation)
o (come)
oe (does)
oo (blood)
ou (double)
u (sun)
wo (twopence)

ä /ä/

a (far)
ea (hearth)
e (sergeant)
oi (memoir)

long e /ē/

ae (Caesar)
ay (quay)
e (be)
ea (beam)
ee (feet)
ei (deceive)
eo (people)
ey (key)
i (machine)
ie (field)
oe (phoebe)
e + e (these)

long i /ī/

ai (aisle)
ay (aye)
ei (height)
ey (eye)
i (ice)
ie (vie)
igh (high)

oi (choir)
oy (coyote)
uy (buy)
y (sky)
ye (rye)
i + e (pine)
y + e (type)

long o /ō/

au (hautboy)
ew (sew)
eau (beau)
eo (yeoman)
o (old)
oa (roam)
oe (foe)
oh (oh)
oo (brooch)
ou (soul, though)
ow (grow)
o + e (home)

long u /ü/ or /ū/

eau (beauty)
eu (feud)
ew (few)
ewe (ewe)

/e(ə)/ or /â/

a (care)
e (there)
ea (bear)
ai (chair)
ay (prayer)
ei (heir)
e'er (e'er)

/i(ə)/ or /ę/

e (here)
ea (fear)
ei (weird)
ee (deer)
ie (bier)
i (fakir)

/(ə)r/

e (ever)
a (liar)
i (elixir)
o (actor)
u (augur)
ou (glamour)
y (zephyr)

/ə/ unstressed short i

a (senate, canoe)
ai (mountain, villain)
ay (always)
ei (forfeit)
eo (pigeon)
e (women)
ie (mischief)
oi (porpoise)
ia (parliament)

ieu (lieu)
iew (view)
ou (you)
ueue (queue)
u (use)
ue (cue)
ui (suit)
u + e (mule)

o or /ȯ/

o (off)
ou (cough)

/ȯ/ or /ȯə/ or /ô/

o (orb)
a (all, walk)
au (caught)
aw (awe)
ah (Utah)
as (Arkansas)
oa (board)
ou (court)
oi (memoir)

ou /au̇/

ou (out)
ow (cow)

/ȯi/

oi (boil)
oy (oyster)

/ə/ or /û/

u (urn)
e (fern)
i (bird)
o (work)
ea (heard̦)
ou (journal)
y (myrrh)
eu (jeu)
o (können)

/o͞o/ or /u̇/

oo (foot)
o (wolf)
ou (should)
u (pull)

/ ü / or o͞o

oo (food)
ew (brew)
ieu (adieu)
o (ado)
wo (two)
oe (canoe)
eu (maneuver)
ue (blue)
u (endure)
ou (group, through)
ui (fruit)
u + e (rule)

The Principle of Position

The second principle to be learned is the principle of position. The sound represented by the vowel letter changes depending upon its position in the word.

The first vowel rule based on the principle of position may be stated thus: *A single vowel letter at the beginning or in the middle of a one-syllable word usually represents its short sound* (am, an, as, at, Ed, if, in, is, it, of, on, up, us, top, hat, pig).* The student needs to be taught that the letter *r* generally modifies the vowel sound (car, her, sir, for, fur).

The vowel letter, however, represents a long sound when a single vowel letter comes at the end of a one-syllable word: a, be, he, she, me, we, I, go, ho, no, so, by, cry, fly, fry, my, ply, pry, sky, sly, spry, spy, sty, try, why, wry.† The second vowel rule may be stated thus: *A single vowel letter at the end of a one-syllable word usually represents a long sound.* This rule is readily applied and is easily learned.

Sometimes the vowel letter occurs in the middle of a word but does not follow the principle of position. The vowel letter represents a long vowel sound.

Long *i*—blight, bright, fight, flight, fright, high, knight, light, might, nigh, night, plight, right, sigh, sight, slight, thigh, tight; bind, blind, find, grind, hind, kind, mind, rind, wind (but note wĭnd); child, mild, wild; pint; climb

Long *o*—bold, cold, fold, gold, hold, mold, old, scold, sold, told; boll, droll, knoll, poll, roll, toll, scroll, stroll; bolt, colt, jolt; gross; ghost, host, most, post; both; comb; don't, won't

* *Or* is an exception. Note that the rule is valid only if a single consonant follows, although the *e* in *egg* is short. The *o* in *off* is long.
† Exceptions are *ha, do, to,* and *who*. These are really not exceptions to the rule, since the vowels are long, but the words are not regular.

Frequently the *o* has the /ò/ sound as in *log; broth, cloth, froth, moth; boss, cross, dross, floss, gloss, joss, loss, moss, toss; cost, frost, lost; gong, long, prong, song, strong, throng, tongs; honk; off, scoff; loft, oft, soft; cough, trough.* The /ŏ/ sound occurs in such words as *bomb, font, golf, pomp, pond, stomp.*

When *a* immediately precedes *ll* or *lk*, it represents /ò/: *all, ball, call, fall, gall, hall, mall, pall, tall, wall, small, stall, squall; walk, stalk, balk, talk, calk, Baltic, fallen, pitfall.*

After *w*, the *a* may represent /ŏ/ or /ò/:

Wa as /wä/—swab, swamp, swan, swap, swat, wad, wand, want, was, wash

Wa as short o—wasp, watch, watt, what, swallow, tightwad, waffle, wallet, wallop, wanting, washing, washrag, washcloth, washer, washroom, watchdog, watchful, watchman, wattage, whitewash

Wa as /ò/—dwarf, swarm, war, ward, warm, warp, wart, walleye, walnut, warble, warden, wardrobe, warlike, warmly, warming, warrant

There are, however, exceptions to the above: *way, sway* and *wag, wax.*

Y as a vowel in the middle of a word usually represents /i/ as in *bicycle.* At the end of a word it may represent /ī/ as in *my* or /ē/ as in *pony.*

The Principle of Silentness

The third principle to be learned is the principle of silentness.* Some vowel letters in words are not pronounced. When the letter *e* comes at the end of a monosyllabic word, it frequently is silent. In addition, the normally short sound in the middle of the word becomes a long vowel. A third rule may be stated thus: *In one-syllable words in which there are two vowel letters, the second one being a silent* e *preceded by a single consonant, the initial vowel letter represents a long vowel sound.* Emans (7) reports that this rule has about 70 percent utility words ending in *le* (ankle) and *ive* (live) are accepted as exceptions to it. Illustrative words are *ape, here, crude, quite, nose.*

Common exceptions include:

are	give	active	justice
have	office	notice	service
live	promise	native	practice

* See Lou E. Burmeister, "Final Vowel-Consonant-E," *The Reading Teacher,* 24 (February 1971), 439–42.

favorite	delicate	assure	lose
representative	purchase	ere	whose
police	manage	there	purpose
automobile	message	where	welcome
marine	passage	were	improve
magazine	village	come	movement
examine	advantage	done	remove
determine	separate	dove	above
machine	sure	love	become
engine	rule	gone	lovely
surface	conclude	move	something
palace	include	none	sometimes
average	measure	one	somewhat
courage	pleasure	some	somewhere
senate	treasure		

A new sound occurs in the following words: bare, blare, care, dare, fare, flare, glare, hare, mare, pare, rare, scare, snare, spare, stare, and ware. This sound of the letter *a* is a more open sound than the long *a* sound and occurs commonly in accented syllables and/or in conjunction with the /r/ sound. There is no great need to distinguish it for the student from the /ā/ sound.

In another group of words the pronunciation of a vowel in the middle of the word is variable. In words like *range, change,* and *strange,* the *a* represents its long sound. In words like *edge, dodge, fringe, singe, tinge, hedge, ledge, wedge, lodge, binge,* and *cringe,* the vowel represents its short sound.

The student must learn further extensions of the principle of silentness. *In certain vowel letter combinations, for example,* ai, ay, ea, ee, oa, oe, ow, *the second letter may be silent and the first represents a long vowel sound.* Table 6-5 shows various monosyllabic words that follow this rule.

In an analysis of vowel-vowel combinations that have one sound, Burmeister (5) found that the *ai* combination has the long ā sound 74 percent of the time; 16 percent of the time, it is followed by *r* and is pronounced /e(ə)/ as in *air, chair, fair, flair, hair, lair, pair,* and *stair.* The other pronunciations should be learned as sight words: *aisle, plaid, said, mountain, villain, again.*

The *ay* combination has the /ā/ sound almost 95 percent of the time (5); common exceptions are *aye, says, yesterday.* The combination *ai* starts some words (ail) and is used in the middle of a word (fail), but at the end of a word the /ā/ is represented by *ay* (play).

The *ee* combination represents /ē/ about 85 percent of the time

(5); the words *beer, cheer, deer, jeer, peer, queer, sheer, sneer, steer,* and *veer* have the /i(ə)/ sound. This is a lowered long *e* sound and occurs only in conjunction with *r*. It occurs about 12 percent of the time (5). A common exception is *been*.

TABLE 6-5

Ai as ā	maize	clay	eel	reel	coal	goes
aid	paid	day	feed	see	coast	hoe
aide	pail	flay	feel	seed	coat	Joe
ail	paint	gay	feet	seem	croak	shoe*
aim	pair	hay	flee	seen	float	toe
ain't	plaid*	may	fleet	seep	foal	
air	plaint	nay	free	sleek	foam	*Ow as ō*
aisle*	praise	play	geese	sleep	gloam	blow
bail	quail	pray	Greek	sleet	gloat	bow
bait	quaint	ray	green	sneer	goad	bowl
braid	raid	say	greet	speed	goal	crow
brail	rain	says*	heed	steed	goat	flow
brain	raise	slay	heel	steel	groan	flown
claim	said*	stay	jeep	steep	load	glow
drain	sail	tray	jeer	steer	loaf	grow
fail	saint	way	keel	sweep	loam	grown
faille	slain		keen	sweet	loan	know
fain	snail	*Ee as ē*	keep	teem	moan	low
faint	staid	bee	knee	teens	moat	mow
fair	stain	beech	kneel	tree	oak	owe
flail	stair	beef	leek	tweed	oat	own
flair	tail	been*	lees	tweet	road	row
gain	taint	beer	meet	wee	roam	show
gait	trail	beet	need	weed	roan	slow
hail	train	bleed	peek	week	roast	snow
hair	trait	breed	peel	weep	soak	stow
jail	waif	creed	peep		soap	throw
laid	wail	creek	peer	*Oa as ō*	toad	tow
lain	waist	creel	preen	boar	toast	
lair	wait	creep	queen	board		
maid		creese	queer	boast	*Oe as ō*	
mail	*Ay as ā*	deed	reed	boat	doe	
maim	aye*	deem	reef	broad*	does*	
main	bay	deep	reek	cloak	foe	

* Aisle (īl); plaid (plad); said (sed); aye (ī); says (sez); been (bin); broad (bröd); does (dəz); shoe (shü); the ee followed by r is always i(ə).

The *oa* combination is sounded like a long *o* 94 percent of the time. The *oa*, pronounced as in *broad*, occurs the remaining 6 percent of the time.

The *oe* combination occurs much less frequently than *oa*, and its pronunciation is much less consistent. It is pronounced as long *o* 60 percent of the time; as long *e* 23 percent of the time; and as /oo/, in such words as *shoe, snowshoe, canoe*, and *horseshoe*, 18 percent of the time (5). A common exception is *does*.

TABLE 6-6

Ea		Ea* Ear			
/e/	/ā/	/i(ə)/	/e(ə)/	/ə/	/ä/
bread	great	clear	bear	earl	heart
breadth	break	dear	pear	dearth	hearth
breast	steak	beard	swear	earn	
breath		ear	wear	earth	
dead		fear		hearse	
deaf		gear		pearl	
dealt		hear		search	
death		near			
dread		rear			
dreamt		sear			
head		shear			
health		smear			
lead		spear			
meant		tear			
read					
realm					
spread					
stealth					
sweat					
thread					
threat					
tread					
wealth					

* Some two-syllable words with ea pronounced as short e are *abreast, headache, ahead, baldhead, behead, blockhead, breakfast, bullhead, deadbeat, deaden, deadeye, deadly, deafen, deafmute, dreadful, feather, headlight, headlong, headstrong, healthful, healthy, heaven, heavy, hothead, instead, jealous, leather, meadow, measure, pleasant, peasant, pleasure, ready, redhead, retread, steady, sweater, threaten, weapon, weather, wealthy.* In *heartbreak* and *heartburn* it is ä. In *impearl, learned, rehearse, searching, unearth,* and *research* it is ə.

The *ow* combination is listed here because in some instances it follows the general principle of silentness. In *ow*, the *w* is not pronounced, and the *o* is given its long sound 50 percent of the time. Forty-eight percent of the time it is pronounced as /aù/ as in *town*.

The principle of silentness also applies to certain words having an *ea* combination. This group of words is by far the least consistent. The student will have to learn many of the words as sight words. In attacking words with the *ea* combination, the student's best guess is the long *e* sound. It occurs about 50 percent of the time (5). The next most common usage is that of the short *e* as in *bread*. The student must learn that *break* and *steak* are pronounced as /brāk/ and /stāk/. The ending *ear* may be pronounced four ways: as /i(ə)/ in *beard;* as /e(ə)/ in *bear;* as /ə/ in *dearth;* and as /ä/ in *heart*. In diagrammatic form the various pronunciations for *ea,* omitting the long *e* sound, may be categorized as in Table 6-6.

The following *ea* combinations are pronounced as long e:

beach	cleave	gleam	leak	plea	seat	teach
bead	creak	glean	lean	plead	sheaf	team
beak	cream	grease	leap	please	sheath	tease
beam	crease	greave	lease	pleat	sheathe	treat
bean	deal	heal	leave	preach	sheave	veal
beast	dean	heap	meal	reach	sleave	weak
beat	dream	heat	mean	read	sneak	weal
bleach	each	heath	neat	ream	speak	weave
bleak	ease	heave	pea	reap	squeal	wheat
bleat	east	jean	peace	reave	stead	wreak
breach	eat	knead	peach	screak	steal	wreath
breathe	feast	lea	peak	scream	steam	wreathe
cheap	feat	lead	peaked	sea	streak	
clean	flea	leaf	peal	seal	stream	
cheat	freak	league	peat	seam	tea	

The Principle of Context

The fourth principle to be learned is the principle of context. When a single vowel letter or a group of vowel letters in a word can represent one of two or three sounds, the word may be described as partially alphabetic. Several different clues must be used to determine which vowel sound to apply in pronouncing partially alphabetic words. If the number of vowel letters and the position of the vowel letter or group of vowel letters in a word do not indicate which vowel sound is to be applied in the pronunciation of the word, word meaning or context must be used as a clue.

For example, the spelling *oo* can represent any of four different vowel sounds: /ō/, /o͞o/, /o͝o/, and /ŭ/. When a student sees *took,* he will tend to reject /tōk/, /to͞ok/, and /tŭk/, since such forms do not exist in his vocabulary, and will be more liable to accept /to͝ok/ as the right pronunciation.

The student should always ask: Does the word make sense in the sentence? What word would make sense in the sentence? The student thus fits the word into its environment and from it may get his first pronunciation clue.

Leary (12) notes that training a learner to anticipate meaning, to infer an unknown word from its total context, or to check the context clue with the form of the word will provide him the most important single aid to word recognition. For, regardless of what word he perceives, if it does not "make sense" in its setting, his perception has been in error.

Dunn (6), in a study with fourth graders, found that context clues made the greatest contribution to the identification of unfamiliar words, followed by initial and final phonic elements. And Olson (14), summarizing the research, concluded that context clues could be used most effectively after students acquired the basic phonic skills, and he suggested that teachers devote more of their instructional efforts to teaching context as a clue to word analysis.

The use of context in deciphering the sound of a vowel is developed slowly because reading is involved. The student must be able to read material on his level fluently before he can make use of context without loss of comprehension. It is nevertheless essential to introduce this means of determining sounds as soon as possible, since many sounds cannot be determined by any other method.

The sequential order of sounds is governed by a multiplicity of nonconsistent phoneme-grapheme conventions which vary with the meaning of the word. The *ough* and *ow* are two graphemes that have several interchangeable phonemes, but a particular phoneme-grapheme association is identifiable only through the meaning of the word in question (2).

The context provides a reliable means for confirming the sounds of all the vowel combinations and is especially useful in dealing with the following variants. If the relationship between a vowel letter and a vowel sound is one that occurs in only a few words, the words should be taught as sight words.

1. Sounds of o	2. Sounds of a
a. /ĭ/ as in *women*	a. /ĕ/ as in *any*
b. /u̇/ or /o͝o/ as in *wolf*	b. /ĭ/ as in *senate*
c. /ü/ or /o͞o/ as in *do, to, who*	c. /ä/ as in *mama*
d. /ŭ/ as in *come*	

3. Sounds of e
   a. /ĭ/ as in *pretty*
   b. /ō/ as in *sew*
   c. /ä/ as in *sergeant*

4. Sounds of *i*
   a. /ē/ as in *ski, broccoli, police, spaghetti, machine, antique, physique, technique, unique, clique, pique, intrigue, fatigue, simile, facsimile, recipe*
   b. /y/ as in *familiar, peculiar, genius, behavior, junior, senior, guardian, Indian, brilliant, Italian, valiant, billion, champion, companion, million, onion, opinion, union, Spaniard, spaniel, congenial, convenience, convenient, Muriel, obedient, Daniel, William, Julia, California, Celia, Virginia, India, Pennsylvania, Columbia, period, Philadelphia, radio, curious, furious, glorious, serious*

5. Sounds of *u*
   a. /ĕ/ as in *bury*
   b. /ĭ/ as in *busy*
   c. /u̇/ as in *bull, full, pull, put, blissful, bulldog, bullet, fitful, glassful, input, pulpit, sinful*

6. Sounds of oo
   a. /ü/ or /ōō/ as in *moon*
   b. /u̇/ or /ŏŏ/ as in *look*
   c. /ŭ/ as in *blood*

7. Sounds of *ou*
   a. /ou/ as in *house*
   b. /ō/ as in *four*
   c. /ȯ/ as in *cough*
   d. /ü/ or /ōō/ as in *you*
   e. /u̇/ or /ŏŏ/ as in *could*
   f. /ŭ/ as in *rough, touch*
   g. /ŏ/ as in *hough*
   h. /ə/ as in *vigorous*

8. Sounds of ow
   a. /ō/ as in *blow*
   b. /ou/ as in *cow*

9. Sounds of *ea*
   a. /ā/ as in *great*
   b. /ĕ/ as in *bread*
   c. /ä/ as in *heart*
   d. /â/ as in *pear*
   e. /i(ə)/ as in *fear*
   f. /ə/ as in *earth*

10. Sounds of *ei*
    a. /ā/ as in *veil*
    b. /ĕ/ as in *heifer*
    c. /ĭ/ as in *foreign*
    d. /ī/ as in *height*

11. Sounds of *ie*
    a. /ĕ/ as in *friend*
    b. /ē/ as in *chief*
    c. /ĭ/ as in *sieve*

12. Sounds of *ew, eu, ui, eu*
    a. /yü/ or /yōō/ as in *new, suit, hue, deuce*
    b. /ü/ or /ōō/ as in *flew, juice, true, maneuver*
    c. /ĭ/ as in *build*

THE COMBINATION Oo *Oo* is pronounced as /ü/ (bloom), as /u̇/ (cook), as /ō/ (door), and as short /u/ (blood). The latter two occur infrequently and should be taught as exceptions. The combination *ook* occurs frequently enough in words so that one may speak of the /ŏŏk/ words. Some examples are *book, brook, cook, crook, hook, nook, rook, shook,* and *took.* Only *spook* is an exception.

The following words are illustrative of the *oo* combinations:

Oo as /ü/—bloom, boo, boom, boon, boast, boot, booth, booze, brood, broom, choose, coo, cool, coon, coop, coot, croon, doom, drool, droop, food, fool, gloom, goof, goon, goose, groom, groove, hoof, hoop, moo, mooch, mood, moon, moose, moot, noose, pooch, pool, proof, roof, room, roost, root, school, scoop, scoot, shoo, shoot, sloop, smooch, smooth, snoop, snoot, snooze, soon, sooth, soothe, spook, spool, spoon, stooge, stoop, swoon, swoop, too, tool, toot, tooth, troop, whoop, zoo, zoom, baboon, balloon, ballroom, bamboo, bassoon, bedroom, behoove, blooming, booby, booster, bootleg, bridegroom, caboose, cartoon, classroom, cocoon, cooler, coolie, disproof, doodle, fooling, foodstuff, foolish, gloomy, home-room, igloo, moonlight, moonshine, mushroom, noodle, noonday, noontime, papoose, platoon, raccoon, reproof, roofing, roomette, roommate, rooster, saloon, storeroom, toothache, toothbrush, toothpick

Oo as /ů/barefoot, bookend, bookmark, bookworm, childhood, cookbook, footstool, football, footbridge, foothill, footnote, girlhood, good-ness, lookout, manhood, redwood, rookie, sooty, woodpile, wood-shed, woodsman, woodwork, lookout, book, brook, cook, crook, foot, good, hood, hook, look, nook, shook, soot, stood, took, wood, wool

Oo as /ō/brooch, door, floor, doorstep, doorway, doorsill

Oo as /short u/—blood, flood, bloodshed, bloodshot, bloodstain, bloody, floodlight

THE COMBINATION EI (EY)   A common pronunciation for *ei* is that of a long *a*. The following words are illustrative: beige, deign, feign, feint, heir, heiress, reign, rein, reindeer, seine, skein, their, veil, vein, eight, freight, neigh, sleigh, weigh, and weight.

In some instances *ei* is simply pronounced as a long *e*, the second vowel letter being silent. Thus we have the following: ceiling, deceive, conceive, receive, perceive, leisure, seize, either, neither.

The *ei* may be pronounced as long *i* as in *height,* short *e* as in *heifer,* and short *i* as in *forfeit* and sovereign).

The *ey* is pronounced as short *i* as in *barley, honey, kidney.* This *ey* is often pronounced as long *e*. It is pronounced as long *a* in *hey, obey, prey, they, whey.* This sound is common in monosyllables and when *ey* occurs in a stressed syllable ending a word: *obey, convey.* It occurs as long *i*: *eye, eyeball, eyebrow, eyelash;* and as long *e*: *key, keyhole, pass-key.*

THE COMBINATION IE   *Ie* generally is a long *e*, a short *i*, or a long *i*. The long *i* sound is common when *ie* is at the end of a word and in the ending *ied*. The following words are illustrative of the various sounds for *ie*:

Long e—bier, brief, chief, fief, field, fiend, fierce, frieze, grief, grieve, lief, liege, mien, niece, piece, pier, pierce, priest, shield, shriek, siege, thief, tier, wield, yield, achieve, backfield, belief, believe, cashier, frontier, grievance, grievous, hygiene, priestly, rabies, relief, retrieve, timepiece, wieldy, handkerchief, mischief, mischievous, reprieve, besiege

Long i—die, fie, fried, lie, pie, tried, vie, allied, applied, belie, implied, tie-up, untie, untried

In plurisyllables when *ie* ends the word, *ie* often represents /ē/: *cookie, prairie, collie, brownie, lassie.*

Short e—friend, befriend, friendless, friendly, friendship

Short i—sieve

THE COMBINATION OU *Ou* has numerous pronunciations: as /ou/ in *blouse,* in which case it represents a diphthong; as long *o* in *course;* as /ü/ in *group;* as /ů/ in *could;* as /ȯ/ in *bought;* as short *u* in *touch;* and as /ȯ/ in *cough.* Certainly, the most common sounds are /ou/, as the schwa sound of *ou* in *rigorous;* as /ü/ in *soup;* and as /ō/.

The following words may be used to teach the various sounds:

Ou as /ou/—blouse, bough, bounce, bound, bout, cloud, clout, couch, count, crouch, douse, drought, flounce, flour, foul, found, fount, gouge, gout, grouch, ground, hound, hour, house, loud, mound, mount, mouse, mouth, noun, ouch, ounce, our, oust, out, pouch, plough, pounce, pound, pout, proud, round, rout, scour, scout, shout, shroud, abound, about, account, aground, aloud, around, arouse, astound, background, blockhouse, blowout, bouncing, bounty, cloudburst, cloudy, compound, counsel, county, devour, devout, discount, doghouse, enounce, flounder, greenhouse, greyhound, guardhouse, housecoat, household, housemaid, housewife, house-work, icehouse, mountain, mounted, mounting, mouthful, ourself, ouster, outboard, outbreak, outburst, outcome, outcry, outdoors, outer, outfit, outing, outlaw, outlay, outlet, outlive, outmost, out-post, output, outrage, outright, outsell, outshine, outside, outskirt, outsmart, outward, outwards, outweigh, outwork, playhouse, pro-noun, pronounce, propound, recount, renounce, rounding, round-ness, roundup, rousing, southwest, stoutness, trousers

Ou as /ō/—course, court, dough, four, fourth, furlough, mould, mourn, pour, soul, source, though, although, doughnut, thorough, courtroom, courtship, courtyard, discourse, fourteen, fourthly, mourning, poul-try, recourse, resource

Ou as /ü/—coup, couth, croup, ghoul, group, rouge, route, soup, through, wound, you, youth, cougar, coupon, detour

Ou as short u—cousin, country, couple, double, enough, tough, rough, roughage, roughen, roughly, roughness, touch, trouble, young, famous, touch-back, touchy, toughen, grievous, jeolous, monstrous, pious

Ou as /ȯ/—bought, brought, cough, nought, fought, ought, sought, thought, wrought

Ou as /u̇/—could, should, tour, would, your

Ou as /ə/—adjourn, journal, journey, flourish

THE COMBINATION OW   The student has already learned the long *o* sound of *ow*. He must also learn the *ou*, or diphthongal, sound of *ow*. This sound at the end of the word is usually written as *ow* and occurs in the following words:

bow, brow, brown, browse, chow, clown, cow, cowl, crowd, crown, down, dowse, drown, drowse, frown, gown, growl, how, howl, jowl, owl, plow, prow, prowl, scowl, sow, town, wow, allow, avow, breakdown, chowchow, cowbell, cowbird, cowboy, cowhide, dowry, endow, flower, Howard, howdy, nightgown, powder, power, powwow, prowess, renowned, towel, tower, township, uptown

THE COMBINATIONS AU AND AW   The combination *au* is pronounced /ȯ/ (ought) 94 percent of the time (5); the principal exceptions are *draught, gauge, aunt, chauffeur,* and *laugh. Aw* is pronounced as /ȯ/ (law) 100 percent of the time (5) when it occurs at the end of the word or syllable or is followed by *k, l,* or *n.* The /ȯ/ sound is represented by *au* or *aw* in the beginning and the middle of the word (*August, awe, cause, crawl*), but at the end of a word it is always *aw* (*law*).

Au as /ȯ/—aught, caught, caulk, cause, craunch, daub, daunt, fault, faun, flaunt, fraud, Gaul, gaunt, gauze, haul, haunch, haunt, jaunt, laud, launch, mauve, naught, naughty, Paul, paunch, pause, raught, sauce, Saul, staunch, taught, taunt, vault, vaunt, applaud, applause, assault, auburn, audit, auger, augment, augur, August, austere, auto, because, caucus, causal, dauntless, default, defraud, laundress, naughty, saucepan, saucer, saucy, slaughter

Aw as /ȯ/—awe, awl, awn, bawl, brawl, brawn, claw, craw, crawl, dawn, draw, drawl, drawn, fawn, flaw, gawk, hawk, jaw, law, lawn, paw, pawn, raw, saw, scrawl, shawl, slaw, spawn, sprawl, squaw, squawk, straw, thaw, trawl, awesome, brawny, awful, awning, bylaw, drawer, drawing, gnawing, hacksaw, in-law, jigsaw, lawful, lawless, lawsuit, lawyer, pawnshop, rawhide, tawny

THE COMBINATIONS EW, UE, UI AND EU   The student has learned two sounds for the long *u*: the /yü/ sound and the /ü/ sound after *j, r, bl, fl, pl, cl, gl,* and *sl.* The /yü/ sound is regularly used after *b, c, f, g, h, k, m, p,* and *v.* He must apply the same principles to the *ew, ue, ui,* and *ey* combinations.

Ew as /yü/—ewe, few, hew, lewd, mew, new, pew, phew, skew, spew, stew, thew, view, whew, sinew, askew, nephew, newly, newness, renew, review

Ew as /ü/—blew, brew, crew, drew, flew, grew, Jew, screw, shrewd, slew, threw, Hebrew, jewel, Jewess

Ue as /yü/—cue, due, hue, imbue, statue, tissue

Ue as /ü/—blue, clue, flue, glue, rue, slue, true, accrue, bluegill, bluegrass, blueprint, construe, gruesome, rueful, untrue, sue, statue, tissue

Ui as /yü/—suit, nuisance

Ui as /ü/—bruise, cruise, juice, sluice, suit, grapefruit, fruitcake, juicy, recruit

Eu as /yü/—deuce, feud, Europe, feudal, Teuton, neural, neuter, neutral, neutron

The *yü* sound of *ew* occurs 61 percent of the time; the *ü* sound, 34 percent (11). *Ew* also occurs as long *o: sew.*

The *yü* sound of *ue* occurs 63 percent of the time; the *ü* sound, 37 percent (5).

The *yü* sound of *ui* occurs 24 percent of the time; the *ü* sound, 29 percent; and the short *i* sound, 47 percent (5). Emans (7) found in his study that *ui* had a short *i* sound 79 percent of the time: *build, built, guilt, guilty, building.* An exception is *suite.*

The *yü* sound of *eu* occurs 72 percent of the time (5).

THE DIPHTHONGS

Diphthongs are digraphs that represent a gliding monosyllabic speech sound. The sound is distinct from that represented by either of the single letters. The most common such combinations are *oi* and *oy.*

The sound of *oi,* as in *boil,* occurs 98 percent of the time (5). It occurs in the following words: boil, broil, choice, coil, coin, droit, foil foist, hoist, join, joint, joist, moist, noise, oil, point, poise, soil, spoil, toil, voice, void, appoint, avoid, boiler, cloister, foible, jointly, jointweed, noisy, recoil, rejoice, rejoin, toiler, toilet, topsoil, uncoil, and unsoiled. A common exception is *choir.*

The sound of *oy,* as in *boy,* also occurs 98 percent of the time. Common words are the following: coy, joy, Roy, soy, toy, Troy, alloy, bellboy, boycott, boyhood, boyish, convoy, cowboy, decoy, deploy, destroy, enjoy, envoy, joyful, loyal, oyster, royal, and tomboy. An exception is *coyote.*

TEACHING THE LONG VOWELS

Burmeister (5) points out that phonemes for vowel pairs tend to fall into the following categories:

1. The first vowel may do the talking, as in *ai, ay, ea, ee, oa,* or *ow,* and say its name. *Ea* may be long e or short e; *ow* may be long o or /ou/.

2. The two vowels may blend: *au, aw, oi, oy, oo; oo* may sound as in *lagoon* or *wood.*

3. The two vowels may create a new sound: *ei, ow, ey, ew.*

According to Burmeister (5), the vowel combinations in order of frequency of occurrence are *ou, ea, ai, oo, ee, ow, au, ie, oa, ay, oi, ei, aw, ey, ew, oy, ue, eu, ui,* and *oe.*

Sabaroff (15) identifies five basic vowel patterns:

1. The single (or short) vowel pattern as in *bat* or *at*

2. The open vowel pattern as in *he, she,* or *me*

3. The vowel with final e pattern as in *rope* or *use*

4. The double vowel pattern as in *rain*

5. The modified vowel pattern as in *bird,* as in *word,* or as in *all*

Exercises such as the following are especially helpful in teaching the various vowel letter and sound correspondences:

1. Have the student circle the correct *a* sound.

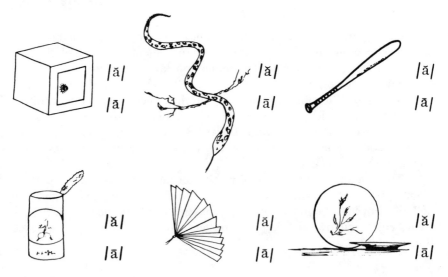

2. Have the student write the missing vowel letters. This exercise is useful in teaching the long vowel sound followed by silent *e*.

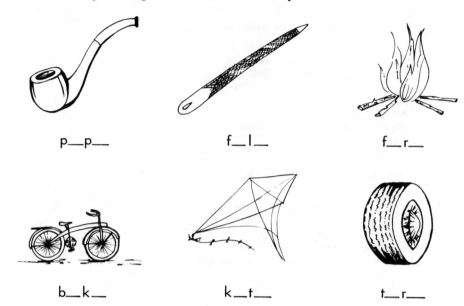

p__p__   f__l__   f__r__

b__k__   k__t__   t__r__

3. Provide a list of words with the vowel letters representing the long vowel sound missing and let students add them:

displ___y,   fl___ght, etc.   p___ceful,   bic___cle,

4. Have students indicate by number the picture that has the same vowel sound as that represented by the underlined letter in a word.

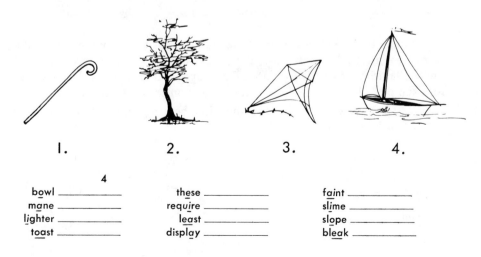

1.   2.   3.   4.

bowl _____	these _____	faint _____
mane _____	require _____	slime _____
lighter _____	least _____	slope _____
toast _____	display _____	bleak _____

5. The student, besides learning to discriminate between long and short vowel sounds and the letters used to represent them, needs to learn how to designate long and short vowel sounds and how to indicate silent letters. An exercise like the following teaches this.

āt̸e	blow	hay	fan
hot	got	duke	jail
dīn̸g	soap	bed	see
gō	sleep	fun	rake
get	joke	fame	brute
fē̸ast	tube	Brad	name
cut	bike	sat	like

6. Present students with the six basic vowel patterns:

a. The single vowel letter pattern as in *bat* or *at*. This is a clue to the short vowel sound.
b. The open vowel pattern as in *be* or *me* (long vowel clue).
c. The vowel letter with a final e pattern as in *rope* or *use* (long vowel clue).
d. The double vowel letter as in *rain* (long vowel clue).
e. The modified vowel pattern as in *bird, word, all, far.*
f. Exceptions or words that do not fit any of the above patterns.

Then present a list of words and let the student indicate which pattern the underlined letters fit.

1

thrush _____	large _____	leave _____
screech _____	lays _____	bored _____
belabor _____	amazed _____	encamp _____
realized _____	justifiable _____	urchin _____
rhubarb _____	reproach _____	burlap _____

Students do not necessarily make the transition from monosyllabic words to multisyllabic words. This means that a lot of practice with multisyllabic words is called for and the application of the rule indicated; for example, silent *e* as in dis*grace*ful, *life*less, inter*fere,* organi*ze*.

7. Have students write out the alphabetic spelling of the *phonetic transliterations* of words:

laf	laugh	fiks _____	
ej	_____	mən _____	
egz	_____	wən _____	
ləv	_____	kyu̇(ə)r_____	
kwilt	_____	kȯ(ə)rn_____	

THE EFFECT OF *R* ON A PRECEDING VOWEL

The student must also be able to cope with *ar, er, ir, or,* and *ur.* The consonant sometimes influences the sound represented by the vowel letter. The letter *r,* when following a single vowel letter, changes the sound of the vowel. The vowel is neither long nor short.

The Sounds of ar

/är/ as in *car*

/âr/ as in *care* and as in *parent* or *Mary* when *ar* is the final letter in an accented syllable and is followed by a vowel

/ãr/ as in *paradise* or *paradox*

/ə/ as in *maroon* when the *a* is the final letter in an unaccented syllable and is followed by an *r*

/ôr/ as in *warm* or *ward*

/ər/ as in *liar, granular, westward, pillar, dollar, orchard, Tartar, circular, lizard, sugar, grammar, collar, wizard, mustard, beggar*

/ĕr/ in the suffix *ary: stationary, legendary, sanitary*

The *a* in monosyllables when followed by *r* or when followed by *r* plus another consonant is the *a* sound as in *bar, car, art, arm, far, mar, farm, jar, tar, bark, hark, lark, mark, park, scar, spar, spark, star.*

Unfortunately, not all *a*'s followed by *r* are pronounced as /ä/. When the *r* is followed by a silent *e* as in *care* or *fare,* or when it is the final letter in an accented syllable and is followed by a vowel as in *parent* or *Mary,* the *a* is frequently pronounced /e(ə)/ or /âr/. The *a,* however, may represent a short vowel in this last instance: *paradise, paradox, charity.* When the *a* is the final letter in an unaccented syllable and is followed by an *r* in the next syllable, it is /ə/: *maroon* and *cataract.*

In the suffix *ar,* as in *ward,* and in some final syllables, *ar* is pronounced /(ə)r/ or /ôr/: *liar, granular, westward, pillar, dollar, orchard, Tartar, circular, lizard, wizard, mustard.* The usage /ôr/ or /(ə)r/ is common when *ar* is immediately preceded by *w: war, warm, warp, ward, dwarf, swarm, wart, warble, warden, wardrobe, warlike, warmly, warming, warrant.* In the suffix *ary, ar* is pronounced as /ĕr/: *stationary, legendary, sanitary.*

The Sounds of er

/ər/ or /ûr/ as in *her, revert, adverb*
/(ə)r/ as in *hotter, baker*
/ĕr/ as in *meridian*
/i(e)/ as in *here*
/e(ə)/ as in *there, where, very*

Er in monosyllabic words (*her*), generally in accented syllables (*revert*), and in unaccented syllables in which the *er* is followed by a consonant (*adverb*) is sounded as /ər/. When it names a person (*baker*) or has a comparative meaning (*hotter*), it is usually pronounced as /(ə)r/. It may also be /ĕr/ as in *meridian*, /i(ə)/ as in *here*, or /e(ə)/ as in *there, where, ferry, herring, very*, or *perish*.

The Sounds of ir

/ər/ as in *firm, firkin*
/ə(r)/ as in *tapir*
/īr/ as in *dire*
/ĭr/ as in *virile*

Ir is sounded as /ər/ in monosyllables (*firm*) and in accented syllables (*firkin*). It may be sounded as /ə(r)/ (*tapir*), /īr/ (*dire*), or /ĭr/ (*virile, irrelevant, irritate*).

The Sounds of or

/ôr/ as in *for or fork*
/ûr/ (ər) as in *word*
/ōr/ as in *more*
/ə(r)/ as in *doctor*

Or is sounded as /ər/ or /ûr/ when *or* follows *w* as in *word, work, world, worship, worm, worse, worth*. In other monosyllabic words it is sounded as /ō/ or as /ô/. The most common pronunciation is /ô/: *born, cord, cork, corn, for, fork, gorge, horn, horse, Lord, morn, Morse, norm, Norse, north, or, orb, scorch, scorn, short, snort, sort, sport, stork, storm, torch, tort, worn*.

When *or* is immediately followed by *e* at the end of a monosyllable, or a syllable in a polysyllabic word, it usually represents /ōr/ as in *store, more, before, soreness*. The spelling *or* also has the sound of /ôr/ in such words as *porch, fort*, and *worn*. The *or* may be pronounced as /ə(r)/ as in *inventor* or may become /är/ or /ŏr/ as in *coral* or *torrid.* It usually is pronounced /ə(r)/ when it names a person (doctor) or a quality or condition (horror).

The Sounds of ur

/ər/ or /ûr/ as in *hurt*
/ə(r)/ as in *liturgy*
/yu̇(ə)r/ as in *cure*
/u̇r/ as in *sure, jury, rural, hurrah*
/ər/ as in *murmur*

Ur is sounded as /ər/ in monosyllabic words and in the accented syllable of polysyllabic words. *Ur* also may be /ə(r)/ (liturgy), /yu̇(ə)r/ (cure), and /u̇(ə)r/ (sure, jury, hurrah, rural).

When *ar, er, ir, or,* or *ur* are followed by a second *r*, the vowel is usually short: *barrel, barren, sparrow, arrest, barrack, derrick, error, terrier, errand, mirror, borrow, horror, sorry, corrupt, torrent, torrid.*

The vowel also is short when the *r* is followed by a vowel: *charity, tariff, lariat, parachute, paratroop, parasol, paradise, paradox, parapet, parallel, parasite, parable, ceremony, America, very, inherit, peril, verity, merit, cleric, spirit, miracle, direct, quorum.*

Sometimes the *r* is separated from the vowel preceding it and has no effect on its pronunciation: *arise, around, arena, spiral, Irish, erect, erupt, hero, irate, siren, uranium, pirate, virus, furious, spirant, wiry, glory, tyrant, mores, oral, story, Tory.*

The spelling *air* represents /âr/ as in *fair, hair, pair.*

The following lists of words illustrate the various common combinations of the vowel with the *r* in monosyllabic words:

Er   as   /ər/—berg, berth, clerk, err, erst, fern, germ, her, herd, jerk, kern, merge, nerve, per, perch, perk, pert, serf, serge, serve, shred, stern, swerve, term, tern, verge, verse, versed

Ir   as   /ər/—birch, bird, birth, chirp, dirge, dirt, fir, firm, first, flirt, firth, gird, girl, girth, irk, Kirk, mirk, mirth, quirk, shirk, shirt, skirt, squirm, squirt, stir, third, twirl, whirl

Or as /ó(ə)r/—born, cord, cork, corn, for, gorge, horn, horse, Lord, morn, Morse, norm, Norse, north, or, orb, scorch, scorn, short, snort, ort, sport, stork, storm, torch, tort, worn

Or   as   /ər/—word, work, world, worm, worse, worst, wort, worth

Ur   as   /ər/—blur, blurb, blurt, burg, burn, burnt, burp, burr, burse, burst, church, churn, curb, curd, curl, curse, curt, curve, durst, fur, furl, gurge, hurl, hurt, lurch, lurk, nurse, purge, purse, scurf, slur, spur, spurge, spurn, spurt, surf, surge, turf, Turk, turn, urge, urn

**TEACHING STRUCTURAL ANALYSIS
SKILLS**

The student rather early needs to develop some skill in structural analysis. Structural analysis, which may logically precede phonetic analysis, is possible with three kinds of words. A word may have an inflectional ending such as *s, es, ed,* or *ing;* it may be a derived word, being constructed from a root, a suffix and/or a prefix; or it may be a compound word.

In the initial stage the student is commonly introduced to two kinds of words which may be analyzed structurally. The student learns that the *s* can change the word in two ways: (1) It changes the verb into third person singular, and (2) it makes a noun plural in form. The teaching of the *s* plural is easier when it is accompanied by another word in the sentence that suggests the plural. The sentence *Tom has ten pet pups* is an example of this.

Betts (3) has outlined the steps in applying phonics skills to the syllables of words:

1. The student must first learn to hear the number of syllables in spoken words.
2. He must learn to identify syllables in printed words. Early in the grades the student needs to learn that some words ending in *ed* have only one syllable (cooked); others have two syllables (landed).
3. He must learn to accent the proper syllable. Accentuation should be taught only after the student has mastered steps one and two and after having learned something about prefixes and suffixes. These latter rarely are accented (intend, fishing).
4. He must learn to apply phonic skills to the separate vowels in words:
   a. He applies the short-vowel rule to the stressed syllable (rabbit).
   b. He identifies such vowel-phonograms as *ar, er, ir, or, ur.*
5. He must check to see if the word makes sense in the sentence.

Let us look more closely at each of the above teaching tasks.

Teaching the Compounds

The student has been introduced to two-syllable words through simple compounds. He needs to learn that one-syllable words have only one vowel sound and that compounds each have two vowels that are sounded and are therefore called two-syllable words. He probably needs to learn this inductively.

A *syllable* is the part of a word that contains a vowel and receives some stress. The syllable is very helpful in attacking new words. After all, monosyllabic words are merely syllables to which we have given a meaning. Hildreth (10, p. 151) notes that "the syllable, not the phoneme, is the basic unit of speech articulation. . . ." There are two kinds of syllabication, one for writing and one for pronunciation. The former is inconsistent and generally one must consult the dictionary to be certain.

Teaching of compounds begins with those compounds that keep the basic meaning of each word making up the compound. For example, a *classroom* is a room where class is held. Other words useful in teaching this skill are *byways, breakdown, campfire, cornstalk, cowboy, earthquake, eyelash, hillside, hilltop, limestone, railroad, rosebush, watchman, weekend, steamboat, workbook, snowshoes, sawdust, sandhill, newsboy, seasick, housework, windshield, newspaper,* and so forth.

Frequently, the meaning of the compound is completely new, such as *broadcast, township, wholesale.* Some compounds are written as two words: *ice cream, living room, dining room, sea power, post office, oil painting, air brake, parcel post, money order, school spirit.*

When a compound word is used as a modifier and occurs before the word that it modifies, it is often hyphenated. We speak of *living-room* furniture. The hyphen is also used with *self* (self-denial, self-confidence, self-control) and with compound numbers from twenty-one to ninety-nine.

Here is a list of common compound words:

airplane	broadcast	eyelash	hillside	milkweed
backbone	broomstick	farmland	hilltop	monkeyshine
bagpipe	byways	fireman	himself	newsboy
barnyard	campfire	fishhook	homesick	nighttime
baseball	cardboard	footprint	horseback	northwest
battlefield	cheapskate	footstep	horsepower	outgrow
bedside	childhood	footstool	hunchback	outline
bedtime	classmate	foreman	inland	outskirts
beefeater	classroom	grandstand	inside	padlock
beehive	cookstove	grapevine	instep	pancake
beeline	corkscrew	graveyard	itself	paperweight
blacktop	cornstalk	gumdrop	kidnap	passport
bobcat	cowboy	halfway	limestone	pinpoint
bobsled	daylight	handrail	lookout	plaything
bobwhite	dragnet	haystack	makeshift	playtime
boldface	drumstick	headfirst	mankind	porthole
bloodshed	earthquake	headstrong	masterpiece	quicksand
bootblack	elsewhere	headwaiter	maybe	quicksilver
boxcar	everything	hedgerow	milkman	racetrack
breakdown	eyebrow	hemlock	milkshake	radioactive

railroad	sidetrack	sunburst	trailways	wigwag
rainbow	signpost	Sunday	treetop	windshield
ransack	skyscraper	sundown	upkeep	wishbone
rattlebrain	smokestack	sunset	uplift	withdraw
roommate	snowshoes	sunshade	upset	within
rosebush	snowstorm	sunshine	vineyard	without
sandhill	soapsuds	sunstroke	warehouse	withstand
sawdust	spillway	sunup	watchman	woodchuck
seacoast	stagecoach	switchboard	watercourse	woodland
schoolroom	starfish	tadpole	waylay	woodpile
seesaw	statehood	thumbtack	weekend	workbook
shipshape	steamboat	toothbrush	whatsoever	yardstick
shopworn	stronghold	touchdown	whenever	yearbook
sideline	subway	township	wholesale	yuletide
sideswipe	sunburn			

The following exercises are helpful in teaching compounds:

1. One exercise consists of two columns of monosyllabic words found in compound words. The student is required to join a word in column I to a word in column II to form a compound word.

I	II	Compound Word
a. bell	top	a. bellhop
b. black	set	b. _____
c. sun	dog	c. _____
d. for	hop	d. _____
e. bull	get	e. _____

2. A second exercise consists of a page containing pictures. Each pair of pictures represents a compound word. Have the student write the word.

fishhook

Teaching -ing

On the elemental level the teacher demonstrates how -ing can be added to verbs to form two-syllable words: hitting, batting, getting, hopping, running, tagging, tugging, nagging, and winning. The student should note that when a monosyllabic word ends in a single consonant letter preceded by a single vowel letter, the consonant is doubled before adding the *-ing* and that the second consonant is silent. The letter *x* is not doubled because it has a double consonant sound (waxing).

In words of more than one syllable, if the last syllable is stressed and ends with a single consonant letter preceded by a single vowel letter, the consonant letter is doubled before adding *-ing* (omitting, regretting). The final consonant is usually not doubled if the accent is on any syllable other than the last (labeling, remembering).

After the student can deal successfully with long vowels in various combinations and after he has mastered the regular uses of *-ing* as discussed above, he needs to expand his uses for *-ing*. Whenever *-ing* is added to monosyllabic words ending in a vowel, diphthong, or double vowel (being, playing, fleeing, hoeing), to monosyllabic words ending in a single consonant preceded by a double vowel (aiding), to monosyllabic words ending in a double consonant (arming), or to words ending in *ow* (blowing), no doubling of the letter preceding *-ing* occurs. Monosyllabic words ending in a silent *e* drop the final *e* before adding *-ing* (bake-baking). The first vowel receives its long sound in reading.

The principles suggested apply not only to *-ing* but to any suffix beginning with a vowel. The most common such suffixes are *able, ably, ability, age, ance, ant, ard, ary, ation, ed, en, ence, ent, er, ern, ery, es, est, ion, ish, ity, ive, or, ous,* and *y*. Words ending in *ce* or *ge* retain the *e* before a suffix beginning with *a* or *o*.

Let us illustrate these principles in all their applications.

1. When *-ing* is added to monosyllabic words ending in a vowel, diphthong, or double vowel and to words ending in *ow*, no doubling of the letter preceding the *-ing* occurs.

being	freeing
doing	seeing
flaying	growing
playing	knowing

2. When *-ing* is added to monosyllabic words ending in a single consonant preceded by a double vowel, no doubling of the letter preceding the *-ing* occurs.

aiding	beating
claiming	floating
creeping	cleaning
feeding	cheating

3. When *-ing* is added to monosyllabic words ending in a double consonant, no doubling of the consonant before *-ing* occurs.

asking	hunting
barking	kissing
drinking	singing
dusting	bunting

4. When -*ing* is added to monosyllabic words ending in a silent e, the e is dropped before adding -*ing* and the vowel in the root word, if it represents a long vowel sound, retains its long sound.

baking	living
biting	making
coming	moving
diving	praising
driving	smiling
giving	smoking
hiding	taking

The words *hoe* and *toe* are exceptions.

The Past Tense with ed

In reading *ed* the student meets certain problems. The *e* is silent (begged, tanned) except after *d* and *t* (batted, nodded), and the vowel in the root word, if it represents a long vowel sound, retains its long sound. The *d* is pronounced as /t/ after the voiceless consonants *c, ch, f* (puffed), *h, k* (peeked), *p* (dipped), *s, sh* (wished), and *th*, but not after *t*. The past participle of *dream, learn,* and *spell* may be pronounced with a /t/ or a /d/ sound.

The following lists of words exemplify the rule:

1. The e in *ed* is silent except after *d* and *t:*

batted	lasted
cheated	nodded
dusted	skidded
folded	started

2. The *d* is pronounced as /t/ after soft *c, ch, f, h, k, p, s, sh,* and *th.*

clapped	dressed
helped	kissed
asked	slashed
baked	laughed
huffed	ached
puffed	touched

Contractions

In sounding contractions the student should learn to focus first on the root word and then blend the sound or sounds of the other letters into this word. The apostrophe is used to denote contractions: *don't* (do not), *let's* (let us), *hasn't* (has not), *didn't* (did not), *can't* (cannot), *I'm* (I am), *I'll* (I will), *I've* (I have), *haven't* (have not), *hadn't* (had not), *isn't* (is not), *wasn't* (was not), *he's* (he is), *he'll* (he will), *she's* (she is), *she'll* (she will), *you're* (you are), *you'll* (you will), *we're* (we are), *we'll* (we will), *they're* (they are), and *they'll* (they will).

The apostrophe indicates that one or more letters have been omitted.

SYLLABICATION

Up to this point we have not emphasized the principles that govern accentuation and syllabication. Glass (8) questions the value of syllabication. He notes that usually the syllabication is done after the sounds in words become known. No one in his study seemed to use syllabication rules to discover the sounds in words; rather, the sounds were used to determine syllable division. Glass adds that word analysis is not needed once the sound of the word is known and asks: "Why syllabicate?" Schell (16) raises the same question. Glass concludes that he can discover no reason why syllabication activities should be included in a word analysis program. Not all specialists agree with these observations. There is the additional confusion in that lexicographers divide words by structure and linguists divided them by pronunciation.

At any rate, the good reader knows how to divide words accurately and rapidly. This does not mean that he divides every word that he comes to in his reading or that he knows the rule for dividing it. The former would slow down his reading and might even interfere with good comprehension. The latter is not necessary for good reading.

The first principle to be learned is that every syllable contains a sounded vowel. At times, a vowel itself constitutes a syllable: a-corn, I, vi-o-let, lin-e-ar, lin-e-al, cer-e-al, o-pen, i-de-a. A *syllable* is thus defined as a unit of pronunciation consisting of a vowel sound alone or with one or more consonant sounds and pronounced with one impulse. It may also be defined as the part of a word that contains a vowel and receives some stress. Phonetically, it is a speech segment having a single vocal impulse.

The student must also learn that a syllable may contain more than one vowel letter. The number of syllables a word has is dependent upon the number of vowels heard, not on the number of vowel letters seen.

The spoken syllable does not always correspond exactly to the written or printed syllable. It is often difficult to determine in speech where one syllable ends and another begins. Furthermore, printing conventions for the division of words at the end of a line have not always followed the pattern of speech syllables. Speech syllables and printed syllables, however, do correspond with enough regularity so that the printed syllable can be used in dividing words into parts which in turn can be readily analyzed and blended to pronounce words. Thus, a *syllable* will be considered as the sequence of letters more or less approximating the syllable of speech. It may be a whole word or a part of a word.

A word of one syllable is called a *monosyllable,* and a word of two or more syllables is called a *plurisyllable.* A word having more than three syllables may be referred to as a *polysyllable.*

Syllables are of two kinds: *closed* syllables and *open* syllables. A closed syllable is one that ends with a consonant: *cat,* ba*sis,* and magne*tic.* The vowel in a closed syllable usually represents a short vowel sound.

An open syllable is one that ends in a vowel: *cry, by.* The vowel in an open syllable is usually a long vowel. At one time, the *y* at the end of a word was often pronounced as a short *i;* today, it is a long *e.* Below is a list of words with the *y* pronounced as long *e.*

ably	cocky	grisly	kingly	pigmy	sloppy
army	copy	grumpy	kinky	pity	smelly
baby	crabby	gusty	kitty	plenty	snappy
badly	cranky	handy	lackey	poppy	soggy
baldy	dimly	happy	lady	pussy	sorry
barley	drafty	hardy	lanky	putty	spotty
belfry	empty	hasty	lassie	rally	study
belly	entry	hefty	lately	Randy	stiffly
berry	flaky	Henry	lily	ruddy	sultry
body	foggy	hobby	madly	rummy	sunny
brandy	folly	holy	manly	rusty	taffy
buddy	fifty	homely	marry	sadly	tally
buggy	filly	humbly	muddy	Sally	tinny
bumpy	funny	hungry	nasty	scabby	tippy
bunny	froggy	jelly	nifty	scanty	tipsy
busy	gladly	jiffy	nippy	Scotty	Tommy
cabby	glory	jolly	pantry	sentry	twenty
candy	grassy	jumpy	pappy	silly	ugly
carry	gravy	Kenny	parley	simply	wiggly
clammy	greasy	kidney	party	singly	windy
classy	greedy	kindly	penny	sissy	
clumsy	grimy				

Rule I

When two consonant letters follow a vowel letter, as in after, kitten, pencil, summer, *and* butter, *the word is divided between the two consonants, and the first syllable ends with the first consonant.* In instances of this kind the second consonant is silent when the consonants are the same except in compounds: *bookkeeper*. Since the first vowel is followed by a consonant, it usually is given its short sound.

The student must be shown that not all double consonant letters can be divided. Consonant blends and speech consonants fall into this category (gam-bler, mi-grate).

Rule II

When only one consonant letter or a digraph follows a vowel letter, as in paper, bacon, prefer, begun, *and* reshape, *the word is usually divided after the first vowel letter, and the consonant or consonant digraph begins the second syllable.* The first vowel letter, in that it ends a syllable, is usually given its long sound (si-lent, no-mad, ba-sin, da-tum, mi-nus, to-tal, ha-zel, si-nus, fa-tal, ca-det, ce-ment).

Exceptions and Observations

One: Not all words follow the rule. For example, *planet, solid, robin, travel, study, record,* river, primer,* cabin, tropic, power, present,* timid, habit, pity, body, quiver, copy, lily, bigot, calico, atom, honor, venom, olive, legend, lemon, valid, limit, dragon, wagon, digit, solid cherish, volume, lizard, snivel, cherub*, and *profit* join the consonant to the first vowel. This makes the first vowel short and the accent is on the first syllable.

Two: The suffix *ed* is a syllable only when it follows the sound *d* or *t*: *bunted*.

Three: Whenever two or more consonant letters appear between two vowel letters, the student must learn to look for consonant blends or speech consonants. These are never divided: *gam-bler, mi-grate*.

Four: Whenever *le* ends a word and is preceded by a consonant, the last syllable consists of the consonant and the *le*. We divide thus: *ta-ble, mid-dle, peo-ple*. When *le* is preceded by *ck, le* is a separate syllable: *freck-le, buck-le*. The *e* in *ble, tle, ple*, and *dle* is silent. Some authors, however, suggest that *le* says /el/ with *e* being shorter than usual and called *schwa*.

Observe that in *tle* the *t* sometimes is silent and at times may be pronounced. Thus, in *battle, bottle, brittle, mantle, cattle, little, rattle*, and *tattle* the *t* is pronounced; in *castle, hustle, jostle*, and *rustle* (words in which the *tle* follows the letter *s*), it is silent.

---

* These may be divided according to both rules, dependent upon their meaning in the sentence.

able	cradle	kettle	raffle	scuttle
ankle	dazzle	kindle	ramble	stable
apple	dimple	little	rattle	steeple
babble	double	mantle	riddle	struggle
battle	fable	maple	rifle	table
beetle	fondle	marble	ripple	tackle
Bible	fumble	mangle*	rubble	tangle*
bicycle	gable	meddle	ruffle	tattle
bobble	gamble	middle	rustle	temple
bottle	gargle	mingle*	saddle	tickle
brittle	gentle	muddle	sample	tingle *
bubble	giggle	muffle	scuffle	title
buckle	grumble	mumble	simple	trample
bugle	haggle	muscle	single*	trifle
bundle	handle	nimble	sizzle	triple
bungle*	humble	nibble	smuggle	treble
cable	hustle	nipple	sniffle	tremble
cackle	jiggle	paddle	snuggle	tumble
candle	jingle*	pebble	spangle*	turtle
castle	little	pickle	sparkle	twinkle
cattle	jostle	pimple	swindle	uncle
circle	juggle	puddle	stubble	waggle
coddle	jumble	purple	supple	wiggle
crackle	jungle*	puzzle	scuffle	wriggle
		rabble		

* When *gle* is preceded by *n*, it is pronounced as /gg'l/.

Five: Sometimes it is necessary to divide between two vowels: cre-ate. Common words in which this occurs are the following:

ai—archaic, laity, mosaic

ea—cereal, create, delineate, fealty, ideal, laureate, lineate, linear, permeate

ei—being, deity, reinforce, reinstate, spontaneity

eu—museum, nucleus

ie—client, diet, dietary, expedient, orient, piety, propriety, quiet, science

oa—coadjutor, coagulate, oasis

oe—coefficient, coerce, coexist, poem

oi—egoist, going

oo—cooperate, coordinate, zoology

ue—cruel, duel, duet, fluent, fuel, gruel, influence, minuet

ui—altruism, ambiguity, annuity, fluid, fruition

Six: In a compound word the division comes between the two words making up the compound: post-man.

Seven: Prefixes and suffixes are usually set apart from the rest of the word: in-sist, go-ing.

Here are exercises useful in teaching word division.

1. Have students read and listen to words and indicate the number of vowels actually heard.

mercury	3	inaccurately	_____
wherewithal	_____	bridge	_____
tuberculosis	_____	humiliate	_____
calculate	_____	thoroughbred	_____
accumulation	_____	arguments	_____

2. Have students divide words of more than one syllable.

witness	wit-ness	allegiance	_____
idea	_____	lonely	_____
pebble	_____	stomach	_____
minstrel	_____	squirrel	_____
completion	_____	camera	_____

3. Have students divide words and then identify the rule that covers the division.

Exercises should enhance the relationship between syllable division and the sound of the vowel. Thus, the student should learn to deal with the short vowel sound in words of more than one syllable where the syllable ends in a consonant: *cos-mic, mas-cot, gym-nas-tic, in-hab-it;* and he needs to be able to deal with the situation where a consonant does not end the syllable: *spi-der, mu-sic, mo-ment, cre-a-tion.*

ACCENTUATION

A word of two or more syllables is generally pronounced with more stress on one syllable. This is termed *accent*. In dictionaries the accent mark (') is placed just after the syllable that receives major stress. In words of three or more syllables there may be a secondary accent, such as in lo'-co-mo'-tive.

The teaching of accentuation is usually put off until the student is well advanced in phonic analysis and word analysis. After the student has learned the meaning of accent and the way the dictionary identifies the accent or stress point, he may gradually be introduced to the following rules:

1. Generally, words of two syllables in which two consonants follow the first vowel accent the first syllable: *after, kitten, puppet, butter.*

2. When a two-syllable word contains two vowels in the second syllable but only one is pronounced, the second syllable is generally accented: *abide, abode, above, about, aboard, delay, proceed.* Usually, the last syllable contains a long vowel sound.

3. Compound words usually carry the primary accent on (or within) the first word: *bellhop, bulldog, carhop, dishpan, godson, humbug, pigpen.* There are many exceptions to this rule: *forbid.*

4. Syllables beginning with a consonant followed by *le* (circle, rabble) are not accented.

5. In three-syllable words in which the suffix is preceded by a single consonant, as in *adviser, exciting, translated,* and *refusal* or in *piloted, traveled,* and *shivered,* the accent may be on the first or the second syllable. It is on the first syllable except when the root word (advise, excite, translate, and refuse) ends in e and the last syllable is accented.

6. In general, the accent is placed on alternate syllables (dis'-ap-point'-ment). Frequently, the accented syllable is followed by two unaccented syllables (san'-i-ty). At times the accent is on alternate syllables and the last two syllables are unaccented (op'-por-tun'-i-ty).

7. Root words when preceded by prefixes or followed by suffixes are usually accented (amuse, amusement).

8. Words ending in *ion, ity, ic, ical, ian, ial,* or *ious* have the accent immediately before these suffixes (consternation, immersion, humidity, athletic, psychological, historian, industrial, harmonious).

9. Words of three or more syllables ending in a silent e usually accent the third syllable from the end of the word (graduate, accommodate, anticipate.

10. Homographs, or words with identical spellings, receive their accent from the context in which they are used (con'-tract—contract', con'-test—contest'; so also object, present, convict, separate, subject, insult, conflict, rebel, record, affix, convert, survey, project, progress, import, combine, confine, protest, impress, reject, extract, conduct, export, produce, rebel, discard, desert, proceed, insult).

In introducing the student to accent and syllabication, the teacher needs to use words that the student knows. Repeated exercise with actual words will help the student to obtain a *functional* knowledge of the generalizations stated above.

Initially the teacher may pronounce a word and may let the pupils indicate by one or two fingers whether the word has one or two syllables or whether the accent falls on the first or the second syllable. Gradually, the student should learn to write a word, divide it, and indicate its accent, and at the upper grade levels he may give the rules that govern its syllabication and accentuation.

SILENT LETTERS

Some time in his reading education the student should learn that certain consonants are not pronounced. When this situation prevails, the word frequently needs to be taught as a sight word. There are, however, some observations that apply consistently. For example, when a consonant is doubled, the first often is silent: *hitting.* The following are other examples in which a consonant is silent:

Silent *b* after *m*:	bomb, bomber, bombproof, bombshell, climb, comb, crumb, dumb, lamb, limb, numb, plumber, plumbing, succumb, thumb, tomb, womb, jamb
Silent *b* before all consonants except *l* and *r*:	bdellium, debt, debtor, doubtful, subtle
Silent *c*:	czar, indict, victuals; and in combinations with *ck* (back)
Silent *ch*:	drachm, fuchsia, schism, yacht
Silent *c* after *s*:	ascend, ascent, descend, descent, scene, scenic, scent, scepter, muscle, science, scissor, transcend
Silent *d*:	adjunct, adjust, handkerchief, handsome, Wednesday
Silent *d* before *g*:	badger, dodger, edge, fudge, bridge
Silent *g* before *n*:	align, arraign, benign, campaign, design, ensign, feign, foreign, malign, assign, gnarl, gnash, gnat, gnaw, gnome, gnu, reign, resign, sign, signer, signpost, diaphragm
Silent *gh*:	eight, freight, neigh, neighbor, sleigh, straight, straighten, weigh, weight
Silent *h*:	aghast, ah, diarrhea, Durham, exhaust, exhibit, forehead, ghastly, gherkin, ghetto, ghost, ghoul, ghoulish, heir, hemorrhage, honest, honestly, honor, hour, hourly, myrrh, oh, rhapsody, rheostat, rhesus, rhetoric, rheumatism, rheumatic, rhinestone, rhinoceros, rhubarb, rhumb, rhyme, rhythm, rhythmic, shepherd, Thomas, Thomism, Thompson, vehement, vehicle
Silent *k* before *n*:	knack, knap, knapsack, knave, knead, knee, kneel, knell, knelt, knew, knickers, knife, knight, knit, knob, knock, knoll, knot, know, knowledge, knuckle, knurl

Silent *l:* almond, alms, balk, balmy, behalf, calf, calk, calm, chalk, em-balm, folk, folklore, half, jaywalk, kinsfolk, palm, polka, psalm, salmon, solder, talk, walk, would, yolk, stalk

Silent *n* after *m:* autumn, column, condemn, damn, damned, hymn, solemn, solemnly

Silent *p:* corps, cupboard, pneumatic, pneumonia, psalm, psalmist, psalter, pseudo, pseudonym, psychiatry, psyche, psychic, psychoanalysis, psychology, psychopath, raspberry, receipt, ptomaine, ptero-dactyl

Silent *s:* aisle, fuchsia, Arkansas, bas-relief, Carlisle, chamois, corps, debris, Illinois, island, isle, Louisville, rendezvous, St. Louis, viscount

Silent *t:* bustle, castle, chasten, chestnut, Christmas, fasten, glisten, christen, bristle, hasten, hautboy, hustle, jostle, listen, Matthew, mortgage, mustn't, nestle, often, rustle, depot, mistletoe, soften, thistle, whistle, trestle, moisten

Silent *th:* asthma

Silent *w:* awry, answer, boatswain, bowler, enwrap, own, owner, play-wright, rewrite, sword, swordfish, swordsman, toward, two, who, whole, wholeness, wholesale, wholesome, wholly, whom, whose, wrack, wraith, wrangle, wrangler, wrap, wrapper, wrath, wreak wreath, wreck, wreckage, wren, wrench, wrest, wrestle, wrestling, wretch, wretched, wriggle, wring, wrinkle, wrist, wristband, writ, write, writer, writing, writhe, wrong, wrongly, wrote, wroth, wrought, wrung, wry, and in the ending *ow* as in snow

MULTISYLLABIC WORDS

Multisyllabic words introduce numerous problems not usually met in mono-syllabic words. For example, in monosyllabic words one expects a long middle vowel sound when the word ends in a silent *e*: *dame, dine, plume.* This rule does not apply in some multisyllabic words. For example:

ace = /əs/ solace, furnace, Horace, menace, palace, preface, surface

age = /ij/ adage, baggage, bandage, bondage, breakage, cabbage, carnage, carriage, cleavage, coinage, cottage, courage, damage, dosage, drainage, forage, garbage, homage, hostage, image, language, leak-age, luggage, manage, marriage, message, mileage, mortgage, orphanage, package, passage, pillage, postage, pottage, roughage, rummage, salvage, sausage, savage, scrimmage, sewage, seepage, soilage, soakage, spoilage, village, vintage, voltage, voyage, wast-age, wattage, wreckage, yardage

ege = /ēg/ renege

ege = /ej/ college

ege = /ij/ privilege

ige = /ēzh/ prestige

ase = /əs/ purchase

ate = /ət/ chocolate, climate, deliberate, delicate, delegate, desolate, duplicate, frigate, palate, prelate, private, senate, separate, temperate

ice = /əs/ chalice, complice, crevice, justice, malice, notice, novice, office, practice, service

ice = /ēs/ caprice, police

ile = /il/ agile, docile, fertile, fragile, futile, hostile, missile, mobile, reptile, servile, sterile, tractile, virile*

ile = /ēl/ automobile, castile

ine = /in/ doctrine, engine, ermine, famine, genuine, urine; but also long *i* as in divine, turpentine

ine = /ēn/ machine, marine, morphine, ravine, routine, sardine, vaccine, vaseline

ise = /əs/ premise, promise, treatise

ise = /ēs/ valise

ite = /ət/ respite

ive = /iv/ active, captive, festive, massive, motive, passive, tractive

ive = /ēv/ naive

uce = /əs/ lettuce

The following are examples of other problems in reading multi-syllabic words:

ain = /ən/   bargain, Britain, captain, certain, chaplain, chieftain, curtain, fountain, mountain, villain

ay = /ē/   always, Monday, yesterday

ia = /i/   marriage, parliament

ience = /shens/   patience

ce, ci, si, ti, as /sh/   ocean; electrician, musician, physician, politician, social, racial, facial, glacial, official, special; ancient, sufficient, efficient; precious, spacious, delicious, conscious, ferocious, cautious, gracious, spacious, vicious; mission, cession, decision, fusion, lesion, occasion, passion, pension, tension, torsion, version; action, attention, auction, caption, caution, definition, diction, edition, faction, fraction, friction, function, junction, ignition, lotion, mention, motion, nation, notion, option, portion, potion,

---

* The chief exception is *gentile;* also note *exile, crocodile, reconcile, juvenile, infantile; mercantile* and *versatile* have both pronunciations.

	sanction, section, station, traction, unction; partial, martial, nuptial, confidential, reesidential, potential; tertian; patient, patience, quotient, transient; ambitious; militia
s = /sh/	mansion, nauseous, issue, tissue
s = /zh/	vision, visual, usury, fusion
sure = /chər; shər; zhər/	censure, measure, pleasure, pressure, treasure, tonsure
du + r = /jər/	procedure, verdure*
tu + r = /chər/	capture, creature, culture, departure, feature, fracture, furniture, future, fixture, gesture, lecture, mixture, nature, pasture, picture, puncture, stature, suture, tincture, texture, torture, venture, vulture; nature is an exception
tu + any other letter = /chə/	actual, mutual, virtue, virtuous
zure = /zhər/	seizure

COMMON SIGHT WORDS

The following list contains words that should be taught as sight words:

above	bury	dove	has	Mr.
again	busy	dozen	have	Mrs.
against	business	eight	heart	none
aisle	buy	enough	hearth	of
already	canoe	eye	his	off
always	choir	father	hour	often
another	come	flood	into	once
answer	coming	four	is	one
anxious	cough	friend	isle	only
any	could	from	knew	own
are	country	front	laugh	other
as	cousin	full	leopard	people
aunt	cover	get	live	pretty
been	do	girl	lived	pull
blood	dog	give	log	push
both	does	glove	love	put
break	done	goes	many	rough
build	don't	gone	mother	said
bull	double	half	move	says

* Common exceptions are *endure* and *mature*.

sew	swat	touch	war	wind
shoe	talk	tough	was	wolf
some	the	tour	wash	women
someone	there	toward	wasp	won
something	thought	trouble	were	won't
sometime	to	two	what	would
son	today	very	where	write
steak	together	walk	who	you
sugar	ton	wand	whom	young
sure	too	want	whose	your
swap				

SUMMARY

It is impossible to suggest at what time students should have mastered the skills taught in this chapter or indeed whether they ever need to master all of them. Teaching must be adjusted to individual needs.

The student needs to learn the phoneme-grapheme system by induction rather than by deduction. Rules should grow out of the situations that the student deals with. Finally, isolated words should always be brought back into the larger patterns and structures that function linguistically and that carry meaning.

In summary:

1. Students should learn from the beginning to associate letter and sound patterns so as to bring about as rapidly as possible an automatic association between them. The relationship emphasized by the linguistic approach is not letter to sound, but rather letter patterns to sound patterns. The first task is to break the alphabet code. The student should learn the letters-to-sound correspondence by actual practice but also use principles that describe or explain the associations.

2. Teaching of reading should separate the study of word form from the study of word meaning.

3. Teaching of reading should emphasize from the start both analysis and synthesis, thus giving greater consideration to individual differences in learning.

4. The student should be taught from the beginning that nearly every generalization has exceptions and that if the word does not make sense in the sentence, he should try another approach. We need to teach him *flexibility*.

QUESTIONS FOR DISCUSSION

1. Discuss two parallel programs for teaching consonant blends and speech consonants.
2. Discuss the principles of variability, position, silentness, and context, and give ways for teaching them at the junior high level.
3. Illustrate the difference between the voiceless *th* and the voiced *th* by describing the mouth geography of each.
4. Develop a sequential program for teaching the *ar, er ir, or,* and *ur* combinations in monosyllabic words.
5. Is there a recommended way for teaching the student to substitute a consonant blend for a single consonant at the beginning of a word? Discuss the various techniques.

BIBLIOGRAPHY

1. BAGFORD, JACK, *Phonics: Its Role in Teaching Reading,* pp. 47–58. Iowa City: Sernoll, Inc., 1967.
2. BANNATYNE, ALEX, "Diagnostic and Remedial Techniques for Use with Dyslexic Children," *Academic Therapy Quarterly,* 3 (Summer 1968), 213–24.
3. BETTS, EMMETT ALBERT, "Issues in Teaching Reading," *Controversial Issues in Reading,* pp. 33–41. Tenth Annual Reading Conference, Lehigh University, April 1961.
4. BURMEISTER, LOU E., "Usefulness of Phonic Generalizations," *The Reading Teacher,* 21 (January 1968), 349–60.
5. BURMEISTER, LOU E., "Vowel Pairs," *The Reading Teacher,* 5 (February 1968), 445–52.
6. DUNN, JAMES, "A Study of the Techniques of Word Identification." Unpublished doctoral dissertation, Brigham Young University, 1970.
7. EMANS, ROBERT, "When Two Vowels Go Walking and Other Such Things," *The Reading Teacher,* 21 (December 1967), 262–69.
8. GLASS, GERALD G., "The Strange World of Syllabication," *The Elementary School Journal* (May 1967), 403–5.
9. HARRIS, ALBERT J., *How to Increase Reading Ability.* New York: David McKay Co., Inc., 1956.
10. HILDRETH, GERTRUDE, *Teaching Reading.* New York: Holt, Rinehart & Winston, Inc., 1958.
11. JOOS, LOYAL W., "Linguistics for the Dyslexic," in *The Disabled Reader,* ed. John Money, pp. 83–92. Baltimore: Johns Hopkins Press, 1966.

12. LEARY, BERNICE E., "Developing Word Perception Skills in Middle and Upper Grades," *Current Problems in Reading Instruction.* Pittsburgh: University of Pittsburgh Press, 1950.

13. NEWBURG, JUDSON E., *Linguistics and the School Curriculum.* Chicago: Science Research Associates, Inc., 1969.

14. OLSON, ARTHUR V., "Applying Research on Word Analysis Skills to Classroom Instruction in Intermediate Grades," *Reading Methods and Teacher Improvement,* pp. 20–26. International Reading Association, Newark, N.J., 1971.

15. SABAROFF, ROSE, "Breaking the Code: What Method? Introducing an Integrated Linguistic Approach to Beginning Reading," *The Elementary School Journal,* 67 (November 1966), 95–102.

16. SCHELL, LEO M., "Teaching Structural Analysis," *The Reading Teacher,* 21 (November 1967), 133–37.

17. SHORE, ROBERT EUGENE, "Programmed Approach vs. Conventional Approach Using a Highly Consistent Sound-Symbol System of Reading," *Reading Methods and Teacher Improvement,* pp. 104–11. International Reading Association, Newark, N.J., 1971.

Developing a
Meaningful
Vocabulary
CHAPTER 7

A READING PROGRAM MUST MAKE PROVISION for the development of meaning by the student. A prime requisite for reading is the association of meaning with a given symbol. Unless the student can associate meaning with a symbol, he has not learned to read. Understanding must escape him, and reading without understanding is verbalism.

The student must also interpret meaning in its broader contextual sense. The word has meaning as part of a sentence, the sentence as part of a paragraph, and the paragraph as part of a story. We will discuss this phase in Chapter 8. In this chapter we will concern ourselves with the association of meaning with the individual symbol. Association of meaning with a symbol cannot occur unless the person has had some experience, whether real or vicarious, with that something represented by the symbol. The word *thermostat,* for example, has no meaning to the student who has never had either a first-hand or a vicarious experience with a thermostat.

Few students have had sufficient experience to appreciate all the connotations of a word. Even if students do have a broader understanding of a word, they are usually content to settle for the first meaning that comes to mind. Poor readers especially tend to accept the first meaning that pops into their heads.

Many students have not learned that words can have more than one meaning. For example, the word *run* can mean to move swiftly; to go back and forth (the boat runs between Georgia and New York); to run in an election; to win a race (the horse ran first); to run into debt; to run (trace) a story back to its source; to run (smuggle) contraband; and to run a store. These are only a few examples. In addition, we speak of a

205

run of fish, a run of bad trouble, a run on the bank, a running brook, the ordinary run of people, and a cattle run.

Multiple meanings and pronunciations are not the only ambiguities of language that hinder communication and that make the apprehension of meaning difficult. Two words may have the same meaning; two words, although pronounced alike, may have different spellings and meanings; and words may have generic or specific meanings. Numerous idiomatic expressions also add to the reader's predicament.

Growth in meaning and vocabulary has many levels. The student must develop precision in meaning; he must become acquainted with multiple meanings; he must learn specific and generic meanings; he must interpret idiomatic expressions; and for successful speech and writing he must be able to call to mind the word needed and then apply it correctly.

The grasping of meaning is obviously important for learning. Educational psychologists have found that students prefer to deal with materials that have meaning. They apply data that bear meaning more easily, and they remember these data for longer periods of time.

TECHNIQUES FOR TEACHING MEANING

Before discussing the techniques for teaching meaning, let us examine a few principles that should guide the teacher in the development of meaning. The following seem especially pertinent:

1. Each new level of meaning requires a corresponding broadening of experience with objective reality.
2. The quality of meaning is greatly influenced by the quantity and quality of previously acquired meanings and concepts. Thus the teacher must build upon the student's previous background of experience.

The teacher's major task in the development of meaning is to select the materials and experiences that will help the student to become more discriminative and learn to generalize. Unfortunately, there is no clear-cut evidence that suggests what materials to use in the teaching of specific concepts. This leaves much to guesswork and taxes the teacher's ingenuity.

The major question then is this: How can the teacher help the student to develop meaning? Generally, the approaches to the teaching of meaning are twofold: (1) the direct experience approach, such as through visiting a farm or acting out an activity, or (2) the vicarious experience approach, such as through looking at pictures, storytelling, or reading explanatory material. The vicarious experience approach in the classroom comes to mean (*a*) direct vocabulary instructions, (*b*) incidental instruction of vocabulary, and (*c*) wide or extensive reading.

The following techniques are frequently used in developing vocabulary skills during the elementary years:

1. Offering direct experience with the concrete object
2. Labeling
3. Learning to read pictures
4. Conversing and storytelling
5. Participating in description, riddle, rhyme, and puzzle games
6. Making use of audiovisual aids
7. Making use of dramatization, marionette and puppet shows, pageants, and operettas
8. Constructing and using picture dictionaries
9. Giving both oral and written directions
10. Fitting objects and words into categories

Each of these techniques can be applied on upper-grade levels. For example, "learning to read pictures" may be "interpreting charts, graphs, and maps" on the fourth- and fifth-grade level. "Labeling" may consist of labeling instruments in a science laboratory.

The following exercise (3) in categorizing can be used on the high school level:

Place each word under the category to which it belongs:

amino acid	ribonucleic acid	DNA
cell chemistry	ionic compound	sucrose
biochemistry	dehydration synthesis	starch
cellulose	molecular compound	carbon
hydrolysis	organic compound	urea
glycerol	glucose	ATP

Carbohydrate	*Fat or Oil*	*Nucleic Acid*
———————	———————	———————
———————	———————	———————
———————	———————	———————
———————	———————	———————
———————	———————	———————
———————	———————	———————

Studies (15, 17) tend to indicate that vocabulary study is beneficial but that students of average or above-average ability profit more than those of below-average ability. Students also tend to learn words better if they have an immediate need to use them. A combination of methods in teaching seems to be better than the use of any one method alone. Some common methods on the high school level include dictionary work, word study in context, use of context clues, attention to multiple meanings and figurative language, study of the history and etymology of words, application of new words in oral and written language, and wide reading.

Let us now look at some of these more advanced meaning skills. Perhaps the first of these is the need for increased competency in the use of the context to arrive at the appropriate meaning.

Study and Analysis of the Context

The pupil's first reading experiences encourage him to use the verbal context in which the word occurs to decipher the meaning of the sentence. Reading teachers have always suggested that the pupil should look at the word, that he should not guess, and that he should see whether the word makes sense in the sentence. The teacher on the high school level should encourage the pupil to *anticipate* and to *predict* meaning. The student needs to think along with the author. If students learn to anticipate probable meaning, they have also learned a most useful means of word identification.

Deighton (4, pp. 2–3) identifies four general principles of context operation: (1) Context reveals the meaning of unfamiliar words only infrequently; (2) context generally reveals only one of the meanings of an unfamiliar word; (3) context seldom clarifies the whole of any meaning; and (4) vocabulary growth through context revelation is a gradual matter. Deighton goes on to note that what the context reveals to a given reader will depend on the reader's previous experiences.

Despite these limitations, the testimonials to the importance of context clues are many. Context is considered one of the most important aids to word identification and to interpretation. Emans (7) notes that context clues help students to (1) identify words they previously identified but forgot, (2) check the accuracy of words tentatively identified by the use of other clues, (3) gain rapid recognition of words by permitting them to anticipate what a word might be, and (4) identify words that are not identifiable in any other way.

Skill in using the context needs constant refinement, and indeed it becomes increasingly more valuable as the student advances through school. Some students, however, rely too much on the context. Their reading makes sense, but sometimes it is not the meaning intended by the writer. Their counterparts are those readers who are so preoccupied with details that they read a word into the sentence that makes little or no sense.

Artley (2), McCullough (12), Deighton (4), Ames (1), and Emans (7) have identified various types of contextual aids or context clues useful in interpreting what one is reading:

1. Typographical aids, such as quotation marks, italics, boldface type, parentheses, and footnotes or glossary references

2. Structural aids, such as appositive phrases or clauses, nonrestrictive phrases or clauses, or interpolated phrases or clauses, indications of comparison and contrast

3. Verbal context or substitute words, such as linked synonyms or antonyms, summarizing words, definitions, examples, modifiers, restatements, description, direct explanation

4. Word elements, such as roots, prefixes, and suffixes

5. Figures of speech, such as simile or metaphor

6. Pictorial representations or illustrations; that is, accompanying pictures, diagrams, charts, graphs, and maps

7. Inference, such as where cause-effect relationships lead the reader to a new meaning

8. Background of experience, where preexisting knowledge sheds direct light upon a new word or expression

9. Subjective clues, such as tone, mood, setting, and intent

10. Presentation clues, such as the position of words, the sequence of a sentence or paragraph, the general organization of a selection, or clues derived from a pattern of paragraph organization involving a main idea and supporting details

Dulin (5), in a study using 315 tenth graders, found that the clues that made the acquisition of meaning the easiest were ranked as follows: language experience, cause-effect relationships, contrast, direct description, and linked synonyms and/or appositives. Contrast functioned better with nouns, and direct description functioned better with adjectives. Verb meanings were more easily generated by cause-effect relationships, language experience, and contrast; adverb meanings were more easily generated by language-experience and cause-effect relationships.

In summary, the student gradually needs to expand both the number and the quality of the meanings that he attaches to a single word. Many words, even in the "simplest" of books, have more than one meaning. Frequently, only by understanding the verbal context can the student select the meaning intended by the writer.

The sentence context often gives the meaning of a word by either defining the word or giving a synonym for it. For example:

Read the following sentences. Select the proper meaning for the underlined word from those suggested to you.

1. The seats upon which we were to sit were *littered* with paper and other trash. In fact, they were absolutely filthy.
   a. put into disorder
   b. a stretcher for carrying sick people
   c. the young as of a cat—a cat's litter
2. The army generals met in secret to plot a *putsch* against the existing government
   a. plot to overthrow the government
   b. drinking party
3. General Motors has the *lion's* share of the car market.
   a. a large carnivorous cat
   b. a man with great courage
   c. largest or greatest
4. Since the undertow on the lake had possibly led to the drowning of two persons in the last three days, we needed no other *deterrent* to keep the kids from wanting to go swimming.
   a. encouragement
   b. discouragement
   c. detergent

At the junior high and high school levels the student's comprehension of what he reads is also aided significantly by the ability to identify the writer's style. Shaw (16, p. 239) points out that a writer's rhetorical and grammatical contrivances characterize his writing. He notes that much like the ice-cream cone which is both container and confection, the contrivances of the writer both support ideas and are digestible themselves. The writer has so many peculiar characteristics that upon rereading some of his work the reader finds that he has a better conception of what the writer is trying to say. The mood of the writer colors the meaning of what is written and frequently can be identified only by reading between the lines.

The reader operates in the context of a special writer, but to get the most out of what he reads he should also become familiar with the rhetorical devices used in a poem, a play, a short story, an essay, a novel, or a bibliography (16). The title, topical headings, topic sentences, graphs, and summarizing sentences are additional clues to meaning. For example, the title at the head of an article helps the reader anticipate what is to come.

Finally, the structure of the phrase, sentence, and paragraph serves as a clue to the fuller meaning of what is written. Rhetorical terms of coherence such as the correlative conjunctions (both—and, not only—but also, either—or) mark pairing of ideas. Subordinating conjunctions signal cause-effect relationships (because, since, so that), conditions (if, unless, although), contrast (whereas, while), and time relationships (as, before, when, after) (16, p. 243).

These words and phrases have meaning only as parts of sentences or paragraphs. The sentence itself has meaning in the larger context of the paragraph.

In such a sentence as "Ed was talkative when Bill remained taciturn" (11), the sentence structure provides the parallelism and the contrast necessary for understanding the word *taciturn*.

But the reader must also be taught that meaning or context clues are seldom adequate alone because they provide only one aid to word recognition. In some instances context may even lead to confusion or error. In general, the reader should be taught to combine the sense of the sentence with phonic or other word-recognition clues. Deducing an unrecognized word from the context should not be chance guessing; it should be more in the nature of inferential reasoning.

Synonyms and Antonyms

The student reaps much benefit from exercises with the synonyms of words. Initially these exercises are oral. The teacher asks: "What word has the same meaning as *azure?*" An exercise is more effective when the student uses the word in a sentence and then substitutes his own synonym.

Synonyms are actually a part of the context. They are defined as one of two or more words or expressions of the same language that have the same or nearly the same meaning. Thus, a synonym for *azure* may simply be *blue,* more correctly the blue color of a clear sky. A synonym may thus be a simple word, or perhaps a phrase or definition. For example:

1. Mary and Bill are sister and brother. They are *siblings.*
2. A *stalactite,* an iciclelike formation hanging from the roof of a cave, is created when limewater drips from the cave ceiling.
3. The first *cartologist* was making maps long before the discovery of America.
4. When the basement floor became run-down, the remainder of the building *deteriorated* too.
5. A *speleologist* is a scientist who studies and explores caves.

An exercise such as the following teaches students to become synonym conscious.

Below is a list of words. Each of the words is a synonym for one of the words in the boxes. Be sure to use each word.

1. conceal	7. impede	13. prohibit
2. throttle	8. eulogy	14. trivial
3. fret	9. miniature	15. prevent
4. detain	10. deaden	16. stifle
5. diminutive	11. whine	17. bewail
6. laud	12. disguise	18. commend

praise	*hide*
muffle	*hinder*
complain	*small*

Antonyms are words opposite in meaning to certain other words. The student perhaps best learns meanings for some words by contrasting them with their opposites. The teacher may ask the student to select the antonym for a given word from a list of three or four words: *tart*—sweet, sour, sharp, caustic.

An exercise similar to the one above can also be used with antonyms.

Below is a list of words. Each of the words is an antonym for one of the words in the boxes. Be sure to use each word.

1. totter	7. exacting	13. succeed
2. palatable	8. guilty	14. topple
3. extravagant	9. wasteful	15. tasty
4. stern	10. stagger	16. prevail
5. delinquent	11. lavish	17. culpable
6. triumph	12. delectable	18. demanding

lenient	*saving*
fail	*disagreeable*
stand upright	*innocent*

Another exercise requires students to match each word with its antonym.

1.	eminent (f)	a.	indolence
2.	docile (h)	b.	light
3.	indigenous (j)	c.	adroit
4.	alacrity (a)	d.	malignant
5.	awkward (c)	e.	include
6.	benevolent (d)	f.	unknown
7.	frugal (g)	g.	extravagant
8.	different (i)	h.	fractions
9.	dusky (b)	i.	confident
10.	exclude (e)	j.	exotic

Qualifying Words

The meaning of a sentence is sometimes dependent upon key qualifying words. Such words are *all, always, almost, many, more, less, few, only, none, nearly, likely, probably, in all probability, true, false, some, usually, frequently, never, sometimes, little, much, great,* and *small.* The ability to interpret these words is especially helpful in taking objective tests.

Exercises like the following teach students the effect that these words have on the meaning of a sentence.

Have students react to the underlined words.

1. The driver rather than the vehicle is responsible for *most* accidents. (How many is most?)
2. Discretion is the *better* part of valor.
3. It is *probably* true that few students study more than a *couple* of hours each day.
4. We are *almost* certain that the Russians will not launch an attack on their Chinese neighbors.
5. I am *absolutely* certain that the United States will *never* use germ warfare under *any* circumstances.

Overworked Words and Phrases

Overworked words and phrases are those that have lost much of their meaning. Some common words in this category are *divine, grand, great, keen, awful, nice, lovely, perfect, swell, terrible, thing, lot, fit,* and *wonderful.*

Such similes and metaphors as *shaking like a leaf, white as snow, eat like a horse, raining cats and dogs, strength of a giant, heart was broken, money to burn, slow as molasses in January,* or *worked like a beaver* are probably overworked.

The following exercise will help students to become more discriminative in their choice of words.

Substitute a more descriptive word for the underlined word in each sentence, or rewrite the sentence keeping the meaning intended.

1. The party was *divine*.
2. We had a *grand* time.
3. Isn't he *keen*?
4. She looked simply *awful*.

Homonyms

Homonyms are words that sound alike but have different spellings and meanings. They frequently lead to recognition and meaning difficulties. To illustrate their difference, the teacher must use them in various contexts. Thus, the difference between *blue* and *blew* is brought out in the following sentences:

1. The wind blew down the house.

2. Mary wore a blue dress.

Following is a list of some common homoynms:

ail-ale	forth-fourth	pair-pare	steak-stake
ate-eight	foul-fowl	peace-piece	steal-steel
arc-ark	four-for	peek-peak	stile-style
awl-all	gail-gale	peel-peal	straight-strait
bail-bale	groan-grown	peer-pier	sun-son
base-bass	hair-hare	plane-plain	sweet-suite
be-bee	hale-hail	pore-pour	tail-tale
bear-bare	haul-hall	praise-prays	teem-team
beat-beet	heel-heal	principal-principle	their-there
bell-belle	here-hear	rain-rein-reign	through-threw
berth-birth	hew-hue	raise-raze	thrown-throne
blue-blew	horse-hoarse	rap-wrap	tide-tied
bored-board	hour-our	read-red	to-too-two
bow-bough	led-lead	read-reed	toe-tow
break-brake	leek-leak	reel-real	tolled-told
bread-bred	loan-lone	road-rode	vale-veil
buy-by	lye-lie	sail-sale	vane-vein-vain
cell-sell	made-maid	sea-see	wade-weighed
cellar-seller	mail-male	seem-seam	waist-waste
cent-sent-scent	mane-main	seen-scene	wait-weight
course-coarse	mantle-mantel	seer-sear	wave-waive
dear-deer	meet-meat-mete	sew-so-sow	way-weigh
do-dew-due	new-knew	sight-site-cite	week-weak
doe-dough	night-knight	slay-sleigh	whole-hole
fair-fare	no-know	sole-soul	wood-would
feet-feat	one-won	some-sum	wring-ring
fir-fur	or-ore	sore-soar	write-right
flee-flea	owe-oh	staid-stayed	wrote-rote
flew-flue	pain-pane	stare-stair	you-yew-ewe
flower-flour			

Labov (10) notes that dialect can increase the number of homonyms in the spoken language, leading to confusion in interpretation of the written language and the need to put extraordinary reliance on context. The omission of the /r/ in *guard* makes homonyms of *guard* and *god;* omission of the /l/ in *toll* makes homonyms of *toll* and toe. The poor academic performance of black youth can often be traced to such confusions. On the secondary level especially, the teacher needs to give particular attention to word endings and letter sound omissions.

Roots, Prefixes, and Suffixes

Apart from using the context to work out the meaning of unfamiliar words, being able to break a word into its root, prefix, and suffix is another valuable skill in developing meaning for a word.

Word analysis of this type generally results in an assigning of fixed values to each part of a word (prefix, root, suffix) and ends up with a literal meaning for the parts. Unfortunately, even the simplest part of a word (*de*) can have multiple meanings. Sometimes the part has lost all its original meaning, with the meaning somehow absorbed by the word, as in *precept.* The *pre* in *precept* has no meaning. Sometimes what looks like a prefix is not a prefix, as in *pre*carious or *pre*datory. The *pre* does not function as a prefix in these words. Clearly, many parts of words do not have fixed, invariant values, but this should not deter the reader from engaging in structural analysis. It simply means that he should be more cautious in equating the literal meaning with the meaning that operates in a given sentence.

In teaching the student the structural skill here indicated, the teacher must follow definite steps. He must show the student that most two- and three-syllable words are composed of a root, prefix, and/or suffix. He next develops meaning for the words *root, prefix,* and *suffix.*

The root is the main part of a word. It is the reservoir of meaning. The prefix is that something that is put before the main part of a word or at the beginning of a word. The word *prefix* is composed of a root and a prefix. It comes from the Latin root *figere,* meaning "to put or fix," and the Latin prefix *prae* meaning "before or at the beginning of."

The teacher should demonstrate to the student that prefixes change the meaning of a word, much as an adjective changes the meaning of a noun. In the sentence "The test was very difficult," the word *difficult* is an adjective, and it changes the meaning of the word *test.* The test could have been described as *easy.* Prefixes work in a similar way. *Circumnavigate* is composed of the prefix *circum* and the root *navigare. Navigare* is a Latin word meaning "to sail." The prefix *circum* means "around," and the entire word, *circumnavigate,* means "to sail around." The prefix *circum* thus changes the meaning of the root by indicating that in this instance *navigate* is not just sailing but is actually a particular type of sailing.

The suffix is another part of many two- or three-syllable words. It comes at the end of the word. It comes from the Latin word *sub* and *figere,* meaning "to add on." The suffix frequently indicates what part of speech the word is. Thus, *ly* in *badly* is a suffix and usually indicates that the word is an adverb. The *ion* in *condition* is a suffix and usually indicates that the word is a noun. This might be termed the grammatical function of the suffix. The suffix also has a meaning function. The suffix *able* means "capable of," as in the word *durable.* Suffixes also serve as an important structural clue and are therefore helpful in the word-recognition program.

Five combinations of root, prefix, and suffix are immediately indicated:

1. Root by itself as in *stand*
2. Prefix + root as in *prefix*
3. Root + suffix as in *badly*
4. Prefix + root + suffix as in *insisting*
5. Root + root as in *cowboy*

Studies have shown that a few Latin and Greek roots are very helpful in deciphering the meanings of thousands of words. Webster's *New International Dictionary* lists 112 words that begin with the root *anthrop* ("man") (14). Numerous other words have this root in the middle of the word: *philanthrophy, misanthrope.* Approximately twenty prefixes account for something like 85 percent of the prefixes used in words. There also are some key suffixes.

Here is a list of nineteen common Latin root words:

Infinitive	Meaning	Examples
agere, ago, egi, actum	to act, do, arouse, set in motion, drive, transact, sue	agent, act, action, actuality, actual, active, actor
cedere, cedo, cessi, cessum	to give ground, yield	seceded, cede, secession
ducere, duco, duxi, ductum	to lead	duct, conduct, ductile, abduct, seduce, deduce

Infinitive	Meaning	Examples
facere, facio, feci, factum	to do, make	fact, factory, benefit, factor, fashion, factual
ferre, fero, tuli, (tolerabilis tollere, tolerare) latum	to bear, carry	ferry, oblation, tolerate, ferret, tolerant, toleration, transfer
legere, lego, legi, lectum	to choose, collect, gather, read	elect, reelect, select, lector, lecture, legendary
mittere, mitto, misi, missum	to send	emit, mission, remit, submit, admit, missive
movere, moveo, movi, motum	to move, arouse, excite	move, mobility, movable, movement, mover, movie
plicare (complicare), complico, complicovi, complicatum	to fold, confuse	complicate, duplicate, plicate, complication
ponere, pono, posui, positum	to put, place	pose, opposite, post, position
portare, porto, portavi, portatum	to carry	comport, port, export, import, report
regere, rego, rexi, rectum	to rule, guide, direct	direct, regular, rector, rectory, rex
scribere, scribo, scripsi, scriptum	to write	script, transcript, manuscript, inscription
specere, specio, spexi, spectum	to see	specious, specter, spectator, inspect, spy
stare, sto, steti, statum	to stand, remain, endure	statue, insist, stationary, station
tendere, tendo, tentendi, tentum (tensum)	to stretch out, extend, march toward	tend, tendency, tension, tender
tenere, teneo, tenui, tentum	to hold, have	tenuto, tenet, tenor, tenaculum
venire, venio, veni, ventum	to come	event, convene, convention
videre, video, vidi, visum	to see	view, vision, visible, visit

Greek roots are also helpful in arriving at the meanings of words. Here are twenty Greek roots, of which the first two are by far the most common.

Greek Root	Meaning	Examples
graphein—grapho, gegrapha	to write, inscribe	graph, phonograph, monograph, graphic
legein, lego	to tell, to say	legend, legendary
aer	air, atmosphere	aerodonetics, aerate
autos	self	automatic, automobile
bios	life	autobiography, biography, antibiotic, biology
geos	earth, land	geologist, geometry, geography
heteros	other	heterodox, heterogeneity
homoios	like, same	homogeneity, homogeneous, homonym
logos	word, thought, study of	geology, biology
micros	small	microscope, microcosm
monos	alone, only, once, one	monochord, monochrome, monotheism
philos	friend	Philadelphia, philanthropy
phone	sound, tone, voice	telephone, phonic, phonetics, phoneme
physis	nature	physics, physical
polys	many	polygamy, polygamist, polynomial
pseudos	lie, false	pseudonym, pseudo-classic
psyche	breath, life, spirit	psychometry, psychopath
sophos	wise, clever	philosopher, philosophy
tele	far	television, telepathy
telos	end	telephone, telegraph

Less frequently used Latin and Greek roots are the following:

Root	Meaning	Examples
acer	sharp, vehement	acrid, acrimonious
ager	field	agriculture
alter	the other (of two)	altercation
amare	love	amatory, amiable
ambo	both	ambidextrous
amicus	friendly	amicable
annus	year	annual, biennial
anthropos	man	anthropology, philanthropist, misanthrope

Root	Meaning	Examples
aqua	water	aquatic, aqueduct, aquaplane
aster	star	asterisk, astronaut
audire	hear	audible, audiometer, audience, audition
avis	bird	aviary
bellum	war	belligerent, bellicose
biblos	book	Bible
bonus	good	bonanza
centum	hundred	percent, century, centennial
cephalo	of the head	encephalitis
chroma	color	chrome, chromosome
chronos	time	chronological, chronometer
corpus	body	incorporate, corporal, corpse, corporation
cosmos	order, harmony	cosmopolitan
credire	believe	credence, creditable, credit, incredible
cryptein	hide	cryptic, cryptogram
demos	people	demagogue, endemic, democracy
derma	skin	hypodermic, pachyderm
deus	God	deism, deify
dexter	right	dexterity, dexterous
dicere	say	dictum, dictionary, predict
dominus	lord, master	dominate, domineer
domus	house, home	domicile
equus	horse	equestrian, equine
eros	love	erotic
ethnos	notion	ethnic, ethnology
facilis	easy	facility, facilitate
fides	faith, trust	confide, confident
fortis	brave, strong	fortitude, fortify
genus	birth, race, type	genealogy, genetic, gender
geras	old	geriatrics, gerontology
glossa	tongue	glossary, polyglot
gyne	woman	gynecologist
gyros	circle	gyroscope
helios	sun	heliotrope, helium

Root	Meaning	Examples
homo	man	homicide
hydor	water	dehydrate, hydroelectric, hydrophobia
ichthys	fish	ichthyology
ignis	fire	ignite
jacere	throw, hurl	projectile, project
lapis	stone	lapidary
liber	free	liberate, liberty
lingua	tongue	language, bilingual
lithos	stone	lithograph
locus	place	location, local
luna	moon	lunar
lux	light	translucent
magnus	great	magnify
malus	bad, ill	malodorous, malefactor, malice
manus	hand	manuscript, manual, manicure
mater	mother	maternity
mega	great	megaphone, megacycle
metros	measure	metronone, barometer
morphos	shape, structure	morphology, metamorphosis
mors	death	mortal, mortuary
nihil	nothing	annihilate, nihilism
omnis	all	omnivorous, omnibus, omniscient
pan	all	pan-Hellenic, pantheistic
pater	father	paternal, patrimony
pathos	feeling, suffering	sympathy, pathology
pes	foot	pedestrian, biped, tripod, pedal
phobia	fear	hydrophobia
phos	light	phosphorous
soma	body	somatic
tempus	time	temporal
terra	land	terrestrial, territory
thermos	heat	thermometer
tres	three	tricycle, triplet
unus	one	unite
via	road, way	viaduct
vir	man	virile
vocare	call	vocal, vocation

The following prefixes are used rather frequently:

Prefix	Meaning	Examples
ab, a	away from, from	abstract, absent, avert,
ad, a, ap, at, as, acc, app, add, al	to, toward	ascend, advent, allocate
be	by, thoroughly, make	beguile, belittle
com, co, cor, con, col, cum	with, joint, equally	cooperate, communication, coauthor, coextensive
de	from	deduce, depress
dis, di, dif	apart, opposite of	discontent, disentangle, differ, dismiss, dissent, digress
epi	upon	epigram, epidermis, epitaph
ex, e, ef, es	out of	exit, exhale, eject, extract
in, en, im, em	in, into	immigrant, impel
in, ir, il	not	inactive, indomitable
inter, enter, intro	between	interchangeable, interpose, interscholastic
mis	wrong	misconstrue, misspell, mislead
non	not	nonreligious, nonconform, nonpayment
ob, op, of, opp, off	against	obstacle, offend, occasion
pre	before	precede, prefect, prefer
pro	in front of	proceed, pronoun
re	back, again	recede, reanimate
sub, succ, suff, susp, supp	under	subterranean, suffix
trans	across	transgress, transcend
un	not, reverse an act	unjust, unfair, unequal, undress, untie, unlock

Used less frequently are the following:

Prefix	Meaning	Examples
a	on, in, at	abed, ablaze, aboard
ambi	about, around	ambiguous
amphi	both	amphibian
an	not	anarch, amoral
ana	up	anatomy
ante	before	antedate, antecedent

Prefix	Meaning	Examples
anti	against	antislavery, antitoxin, antisocial
apo	away from	apostasy
archi	chief	architect
auto	self	automatic
bene	well	benefactor
bi	apart, two, twice	bicycle, biennial, biweekly
cata	down	catalog
circum	around	circumference, circumnavigate
contra	against	contradict
di	twice	dilemma
dia	through	diagnose, diameter
dys	ill, hard	dysentery
ec	out of	eccentric
en	in, into	enchant
enter	to go into, among	enterprise
equi	equally	equidistant
extra	beyond	extraordinary
for	away, off	forbid
fore	before	forearm, foreground
geo	earth, ground, soil	geography
hemi	half	hemisphere
hyper	over, above	hyperbole, hypertension
hypo	less, under	hypotenuse, hypoactive
inter	among, between	intercede, interstate
intra	within	intramural
meta	between, after	metamorphosis
mono	single, one	monotone
multi	much, many	multiform
off	away, apart	offset
para	alongside of, beyond, against, amiss	paraphrase
per	through, throughout	percolate
peri	around, about	periphery
phono	voice, sound	phonograph
poly	many	polysyllable
post	behind, after	postscript, postpone
pre	before, in front	precede, prediction
preter	past, beyond	preternatural
retro	back, backward	retroactive, retrospect
se	without, aside, apart	seclude, secure

Prefix	Meaning	Examples
semi	half	semicircular
super	above	superstructure
syn	together	synonym, symmetry, synagogue
ultra	beyond	ultramontane
under	beneath, less than	underbid, undervalue, undergo

Exercises

1. Have students underline the prefixes in a list of words, such as *un*willingly, *sub*station, *in*vincible, *com*bining, *dis*respectful.

2. Require the student to work out the meaning of a word when the prefix and its meaning are given:

Prefix	~~Meaning of~~ Prefix	Meaning of ~~Word~~ *Prefix*
transport	trans	across
deduct	de	from, away from
import	im	into
subscript	sub	under
invisible	in	not
inactive	in	not
unable	un	not
adduce	ad	to, toward
compose	com	with
export	ex	out of

3. Require the student to identify the word when the meaning and the prefix are given:

a. To send out of the country (ex)   (export)
b. To send into the country (im)
c. To turn a pupil away from school (ex)

4. Require the student to give a synonym for an underlined prefixed word used in a sentence:

a. We have a <u>semimonthly</u> meeting (*twice a month*).
b. It is questionable that we can <u>disentangle</u> ourselves from the internal strifes of other peoples.
c. Is there really so much virtue in being a <u>nonconformist</u>?
d. The film was clearly <u>overexposed</u>.

5. Require the student to select the word that means the same as the underlined words in a sentence:

   a. The virtuosa announced her encore, but because of the applause her words were _only half heard_.
     (1) audible
     (2) semiaudible
     (3) inaudible
   b. Randy thought of trading in his Fury I on a GTO, but the dealer obviously _put too low a value on_ his car.
     (1) valueless
     (2) undervalued
     (3) invaluable
   c. The teacher was _extremely critical_ of my performance.
     (1) uncritical
     (2) ultracritical
     (3) overcritical

Many suffixes are also helpful in working out the meanings of words. The following are common:

Suffix	Meaning	Examples
able, ible, ble	capable of, worthy	durable, credible, detachable, insoluble
ac, ic	relating to	maniac
aceous	names of orders	herbaceous
acy	quality or state of	piracy, lunacy
age	act or state of	dotage, bondage
al, eal, ial	relating to that which	naval, terminal, regional, judicial, regal
an, ian	relating to, belonging to	urban, Christian, metropolitan
ance, ancy, ence, ency	quality or state of	temperance, violence
and	to be	multiplicand
ant	quality of (adj.)	reliant
	one who (n.)	truant
ar, er, or	related to (adj.)	popular
	one who (n.)	scholar, author
arium	a place for	aquarium
ary	related to (adj.)	planetary
	signifying office	notary
	a place for (n.)	granary

Suffix	Meaning	Examples
at(e)	cause to be (v.)	liberate
	quality of (adj.)	moderate
	office (n.)	pastorate
ation	cause to be, or the act of	creation
ative	tending to, or of the nature of	palliative
cle	diminutive ending	particle
cy	state of (n.)	bankruptcy
	quality of	constancy
	office of	superintendency
	rank of	captaincy
dom	fact of being, state, condition	kingdom, wisdom
ee	recipient of an action	nominee, assignee, employee
eer	one who deals with, is connected with	auctioneer
el	diminutive ending	hovel
en	made of	woolen
en	to make	lengthen, strengthen
en	to make plural	oxen
end	to be	subtrahend
ent	being	adjacent
er	one who, that which	pointer
esce, escent, escence	beginning to be, becoming	adolescent
esque	in the manner or style of	statuesque
ess	feminine ending	actress
est	superlative degree	slowest
et	diminutive ending	cornet
eur	one who	amateur
ful	full of	graceful, blissful, merciful, spoonful
fy	to make	glorify, falsify, classify
ial	pertaining to	official
ic	pertaining to	classic, metallic
	belonging to	Germanic
	connected with	domestic
	of the nature of	philosophic
ical	belonging to	comical
	related to	medical
ice	act, quality, or condition of	service

Suffix	Meaning	Examples
ier	one who	carrier
ile	connected with appropriate to	docile, ductile virile
ine	like, characterized by nature of	marine crystalline
ion	act of, process of, state of	vision, suspension
ish	like	foolish
ism	act or fact of doing or fact of being doctrine or teaching	baptism, barbarism Judaism
ist	one who	communist, violinist
ite	native of	Gothamite
itis	signifying inflam- mation	bronchitis
ity, ty	state of	unity, ability
ive	having the nature or quality of that which	suggestive abusive, destructive
ize	to subject to the action or treatment denoted by the verb to make	modernize memorize
	to treat or combine	oxydize
	to practice	temporize
less	without	motionless
let, et	small	cornet, hamlet
ly	like in appearance characteristic	brotherly, ably, gently slowly, lastly
ment	result of, act of doing state or quality of	astonishment, increment enjoyment
mony	denoting resulting things or conditions	testimony
ness	state, quality of, degree of	preparedness, blindness
oid	like, resembling, having the form of	spheroid
on	ultimately small particles	proton
or	agent or doer state or quality of	editor candor
orium	place for	auditorium
ory	of or belonging to, place of	auditory, laboratory
ose, ous	full of	comatose, piteous

Suffix	Meaning	Examples
ous, ious, eous	full of or abounding in	joyous, courteous
ry	quality, character	foolery
	conduct of, place of	bakery
	art or trade	archery
sis	state or condition of	peristalsis
tion, sion, xion	act, state, result of	contention, condition
tude	quality or degree of	servitude
ty	quality or state of	liberty
ure	act of being	censure
	result of an act	picture
	state	judicature
	body	legislature
ward	toward	southward

Exercises

1. Some suffixes when added to a word form a personal noun and mean "one who." For example, *farmer* refers to one who farms. What noun may be formed from each of the following definitions?

   One who manages . . . . manager One who theorizes . . . .

   One who speaks . . . . One who paints . . . .

   One who exports . . . . One who organizes . . . .

2. Some suffixes when added to a word form an adjective. For example, *teachable* pertains to someone who can be taught. Give the meanings of the following words.

   childish . . . . acting like a child honorary . . . .

   poetic . . . . compulsory . . . .

   illusory . . . . dreamy . . . .

   peerless . . . . spacious . . . .

3. Give the suffix, suffix and word meanings, and part of speech for each of the following words.

	Suffix	Meaning of Suffix	Meaning of Word	Part of Speech
cherubic	ic	pertaining to	pertaining to a cherub	adjective
falsify	fy	to make	to make false	verb
occurrence				
motherhood				
feverish				
usually				
generous				
braggart				

4. Using the list of suffixes and the meanings provided, select the word or words that say the same thing as the italicized words in the sentence.

   a. The dog was *watching carefully* lest the child wander onto the street.
      (1) watchful
      (2) watcher

   b. The Democrats put on an intensive campaign *to make* their candidate *popular* with the people.
      (1) popularity
      (2) popular
      (3) popularize

   c. The man *did not move a muscle*. He waited for the judge's verdict.
      (1) was movable
      (2) was motionless

   d. The water in the lake was *somewhat brown* after the storm.
      (1) brownish
      (2) browner

   e. The United States is constantly forced to *bring* its armed forces *up to modern standards*.
      (1) modern
      (2) modernize

Compound Words

The student must also learn that sometimes root and root are combined to form compound words. Some of these keep the basic meaning of each root; others have a completely new meaning. We discussed the problems and techniques of teaching compounds in Chapter 6.

Figurative and Idiomatic Expressions

We have already indicated that numerous idiomatic expressions also add to the reader's predicament. We speak (6, p. 245) of facing the music, leaving no stone unturned, or breaking the ice with someone. We say that someone's hands are tied or that he is cutting the ground from under someone. We speak of a Jack-of-all-trades, of a devil-may-care attitude, and of someone being penny-wise and pound-foolish. We speak of George Washington as the Father of our country, we are as cozy as a bug in a rug, the wind whistles and the rain patters, and someone jumps up as if he had been shot or runs out the door like a shot. A bill is thrown into the legislative hopper, a candidate sweeps the field, the United States is a melting pot, and someone almost dies laughing (14). Embler (8) lists numerous idiomatic expressions: to be down-and-out, to be looked down upon, to be at the bottom of the heap, high living, ladder to success, social climber, too keyed up, to settle down, down to earth, going to the root of the matter, big wheel, great guy, soft drink, hot-headed, cold-headed, be in hot water, frozen with fear, square meal, dead pan, kiss of death, to be out of line, open minded, and heavy heart. Other examples might include the following: young at heart, don't cry over spilt milk, cost a pretty penny, burn the candle at both ends, blow off steam, birds of a feather flock together, between you and me and the lamppost, to play with fire, rose between two thorns, bed of roses, beat about the bush, get down to brass tacks, have an ax to grind, cast one's bread on the waters, cook someone's goose, talk through one's hat, sit on the fence, put through the mill, something rotten in Denmark, read between the lines, raining cats and dogs, take with a grain of salt, take the bull by the horns, snake in the grass, and smell a rat.

Figurative language differs from the literal or standard construction; figures of speech are the various types of departures from the literal form (see Table 7-1).

The following sentences illustrate the various figures of speech:

1. George Washington was the *Father of our country*. (metaphor)
2. I laughed until I thought *I would die*. (hyperbole)

TABLE 7-1   FIGURES OF SPEECH

Figures of Resemblance	*Figures of Contrast and Satire*	*Others*
Allegory	Antithesis	Hyperbole
Onomatopoeia	Epigram	Euphemism
Personification	Irony	Synecdoche
Metaphor	Apostrophe	
Simile		
Metonomy		

An *allegory* is the prolonged metaphor, e.g., *Pilgrim's Progress*
Onomatopoeia is the use of words whose sounds suggest the meaning.
A *metaphor* is simply an analogy or an expression of comparison: unlike the simile, the metaphor does not use *as* or *like* (You're a clumsy ox).
Personification is the endowment of an inanimate object or abstract idea with personal attributes.
A *simile* compares two objects or actions and usually joins them with *as* or *like*, for example: My car goes like the wind.
Antithesis is the contrasting of ideas.
An *epigram* is a short, terse, satirical, or witty statement.
Metonomy is the use of one word for the other, the first word being suggestive of the other, for example: The woman keeps a good table.
A *hyperbole* is an exaggeration; *euphemism* is the substitution of an inoffensive expression for one that is unpleasant; *apostrophe* is the addressing of the living as dead or the absent as present; and *synecdoche* is the use of the part for the whole.

3. I was just *tickled to death.* (hyperbole)
4. Her face turned *as red as a beet.* (simile)
5. The summer months sure *fly by.* (personification)
6. The squirrel *froze in its tracks.* (metaphor)
7. *Long fingers* of early sunlight came through the trees. (metaphor)
8. I came within sight of *the forks of the road.* (metaphor)
9. *"Zzzingg! Yowww!" howled the saw.* (onomatopoeia and personification)
10. Neighbors from *near and far* gathered there. (antithesis)
11. *Arise dead sons* of the land and sweep the enemy from our shores. (apostrophe)
12. She *gave her hand in marriage.* (synecdoche)
13. The midsummer eve *brought roses in her lap.* (personification)
14. Garden flowers *laughed merrily.* (personification)
15. Leaves drifted down from the large tree *like tiny parachutes.* (simile)
16. We *zipped up* our summer cottage and headed for home. (metaphor—cottage (described as a garment)
17. Lightning flashes were seen in the sky and thunder *applauded* in the distance. (metaphor—thunder described as an audience)
18. *Lend me* your ears. (synecdoche)
19. *I bought two seats* for the play. (metonymy)

You might want to try the following:

1. An icy chill *ran up his spine.*
2. The tightrope walker *held his breath.*
3. She had a *lump in her throat.*
4. His hands were *frozen* on the steering wheel.
5. He is a *pig-headed* fool.
6. His eyes almost *popped out of his head.*
7. Some characters constantly parade around with a *chip on their shoulder.*
8. The old miser had *money to burn.*
9. It was terribly hard for him to *hold his tongue.*
10. With a lot of hard work, Mary and Jim *kept the wolf from their door.*
11. He got the car *for a song.*
12. The comic *brought down the house* with his pointed barbs.
13. The spectators were *yelling their heads off.*
14. Her head was *in the clouds.*

15. She went *into a tailspin.*
16. His *lips were locked.*
17. He *threw in the sponge.*
18. *Weep no more, sad* fountains.
19. The glassy brook *reflects the day.*
20. That *orbèd maiden* with white fire laden, Whom mortals call the Moon, Glides glimmering o'er my fleece-like floor.
21. The road was a *ribbon of moonlight* over the purple moor.
22. The house, *ashamed* of its dilapidation, *was hiding* behind the giant oak.
23. He approached quietly, *moving like a wary cat.*
24. The waves *played tag* with each other.
25. The waves *kept turning somersaults* all afternoon.

The student will also benefit from exercises such as the following, which require him to ascertain the meaning of the italicized word (9):

1. You cannot trust him. *He's a wolf in sheep's clothing.*
   a. He howls like a wolf.
   b. He looks like a wolf, but dresses well.
   c. He is mean and cunning but pretends to be meek and innocent like a sheep.
2. *I'll stand by* you whenever you need me.
   a. I'll wait alongside.
   b. I'll be ready to help.
   c. I'll be near.

Developing Skill in Using Punctuation Marks as Clues to Meaning

Punctuation is frequently looked upon merely as a discipline in writing rather than as a help in reading. Yet, the writer punctuates not for himself but for his reader. Punctuation is not only a set of rules to be learned but also a way to facilitate the grasp of meaning.

Punctuation replaces the intonation pattern in speech—the pauses, pitch, and stress. Intonation in speech is used to convey surprise, anger, or satire; it also indicates whether the utterance makes a statement, gives a command, or asks a question. In written language the comma and the semicolon indicate a pause. The comma is also used to set off a nonrestrictive clause, to note a series, and to set off an appositive. The period is used to end a statement; the question mark, to end a question; and the exclamation point, to end a command. The question mark indicates that in speech there would be a sharp rise in voice and then a drop back to the normal level. The colon indicates that something additional is about to follow:

Here is an example of how punctuation can affect meaning:

1. The school, kitchen, cafeteria, and auditorium are off bounds during regular school hours.
2. The school kitchen, cafeteria, and auditorium are off bounds during regular school hours.

The comma after the word *school* in sentence 1 falsifies the intended meaning.

Study of the Dictionary, Text Glossaries, and Word Lists

Glossaries become important as soon as students engage in any type of content-area reading. The teacher discusses the new words that will be met in the day's lesson. He identifies the word through its visual form, pronunciation, accent, and meaning. The discussion is completed when the word is met in its contextual setting. In this way teacher and student develop their own glossary.

Although the student has learned to use the context and other clues to decipher the meaning of words, he must sometimes go to the dictionary. In the junior high and high school, the dictionary becomes a very useful tool. To be able to use it correctly, the student should do the following:

1. Develop alphabetization skills.
2. Understand the use of guide words and be able to locate entry words quickly.
3. Understand dictionary symbols—the breve, macron, circumflex, tilde, etc., and understand each item included in an entry. To do this the student needs to be able to deal with such abbreviations as *cap* (capitalized), *cf* (compare, see), *esp* (especially), *exc* (except), *fr* (from), *i.e* (that is), *Illus* (illustration), *mod* (modern), *opp* (opposite), *orig* (originally).
4. Use the dictionary to work out the pronunciation of words to help him in his spelling, and to identify accents, derivations, and parts of speech.
5. Use the dictionary to learn the various meanings of words and to select the definition that applies to a word as it is used in a sentence.

The following exercises are designed to teach dictionary skills.

1. Have students alphabetize a list of words and indicate the alphabetization by numbering the words in proper sequence:

shear _____	shindig _____
shingle _____	Shilluk _____
shibboleth _____	shoal _____
Shingon _____	setaceous _____
settee _____	shifty _____

2. Have students identify the correct pronunciation of words by checking them in the dictionary:

a. mackinaw

mak-ə-nou
mak-ə-nȯ

b. mosquito

mə-skēt-ō
mos-skwēt-ō

3. Have students underline the words in a list that would appear between given guidewords, such as *gust* and *haet*:

guttural	haggle
gunpowder	hackney
gyroscope	hockey

4. Have students do an exercise like the following: *

Below is a list of numbered, italicized words. Opposite each are four words, two of which might serve as *guide words* for the italicized word. Put a ✔ in the column *between the correct guide words*. (Note: Number one has been done for you.)

Guide Words

		A	B	C
1. *medicable*	mazzard	___meaninglessness___ medalist		✔_mediocrity
2. *brachial*	bouse	___ box	___ Brachiopoda	___brachium
3. *inordinate*	inobservance	___ inscription	___ insinuate	___instantaneous
4. *monandry*	mollifying	___ monarchy	___ monism	___monody
5. *debauch*	datura	___ dayspring	___ deal	___debility
6. *orrery*	organdy	___ origin	___ Orozco	___ortolan
7. *urbane*	upright	___ uraninite	___ uriniferous	___use

5. Have students put a check (✔) opposite words that are incorrectly accented: *

* *Listen and Read*, MN, Educational Development Laboratories, p. 22.

_____a. se'·ri'·ous
_____b. ge·og'·ra·phy'
_____c. neg'·a·tive'
_____d. cor'·rec'·tion
_____e. sanc'·tu·ar·y'
_____f. throt'·tle'
_____g. in'·te·ri·or'
_____h. tem'·po·rar'·i·ly
_____i. dec'·la·ra'·tion
_____j. his·to'·ri·an

6. Have students select from the dictionary the definition that fits the specific use of the word in the sentence:

> **man·da·rin** \'man-d(ə-)rən\ *n* [Pg *mandarim,* fr. Malay *měntěri,* fr. Skt *mantrin* counselor, fr. *mantra* counsel — more at MANTRA] **1 :** a public official under the Chinese Empire of any of nine superior grades **2** *cap* **a :** the primarily northern dialect of Chinese used by the court and the official classes under the Empire **b :** the chief dialect of China that is spoken in about four fifths of the country and has a standard variety centering about Peking 3 [F *mandarine,* fr. Sp *mandarina,* prob. fr. *mandarin* mandarin, fr. Pg *mandarim:* prob. fr. the color of a mandarin's robes] **a :** a small spiny Chinese orange tree (*Citrus reticulata*) with yellow to reddish orange loose-skinned fruits; *also* **:** a cultivated selection or hybrid of the Chinese mandarin **b :** the fruit of a mandarin — **man·da· rin·ate** \-ˌāt\ *n* — **man·da·rin·ism** \-ˌiz-əm\ *n*
> ²**mandarin** *adj* **1 :** of, relating to, or typical of a mandarin <~ graces> **2:** marked by polished ornate complexity of language <~ style>

Example: He ate the mandarin, but he would certainly have preferred a California orange. What does *mandarin* mean in the preceding sentence? Which definition applies?

7. A variant of the exercise above requires the student to write the number of the correct definition for an underlined word.*

> **ma·trix** (mā'trĭks, măt'rĭks), *n., pl.* **matrices** (mā'trĭsēz', măt'rĭ-), **matrixes. 1.** that which gives origin or form to a thing, or which serves to enclose it. **2.** *Anat.* a formative part, as the corium beneath a nail. **3.** *Biol.* the intercellular substance of a tissue. **4.** the womb. **5.** the rock in which a crystallized mineral is embedded. **6.** *Mining.* gangue. **7.** *Print.* **a.** a mold for casting type faces. **b.** mat¹ (def. 6). **8.** (in a punching machine) a perforated block upon which the object to be punched is rested. [t. L: breeding animal, LL womb, source]

a. The very first time he was allowed to use the punch press, the apprentice machinist succeeded in damaging the underline{matrix.}

* *Listen and Read.*

sub·due (səb-dū′, -dōō′), *v.t.*, **-dued, duing. 1.** to conquer and bring into subjection. **2.** to overpower by superior force; overcome. **3.** to bring into moral subjection, as by persuasion or by inspiring awe or fear; render submissive (to). **4.** to repress (feelings, impulses, etc.). **5.** to bring (land) under cultivation. **6.** to reduce the intensity, force, or vividness of (sound, light, color, etc.); tone down; soften. **7.** to allay (inflammation, etc.). [ME, through AF, t. OF: m. *so(u)duire* seduce, g. L *subdūcere* remove by stealth; sense development in AF affected by L *subdere* subdue] **—sub·du′able,** *adj.* **—sub·dued′,** *adj.* **—sub·du′er,** *n.* **—Syn. 1.** See defeat. **—Ant. 4.** awaken, arouse. **6.** intensify.

b. With the aid of antibiotics, the physician was able to <u>subdue</u> the fever.

c. The decorator advised us that <u>subdued</u> colors would make the room appear larger.

d. Our soldiers fought bravely but were <u>subdued</u> by the large enemy force.

8. For each of the underlined words in the following sentences, have students indicate the entry word that they would look for in a dictionary:

a. He was <u>terribly</u> confused about the whole situation. <u>terrible</u> _____

b. As the candle burned lower, the light in the room became <u>dimmer</u>. _____

c. Jack was <u>unearthing</u> some fossils. _____

9. Have students develop skill in *using* (not rote memory) the reference materials in the dictionary by asking them to locate such information as

a. Abbreviations:
(1) CBD
(2) CSF
(3) Ark
(4) Ci
(5) KKK
(6) id
(7) fm
(8) pizz
(9) MP

b. Arbitrary signs:
(1) △
(2) ≠
(3) ℨ
(4) Σ
(5) ⌢
(6) β

c. Biographical names:
(1) Baring
(2) Charlemagne
(3) Cézanne
(4) Dreyfus
(5) Kipling
(6) Lombard

d. Pronouncing gazetteer:
(1) Ardennes
(2) Baton Rouge
(3) Dvinsk
(4) Djakarta
(5) Oshkosh
(6) Shantung

e. Colleges and universities:
(1) Dekalb College
(2) Erskine College
(3) Fairleigh Dickinson University
(4) Puget Sound University

10. Have students learn the meanings of each item in a dictionary entry:

a. Main entry

en·grave \in-'grāv\ *vt* [MF *engraver*, fr. *en-* + *graver* to grave, of Gmc origin; akin to OE *grafan* to grave] **1 a :** to form by incision (as upon wood or metal) **b :** to impress as if with a graver **2 a :** to cut figures, letters, or devices upon for printing; *also :* to print from an engraved plate **b :** PHOTOENGRAVE — **en·grav·er** *n*

b. Pronunciation

en·grave \in-'grāv\ *vt* [MF *engraver*, fr. *en-* + *graver* to grave, of Gmc origin; akin to OE *grafan* to grave] **1 a :** to form by incision (as upon wood or metal) **b :** to impress as if with a graver **2 a :** to cut figures, letters, or devices upon for printing; *also :* to print from an engraved plate **b :** PHOTOENGRAVE — **en·grav·er** *n*

c. Part of speech

en·grave \in-'grāv\ *vt* [MF *engraver*, fr. *en-* + *graver* to grave, of Gmc origin; akin to OE *grafan* to grave] **1 a :** to form by incision (as upon wood or metal) **b :** to impress as if with a graver **2 a :** to cut figures, letters, or devices upon for printing; *also :* to print from an engraved plate **b :** PHOTOENGRAVE — **en·grav·er** *n*

English toy spaniel *n* any of a breed of small blocky spaniels with well-rounded upper skull projecting forward toward the short turned-up nose

d. Other forms of entry word

en·grave \in-'grāv\ *vt* [MF *engraver*, fr. *en-* + *graver* to grave, of Gmc origin; akin to OE *grafan* to grave] **1 a :** to form by incision (as upon wood or metal) **b :** to impress as if with a graver **2 a :** to cut figures, letters, or devices upon for printing; *also :* to print from an engraved plate **b :** PHOTO-ENGRAVE — **en·grave·er** *n*

en·gram *also* **en·gramme** \'en-,gram\ *n* [ISV] : a memory trace; *specif :* a protoplasmic change in neural tissue hypothesized to account for persistence of memory — **en·gram·mic** \en-'gram-ik\ *adj*

e. Derivation or history

en·grave \in-'grāv\ *vt* [MF *engraver*, fr. *en-* + *graver* to grave of Gmc origin; akin to OE *grafan* to grave] **1 a :** to form by incision (as upon wood or metal) **b :** to impress as if with a graver **2 a :** to cut figures, letters, or devices upon for printing; *also :* to print from an engraved plate **b :** PHOTOENGRAVE — **en·grav·er** *n*

f. Definitions

en·light·en·ment \in-'līt-ən-mənt\ *n* **1 :** the act or means of enlightening : the state of being enlightened **2** *cap :* a philosophic movement of the 18th century marked by questioning of traditional doctrines and values, a tendency toward individualism, and an emphasis on the idea of universal human progress, the empirical method in science, and the free use of reason — used with *the*

g. Special usage

en·gross \in-'grōs\ *vt* [ME *engrossen*, fr. AF *engrosser*, prob. fr. ML *ingrossare*, fr. L *in* + ML *grossa* large handwriting, fr. L, fem. of *grossus* thick] **1 a :** to copy or write in a large hand **b :** to prepare the usu. final handwritten or printed text of (an official document) **2** [ME *engrossen*, fr. MF *en gros* in large quantities] **a :** to purchase large quantities of (as for speculation) **b** *obs* : AMASS **c :** to take the whole of : MONOPOLIZE — **en·gross·er** *n*

en·light·en·ment \in-'līt-ən-mənt\ *n* **1 :** the act or means of enlightening **:** the state of being enlightened **2** *cap* **:** a philosophic movement of the 18th century marked by questioning of traditional doctrines and values, a tendency toward individualism, and an emphasis on the idea of universal human progress, the empirical method in science, and the free use of reason — used with *the*

h. Synonyms

enig·ma \i-'nig-mə\ *n* [L *aenigma*, fr. Gk *ainigmat-, ainigma,* fr. *ainissesthai* to speak in riddles, fr. *ainos* fable] **1 :** an obscure speech or writing **2 :** something hard to understand or explain **3 :** an inscrutable or mysterious person **syn** see MYSTERY

i. Key to symbols

ə abut; ə kitten; ər further; a back; ā bake; ä cot, cart; aú out; ch chin; e less; ē easy; g gift; i trip; ī life; j joke; η sing; ō flow; ȯ flaw; oi coin; th thin; th this; ü loot ú foot; y yet; yü few; yú furious; zh vision

The student also needs to learn to analyze the definitions given in a dictionary. A good definition puts something into a class of things and then differentiates that something from all other members of that class. Thus the word *rocket* is defined as a firework (this is the class concept) that consists of a case filled with combustible material and that is fastened to a guiding stick (these are the aspects that differentiate it from other fireworks).

An exercise requiring the student to look up the word in the dictionary and to note both its class aspects and its *differentia* is helpful in teaching the dictionary as a device for broadening meaning. Thus:

Term	Class	Differentia
raccoon		
plow		
potash		
echidna		
eel		

Study of Technical Vocabularies

The student should become familiar with the technical vocabularies of the content areas. Only by knowing them can he read with meaning in those areas. We will discuss this aspect in some detail in Chapter 9. Let us concentrate here on some of the new words and words with new meanings that have been added to the language in the last few decades:

ack-ack	bamboo curtain
amtrac	bazooka
antinatalist	beachhead
audiophile	bebop
babushka	bellyland

big wheel
Black Panther
blitz
Blue meanie
boogie-woogie
brainwashing
cherrypick
chicken dog
chopper-copper
cloverleaf
commune
dartchery
deicer
deltiology
discophile
ecocide
ecofreak
ecophobia
ecosystem
emcee
freeway
frozen rope
genocide
ghetto
goldbrick
grasshopper
grass roots
hardtop
hi-fi
imploit
intercom

jawboning
Jesus freak
junkie
liquidate
LSD
maxi
meat packer
megaton
me-tooism
mini
Molotov cocktail
needle (v.)
no-no
Oscar
pedal pusher
ponytail
poodle cut
prefab
rabbit ears
rev
rhubarb
satellite
schmo
sexism
snow (television)
spelunker
split-level house
transsex
tripsit
Uncle Tomahawk
urbicidal

A CHART FOR THE CLASSROOM

The junior high–high school student should have before him a constant reminder of the techniques and principles useful in building a vocabulary. A summary chart such as the following might be adapted for display in the classroom.

How to Improve Your Vocabulary

1. Broaden your experiences. Be alert for new ideas and always learn to describe them in clear terminology. Read and discuss. Listen and write!
2. Develop a regular and systematic method of studying words.
3. Keep a vocabulary notebook, or three-by-five-inch cards, in which you write the words you want to master. Include the pronunciation and the meanings of the word.

4. Learn first the common meaning of the word. Gradually expand your knowledge to include special meanings.
5. Study the word in its context.
6. Associate the word with a mental picture.
7. Break the word into its basic elements—the root, prefix, and suffix. Break a compound word into its simple words.
8. Associate the root word with its synonyms (words with similar meanings) and antonyms (words with opposite meanings).
9. Study carefully those words that are pronounced alike but have different spellings. Such words are called homonyms: f-a-r-e—f-a-i-r.
10. Use the new words in writing and in speech.
11. Develop an interest in the origin of words.
12. Introduce yourself to the new words in the language, for example, *chunnel, Custerism, gasbaggery, iongage, quadplex, snopolo, telediagnosis, vege-burger.*
13. Learn the fine shades of meanings of words. Instead of the word *little,* you may at times wish to use *small, minute, microscopic, puny, tiny, petty, dwarfed, stunted, diminutive, Lilliputian, short,* or *miniature.*
14. Study the technical vocabulary of your subject matter.

SUMMARY

To be a reader the student must be able to identify words and to associate some meaning with them. Unfortunately, he cannot do this unless he has had the opportunity to develop meaning. Meaning is generally acquired through some form of direct or vicarious experience. Perhaps our emphasis on learning from experience is too great. We might emphasize more learning from instruction, and this has been the intent of this chapter.

Ideas and experiences can be expressed in many ways. Each writer has his own modes of expression. Because of this the teacher must develop in students the ability to gather meaning from the context and to decipher the author's rhetorical and grammatical contrivances.

QUESTIONS FOR DISCUSSION

1. What are some of the hindrances to the easy development of meanings for words?
2. What is *conceptualization?*

3. Describe the characteristic pattern in the development of meanings or concepts.
4. Distinguish the three meanings for *percept*.
5. What are some appropriate techniques for teaching meaning at the high school level?
6. Discuss and illustrate the various ways that the context may be used to infer the meaning of a word.
7. Discuss ways of developing meaning for figurative expressions.
8. What dictionary skills should the student develop in the high school years?
9. What is meant by the *class* and *differentia* aspects of a definition? Illustrate your answer.
10. Discuss:
    a. Facility in conceptualization is a function of previous experience in concept formation. This progression in concept formation is from simple to complex, from diffuse to differentiated, from egocentric to objective, from specific to general, and from inconsistent to consistent.
    b. Concepts are possible only when the student has had experience with the actual phenomena that are to be conceptualized.
    c. Concepts are formed when the individual perceives the commonality of characteristics among a variety of changing aspects. He perceives likenesses and differences.

BIBLIOGRAPHY

1. AMES, W. S., "A Study of the Process by Which Readers Determine Word Meaning through the Use of Verbal Context." Unpublished doctoral dissertation, University of Missouri, 1965.
2. ARTLEY, A. S., "Teaching Word-Meaning through Context," *Elementary English Review*, 20 (February 1943), 68–74.
3. BARRON, RICHARD F., "The Use of Vocabulary as an Advance Organizer," *Reading in the Content Area*, ed. Harold L. Herber and Peter L. Sanders, pp. 29–39. Syracuse, N.Y.: Syracuse University, 1969.
4. DEIGHTON, L., *Vocabulary Development in the Classroom*. New York: Teacher's College Press, Columbia University, 1959.
5. DULIN, KENNETH LA MARR, "New Research on Context Clues," *Journal of Reading*, 13 (October 1969), 33–38.
6. DURRELL, DONALD D., *Improving Reading Instruction*. New York: Harcourt, Brace & World, Inc., 1956.
7. EMANS, ROBERT, "Context Clues," *Reading in the Total Curriculum*. International Reading Association Proceedings, (1968), 13.
8. EMBLER, WELLER, "Metaphor in Everyday Speech," *Etc. A Review of General Semantics*, 16 (Spring 1959), 323–42.
9. GAINSBURG, JOSEPH C., and LILLIAN G. GORDON, *Building Reading Confidence*, p. 45. Maplewood, N.J.: C. S. Hammond and Company, 1962.

10. LABOV, WILLIAM, *Some Sources of Reading Problems for Negro Speakers of Non-Standard English*. National Cash Register Company, 4936 Fairmont Avenue, Bethesda, Md. 20014. 1966.

11. MCCULLOUGH, C. M., "Context Aids in Reading," *The Reading Teacher*, 11 (April 1958), 225–29.

12. MCCULLOUGH, CONSTANCE M., "Learning to Use Context Clues," *Elementary English*, 20 (1943), 140–43.

13. MILLIGAN, JERRY L., and RAYMOND J. O'TOOLE, "Breaking the Word Barrier in Science," *Elementary School Journal*, 70 (November 1969), 86–90.

14. National Association of Secondary-School Principals, "Teaching Essential Reading Skills," *Improving Reading Instruction in the Secondary School*, II, 34 (February 1950), 39–130.

15. SEVERSON, EILEEN, "The Teaching of Reading-Study Skills in Biology," *American Biology Teacher*, 25 (1963), 203–4.

16. SHAW, PHILIP, "Rhetorical Guides to Reading Comprehension," *The Reading Teacher*, 11 (April 1958), 239–43.

17. VANDERLINDE, L., "Does the Study of Quantitative Vocabulary Improve Problem Solving?" *Elementary School Journal*, 65 (1964), 143–52.

Advancing the Student's Comprehension Skills

CHAPTER **8**

THE GOAL OF ALL READING is the comprehension of meaning. The *initial* step in this process (which we discussed in the preceding chapter) is the association of an experience with a given symbol. This is absolutely necessary, but it is the most elemental form of comprehension. Complete meaning is not conveyed by a single word. The good reader learns to interpret words in their contextual setting. He comprehends words as parts of sentences, sentences as parts of paragraphs, and paragraphs as parts of stories.

Effective reading includes not only a literal interpretation of an author's word but also an interpretation of his mood, tone, feeling, and attitude. The reader must comprehend the implied meanings and prejudices of the writer. He must recognize summary statements, make inferences and applications, and see the broader implications of a passage. He must familiarize himself with the time and place in which the words were written. He must use the periods, commas, quotation marks, and questions as aids to interpretation.

Too often we involve the student in the retrieval of the trivial factual data of a story. Comprehension questions asked are often directed at literal comprehension rather than at getting broad understandings. The student quickly learns to parrot back an endless recollection of trivia. The purpose of this chapter then is to help teachers to instruct the student to look for intricate relationships, implications, subtle meanings, conjectures, evaluations, and inferences.

Children learn to read so they can read to learn. As the youngster progresses from the primary through the elementary level and into the junior high and high school, more emphasis is placed on learning to learn, and the concept load of what needs to be read becomes more difficult.

Few students are satisfied with simple word calling. We expect the student to be a comprehender, and yet perhaps one student in four on the high school level cannot adequately understand his reading assignments or the textbooks on which his assignments are based. Let us look more closely, then, at what comprehension is all about.

COMPREHENSION SKILLS

Comprehension involves a complex of abilities. The good comprehender possesses the ability to:

1. Associate experiences and meaning with the graphic symbol.
2. React to the sensory images (visual, auditory, kinesthetic, taste, smell) suggested by words.
3. Interpret verbal connotations and denotations.
4. Understand words in context and to select the meaning that fits the context.
5. Give meaning to units of increasing size: the phrase, clause, sentence, paragraph, and whole selection.
6. Detect and understand the main ideas.
7. Recognize significant details.
8. Interpret the organization.
9. Answer questions about a printed passage.
10. Follow directions.
11. Perceive relationships: part-whole; cause-effect; general-specific; place, sequence, size, and time.
12. Interpret figurative expressions.
13. Make inferences and draw conclusions, supply implied details, and evaluate what is read.
14. Identify and evaluate character traits, reactions, and motives.
15. Anticipate outcomes.
16. Recognize and understand the writer's purpose.
17. Recognize literary and semantic devices and identify the tone, mood, and intent or purpose of the writer.
18. Determine whether the text affirms, denies, or fails to express an opinion about a supposed fact or condition.

19. Identify the antecedents of such words as *who, some,* or *they.*
20. Retain ideas.
21. Apply ideas and integrate them with one's past experience.

This chapter, being intended to help the youngster to move from elemental comprehension to the higher-level skills mentioned above, describes the development of comprehension skills, location skills, and ability to read charts, maps, and graphs.

DEVELOPING COMPREHENSION SKILLS

Of major importance for interpretative reading is a purpose for reading. The purposeful reader is an interested reader. If the student is to understand what he is reading, he must know why he is reading. He must know whether to read for information, to solve a problem, to follow directions, to be entertained, to obtain details, to draw a conclusion, to verify a statement, to summarize, or to criticize. As already mentioned, learning to comprehend involves a complex of skills. In the preceding chapter the first of these skills was discussed. Let us add a few words here about the significance of word meaning.

Word Meaning

Studies generally indicate that vocabulary is highly related to comprehension. Vineyard and Massey (35) found that even when intelligence is held constant there still is a sufficiently high relationship between comprehension and vocabulary proficiency to justify attempts to improve comprehension through vocabulary training. To comprehend, the student must have a knowledge of word meanings and be able to select the correct meaning from the context.

Certain principles should guide the teacher in the development of word meanings.

1. *Words by themselves are not valid units of meaning.* The meanings connoted by a word have been arbitrarily assigned to the symbol.
2. *Most words have more than one meaning.* Generally, the more frequently a word is used, the more meanings it tends to have.
3. *The specific meaning elicited by a word is a function of the context in which the word occurs.* It is a function of the environment of the word. This is not only the verbal context but also the cultural and structural context.
4. *The number of meanings actually elicited by a word depends on the number and quality of experiences that the reader has associated with the word.*

5. *The student has numerous means at his disposal for developing word mean-ings.* These were discussed in Chapter 7. He may use the context. The word may be explained to him by giving a synonym, by classifying the word, and by pointing out differences and similarities. Or, the meaning of the word may be illustrated through activities, picture clues, structural analysis, and the dictionary.

Perhaps we have not paid enough attention to the sense appeal of words. Words make the reader touch, see, hear, taste, and smell. The following words are examples:

Touch (Feeling)	Sight	Sound	Taste	Smell
cold	green	mellow	sweet	fresh
warm	rippled	bang	sour	pungent
hot	spotted	crash	bitter	stuffy
rough	glistening	thud	salty	fragrant
bumpy	ruffle	bellow	smoky	choking
sandy	pale	thumping	ripe	clean
soft	grassy	thrashing-	tender	stifling
sticky	whirling	around	tasty	aroma
wet	weather-	stampeding	well-	burning
limp	beaten	splash	seasoned	
sturdy	shadowy	shuffle	tart	
smooth	billowing	honk	spicy	
sleek	lightning	snort	sage	
frozen	darkness	peal	peppery	
steamy	shiny	rumble		
sharp	dense	lapping		
waxy	bright	growl		
damp	swirling	murmuring		
gentle	hair-	rustle		
crisp	raising	buzzing		
frosty	crouching	purring		
thick	trembling	moan		
tender	fluffy	howl		
stinging	foamy	chirp		
snapping	blossoming	hissing		
icy	brilliant	creaking		
icy cold	windblown	thunderous		
thin	snowy	whine		
	grotesque	buzz		
	resplendent	tinkle		
	battered	clatter		
	glowing	snarl		
		shrill		
		squeaky		
		hoarse		
		dripping		
		wailing		

The underlined words in the following sentences are examples of words that appeal to the senses.

1. The *bumpy* highway caused the car to <u>creak</u> and <u>rattle,</u> but we went merrily on our way.

2. Icicles, hanging from the roof of our battered cabin, <u>dripped</u> and <u>peppered</u> the snow beneath <u>with holes</u> where the melted water fell.

The student will learn multiple meanings of words from an exercise such as the following which requires him to look up the underlined word in the dictionary and to associate the proper meaning with it.

1. The <u>majority</u> of boys and girls still adhere closely to parental values. (*greater part*)

2. When John reached his <u>majority</u> he got a brand new car. (*legal age of responsibility*)

Phrase Meaning

Phrase reading is not synonymous with word meaning. A phrase is more than the sum of the individual words that it contains. The meaning of phrases like *to spin a yarn, to throw away one's money,* or *to pitch a tent* cannot be deciphered from individual words. In the preceding chapter we gave numerous examples of similar idiomatic and figurative phraseology.

In developing the student's phrase-reading skill, an exercise like the following is useful:

Phrase	*Synonym*
1. big wheel	
2. great guy	
3. open-minded	
4. pig-headed	
5. cold-hearted	

Phrase reading becomes especially difficult when one has to deal with idiomatic expressions and with proverbs. Examine the following proverbs:

1. Many hands <u>make light</u> work.

2. A rolling stone <u>gathers no moss.</u>

3. Smooth seas <u>make</u> poor sailors.

4. If you would enjoy the fire, you must *put up with the smoke*.

5. Everyone *can master a grief* but he who has it.

Identify similar proverbs and let students put on paper in their own words the meaning intended.

Sentence Meaning

Effective reading implies an understanding and an interpretation of language patterns. The full meaning of a sentence depends on the punctuation, the word order, and the grammatical inflections signaling tense, number, and possession and on such key words as *because* or *nevertheless*. Until the reader correctly translates the printed text into the intonation pattern of the writer, he may not be getting the meaning intended.

The following exercises help the student to decode simple sentences and to formalize the teaching of language patterns: *

1. Below are some word-for-word translations of French sentences. Beneath each translation rewrite the English sentences in the correct patterns.

   a. *Je lui ai donné le chien noir.* (I her gave the dog black)

   b. *Elle lui a parlé de la porte cassée.* (She to him spoke about the door broken)

2. Put the following groups of words into English sentence patterns.

   c. the out cat fat red went

   d. of gone some the were cookies

Before exercise number 3 is used, the student must first become familiar with the basic sentence patterns. Figure 8-1 illustrates the four different types: subject–verb, subject–predicate–object, subject–linking verb–adjective, and subject–linking verb–noun.†

FIGURE 8-1   BASIC SENTENCE PATTERNS

Pattern 1.

Subject—Verb which can also be expressed		Examples—Pattern 1	
Noun—Verb		N	V
or		Birds	fly
Who, What—Action, Being		Fish	swim
		(The) dog	barked

* *Listen and Read,* MN, Educational Development Laboratories, p. 26.
† *Ibid.,* p. 27.

Pattern 2.

Subject—Predicate—Object	Examples—Pattern 2		
or	S	V	O
Noun (one)—Transitive Verb—Noun (two)	Mary	hit	Jack
or	Bill	studies	English
Who, What—Action—Receiver	(The) cat	caught	mice

Pattern 3.

Subject—Linking Verb—Adjective	Examples—Pattern 3		
or	S	LV	A
Noun—Linking Verb—Describer	Games	are	interesting
or	Roses	smell	sweet
Who, What—Linking Verb—Modifier	Jane	is	studious

Pattern 4.

Subject—Linking Verb—Noun	Examples—Pattern 4		
or	S	LV	N
Who, What—Linking Verb—Who, What	Jane	is	(my) sister
	(the) building	was	(a) church

---

3. The following exercise requires the student to identify the sentence pattern of a series of sentences.* The student is required to indicate whether the pattern is 1, 2, 3, or 4.

_____a. The children skated all day.

_____b. The new exhibit showed this year's autos.

_____c. He became president of our club.

_____d. Janice practiced the piano faithfully.

_____e. This is fun!

_____f. An eclipse of the moon occurred last night.

Reading materials usually do not come in single word or phrase units. The meaning of a sentence is not obtained by piling up, as it were, the meanings of individual words. The student must learn to master the skills of relating the various words that form a logical sequence in a sentence. Unfortunately, the dynamics of converting single word meanings into the total thought of a sentence or paragraph has not been sufficiently investigated.

The student must learn that all sentences have a *who* or a *what* and that they often answer the questions *where, when, why,* and *how.* The reader may realistically be described as a news reporter. The good reporter answers the above questions in his story, and the good reader identifies the answers in print.

* *Listen and Read.*

The following sample exercises teach the student to look for answers to *who, what, when, where,* and *how* in his reading:

Read the sentences below. Then answer the questions that follow in the blanks provided.

1. Late last night a burglar entered the home of Jack Perkins on Market Street apparently to steal several valuable paintings.

   Who or what? _____

   What happened? _____

   Where? _____

   When? _____

   Why? _____

2. Anxious passengers waited in Kennedy terminal on this cold stormy night, watching the lights of the big 747 and wondering whether the pilot could land the huge craft.

   Who or what? _____

   What was happening? _____

   Where? _____

   How? _____

Sentences are parts of paragraphs and not only receive their full meaning from the context in which they occur but give meaning to the sentences that surround them. Thus, some sentences are introductory or lead-in sentences; some are transitional sentences; and some are concluding sentences. An exercise similar to the following will teach the student to identify the type of sentence being used and to read for implied meaning:

Select from the three choices (I, T. C.) the one that best describes each of the following sentences.
   I—Introductory Sentence
   T—Transitional Sentence
   C—Concluding Sentence
1. There are three chief reasons for studying government.
2. Finally, democracy is based upon the acceptance of these responsibilities.
3. In addition to knowledge and skills there must be the willingness to work with one's talents.

The meaning of a sentence can also be identified
By context:
He *brandished* his sword fiercely, but the enemy soldier also waved his own sword in a threatening manner. (The word *brandished* is defined.)

By opposites:

Being *nocturnal* in his flying habits, the owl seldom flies during the day. (*Day* is the opposite of *nocturnal.*)

By reasoning:

It was so *frigid* outside that I quickly buttoned up my coat. (It is logical that the reason I buttoned up my coat was that it was cold.)

Paragraph Meaning

Paragraphs are basically a series of sentences that give one basic idea. All the sentences are written in such a way that they relate to one another. The *Administrator's Guide,* published by the Reading Laboratory, Inc., points out that

> Each paragraph is constructed around a topic idea which is implied or stated; the separate paragraphs, however, frequently serve different functions; some narrate, others describe; some compare, others contrast; some reason, others illustrate; some persuade, others define; some classify, others divide.
>
> In order to read most effectively, the student should have more than a passing acquaintance with this fact. He should have developed sufficient familiarity with the several different kinds of paragraphs to be able to appraise, while he reads, the legitimacy of the reasoning the author uses in arriving at his conclusions.
>
> An additional means of making the students conversant with paragraphs, their purposes, and their varieties is to have them analyze paragraphs frequently during the training. . . . The following are suggestions for conducting the practice in PARAGRAPH ANALYSIS. Have the students:
>
> 1. Locate the topic sentence of the paragraph.
> 2. Write a topic sentence for the paragraph, if one is not provided.
> 3. Restate the topic sentence in their own words.
> 4. Determine the nature of the paragraph; which of the above purposes does it attempt to achieve?
> 5. Write a title for the paragraph.
> 6. Locate crucial words in the paragraph: *Therefore, however, on the contrary, but,* and *although* are logical connectives that move the discussion on to its next point, and, as such, they signal the need for a close and critical reading.
> 7. Outline paragraphs.
> 8. Read an essay to find the major and minor paragraphs. Major paragraphs are to the whole essay what the topic sentence is to the paragraph. Topic paragraphs are the foundations of the essay.
> 9. Outline essays by: (a) finding the topic sentences of all the paragraphs, (b) deciding which of these reflect a major change in the trend of thought, (c) using these as headings in the outline, (d) using as sub-headings, the key words of the *topic sentences* of the minor paragraphs.
> 10. PRE-READ essays, trying to decide in the case of each paragraph whether or not its first sentence *is* the topic sentence of that paragraph. (If using

their own texts, they can put a check beside those which they believe to be topic sentences.) When they re-read the essays, they will be able to check the accuracy of their beliefs. This particular exercise will be found most helpful in training them to PRE-READ thoughtfully instead of by recipe.*

The following illustrative exercises present additional ways of teaching paragraph interpretation:

1. *Have pupils select from a series of sentences the one that doesn't stay on the topic.*

   Visitors to Holland are more often than not disappointed by the rarity of wooden shoes. At one time Holland boasted of 3,884 clog-making establishments; today very few such establishments exist. In autumn there is usually a lot of rain and mud in Northern Europe. The Dutch refer to clogs as *Klompen.* Klompen fashions vary from region to region and appear as high-heeled, low-heeled, broad, thin, blunt, pointed, carved, smooth, painted, and plain.†

2. *Have pupils select the topic sentence or the sentences which best summarize the main idea of a paragraph.*

   Bamboo is one of the most useful grasses in the world. In fact, it may be more like a tree than like grass. It has leaves and often reaches great heights, and the bamboo stems may even grow as thick as a tree. It can be used to make fences, ladders, houses, toys, boat masts, umbrellas, and rafts. Its leaves are used as food for animals or to make paper. From the stem are made buckets, water pipes, flutes, and flowerpots. The juice from bamboo is turned into medicine and the young tender stems are eaten as vegetables. There are literally hundreds of uses for bamboo.

3. *Have pupils identify the technique that the writer is using to get his point across. Is he piling up details? Does he open with a generalization and then go on to list supporting details? Does he use repetition or contrast to get his point across? Does he use a chronological sequence?*

   a. *Piling Up Details*

   The kiwi is a strange bird from New Zealand, perhaps the least bird-like of birds, that sleeps while it stands on its head. It is not at all like other birds. It can't fly, it sleeps during daylight, and its feathers are so thin that they look like hair. The kiwi female lays eggs, but the male kiwi has to hatch them. The egg itself is monstrous, being one-fourth the size of the mother.

* *Administrator's Guide,* Developmental Reading Program (New York: The Reading Laboratory, Inc., 1966), pp. 36–37.
† Adapted from I. Stenker, *The New York Times Magazine,* June 1954, p. 76.

b. *Chronological Sequence*

On June 7, 1896, Samuelson and Harbo, in an eighteen-foot boat, rowed out of New York on the evening tide. They wanted to cross the Atlantic by rowboat. They rowed for nine hours and then rested for an hour; at night each man rowed for three hours while the other rested. A month out of New York the boat was overturned, but they managed to right it. Fifty-two days after leaving New York harbor they landed on the Scilly Islands, near France.

Reading for the Main Idea

The ability to identify the main idea is necessary for interpretation and understanding of what is written. It is based on an accurate comprehension of the word, the phrase, and the sentence. All the other interpretative reading skills are secondary. Students who do not get the main idea cannot identify the theme of a paragraph, do not understand the implied meanings, and usually cannot organize or summarize what they have read.

To help the student find the main idea, Dawson and Bamman (7, pp. 178–79) give the following list of suggestions in order of difficulty:

1. Read a short selection and select the best title, from several listed for the selection.
2. Read a short selection and give it a title, in the pupil's own words.
3. Read the title of a chapter and attempt to predict what the author is going to say.
4. Read the introduction of a chapter and note carefully just what the author has outlined.
5. Read the summary of a chapter and tell, in a simple sentence, what the chapter covered.
6. Read a paragraph and reduce it to a simple sentence, by paraphrasing the author.
7. Rapidly skim the titles and the subheads of a selection and attempt to list details which will give a general impression of the entire selection.
8. Read the first and last sentences of an entire selection.
9. Turn each subhead or subtitle into a question. The answer to that question will be the main idea of the paragraph or paragraphs.
10. Give the students a newspaper and present them with a clearly stated problem. Ask them to skim rapidly for a solution to that problem. In the beginning, it is best to confine the exercise to a single selection from the newspaper.
11. Have students select a headline that best describes the narration of an incident in a newspaper.

12. Have students select from a series of proverbs or sayings the one that best fits a written passage.*

Other means are the following: Look for comparisons that the author is making, study his use of vocabulary, look for analogies, study the figurative language, read between the lines, and study the topic sentence.

Robinson (27) suggests that the student be taught to identify the main idea of a sentence by being required to underline key words. He then moves to identifying the key sentence in a paragraph. This is the topic sentence. Some paragraphs, however, do not have a single sentence that summarizes the main idea. Thus the third step consists of teaching the student to make an inference from a series of sentences as to what the basic idea is. Eventually the student needs to learn that a main idea may be spread over two or three paragraphs.

The following exercises illustrate how some of these suggestions may be put into practice:

1. *Select the best title.*

It was a hot summer afternoon. The sun blazed down on the ripening fields and the roaring combines. It would have been hot anywhere on that day, but on the combines it must have been doubly so.

a. A Hot Afternoon

b. The Noise of the Combines

2. *Select the topic sentence.*†

The thermostat, an invention of the twentieth century, has been designed to substitute machinery for man's brain and nervous system. This device is an example of the simple analog computer and controls the temperature of a room automatically. When the temperature of a room changes, a signal is sent to the starting switch of the furnace. What makes the switch work? The signal sent by the thermostat turns on the switch when heat is needed or turns it off when enough heat has been manufactured.

Mark the topic sentence of the paragraph.

_____a. "The signal sent by the thermostat turns on the switch. . . ."

_____b. "The thermostat . . . has been designed to substitute machinery for man's brain and nervous system."

_____c. "What makes the switch work?"

_____d. "When the temperature of a room changes, a signal is sent to the starting switch of the furnace."

† *Listen and Read,* GHI (1), 12.

3. *Find the answer to a question.*

In May 1883 the volcano Krakatoa on an Indonesian island began to spit forth dust and rocks, but nobody paid much attention. Then, in August, Krakatoa threw forth a block of earth one cubic mile in size, producing a hole one thousand feet deep. Windows were blasted out of homes one hundred miles away, and a wall of water, reaching one hundred feet into the sky, destroyed entire villages and killed some thirty thousand people.

a. What was the size of the block of earth that emerged from the crater?

b. Were the people prepared for the volcanic eruption?

4. *Look for comparisons.*

"Pursue, keep up with, circle round your life, as a dog does his master's chaise. Do what you love. Know your own bone. Gnaw at it, bury it, unearth it, and gnaw it still" (Thoreau).

Can you in one sentence describe Thoreau's philosophy?

5. *Identify the main idea of a poem.*

America

My country, 'tis of thee,
Sweet land of liberty,
    Of thee I sing;
Land where my fathers died,
Land of the pilgrims' pride,
From every mountainside
    Let freedom ring.

My native country, thee,
Land of the noble free;
    Thy name I love;
I love thy rocks and rills,
Thy woods and templed hills;
My heart with rapture thrills
    Like that above.

Let music swell the breeze,
And ring from all the trees
    Sweet Freedom's song;
Let mortal tongues awake,
Let all that breathe partake,
Let rocks their silence break,
    The sound prolong.

Our fathers' God, to Thee,
Author of Liberty,
    To Thee we sing;
Long may our land be bright
With Freedom's holy light;
Protect us by Thy might,
    Great God, our King.

—Samuel Francis Smith

a. "America" ought to be sung on all national holidays.
b. You are not very patriotic if you do not sing "America."
c. America is a good land because it is the land of liberty and justice.

Poetry presents thousands of opportunities to practice reading for main ideas. For example:

The night shall be filled with music,
And the cares that infest the day
Shall fold their tents like the Arabs,
And as silently steal away.

    —Henry Wadsworth Longfellow

If you wish in this world to advance,
Your merits you're bound to enhance;
You must stir it and stump it,
And blow your own trumpet,
Or, trust me, you haven't a chance.

    —W. S. Gilbert

Life's but a walking shadow; a poor player,
That struts and frets his hour upon the stage,
And then is heard no more: it is a tale
Told by an idiot, full of sound and fury,
Signifying nothing.

—William Shakespeare

'Tis an old maxim in the schools,
That flattery's the food of fools;
Yet now and then your men of wit
Will condescend to take a bit.

—Jonathan Swift

Reading for Details

After the student has had some success in reading for and stating the main idea, he is ready to read for details. Reading for details becomes especially important in science, geography, arithmetic, home economics, and history.

Learning to follow directions through reading is essentially reading for details. In directions every little step is significant. The student must give full attention and must look for a definite sequence of data (7, p. 182). This process is particularly important in doing arithmetic and in carrying out experiments.

Perhaps you might want to give the following test to your students. Students should read the nine directions on their own and should complete the exercise in two minutes:

1. Cross out all the letters in this sentence.

2. If a brother is older than his sister and his sister is older than her brother, what is the least number of children in the family?

3. Write the abbreviation for the shortest month in the year at the end of this sentence.

4. Write the first letter of the last name of the oldest living president of the United States now in office.

5. Is the temperature at zero degrees Fahrenheit or freezing cold higher on a thermometer?

6. If there are 62 weeks in the year, underline the third word in this sentence.

7. If the hour hand of a clock is at 7 and the minute hand at 4, what time is it?

8. Draw a circle around the longest word in this sentence.

9. If awkward and graceful mean the same, write the figure seven after this sentence; if they are the opposite, write twice seven.*

* From Donald E. P. Smith *et al., Learning to Learn* (New York: Harcourt, Brace & World, Inc., 1961), p. 2.

If the student made any errors, a problem in reading directions may well exist.

The *Specific Skill Series* by Barnell Loft, Ltd., provides numerous exercises in reading for details. It contains books entitled *Following Directions, Locating the Answer, Getting the Facts.* The upper level of these books is sixth grade, but they may well be used on the junior high level.

The following activities promote reading for detail:

1. Ask students to note the details in a paragraph after you have stated the main idea.
2. Have students read a paragraph into which have been inserted some irrelevant sentences and let them identify these sentences.
3. After the students have read a paragraph, let them choose from a prepared group of sentences those that agree or disagree with the paragraph.
4. Present three paragraphs and let the students determine which of the last two supports and logically follows the first paragraph.
5. Analyze a written paragraph into its main and supporting ideas by making a formal outline of it.
6. Ask questions about the paragraph; multiple-choice, completion, and true-false questions are especially appropriate in eliciting answers concerning the details of a paragraph.
7. Develop a chart, diagram, or map of the sequence of events.

Reading for Organization

The good reader also comprehends the organization of what is being read. He thinks with the reading material, outlining it as he goes along. He sees the relationship between the main and the subordinate ideas and arranges these in some logical order. He uses materials from many sources and is able to draw conclusions.

Bruner (5) notes the importance of structure for learning. It makes it easier to understand by simplifying information, by generating new propositions, and by increasing the manipulability of a body of knowledge. Without structure, knowledge is more readily forgotten. Bruner (4) notes that the key to retrieval (or recall of the information) is organization. Organization of information reduces the aggregate complexity of material by embedding it into a person's cognitive structure.

Reading in the content areas especially depends upon proficiency in organization skill. Textbooks have a characteristic paragraph organization. The topic sentence sets the theme of the paragraph. A sequence of details follows. The paragraph is concluded by a summarizing sentence.

Numerous activities help the student to learn how to organize what he is reading. For example:

1. Have the student group a series of details about a main idea.
2. Have the student develop an outline for a story, with headings and subheadings.
3. Have the student arrange records, directions, or ideas in a sequential order.
4. Have the student assemble various bits of information and group them into an informative story.

Niles (22) suggests the following patterns of organization: enumerative sequence, time sequence, cause-effect, and comparison-contrast. Other authors speak of organization by size and distance, according to sequence of events, from general to specific ideas, or from specific to general.

Birkley (3) speaks of the thesis-proof pattern (begins with a thesis and is followed by a series of proofs), the opinion-reason pattern (this is most common in editorials), the problem-solution pattern, the information pattern, and the narrative pattern. Niles adds that efficient study is a matter of perceiving these organizational patterns as one reads and responds to what one has read.

The student should be taught to watch for time sequences in paragraphs (indicated by such words as *next, while, when, later*), to look for organization according to position or degree, to look for categorization (hoofed mammals, winged mammals, toothless mammals, sea mammals), and to look for comparisons, contrasts, and cause-and-effect organizations.

Paragraphs may thus be described as narration and description paragraphs, comparison and contrast paragraphs, cause and effect paragraphs, definition paragraphs, example paragraphs, reasons paragraphs, and classification and division paragraphs.* These are often introduced by anticipatory words or phrases such as the following:

Narration and Description		*Comparison and Contrast*	
after, afterward	over	but	in spite of
at last	under	however	despite
during	around	nevertheless	still
in the meantime	looked like	on the other hand	on the contrary
subsequently	appeared	rather	yet
besides	went	in comparison	notwithstanding
here	at that time	although	in contrast
there		conversely	at the same time

* *Administrator's Guide*, p. 31.

Cause and Effect	*Definition*
therefore	defined as
accordingly	means
it follows	is
thus	
as a result	*Example*
hence	for example
consequently	for instance
in conclusion	to demonstrate
	an illustration of
Reasons	
because	*Classification and Division*
the reason for	classified
the purpose was	belongs to
in order that	part of
aim was	divided
so	broken down

Let us illustrate a few types of organization:

Organization according to Contrast:

> The speed of animals varies greatly. Land animals generally are more speedy than water animals, but less so than air animals. Nevertheless, individual differences within each group are considerable. A goldfish swims about four miles an hour; a trout, five miles an hour; a sailfish and a barracuda, thirty miles an hour.
>
> Among land animals, the slowest is the turtle, which travels about one-tenth of a mile an hour, and the fastest is the cheetah, which travels up to 65 miles an hour. Man can swim about 5 miles an hour but can run 20 miles an hour. Among air animals, the housefly is the slowest, traveling about 5 miles an hour; the duck hawk flies 175 miles an hour.

Organization on a Cause-Effect Basis:

> What causes a cyclone, a tornado, and a hurricane? A cyclone is caused by a low-pressure area in which the winds move counterclockwise in a spiraling upward fashion. A tornado also is a low-pressure area, but smaller and more violent than a cyclone. A hurricane is a huge mass of air whirling about a calm center.

The organizing of what is read is also an important part of effective learning or integrative reading. There are various approaches to this task. Summarizing, outlining, note making, and combinations of these have been recommended. The specific approach used is not so important as that the student perceive the interrelationship of the various elements.

SUMMARIZING   Summaries help to preserve the essential facts and the main ideas in capsule form. They are especially necessary when the student is not using his own book.

Summaries are particularly useful when reading literature, essays, or social science materials; they are not so useful in chemistry, physics, or biology. A summary or synopsis is all that may be necessary in reading the former. As for the latter, a summary is usually longer than the original.

Exercises similar to the following teach the summarizing skill.

1. *Have students select the main idea of a paragraph from four possible choices.*

Transportation developed step by step. In the beginning man used logs to move down the stream. The lake or stream was the first roadway. Then man taught the animal to pull heavy loads on sledges. The land became the natural roadway. Finally, man discovered the wheel. This led to the invention of the stagecoach.

A good summary for the paragraph might be:

    a. Man used logs to move down the streams.
    b. The problems of transportation were overcome by the invention of the wheel.
    c. Transportation passed through the stages of log travel, sledge travel, and stagecoach travel.
    d. The land became the natural roadway.

2. *Have students note how various writers introduce the topic or summarizing idea.*

In the following paragraph the writer asks a question, and his answer to the question summarizes the paragraph:

What is success? Was Napoleon successful? What about Stalin, Hitler, or Michelangelo? Is that man successful who accomplishes the task that he set for himself? In other words, does success consist in getting what one wants? I doubt it. I believe success consists in being the best that one can be. Success must be measured by its effects upon man and society. The emphasis must be on being the best, not necessarily on getting the greatest rewards. The good plumber is a success; the lousy philosopher is a failure. And, the good plumber is an asset to both himself and society.

A good summary for the paragraph might be:

    a. That man is successful who accomplishes the task that he sets for himself.
    b. Success consists in being the best that one can be, and it must be measured by its effects on man and society.
    c. Rewards are a significant aspect of success.

3. *Have students read poetry and select the best summary from a series of three choices.*

Poetry usually presents one main idea or moral, and that main idea summarizes what the poem has to say. In poetry all the words are so interrelated that they dovetail into one main idea. Thus:

Not enjoyment, and not sorrow,
Is our destined end or way:
But to act, that each to-morrow
Find us farther than to-day.
        —*Psalm of Life*, Longfellow

A summary of this poem might be:

a. Man must take what comes.
b. Man can do something about his destiny.
c. All of us are doomed to sorrow.

4. *Have students outline graphically a paragraph on a scientific topic.*

Scientific materials are difficult to summarize. Graphs, charts, maps, formulas, and definitions can rarely be summarized.

Trees

There are two kinds of trees. Some have leaves that drop off during one particular season of each year. Others keep their leaves for much longer periods of time. The latter are called evergreens.

Evrgreens are of various types. Those with very narrow leaves are the pine, the cedar, the spruce, and the hemlock. Broad-leaved evergreens are the palm and the live oak.

Graphical Outline

Trees

Some lose leaves annually   Some do not
                                             (evergreens)

                    Narrow Leaves   Broad Leaves
                        pine   palm
                        cedar   live oak
                        spruce
                        hemlock

Other techniques useful in developing the summarizing skill are the following:

1. Have students summarize a message so that it will be suitable for sending by telegram (reduce a fifty-word message to a twenty-word message).
2. Have students write summaries of stories that they have read.
3. Have students select from three summaries that which best summarizes a series of paragraphs.
4. Have students organize and summarize materials from a variety of sources.
5. Have students write headlines for the school paper.

OUTLINING　Outlining is just another way of organizing information. It is closely related to summarizing. When the reader owns the book, he sometimes outlines by underlining and by using letters and numbers to designate main and subordinate points.

Outlining is not easy. Many speakers and writers do not have a clear-cut outline. Others, because not all students immediately grasp what is said, repeat or elaborate at great length. This may tend to make their presentation seem unorganized. As the student attempts to outline such a presentation, he needs to ignore the unimportant details. He must select the essentials from the nonessentials.

Once the student understands the organization, he is ready to put this organization into an outline form. He starts by listing the major points. Points of lesser importance that support the main ideas are indented. Indentation gives clues to the organization.

Sometimes the student may want both to indent and to letter and number the headings. Roman numerals represent major headings; headings of next-highest significance, or second-order headings, are indented and prefaced by capital letters; headings or points that support second-order headings, hence third-order headings, are preceded by arabic numerals; finally, fourth-order points are preceded by lowercase letters.

The student may use a topic approach or a sentence (or question) approach in outlining. Thus, the first major point may simply be "A definition of photosynthesis." Or, it may be put into a complete sentence, such as "What is the definition of photosynthesis?" Either technique is satisfactory.

The outline, like any other summarization, has certain limitations. It does not contain the original material. It cannot contain everything that was said or written. But, in the beginning at least, it may be better for the student to write too much rather than not enough. An outline that is too skimpy is not very useful. It must contain enough material so that the student will see the relationships between the facts, ideas, or statements made. The perceiving of relationships is true organization.

Teaching the student to outline may be done in many ways:

1. Have students organize a series of objects into specific categories.
2. Have students select the two or three main ideas in a series of paragraphs.
3. Have them group details about each of several main ideas.
4. Teach outline form.
5. Have students check their outlines against teacher-prepared outlines of the same material.
6. Have students fill in the details in an outline for which they have been given the major ideas.

I.
    A.
    B.
II.
    A.
    B.

This exercise may be simplified by giving the students the four statements that should be used to complete the paragraph, but requiring them to put them in the proper order.

UNDERLINING   Another form of organizing information is underlining. Many students use underlining of key words and phrases in a book to organize what they have read. Unfortunately, the technique used is frequently not good. The student reads and underlines words and phrases in a hit-and-miss fashion. He finds out too late that his underlining was not planned. In short, it does not show the organization of what was read. When the student returns to the underlining later, he finds that he can no longer decipher the reasons for underlining. Underlining thus may become a poor substitute for the thinking and organizing that accompanies good reading.

Proper underlining requires the student:

1. To survey the chapter
2. To read the chapter
3. To mentally familiarize himself with the organization of the chapter
4. To underline main ideas and supporting details after having read each paragraph
5. To underline only those words and phrases that actually indicate the organization of the paragraph

The student should usually underline the topic sentence. This sentence gives him the main idea of the paragraph. Frequently, he may want to underline only a key word or a phrase in the topic sentence. The good reader, using a skimming technique, learns to know the major content of a book simply by detecting the topic sentences and then associating them with one another.

Proper underlining also means that the student must underline the key subtopics or supporting ideas. This includes key words or key phrases.

A useful technique is to number the subpoints or facts that support the main idea. The student's memory for these facts will be improved, and in review they will stand out more forcibly if he numbers them.

When underlining, the student should have a code of symbols that he can use consistently. Thus, the topic sentence may have two lines under it; the supporting details have only one line under the key words.

Students frequently use a vertical bar in the margin to indicate an area of importance. An *S* in the margin may indicate that at that point the writer has summarized what he has said. A question mark in the margin indicates that here is a section that the learner does not understand. A circle is frequently used to indicate new and technical words in the paragraph.

Some writers disparage underlining; however, one might ask: Why spend time taking notes on something that one can have in its entirety? Underlining prevents the learner from taking too few notes. It also permits him, during review, to again read the entire paragraph if, in the meantime, he has lost the trend of thought.

NOTE MAKING   Effective note making is a high-level study or integrative reading skill.* It requires attention, concentration, skillful reading and listening, and the putting into practice of one's organizing abilities.

The making of good notes whether in reading or in listening requires the student to learn to write notes and to pay attention at the same time. The making of notes is certainly more than a secretarial job. Digestion and learning should be taking place. However, all notes do not need to be in the student's own words. Usually there is nothing wrong with the teacher's words, if the student understands them. Comprehension is the prime consideration. The student should learn to listen and read for meaning rather than for mere words.

The student needs to be taught to focus on the main idea and on those points that support the main idea. The student's notes should be a clue to the organization of the original material.

There are three basic forms of note making:

1. *The Paragraph*—This is probably most easily developed, but it frequently is not the best organized. Each paragraph represents a new idea.

2. *The Sentence*—This is better than the paragraph form in that it attempts to organize the material by stating a series of sentences. It thus may also be easier to use in review.

3. *The Outline*—This provides the best opportunity for organization.

Kollaritsch (17) suggests an outline method of note-making that involves relatively little writing. Instead of detailed description, the method consists of (1) stating the section heading of a chapter, noting the page on which it is found; (2) noting what each paragraph in the chapter is

* See Robert A. Palmatier, "Comparison of Four Note-Taking Procedures," *Journal of Reading,* 14 (January 1971), 235–40; and Don Butcofsky, "Any Learning Skills Taught in High School?" *Journal of Reading,* 15 (December 1971), 195–98.

about, and what kinds of things the student needs to remember from the paragraph without writing out the details (e.g., definition of *parapsychology*); (3) reviewing immediately after reading and indicating by a check if he can recall what each written heading elicits without referring to the text. The same procedure is used for review.

Obviously, the best notes seem to be written in outline form. Charts, diagrams, and illustrations should be included in the outline, or at least it should indicate where they are located. The writer or speaker frequently summarizes in a simple drawing hours of lecture or written material. Charts frequently show the organization of an entire discussion.

The student should learn to read for the topic sentence. He also must read for the supporting details, for the speaker's organization, and for transitional words that give clues to the entire paragraph or chapter.

Such cue words as *The main point is, There are three major ideas represented here, I will discuss three major issues,* and *The uses of lye are* indicate that the writer is about to present major ideas.

Words like *and, besides, furthermore, moreover, likewise,* and *in addition* indicate that a supporting idea is about to be introduced. Words like *first, in the first place,* and *second* indicate that a number of subpoints will be introduced. Words like *consequently, therefore, hence, thus, it follows, in conclusion, thereupon,* and *accordingly* indicate that the point now being made flows from previous statements or describe a cause-effect relationship. Words like *finally* and *in conclusion* indicate that a summary is about to be made.

Words like *but, however, whereas, nevertheless, on the contrary, yet, on the other hand, rather, in comparison, although, conversely, in spite of, still,* and *in contrast* indicate that a contradictory or contrasting statement or point of view is about to be introduced.

Words like *classified, belongs to, broken down, part of,* and *divided* indicate a classification or a division. *For example, for instance, to demonstrate,* and *an illustration of* introduce an example. Words like *defined as, means,* and *is* often introduce a definition.

It is not uncommon to find a conscientious student failing to get significant results from note making. Perhaps the notes themselves are adequate, but the student has not taken the pains to organize them. He has written them on any piece of paper available. Unfortunately, when the time comes for review, he can no longer locate the odd bits of paper or, if he can find them, he no longer knows what comes first and what comes next.

Some students may be too wordy. Simplicity is the key to good note making. Thoroughness, however, should not be ignored. The student must learn to take enough notes so that if after the lecture he spends a few moments on them, he can organize them into a representation of the lecture or of his reading. This is impossible when he takes notes only over those elements that he does not understand.*

Finally, notes must be reworked. They should not be rewritten, but as soon as possible they should be revised. The more recently the student has written them, the better will be his memory for the content that they contain and the more easily will he be able to organize them. Notes do not change physically, but unless the student rereads them and reworks them immediately, he will lose much information. It is the student who loses that "something" required to make notes meaningful.

In summary, let us suggest a few guidelines for effective note making. The student should learn to:

1. Use a standard 8½" × 11" notebook.
2. Use a loose-leaf notebook, not clipboards, small pads, or ordinary writing tablets.
3. Divide his paper into two sections: the right side of the page to be used for actual note-making, the left margin for personal comments. Below the notes and personal comments may be written the summary.
4. Number each page, entitle notes, and begin each new topic on a new page.
5. Keep notes from different classes in separate notebooks, or separate them with dividers or tabs.
6. Take notes in ink.
7. Use only one side of the page.
8. Make notes brief and to the point.
9. Use quotation marks whenever the writer's or the speaker's words are quoted.
10. Copy definitions, formulas, and statistics exactly. They usually cannot be shortened.
11. Move on if a point is missed. Allow room to add it later.
12. Combine notes on the same topic.
13. Make notes of those items that are emphasized, that are frequently repeated, on which there will be an examination, and that are written on the chalkboard.
14. Make a table of contents for the notebook.
15. Organize notes, indenting supporting points and subtopics.

* Eisner and Rohde (9) found that making notes after the lecture was just as effective as making them during the lecture. Perhaps if students were trained to delay note making, retention would generally improve. Notes are only an aid to learning, not learning.

READING FOR EVALUATION
(CRITICAL READING)

Critical reading involves literal comprehension, but it also demands that the reader evaluate—pass personal judgment on the quality, value, accuracy, and truthfulness of what is read (32). It involves the evaluation of the validity, accuracy, and intellectual worthwhileness of printed materials (10). It means that the reader must be able to recognize the author's intent and point of view, to distinguish fact from opinion, and to make judgments and inferences (23).

Larter and Taylor (19), in a study of 197 students in grades ten to twelve in Winnipeg, found that IQ and academic achievement were the best predictors of an individual's ability to think critically. The critical thinkers were aggressive, daring, incisive; they were interested in power, influence, and renown; their fathers were well educated and had a prestigious position; they were alert and poised.

Relatively few instruments are available to appraise critical thinking abilities (6). The *Gans Selection Rejection Test* measures the ability to detect relevancy and irrelevancy. It is usable with intermediate-grade pupils. The *Ginn Basic Reading Tests* measure the ability to interpret the writer's suggestions and to recognize propaganda devices; Mancy's *Intermediate Reading Test* measures critical interpretation of science materials, and Sochor's *Intermediate Reading Test* does the same thing for social studies materials. The *Watson-Glaser Critical Thinking Appraisal* and *Kay's Critical Reading Test* evaluate critical thinking abilities of junior and senior high school students.

The student must constantly read to evaluate. The good comprehender is a critical reader. He checks the truth, logic, reliability, and accuracy of what is written. He looks for contradictory material. He relates the material to his experience. He distinguishes fact from fiction, is concerned with the timeliness of the material, and tries to understand the author's motives.

The critical reader is as much interested in why something is said as in what is said. He is sensitive to how words are used and is slightly suspicious of the author's biases. He pays particular attention to words with several meanings. He checks the copyright data, the author's reputation, and the publisher's past performance. He looks for errors of reasoning, of analogy, of overgeneralization, of oversimplification, and of distortion. He looks for one-sided presentations, prejudices, biases, faulty inferences, and propaganda. He avoids jumping to quick conclusions.

The critical reader examines the arguments and the language.* He

* *Administrator's Guide,* pp. 42–43.

needs to be able to follow inductive and deductive argument, to spot generalizations, to be sensitive to analogies and such simple devices as guilt through association. He needs to know the functions of language: to inform (the informative), to vent or excite feelings (the expressive), to move people to do things (the incitive).

The teacher can and must lessen the difficulties of critical reading, among which are the following (23): the use of a single textbook, the halo effect that is attached to the printed word, the desire on the part of school people to avoid controversial subjects, the emphasis on conformity, and the natural involvement of personal prejudices and emotions.

Huelsmann (15) mentions three ways of teaching critical reading: the direct approach, the incidental approach, and the functional approach. Kottmeyer (18) experimented with a direct approach. Newspapers, magazines, editorials, and cartoons were read critically. Students were given definitions of propaganda techniques and sought to discover their presence in the materials read. The functional approach is one in which class materials are taught with the definite purpose of promoting critical skills. The least effective is an incidental approach. It refers to the training in critical reading that may come as a mere by-product of social studies learning.

Russell (31) recommends group discussion as a way of getting at assumptions or preconceptions. Artley (1) suggests that the essential process is one of raising questions or of setting up situations based on reading that require an evaluative response and then, by a process of guidance, helping the student to think his way through to an answer. A simple technique is to stop the student before he comes to the writer's conclusion and to let him state all the possible solutions.

Harvison (13) points out that teachers will have to depend upon their own creativity and initiative in teaching critical reading. Activities are as many and as varied as the teacher's imagination permits. In the intermediate grades and in the junior-senior high school years the student may be encouraged to read many texts to find answers, with the emphasis being on problem solving, inductive thinking, and frequent verbal expression among students.

The critical reader reads all materials in a questioning way. He constantly asks: Why? He is constantly concerned lest the writer's prejudices, biases, or assumptions may be coloring his presentation and consequently lead to an acceptance of a wrong point of view.

The critical reader reads beyond the materials. He is not satisfied with the simple statements. He uses his previous experiences and previous learning to understand fully what he is reading.

The critical reader thinks with the writer. He formulates the question clearly, checks the authenticity of the materials, evaluates the author's credentials, looks for errors in reasoning, and develops a sensitivity to the rightness or wrongness of what is presented.

The critical reader suspends judgment until the writer has finished his argument. As he proceeds with the material he asks himself: Is the author consistent? Is he logical? Are his motives noble? Are his facts true? Are his conclusions correct?

Critical reading is slow, sentence by sentence, and thought by thought reading. It requires the reader to analyze carefully the writer's words, his purpose, and his implications.

Let us look at these:

WORDS   Many words can be used by writers to arouse unfavorable feelings toward a person or an idea. For example, the words *fascist, communist,* or *socialist* usually arouse antagonism and distrust. In some circles, to be labeled *black, Jew,* or *Catholic* may leave similar impressions. The words *conservative, capitalist, warmonger, isolationist, progressive educator, selfish, conformist, world-minded, idealist, overzealous,* and *liberal* similarly mean many things to many people.

PURPOSE   What is the writer's purpose? Does he wish to inform or to entertain, to teach or to move emotionally? Is his motive open or hidden? The reader should constantly ask: Who would benefit if I agreed with the speaker or writer? What kind of evidence does he bring forth?

IMPLICATIONS   It is obvious that the reader must prepare himself so that he can detect generalities, fallacious reasoning, and unwarranted clichés. As citizens, as buyers of somebody's products, or as students in a classroom, individuals are constantly subject to writings that attempt to make them think in a given way. They are asked to give allegiance to one thing and to turn against something else.

Some common techniques used by speakers and writers to sway public opinion are the following:

1. False or glittering generalization.
2. Bias or prejudice.
3. Unwarranted inference or cliché.
4. Confusion of fact and opinion.
5. Distortion of truth.
6. Begging the question.
7. False analogy.
8. Error in inductive or deductive reasoning.
9. Ignoring alternatives.
10. Oversimplification.

11. Changing the meaning of terms.

12. Misleading headline.

13. Failure to cite sources for one's information.

14. Using prominent names to bolster one's point of view (testimonial).

15. Assuming all relationships are casual.

16. Use of bandwagon appeals.

17. Use of questionable sampling.

18. Appeal to emotion rather than to intellect.

19. Relating only one side.

20. *Argumentum ad hominem*—Getting the reader to accept a conclusion by ridiculing the opposition, by snubbing it, or by ridiculing the person who holds the argument rather than by attacking the argument. Name-calling is such a technique.

21. Use of straw men, straw issues, outright lies, digs, and snide remarks.

22. Transfer techniques (I'm Jimmy Jackson, I drink Mayberry).

The teacher may develop the critical reading skill with exercises similar to the following:

1. Teach students to differentiate between factual news reporting and editorial writing.

2. Have students identify the types of writing that are more likely to state the facts, that indulge in the bantering about of personal opinion, or that specialize in propaganda.

3. Have students select from three or four stated purposes the one that best represents the writer's purpose.

4. Have students select from a list of words those that tend to arouse the emotions of the reader.

5. Have students match given propaganda techniques with statements such as the following:

Propaganda Techniques

a. Citation of an authority or a testimonial

b. Bandwagon or everybody-is-doing-it technique

c. Glittering generality

d. Transfer technique (similar to testimonial, but the person does not say anything directly associated with what is being advocated or recommended)

e. Name-calling

Statements

_____ 1. Mr. Bott says there is no need to fear snakes.

_____ 2. Everybody is going to Lakewood Park on Sunday afternoon.

_____ 3. Grand Park is the finest park in central Missouri.

_____ 4. Don't be a wallflower.

_____ 5. A and B tastes best. Everybody drinks A and B.

_____ 6. We have the finest and the world's largest industrial facilities.

_____ 7. When you wear a hat you are more of a man and people hire men.

_____ 8. There's nothing like wood to add to the decor of your home.

_____ 9. The best music comes from a Cunningham radio.

_____10. People who know drink their beer out of a glass.

_____11. Theresa Pond, movie star, uses Market soap.

_____12. You will look better in a Manor shirt.

_____13. Fifty million people carry Blue-White insurance.*

6. Have pupils read a paragraph and learn to make the proper inferences: †

> Yet the Australian bushmen (horse thieves and highwaymen) enjoyed much popularity and sympathy; they represented pluck and courage; they were under-dogs fighting the law (which is rarely highly respected in pioneer communities) and attacking property, often looked upon as "fair game" by those who have none.

1. A certain disrespect for the law is a common feature of many pioneer communities.   a. _____

2. The Australian pioneers had a special reason for restlessness and discontent under the law.   b. _____

3. It is improbable that any Australian pioneer disagreed with the assumption that property is "fair game" for those who have none.   c. _____

4. Although the Australian bushrangers were thieves and high-waymen, they had the admiration and sympathy of many of the pioneers.   d. _____

5. In some pioneer communities courage and daring were held in higher regard than honesty and respect for the law.   e. _____

* This exercise is effective only if the students have been taught the various propaganda techniques.
† Exercise 6 is from Doris Wilcox Gilbert, *Study in Depth* (Englewood Cliffs, N.J.: Prentice-Hall, Inc., 1966), p. 41.

READING FOR LEARNING

Complete reading is said to involve four steps: recognition, understanding, reaction, and integration. Ideally, the reading a student does will influence and direct some future activity. In a very real sense, then, whenever the student integrates what he is reading, he is studying. This may be the ultimate in comprehension. Gray (12) points out that integration is "the heart of the learning act in reading."

Integrative reading is commonly identified with study-type reading. Herber (14) defines study skills as work skills that produce useful knowledge for a learner; they are reading skills especially adapted to execute particular tasks. They help us to develop ideas, to remember ideas, and to use ideas. Russell (30) defines study skills as including skill in locating, selecting, using, and evaluating information, ability to adjust method and rate of reading to the purpose for reading and to the nature of the material and skill in retaining what is read.

Study habit inventories typically measure four study variables: morale or self-confidence, scholarly drive and values, study mechanics, and planning for study.

Berg and Rentel (2) note the general lack of agreement as to what study techniques to teach and state that at least some evidence shows that both failing and successful students use about the same study skills, but they nevertheless conclude on the basis of their evaluation of studies in this area that instruction in study skills does produce significantly higher study skill levels than were obtained through trial-and-error methods.

Let us look at a method of integrative reading, such as that proposed by Robinson (28, pp. 13–14). It involves five steps: survey, question, read, recite, and review (SQ3R). The SQ3R method is especially designed for history, social science, science, and prose materials.

How good is the SQ3R method? Donald (8) found that the use of the SQ3R method on the junior high level resulted in a significant difference in factual type of knowledge of content material. The method seemed to develop better powers of organization, association, and critical thinking.

Various modifications of the SQ3R method are available today. Pauk (24) developed a reading technique for prose, poetry, and drama called the EVOKER system—explore, vocabulary, oral reading, key ideas, evaluations, and recapitulation. Later he developed the OK4R (25) method—overview, key ideas, read, recall, reflect, and review. Johnson (16) developed the Three-Level Outlining Method. It requires the student to outline and to locate information.

Survey

BROAD OUTLINE

Surveying is the first step in the SQ3R method and is the process of becoming familiar with the broad outlines, the chapter title, the main headings, the topic sentences, and the summary.

The good student gets an overall picture of what he is reading or studying. The reason is obvious. The driver consults a road map before venturing on a trip. The race driver drives the course many times before the actual race. The diner surveys a menu. In rapid fashion he notices the dinners, sandwiches, appetizers, and drinks, and the prices do not escape him. The baseball player checks the infield for chuckholes, and the general surveys the terrain before initiating his attack. Each of these persons wants to know what lies ahead so he may proceed with the proper technique. The student must know what type of article he is reading before he can choose his techniques well.

In surveying a book, the *title* tells in general what the book is about; the *preface* gives a more detailed statement. In it the writer tells why he wrote the book and what he seeks to accomplish.

The *table of contents* gives a more detailed outline of the book. It gives clues to the writer's organization.

The chapter *titles, headings,* and *summaries* should come next. The headings are especially important. They are the clues to the chapter organization. In general, the chapter title tells the main idea. The major headings give the broad outlines of the chapter and show how the writer supports the main idea. Under each major heading may be one or more side headings.

The *topic sentence* in each paragraph is especially important. It summarizes the paragraph. It contains the main idea of the paragraph and usually is the first sentence in a paragraph. Sometimes, however, it occurs at the end of the paragraph or in the middle of the paragraph, or it may even not be stated.

Surveying thus allows the reader to "warm up" to the reading task ahead. It gives an overall view of the material.

Elementary teachers have always prepared the pupil for the reading task. They have made certain that the child had the necessary experience for understanding and that he had a purpose for reading. This is what surveying accomplishes for the more mature student.

Smith and Hesse (33), in a study of 340 eleventh-grade students in Madison, Wisconsin, found that listening to a cognitive organizer or preview had a positive effect on the attitudes of poor readers and on their ability to identify the main idea. It did not have the same effect on good readers. It seemed that the good readers had reasonably well-developed styles of organizing themselves cognitively to comprehend what they read, and in fact, an organization different from the one that they might naturally develop might even hinder comprehension.

Skimming is frequently used in previewing. Skimming gives a quick glimpse at the organization. It is a sort of threshing process in which the wheat is separated from the chaff. The reader is after certain information or perhaps wishes to decide whether or not to read the selection more intensively.

Question

The second step in integrative reading is the *question*. Sometimes the writer poses questions at the beginning or at the end of the chapter. The teacher may suggest questions as a part of the assignment. The student should become able to make his own questions. In doing this, he may turn the main headings or italicized words into questions. The teacher has many questions at his disposal. His questions may call for memorization, evaluaton, recall, recognition, comparison, summarization, discussion, analysis, decision making, outlining, illustration, refutation, and inductive or deductive thinking.

Melnik (21) notes that questions establish a basis for identifying and clarifying the purpose for reading. Taba and others suggest that the teacher's questions circumscribe the mental operations that students can perform and determine what points they can explore and what modes of thought they can learn (34). Frederick (11), however, found that the introduction of vocabulary terms and questions prior to reading did not result in better learning or retention on the part of students. Rothkopf (29) suggests that the set of questions that students *expect* largely determines what they learn. He feels it is the inspection activities that determine learning rather than immediate feedback of knowledge of results and that questions asked after the reading are more important for understanding and retention than those asked before.

Nevertheless, it would appear that questions provide a certain "readiness" for reading and guide the student's reading by creating a set to respond in a particular manner. They are motivational stimuli, permitting the selection of relevant information and the rejection of incidental information.

Melnik lists two main functions of questions. As a diagnostic tool, the unstructured question permits the teacher to observe the variety of individual responses: how the student approaches the reading passage; his tendency to relate ideas or perhaps to focus on isolated details; his ability to organize; his tendency to let emotions and prejudices influence his comprehension. As an instructional tool, the question helps the student to identify the author's pattern of thought or to clarify meaning. Questions are most effective in enhancing delayed and immediate recall for the largest number of meaning values. The question technique tends to surpass both careful reading without questions and rereading of the same material (2).

Formulating questions encourages the reader to seek answers as he reads. Many writers believe that students should write down these questions as a basis for review. Additional questions may be added during the actual reading.

Here are a few suggestions about asking questions:

1. The student should ask questions both before and after he reads. He must turn the chapter title, headings, unfamiliar terms, etc., into questions.
2. He should ask questions during reading.
3. He should try to answer his questions before actually beginning reading.

Read

The third step of an effective study procedure is *purposeful reading.* Let us examine some of the objectives of purposeful reading. The reader should do the following:

1. Have a definite reason for his reading
2. Define clearly the problem that he wishes to solve
3. Focus his attention on the main points
4. Try to group the supporting details with the main idea
5. Keep in mind the nature of the assignment
6. Pay special attention to illustrations of all kinds, graphs, maps, charts
7. Be a flexible reader, adjusting his rate to the purpose of the reading and the nature of the material
8. Try to remember that he is seeking to answer questions

Study-type reading frequently is intensive reading. It is careful, rather slow reading with emphasis upon remembering details. Intensive reading requires that upon reaching the end of the chapter the reader recognize the main idea. He should know where the author was heading and how he got there. He tends to form an outline of what he has read. He sees the major and supporting points.

Recite

The fourth step of Robinson's SQ3R study method, *recite,* is literally a self-examination. Here the student attempts to answer the questions that he has posed without referring to his notes or other aids. Only when he fails should he consult his notes or refer to the book. One study method has been labeled a "self-recitation method" because of the great importance of recitation in learning. Recitation directs our attention to specific questions, thereby aiding concentration. Concentration is a by-product of having a goal that challenges the person's whole mind (26).

Self-recitation makes a number of contributions to effective learning. The student is immediately aware of how well he read, how accurately he accomplished his purposes, and whether he can express his newfound knowledge in his own words. If he can verbalize his knowledge to his own satisfaction, he can generally explain or recite to another. Recitation is the heart of effective study; it is the seeking of answers to self-imposed questions and of putting new learnings into one's own words.

Review

The fifth and final step of Robinson's method is *review*. Study is not complete until it includes a plan for retention. If learning is to be of any use in later situations, the student must remember what he has learned. Actually, remembering itself is defined in various ways. We say that one remembers data if he can recall them, relearn them more quickly, recognize them, use them in test situations, or use them to learn something else more easily. Perhaps the most important criterion of retention is the transfer that is made from the school situation to the life situation, to future acquisition of knowledge, and to future behavior.

Review becomes a relatively simple process if the reading has been done correctly. If the student developed an outline, wrote out questions for himself, developed the textbook into an outline, or made a summary, he might use any one of these as the basis for a good review.

Review, whether through notes or through rereading, should be an exercise in critical reading and thinking. Basically there are two methods of review: symbolical review and review by reimpression. Reimpression is the type of review that occurs when the person rereads. Symbolical review is done through recall, self-recitation, class discussion, tests, summaries, and lecture notes. This type of review encourages thinking, assimilation, integration, and organization. It is review with a purpose and with an eye on application.

Pauk provides the following outline of the OK4R method:

The OK4R Method of Reading

BEFORE

O 1. Overview. Take about five minutes to read introductory and summary paragraphs of the assignment. Then read center and side headings, or topic sentences if there are no headings, to determine general content and sequence of topics. Locate the main divisions.

K 2. Key Ideas. Distinguish key ideas from secondary ideas and supporting materials. Convert headings or topic sentences into questions—a sure way to become involved in the author's ideas.

DURING

R¹ 3. Read. Read the sections or paragraphs consecutively to answer your questions and to see *how* supporting materials clarify or prove key points. Pay close attention to transitional words and phrases. If you are reading persuasive materials, keep asking yourself: What is the evidence? Does is prove the point? Is there enough support? Do I believe this? Why or why not? If you are reading exposition, ask yourself the following questions: What is the main point in this section? Does this example make the main point clear? How? Can I think of other examples?

AFTER

R² 4. Recall. After reading, test your memory and understanding. Without looking at the book, try to say or write the main points and supporting materials in your own words. If you cannot do so immediately after reading, you cannot hope to tomorrow in class or next week in an exam. Now—but not before—take brief summary notes in your notebook or underline key points in your book and make "recall" notes in the margins. Remember to *understand first*, then write.

R³ 5. Reflect. Step 4, Recall, will help fix the material in your mind. To make it really yours, go further: Think about it. Relating new facts and ideas to others you already know gives added meaning to new and old knowledge and establishes both more firmly in your mind. This is the essence of all creative thinking: the discovery of new relationships and new significance.

R⁴ 6. Review. To keep material fresh in mind, review it periodically. Re-read your notes and say over the sequence of main ideas and supporting materials until you have them once more firmly in mind. Mastery is a never-ending process.*

* Walter Pauk, "Techniques for Textbook Study," *Reading Improvement*, 6 (Spring 1969), 7–10.

Developing Study Skills

Educational Developmental Laboratories supplies a study skills library designed to help the student to develop the essential study skills and to improve his reading in the content areas. The program is planned as a sequential twelve-year program. It emphasizes reading in science and social studies and provides training in reference skills. At present materials are available for grades four through nine. A similar program is offered by Science Research Associates.

Mahoney (20) outlines various study skills, estimates the grade level on which they are to be taught, and suggests tools and methods to be used in teaching them. She covers teaching of the alphabet, dictionary, parts of a book, encyclopedia, library skills, study methods, and research skills.

Location Skills

The good student is one who has learned "to find the facts." He knows how to locate information. This means a familiarity with library aids and with such library resources as the Dewey classification system and card catalog, the various indexes, encyclopedias, and almanacs, but it also means the ability to find the desired material within a book, a chapter, a paragraph, or a sentence. It means that he knows how to use a table of contents, an appendix, and the footnotes. There is a high degree of relationship between a student's ability to locate and use reference materials and the grades that he gets in school.

READING MAPS, GRAPHS, TABLES, AND CHARTS

Sometimes the writer cannot accurately put into words what he wants to say. Writers thus frequently use pictures, maps, graphs, tables, and charts to explain more fully than is possible through words. Unfortunately, the student gets from these materials what is intended only if he can read the symbols, terms, and colors that the writer incorporates into these illustrations.

Reading Maps

Map reading requires numerous skills. The student needs to identify natural features such as rivers and lakes; land shapes such as continents and islands; and man-made features such as railroads and highways. He needs to know the meaning of gulf, bay, earth, distance, scale, latitude, longitude, sphere, hemisphere, pole, and equator. He needs to be able to read map symbols.

He needs to read physical and political maps of the United States, of North America, and of the world. He needs to read maps depicting crops, rainfall, population, vegetation, wind belts, and ocean routes. He must learn to read maps of cities. And he should be able to read topographic and polar maps.

At the earliest level the pupil will learn simple concepts of direction (north, south, east, west), of distance, and of scale. He next advances to a recognition of large land and water forms on the globe, and he may learn to identify water, land, forests, and mountains by their color designation. Gradually, his learning becomes more specific. He will learn to locate continents, seas, oceans, and countries on a map.

In the upper elementary grades and on the junior high level the student usually learns to use map symbols, scales, and legends. He learns to find and use the equator, longitude, and latitude, and he can understand the causes of night and day and of the seasons. He translates latitude into miles and longitude into time. He becomes familiar with the poles, the arctic and antarctic circles, the Tropic of Capricorn and the Tropic of Cancer. He understands meredians and parallels. He develops skill in location, in direction (upstream, downstream, etc.), and in identification of natural features (continents, countries, islands, peninsulas, oceans, rivers, lakes, gulfs, mountains, plains, deserts) and cultural features (cities, capitals, railroads, industries, crops).

He learns that in the tropics it is warm all year; that between the tropics and the arctic-antarctic circles the temperature varies from season to season; that near the poles it is cold all year.

Teaching the student to read maps includes the following steps:

1. Studying the title of the map
2. Studying each symbol (the legend)
3. Noting direction on the map
4. Analyzing and applying the map scale
5. Relating the area under study to a more general or larger area (Kansas in relation to the United States)

The following exercises are helpful in teaching map skills:

1. Relate map study to pictures and aerial photographs.

2. Demonstrate how a small map or globe represents a large territory.

3. Make a map of the student's hometown or of his immediate environment (school building, school grounds).

4. Teach that shading from green through yellow, brown, and red indicates an increase in altitude.

5. Require students to find answers for questions such as the following:

    a. How many continents are there?
    b. How do you know that the earth is round?
    c. What route did Balboa take?
    d. What changes have occurred in the map of Europe as a result of World War II?
    e. What time is it in Tokyo and in London when it is 6 P.M. in New York?

6. Require the student to locate on the map an example of each of the following:

archipelago	coastline	highland	ocean
basin	continent	inlet	peninsula
bay	delta	island	plateau
boundary	desert	isthmus	port
branch	dike	jungle	reef
canyon	divide	lake	river
cape	estuary	marsh	sea
channel	fiord	mesa	strait
city	gulf	mountain	swamp
cliff	harbor	oasis	tributary
			valley

A chart such as Figure 8-2 is useful in teaching the meaning of these terms.

7. Require the student to match picture symbols with word symbols (Figure 8-3).

8. Teach the representation of elevation and slope through contour lines.

9. Study the meanings of such terms as

apogee	isobar	altitude
contour line	isotherm	longitude
divide	meridian	parallel
equinox	perigee	meridian
international date line	satellite	Mercator projection

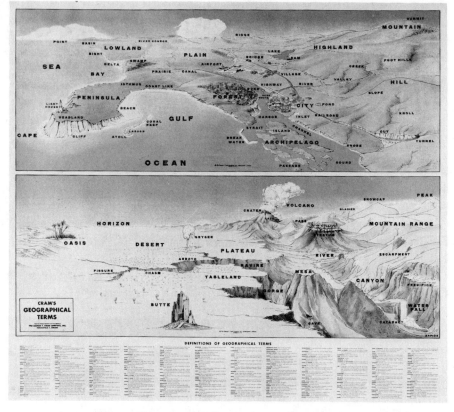

FIGURE 8-2   GEOGRAPHICAL TERMS. This "Geographical Terms Chart" is published by the George F. Cram Company, Inc., Indianapolis, and is reproduced by permission.

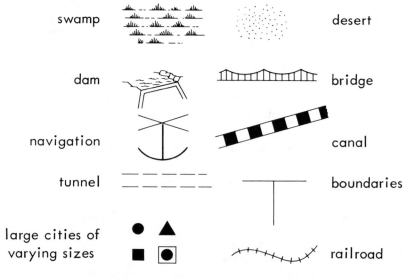

FIGURE 8-3   GEOGRAPHICAL SYMBOLS

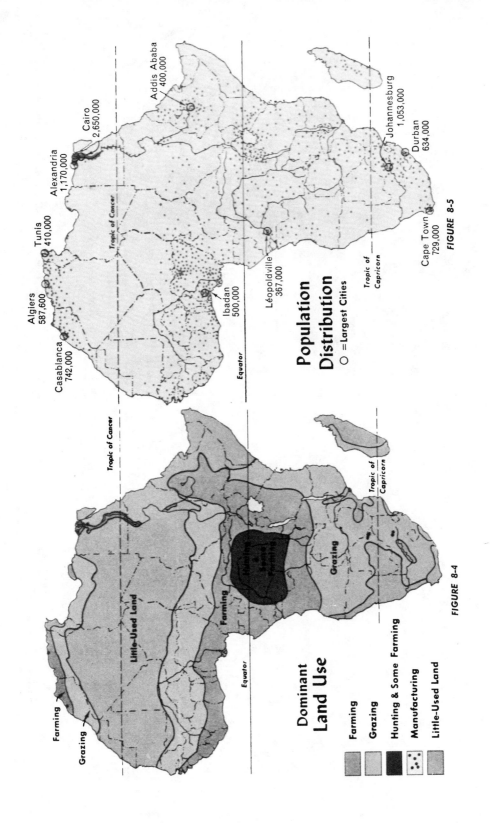

**Population
Distribution**

○ = Largest Cities

Casablanca
742,000

Alglers
587,600

Tunis
410,000

Alexandria
1,170,000

Cairo
2,650,000

Addis Ababa
400,000

Tropic of Cancer

Ibadan
500,000

Léopoldville
367,000

Equator

Johannesburg
1,053,000

Durban
634,000

Tropic of
Capricorn

Cape Town
729,000

FIGURE 8-5

**Dominant
Land Use**

Farming

Grazing

Hunting & Some Farming

Manufacturing

Little-Used Land

Tropic of Cancer

Farming

Grazing

Little-Used Land

Farming

Hunting
& Some
Farming

Farming

Grazing

Grazing

Equator

Tropic of
Capricorn

FIGURE 8-4

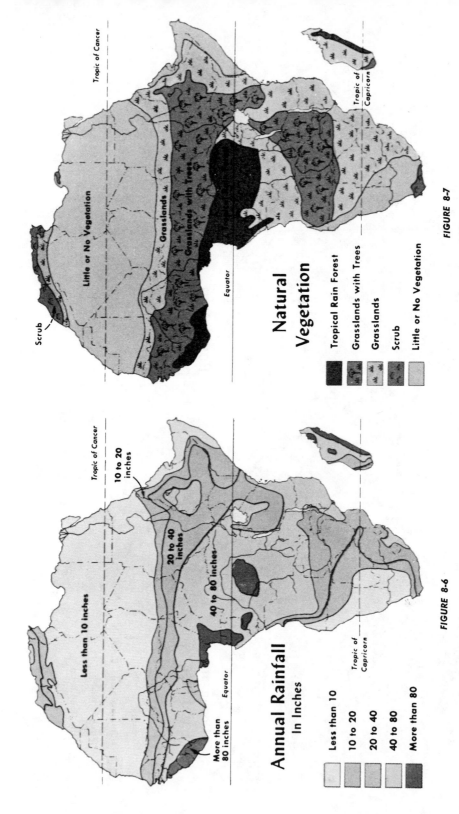

Natural Vegetation

Tropical Rain Forest
Grasslands with Trees
Grasslands
Scrub
Little or No Vegetation

Scrub

Grasslands

Grasslands with Trees

Little or No Vegetation

Tropic of Cancer

Tropic of Capricorn

Equator

FIGURE 8-7

Annual Rainfall
In Inches

Less than 10
10 to 20
20 to 40
40 to 80
More than 80

Less than 10 inches

10 to 20 inches

20 to 40 inches

40 to 80 inches

More than 80 inches

Tropic of Cancer

Tropic of Capricorn

Equator

FIGURE 8-6

Maps are from *Exploring the Old World,* © 1957 by O. Stuart Hamer, Orlando W. Stephenson, Ralph S. Yohe, Ben F. Ahlschwede, Dwight W. Follett, and Herbert H. Gross. Used by permission.

10. Require the student to answer questions based on maps. For example:

a. In Africa, the rainfall around the equator (see Figure 8-6) is generally heavier than either north or south of the equator.

_____true

_____false

b. North of the equator there is very little vegetation (see Figure 8-7).

_____true

_____false

c. Farming is most common near the equator (see Figure 8-4).

_____true

_____false

d. The population near the Tropic of Cancer is more dense than near the equator (see Figure 8-5).

_____true

_____false

Reading Charts

Another important skill is the ability to read graphs. There are four kinds of graphs. The *pictorial* graph (see Figure 8-8) in which the units are expressed in picture form is the easiest to read. It uses pictures to show relationships between realities. The *bar* graph (see Figures 8-9 and 8-10) compares the size of quantities. It expresses amounts. For example, one may want to compare the heights of various buildings or dams in the United States; the number of ticket sales made by the boys and girls in a class; or the number of deaths that are attributable to various causes, such as drowning, car accidents, and airplane accidents. In each instance, the bar graph shows how much more or less one type is than another. A bar graph may be either vertical or horizontal.

The *line* graph (see Figures 8-11 and 8-12) shows changes between quantities. It indicates what has happened over a period of time. It indicates whether there has been an increase or a decrease, for example, in the amount of rain each month of the year, in the price of foods, in daily temperature.

The *circle* graph (see Figure 8-13) shows the relation of parts to a whole. It may be used, for example, to indicate the percentage of A's, B's, C's, and D's in a certain class; how much of the family budget goes to food, clothing, shelter, savings, car, miscellaneous; or the percentage of the school budget that is allotted for salaries, maintenance, and the general operation of the school plant.

To read graphs of one kind or another the student should learn to observe the following steps:

1. Read the title of the graph—this tells what the graph is about.
2. Discover what is being compared—persons, places, or things.
3. Be able to interpret the legend and the meaning of the vertical axis and the horizontal axis.
4. Identify the scale of measure that has been used. What does each figure represent?
5. Discover what conclusions can be drawn from the graph.

   Figures 8-8 through 8-13 illustrate the various types of graphs.* There is a set of questions with at least one of the different types of graphs that checks up on the student's ability to *read* it.

FIGURE 8-8   PICTORIAL GRAPH (PICTOGRAPH)

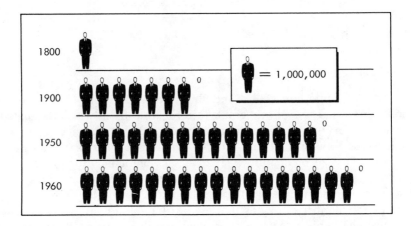

1. The population of the United States in 1900 was more than seven times that in 1800.
   _____true
   _____false

2. Between 1950 and 1960 the population grew approximately twenty million.
   _____true
   _____false

1. The population of New York City is about
   a.   8,000,000
   b.   7,000,000
   c.   800,000
   d. 8,000,000,000

* Figures 8-8 through 8-13 are reprinted by permission from the *Listen and Read Workbook,* copyright 1961, and *Listen and Read,* MN, copyright 1969, by Educational Developmental Laboratories.

FIGURE 8-9

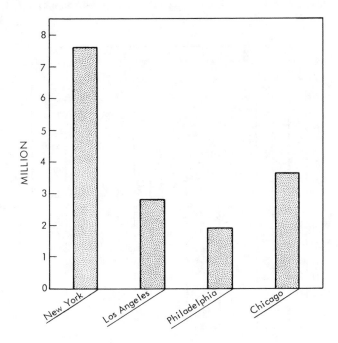

2. The city of Los Angeles has more people than the city of Philadelphia.
   _____true
   _____false

3. The city of New York is more than twice as large as the city of Chicago.
   _____true
   _____false

The teacher may require the student to develop:

1. A bar graph showing the ticket sales of the following groups: sixth graders, 200; seventh graders, 350; eighth graders, 300; fourth graders, 220.

2. A bar graph showing the percentage of voters who turned out in various countries in recent elections: Austria, 95 percent; Greece, 85 percent; Korea, 80 percent; United States, 60 percent.

3. A bar graph showing the death rates per 100,000 occurring in 1970 as a result of various illnesses: influenza and pneumonia, 305; heart, 360.3; all accidents, 54.2; malignant neoplasms, 162.0; cerebrovascular diseases, 101.7.

4. A bar graph showing the battle deaths in World War II for the following countries: Austria, 380,000; China, 1,325,000; Germany, 3,250,000; Japan, 1,270,000; Poland, 664,000; Rumania, 350,000; Russia, 6,115,000; England, 357,000; United States, 291,000.

5. A graph showing the number of students reporting different types of problems is included here because it illustrates another type of bar graph.

FIGURE 8-10

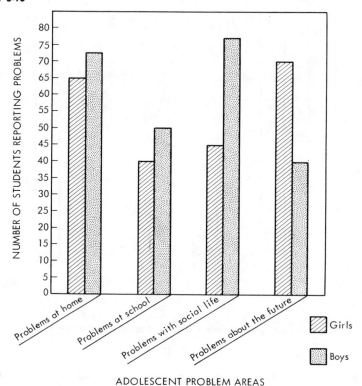

ADOLESCENT PROBLEM AREAS

FIGURE 8-11   LINE GRAPH

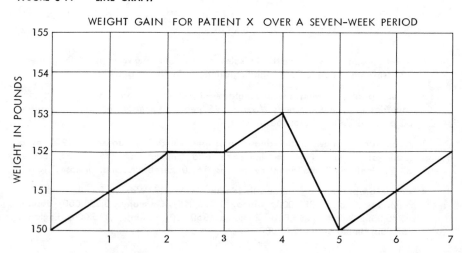

WEIGHT GAIN FOR PATIENT X OVER A SEVEN-WEEK PERIOD

1. Patient X weighed the least during the second week.
   _____true
   _____false

2. Patient X weighed the most in the fourth week.
   _____true
   _____false

3. Patient X weighed eleven pounds more at the end of the seven-week period.
   _____true
   _____false

Have the pupils draw the following:

1. A line graph showing John's percentile scores on four weekly tests: week 1, 92; week 2, 85; week 3, 65; week 4, 98.

2. A line graph showing the increase and decrease in battle deaths in various wars in which the United States was involved: Revolutionary War, 4,435; War of 1812, 2,260; Mexican War, 1,733; Civil War, 140,414; Spanish-American War, 385; World War I, 53,402; World War II, 291,557; Korean War, 33,629.

FIGURE 8-12

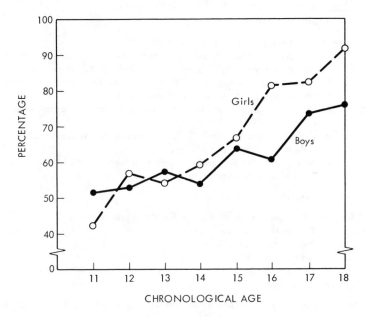

The relationship between chronological age and percentage of boys and girls choosing the same person as their best friend on two occasions separated by a two-week interval.

The Development of Friendships

The 969 subjects used in this study were obtained from one city in Pennsylvania. Girls were studied from families of approximately average socioeconomic status; a similar condition prevailed in the earlier study of rural adolescents. A comparison of the rural and urban boys in their fluctuations indicates a slightly greater stability in friendships among urban than among rural adolescents, although the differences found were not statistically reliable. The relationship between age and percentage of boys and girls choosing the same person as their best friend is shown. For both boys and girls there is a decided tendency toward an increased stability of friendship, with the girls showing the greater increase.

1. The overall and most significant conclusion to be drawn from this graph is
_____a. that boys at age 13 have more lasting friendships than girls of the same age.
_____b. that girls show a greater increase in stability of friendships.
_____c. that both boys and girls, as they grow older, show a decided tendency toward an increased stability of friendship.
_____d. that boys and girls at age 15 are about equal in their ability to maintain friendships.

2. The greatest difference between boys and girls in ability to maintain stable friendships occurs at the age of
_____a. 12.
_____b. 14.
_____c. 16.
_____d. 17.
_____e. 18.

3. Four of the following statements are true. Mark them.
_____a. At ages 11 and 13, the percentage of boys who maintained stable friendships was higher than for the girls of the same age.
_____b. At age 18, slightly more than 90% of the girls maintained stable friendships for at least a two-week period.
_____c. Between ages 11 and 16, the girls showed an approximate 80% increase in stability of friendships.
_____d. Between ages 11 and 18, boys showed an approximate increase of 30% in stability of friendships.
_____e. At age 15, the percentage difference between boys and girls was the least of all other ages considered.

Put a ✔ beside the correct answer.

1. The greatest single source of income for the government is
_____a. Corporation Income Taxes.
_____b. Individual Income Taxes.
_____c. Social Insurance
_____d. Excise Taxes.
_____e. Borrowing.

2. The share of each dollar spent for Education and other Major Social Programs is
_____a. 20¢.
_____b. 22¢.
_____c. 11¢.
_____d. 43¢.
_____e. 3¢.

FIGURE 8-13 **CIRCLE OR PIE GRAPH** *(Listen and Read, MN, p. 105.)*

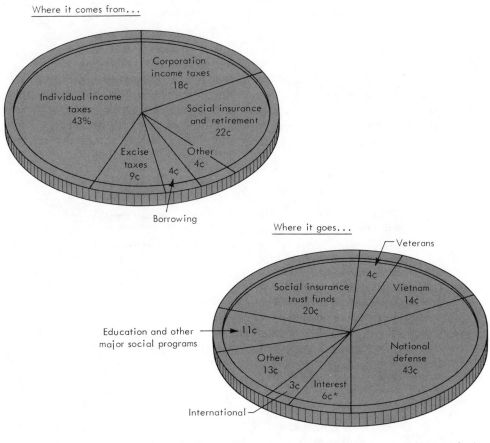

Where it comes from...

Where it goes...

*Excludes interest paid to trust funds

3. The greatest share of the National Dollar is spent
    _____a. for Education.
    _____b. for National Defense.
    _____c. for Social Insurance.
    _____d. for International Relations.

Students may be required to draw graphs for the following:

1. A hotel spends 28¢ of each dollar for services and supplies; 19¢ for food; 37¢ for payroll; and 16¢ for maintenance and repair.
2. In 1971 the world population was 3,700 million. Of these 354 million were in Africa; 322 million in North America; 291 million in Latin America; 2,100 million in Asia; 462 million in Europe (plus 241 million in the USSR), and 19 million in Oceania.

Requiring the student to construct his own graphs is an effective teaching technique. The teacher should prepare for students a guide both for the development of graphs and for the interpretation of them.

Reading Tables

A table is a simple listing of facts and information. In reading a table the student should first look at the title. He should then look at the headings of the various columns with their major headings and subheadings, if there are any. Finally, he must read the details. These are usually written in the left-hand column. Figure 8-14, from *Listen and Read,* MN, p. 107, teaches all of these skills.

GOING TO EUROPE: WHO SPENDS WHAT

Family Income	Number of Travelers	Number of Days	Amount Spent Per Day	Total Spent
$5,000 or less	181,500*	51	$ 9.60	$495
$5,000–$10,000	557,700	36	$13.20	$474
$10,000–$15,000	435,160	32	$15.10	$487
$15,000–$20,000	305,140	29	$16.54	$473
$20,000 and up	720,500	26	$25.39	$671
All Travelers	2,200,000	33	$16.73	$552

* All figures are for 1967   Source: U. S. Treasury

FIGURE 8-14

1. Mark those questions WHICH CAN BE ANSWERED by referring to the table.
   _____a. How many travelers went to Europe in 1967?
   _____b. How much did travelers in various income groups spend per day?
   _____c. What countries in Europe received the greatest percentage of the traveler's dollar?
   _____d. What percentage of each traveler's dollar was spent for transportation?
   _____e. Which income group did the greatest number of travelers come from?

2. Two of the following statements show trends and two show extremes. Write T beside those statements which are TRENDS. Write E beside those statements which are EXTREMES. (The statement which shows neither a trend nor an extreme is not true.)
   _____a. The amount of money spent per day increases as the family income of the traveler increases.
   _____b. The least amount of money spent per day is $9.60 and the most spent per day is $25.39.
   _____c. The number of travelers per income group steadily increases as the family income increases.

————d. The number of days in Europe steadily decreases as the family income increases.

————e. The traveler from the highest family income group spends the least number of days and the greatest amount of money.

Reading Charts

Possibly the most common type of chart is the *flow chart,* which shows the flow of organization. The student needs to be able to read it in social studies. Figure 8-15 illustrates one such chart.

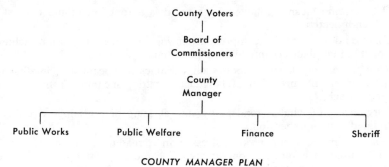

COUNTY MANAGER PLAN

FIGURE 8-15

SUMMARY

In this chapter we examined such skills as the ability to comprehend words, phrases, sentences, and paragraphs; the ability to read the context; and the ability to read for main ideas, for details, and for organization. We also examined critical reading, reading for learning, and the reading of maps, graphs, tables, and charts.

We must lead the students from literal comprehension through inferential comprehension to evaluation and appreciation. Appreciation involves all the other cognitive dimensions of reading.

QUESTIONS FOR DISCUSSION

1. What comprehension skills seem not amenable to training? Which seem most amenable to training?
2. What principles in addition to those mentioned in this chapter should guide the teacher in the development of word meanings?

3. What types of organization do paragraphs normally fall into? Either write or locate materials that illustrate various organizations and that might be used at junior high or high school level.
4. What is critical reading? How might newspapers be used to develop critical-reading skills?
5. Discuss Robinson's SQ3R method and its appropriateness in the high school years.
6. Discuss the special problems of map reading.
7. Discuss four kinds of graphs and the problems they present in interpretation.
8. Discuss:
   a. The specific meaning elicited by a word is a function of the context in which it occurs.
   b. Drill and training in comprehension increase comprehension achievement rather than comprehension potential.
   c. Comprehension depends upon such variables as vocabulary, intelligence, perception, interpretation of language, (getting meaning from context), and speech.
   d. Organizing of what is read as by summarizing or outlining is positively related to comprehension.
   e. The closer the reading skills stressed in a reading program are to the skills used in a specific content area, the more transfer occurs and the more the student tends to learn when reading in that area.

BIBLIOGRAPHY

1. ARTLEY, A. S., "Implementing a Critical Reading Program on the Primary Level," *Reading and Inquiry.* International Reading Association Proceedings, 10 (1965), 111.
2. BERG, PAUL C., and VICTOR M. RENTEL, "Improving Study Skills," *Journal of Reading,* 9 (April 1966), 343–48.
3. BIRKLEY, MARILYN, "Effecting Reading Improvement in the Classroom through Teacher Self-improvement Programs," *Journal of Reading,* 14 (November 1970), 94–100.
4. BRUNER, J. S., "The Act of Discovery," *On Knowing,* pp. 81–96. Cambridge: Harvard University Press, 1962.
5. BRUNER, J. S., *Toward a Theory of Instruction,* p. 41. Cambridge: Harvard University Press, 1966.
6. CIANCIOLO, PATRICIA J., "Discriminating Readers Are Critical Thinkers," *Reading Horizons,* 9 (Summer 1969), 174–80.
7. DAWSON, MILDRED A., and HENRY A. BAMMAN, *Fundamentals of Basic Reading Instruction.* New York: David McKay Co., Inc., 1959.
8. DONALD, SISTER M., "The SQ3R Method in Grade Seven," *Journal of Reading* 11 (October 1967), 33–35, 43.

9. EISNER, SIGMUND, and KERMIT ROHDE, "Note Making During or After the Lecture," *Journal of Educational Psychology,* 50 (December 1959), 301–4.

10. ELLER, WILLIAM, and JUDITH G. WOLF, "Developing Critical Reading Abilities," *Journal of Reading* (December 1966).

11. FREDERICK, E. C., "A Study of the Effects of Certain Readiness Activities on Concept Learning." Unpublished doctoral dissertation. Syracuse University, 1968.

12. GRAY, W. S., "Is Your Reading Program a Good One?" University of Kansas Conference of Reading, International Reading Association, October 12, 1957.

13. HARVISON, ALAN R., "Critical Reading for Elementary Pupils," *The Reading Teacher,* 21 (December 1967), 244–47, 252.

14. HERBER, HAROLD L., "Study Skills: Reading to Develop, Remember and Use Ideas," *Reading in the Content Areas,* pp. 13–21. Syracuse, N.Y.: Syracuse University, 1969.

15. HUELSMANN, CHARLES B., JR., "Promoting Growth in Ability to Interpret When Reading Critically: In Grades Seven to Ten," *Promoting Growth toward Maturity in Interpreting What Is Read,* Supplementary Educational Monographs, No. 74, pp. 149–53. Chicago: University of Chicago Press, 1951.

16. JOHNSON, HARRY W., "Another Study Method," *Journal of Developmental Reading,* 7 (Summer 1964), 269–82.

17. KOLLARITSCH, JANE, "Organizing Reading for Detailed Learning in a Limited Time," *Journal of Reading,* 13 (October 1969), 29–32.

18. KOTTMEYER, WILLIAM, "Classroom Activities in Critical Reading," *School Review,* 52 (November 1944), 557–64.

19. LARTER, S. J., and P. A. TAYLOR, "A Study of Aspects of Critical Thinking, *The Manitoba Journal of Education,* 5 (November 1969), 35–53.

20. MAHONEY, SALLY, "Basic Study Skills and Tools," *Elementary English,* 42 (December 1965), 905–15.

21. MELNIK, AMELIA, "The Formulation of Questions as an Instructional-Diagnostic Tool," *Reading and Inquiry.* International Reading Association, 10 (1965).

22. NILES, O. S., "Organization Perceived," *Developing Study Skills in the Schools,* Perspectives in Reading #4, pp. 57–76. International Reading Association, 1965.

23. OLSON, ARTHUR V., "Teaching Critical Reading Skills," *Reading Improvement,* 4 (Fall 1966), 1–4, 19.

24. PAUK, WALTER, "On Scholarship: Advice to High School Students," *The Reading Teacher,* 7 (November 1963), 73–78.

25. PAUK, WALTER, "Techniques for Textbook Study," *Reading Improvement,* 6 (Spring 1969), 7–10.

26. PERRY, WILLIAM G., JR., and CHARLES P. WHITLOCK, "The Right to Read Rapidly," *Atlantic Monthly,* 190 (November 1952), 88–96.

27. ROBINSON, ALAN, "A Cluster of Skills: Especially for Junior High School," *The Reading Teacher,* 15 (September 1961), 25–28.

28. ROBINSON, FRANCIS P., *Effective Study* (rev. ed.). New York: Harper & Row, Publishers, 1961.
29. ROTHKOPF, ERNEST Z., "The Concept of Mathemagenic Activities," *Review of Educational Research,* 40 (June 1970).
30. RUSSELL, DAVID H., *Children Learn to Read,* p. 359. New York: Ginn and Company, 1961.
31. RUSSELL, D. H., "Research on the Process of Thinking with Some Implications to Reading," *Elementary English,* 42 (1965), 375.
32. SMITH, NILA B., "Reading for Depth," *Reading and Inquiry.* International Reading Association Proceedings, 10 (1965), 118.
33. SMITH, RICHARD J., and KARL D. HESSE, "The Effects of Prereading Assistance on the Comprehension of Good and Poor Readers," *Research in the Teaching of English,* 3 (Fall 1969), 166–77.
34. TABA, HILDA, *et al., Thinking in Elementary School Children.* Cooperative Research Project, No. 1574, p. 53. San Francisco: San Francisco State College, 1964.
35. VINEYARD, EDWIN E., and HAROLD W. MASSEY, "The Interrelationship of Certain Linguistic Skills and Their Relationship with Scholastic Achievement When Intelligence Is Ruled Constant." *Journal of Educational Psychology,* 48 (May 1957), 279–86.

Teaching Content-Area
Reading Skills

CHAPTER **9**

IN CHAPTERS 6–8 WE DISCUSSED THE SKILLS that each learner should acquire if he is to become a competent high school reader. This chapter elaborates on the specific skills needed in each of the content areas.*

Although reading in each of the content areas requires certain specific skills, this by no means reduces the importance of the general reading skills. As the student advances through the school grades, it becomes increasingly difficult for him to be weak in reading and strong in the content subjects. We should expect this to be true.

Good readers generally are more fortunate than poor readers in a number of ways. They have found reading interesting, they have good vocabularies, and they are usually of higher intelligence. These traits, as well as their better basic reading skills, should help them to become good readers in each content area. There is considerable evidence that this actually happens.

Writers have sought to identify those general reading abilities that are needed in all content-area reading. These include the ability to interpret data, to apprehend the main idea, to identify the sequences, to organize ideas, to draw conclusions, to appreciate the literary devices of the writer, to evaluate ideas for relevancy and authenticity, to interpret graphs and charts, to follow directions, and to remember and use the ideas. In addition, students should be able to survey materials, choose appropriate reading techniques, and acquire a flexible reading rate.

* See Leo Fay, *Reading in the Content Fields: Annotated Bibliography,* International Reading Association, 1969.

The acid test of a high school reading program is the transferability of the learnings it provides to content areas. The goal has to be the infusion of reading skills instruction into every subject area where reading is a prime medium for learning (7). Research shows that general reading ability alone is often not enough to assure reading improvement in content courses; the student must be equipped with special skills to meet his needs. And, he must be taught these skills.

The assumption in the recent literature has been that certain reading-study skills are nontransferable—that certain skills are peculiar to specific subject areas and are inappropriate to others. We have assumed that transfer occurs within subject areas but not from subject to subject. Even though Herber (11) challenges this assumption, the evidence is such that it still seems wiser to distinguish between general reading skills that do transfer and those skills that do not.

At one time reading was considered to be a general ability applicable to any reading material, reading instruction occurred only in the reading class, often the first four elementary grades, and ability to read was measured by a general reading test. Today we realize that reading consists of many skills, reading comprehension in a given subject area can be broken down into many subskills and abilities, and the student might read exceptionally well in a given content area, but extremely poorly in another.

Content-area reading presents many problems. For example: Vocabulary in the content fields is usually more difficult; new terms are introduced faster and with fewer repetitions; more facts are presented to the reader; and greater retention and application are expected.

Each reader's background of vocabulary and experience will vary from one content area to another. Consequently, in a given content area equally intelligent readers may greatly differ in readiness for reading. And each area possesses its own problems. Specialized vocabulary, maps, tables, graphs, abbreviations, indexes, diagrams, and footnotes are but a few of the new problems that the reader must deal with as he learns to read effectively in the content areas.

In the content areas the emphasis is on *purposive* reading. The specific purpose for reading should determine both the degree of comprehension that is required and the rate at which the reading is done. A recognized purpose promotes concentration and attitudes favorable toward reading.

The content-area teacher helps the student to develop his reading and study skills by formulating questions that require the application of specific comprehension skills. Sometimes it is desirable that the student get only the general import of a selection; at other times he needs to get its literal meaning. Sometimes he must make inferences and applications, see implications and connotations, or understand the specific meaning of a word in the context. Through appropriate questions, the skillful teacher encourages the student to form summary statements, examine the authority of the writer, and to bring to light misconceptions or gaps in knowledge that should be remedied.

Teachers need to relate the teaching of reading to the teaching of a sensitive and accurate response to written materials. They need to differentiate between reading and the teaching of reading, between literature and the reading of literature.

KNOWLEDGE OF VOCABULARY AND CONCEPTS

Although Chapter 7 was devoted to vocabulary development, it may be apropos to outline vocabulary study in the content areas. The teacher cannot simply be satisfied with a student answer such as "I know what it means, but I can't really tell you." The student needs to develop exact meanings, and he must be able to translate these meanings into exact words.

That vocabulary development is particularly significant in content-area reading is hardly debatable. Words are "advance organizers" and provide cues to the structure of the materials. Ausubel (2) noted that the learning and retention of unfamiliar, but nevertheless meaningful, verbal material can be facilitated by the advance introduction of relevant subsuming concepts. These concepts and the words that represent them help the learner to mobilize the most relevant existing concepts that the learner already possesses (past learning) and provide anchorage for the learning material (help him to organize).

The following techniques are generally useful in developing vocabulary skills:

1. Arouse interest in word study by an experiment or a curiosity-arousing question.
2. Help students to become collectors of words—have them develop their own dictionary.
3. Require students to use the word.
4. Create opportunities for frequent contact with or review of the words.
5. Teach the skill of deriving meaning from the context.
6. Encourage frequent use of the dictionary.

COMPREHENSION IN A SPECIFIC
CONTENT AREA

In the preceding chapters we have discussed numerous reading skills. We have emphasized the importance of grasping the main idea, of surveying materials, of choosing appropriate reading rates, of interpreting graphs, maps, charts, tables, and diagrams, of reading for a purpose, of organizing what one reads, of drawing inferences, and of retaining and applying what has been learned.

In the content areas, these and all the other reading skills are needed for successful comprehension. In addition, in the individual content areas each of these reading skills must be applied in a specific way.

Let us take a look at some of the major content areas, and let us attempt to identify some of the causes of reading difficulties.

Literature

Reading literature requires special appreciation of the mood and style of the author.* It requires the reader to respond to form, to connotative meanings, to rhyme, and to emotional overtones. It requires interpretative reading and emotional involvement. It requires the reader to deal with such literary forms as the sonnet, the essay, and the metaphor. The reader needs to read with his mind and with his emotions. He must find in literature splotches of the ever-flowing stream of human behavior and emotions. He must analyze the characters, appreciate the style, and digest the sequence of development (26). Reading literature requires literal understanding, analysis, appreciation, symbolic interpretation, and recognition of the relevance of literature to life (18). Students need to go beyond mere passive acceptance of literal comprehension; they must do something with what they read (23). They need to get involved. Reading includes not only word perception and comprehension but also reaction and assimilation. Literature is the basis for good reading instruction when it serves as a vehicle for critical insight and aesthetic revelation (23).

Literature allows for identification between reader and character or with a particular group, assists in the solution of personal problems, reinforces views already held, teaches appreciation of beauty, and permits escape. Literature has effects that are personal and often original. The

---

* See Helene W. Hartley, "Teaching the Reading of Literature in the Elementary School," *Challenge and Experiment in Reading,* International Reading Association Conference Proceedings, 7 (1962), 43–45; and J. W. McKay, "Developing Reading Skills through Literature," *Reading Children and Young People through Literature,* International Reading Association, 1971, pp. 50–57.

same passage may produce different effects at different times on the same student and different effects on different students.

Fiction is a biography of conflict in human motives (16). It traces the conflict from its inception to its conclusion. Since motives are "within" the individual, the writer must "psychoanalyze" the fictional character, report what the character is saying to himself, use soliloquies or asides in which the character tells the audience what his motives are, or portray the character's motives through his appearance, speech, or action. The successful reader of literature must understand these literary contrivances of the author and read between the lines for a comprehension of the basic meaning.

Each literary form has its own mode of expression. In *poetry* the writer communicates through words and concepts and also through tone, mood, repetition, rhythm, and rhyme. Poetry is literary work in metrical form. It is the art of rhythmical composition (21).

Poetry presents all kinds of grammatical and structural difficulties. The syntax is irregular; it is sometimes difficult to identify the verb; the juxtaposition of words for auditory and aesthetic effects is peculiar; and the writing is littered with irregular constructions. It is absolutely necessary to understand metaphors.

In reading *drama* it is necessary to understand the action and the setting. The latter is largely supplied by stage directions which break up the dialogue, making it more difficult to follow the sequence of events. The student must also learn to visualize various actions going on at the same time.

In *essays* the mood may take a formal, pedantic, humorous, satiric, philosophical, inspirational, persuasive, or political form. The *short story* presents its own literary contrivances. It is characterized by uniformity of tone and plot and by dramatic intensity.

To appreciate novels, short stories (12), poems, and plays, the student must learn to analyze the elements of plot, characterization, style, and theme.

Plot. The student must learn to ask himself a series of questions. Did I like the ending? How would I have changed it? Did the writer use surprise, suspense, or mystery to keep me interested? What was the conflict or the major motive of the story? What are the time and place settings? Is it fanciful or realistic literature?

An exercise similar to the following teaches the student to appreciate plot:

Read the following sentences and select the word that best characterizes the plot:

1. We stood on the bridge not knowing whether to go forward, backward, or just remain where we were. In front of us and behind, the flood waters were

rushing across the highway. Broken tree limbs, barrels, and household goods were floating by.

This series of sentences indicates that the plot is based upon
   a. Surprise
   b. Suspense
   c. Adventure
   d. Intrigue

2. How wonderful it would be if the world were really at peace. There wouldn't be this constant distrust among all of us. People could intermingle freely. The fear of atomic destruction would disappear.

This series of sentences indicates that the plot is
   a. Fanciful
   b. Realistic

Characterization. The student should ask: What character did I like best? Which one would I like to be? Were the characters true to life?

The student learns characterization skills by analyzing statements and answering certain questions about them. For example:

1. The man just sat. His eyes stared into empty space. No smile or grin ever adorned his face. When he' spoke, it was about the wickedness of man and the burning fires of hell.

This series of sentences describes a person who is probably
   a. Discontented with life
   b. Satisfied with life
   c. Successful in life
   d. Proud of living

2. The wrinkled old man with curved back was ambling toward the park. Behind him in droves came the pit-pat of little feet. Little ones and not-so-little ones were laughing and jumping trying to get his attention.

This series of sentences describes an old man who
   a. Is discontented with life
   b. Enjoys the little things of life
   c. Has few friends
   d. Is considered on old fogy

Or, the teacher may require the student to underline one of three words that best characterizes the person described in key sentences. For example:

1. Jim grabbed Johnny by the shoulder and threw him against the wall. "That's for ratting on me."
Jim is generous, <u>unethical</u>, brave.

2. Mary's eyes shot darts of fire at anyone who in the slightest way disagreed with her.
Mary is rude, generous, <u>opinionated</u>.

Style. The student should ask: What was the writer's style? What is his distinctive manner of presentation? What figures of speech did he use? What was the general mood or tone of the writing?

Exercises such as the following may teach the student to read for style.

1. We were awakened by the sound of a man trying to break open the door. Quietly my father peered out of the window but there was only darkness. The noise continued. My father got his revolver from the closet and loaded it, and we advanced toward the door with trepidation.

   This series of sentences describes a set of circumstances characterized by
   a. Annoyance
   b. Dismay
   c. Fright
   d. Anger

2. Lori wiggled and crawled and splashed in the pool. It was her first outing for the summer, and what an occasion it was!

   This series of sentences describes a little girl who is
   a. Comfortable
   b. Contented
   c. Joyful
   d. Successful

3. All afternoon Marie thought of what would happen when her father came home. She had just broken her father's favorite pipe. Then the moment arrived. Dad was just pulling up his ashtray and said, "Honey, where is my pipe?"

   This series of sentences describes a girl who is
   a. Ashamed
   b. Embarrassed
   c. Guilty
   d. Shy

Theme. The student should ask: What was the moral of the story? Which character best exemplified the morals and ideals of the writer? How do the morals and ideals portrayed fit with the reader's morals?

Social Studies

Reading in the social studies involves a special skill, and it is one that the student is obliged to use innumerable times.* The student must learn a new verbal vocabulary. He must be able to deal with detailed

---

* For additional discussion see Paul A. Witty, "The Role of Reading in the Social Studies," *Elementary English,* 39 (October 1962), 562–69; also Helen Huus, "Antidote for Apathy—Acquiring Reading Skills for Social Studies," *Challenge and Experiment in Reading,* International Reading Association Conference Proceedings, 7 (1962), 81–88.

information in historical sequence and with cause-and-effect relationships. He must be able to organize materials, locate facts, interpret abstract ideas, and understand concepts of time, space, and chronological order. He must also learn to handle new symbols: maps, charts, diagrams, and graphs (24). And, he must be a critical reader.

Simmons (22) equates critical reading with critical thinking and uses the description of Pingry (19) to state the various aspects of critical thinking: (1) collecting data, organizing data, and formulating hypotheses from data; (2) use of correct principles of logic and understanding the nature of proof; (3) criticism of thinking; (4) understanding of the psychology of propaganda and advertising techniques; (5) problem solving.

Simmons then identifies the characteristics of critical reading. He notes that it is a skill involving cumulative comprehension (a student must understand, reorganize, and find the main idea of a selection, and in that order before critical reaction to it is possible); it includes the understanding of that which is explicit in the selection read and the use of higher mental processes (certainly in the secondary school students must develop the ability to use and understand association, generalization, symbolic revelation, and the like); it can be contrasted with literal reading (critical reading goes beyond the passive acceptance of ideas and information stated in print); and it is the habit of examining printed statements and attacking problems in the light of related objective evidence.

In teaching the student to read social studies content one must begin with social studies materials. The teacher must know what specific skills to teach and how they should be taught.

Let us dwell on the *how*:

1. Call attention to the new words, duplicate them for the student, have the student consult the dictionary definition, use them in the appropriate context, give attention to root words and shades of meaning, use Latin derivatives and prefixes to increase vocabulary, pay special attention to words of foreign origin, and require students to use them in meaningful sentences (6).

2. Use films, charts, pictures, recordings, dramatizations, cartoons, models, exhibits, etc., to illustrate new concepts.

3. Teach students to comprehend social studies materials.
   a. Common words in social studies often take on technical meanings: gold rush, cold war, diet, raw materials, etc.
   b. Social studies textbooks are full of abstract terms: latitude, longitude, democracy, etc.

4. Require students to read for special purposes: to answer a question, to identify the cause, to locate a certain fact, to verify an opinion, to compare different points of view, and to adjust speed of reading to purpose and type of content.

a. Teach the value of skimming in preparation of assignments.

b. Encourage students to experiment with different rates for different materials and purposes.

c. Require intensive SQ3R reading of textbook.

d. Have those who experience difficulty understanding or retaining the material take notes or make outline.

5. Teach students how to locate materials. Teach library usage, use of *Readers' Guide,* card catalog, and sources of social studies materials.

6. Provide numerous activities that stimulate critical thinking and analysis and that teach students to infer, to evaluate, and to integrate what they read.

a. Discuss steps to follow in problem solving.

b. Teach students how to develop their own point of view.

c. Use the discussion method and require students to state their own opinions and how they arrive at them.

d. Use debate-type presentation of beliefs and supporting factual evidence to teach students how to collect and evaluate facts and how to relate facts to points in an outline (6).

7. Make assignments specific enough so the student will know how to read (25, p. 149). For example, the teacher may require the student to identify the author's point of view.

8. Test and constantly evaluate the student's proficiency in reading social studies materials (25, p. 147).

a. Prepare a self-evaluation checklist, use class evaluation of oral and written reports, and evaluate the adequacy of outlines and summaries.

b. Organize interrogation periods in which student leaders ask questions about material read and evaluate responses (6).

9. Teach students to perceive the organization of materials.

a. Have them identify main idea-detail structure of writing.

b. Have them find and understand the purpose of cue words, such as *furthermore, nevertheless, moreover, since, because.*

c. Have students differentiate between chronological organization and fictional approach where events lead to a climax.

d. Have them use the SQ3R approach.

Mathematics

Reading in mathematics requires the student to comprehend a new set of symbols.* He must react to numerical symbols that synthesize verbal

---

* *Academic Therapy,* Fall 1970, is entirely devoted to the teaching of and reading in mathematics.

symbols. He must be able to read *and* to compute. He must know both the individual and combined meanings of verbal symbols and mathematical signs. He must read deductively. He must translate formulas into significant relationships, and, generally, he must read slowly.

Fay (8), in a study in which he controlled chronological and mental age, found no differences in arithmetic achievement between good and poor readers. Lessenger (13) analyzed errors on the Stanford Achievement Test to determine loss in arithmetic as a result of faulty reading. He found that among sixty-seven poor readers, the average loss was 10.1 months of arithmetic age. After one year of instruction in specific reading skills, the loss was all but eliminated. Russell (20) also reported that the correlation between problem solving and general reading ability was relatively low. Hansen (10) found that poor achievers were, on the average, faster readers. Balow (3), after an analysis of this research, noted that whenever reading skill was important in problem-solving ability, each increase in reading ability might well be accompanied by an increase in problem-solving achievement. It might also require a minimum level of reading ability to do well in problem solving at any given grade level.

From his own study, involving fourteen hundred sixth graders, Balow concluded that general reading ability had an effect on problem-solving ability; that much of the degree of relationship between reading and problem-solving ability was the result of the high correlation of each of these factors with IQ; that computation ability did have a significant effect on problem-solving ability; and that one should consider children's reading ability as well as computation ability when teaching problem-solving skills.

In mathematics, comprehension is not limited to the understanding of a story. It is not even limited to the understanding of one experiment. One concept is built on another in mathematics and can have meaning only on the basis of the understood meaning of the former. In no other area is it more true than in mathematics that new learning depends upon previous learning.

Reading in mathematics also requires other rather diverse skills. Smith (24) identified the following writing patterns in mathematical textbooks: classification, explanation of a technical process, instructions for an experiment, detailed statement of facts, descriptive problem solving, abbreviations and equations, mathematical problems, and various combinations of each of these. Such patterns point up the diverse reading task a student must be prepared to handle.

The student should early be introduced to the procedures involved in reading mathematics. Bond and Wagner (4, p. 317) point out that the student must know what the problem calls for, what facts are needed for the solution, what steps are appropriate in leading to a solution, and what is the probable answer.

Aaron (1) notes that the mathematics teacher must develop the mathematical vocabulary, teach the student to select appropriate rates for reading various materials, provide training in reading word problems, equations, charts, graphs, and tables, and develop skill in dealing with mathematical symbols and abbreviations.

Mathematics texts are full of technical terms: *addend, factor, exponent, isosceles, reciprocal.* Some of these terms are peculiar to mathematics; others are common words used with a different meaning: *axis, chord, cone, set.*

Because what the reader takes to the printed page determines in large measure what he gets from the page, the teacher of mathematics needs to provide students with the understandings and the prelearning necessary to read the mathematics textbook. He must be sure that the student has the necessary background to understand mathematical concepts. He needs to ascertain the student's readiness for the materials: Can he read the mathematical symbols? Can he read the graphs, tables, and diagrams which help to develop concepts?

In learning to read in mathematics, the student should do the following:

1. Read the problem quickly to get an overview.
2. Read for main ideas or the specific question asked.
3. Learn technical mathematical terms.
4. Read for organization, listing perhaps in one column the points given and in the second the points needed.
5. Translate the verbal symbols into mathematical symbols and formulas.
6. Read for relationships and translate these into an equation.
7. Analyze carefully all mathematical symbols and formulas.
8. Analyze carefully all graphs, figures, illustrations, etc.
9. Follow a definite procedure:
   a. Learn the meaning of all words.
   b. Find what the problem asks for.
   c. Decide what facts are needed to find a solution to the problem.
   d. Decide what mathematical process is required (addition, subtraction, etc.).
   e. Identify the order for solving the problem.
10. Make a drawing of the problem. A problem such as the following can be easily represented by a drawing:
    Harry has fifteen pictures. If he can paste three pictures on each page of his scrapbook, how many pages will be filled?

11. Study the contrast between the way words are used in mathematics and the way they are used in other areas.
12. Learn the proper symbols and abbreviations: ft. = foot; $7^3 = 343$.
13. Proceed slowly and be willing to reread.
14. Learn to follow directions.

Does direct instruction in reading help in mathematics? Call and Wiggin (5) devised an experiment to answer this question. They concluded that teaching specialized mathematical reading-study skills had a definite effect on the ability to solve mathematical word problems. The experimental group did better even when reading abilities and mathematical aptitude were controlled. Their procedures are described in sufficient detail to permit replication.

Science

Reading in science requires the ability to follow a sequence of events.* It requires an orderly, systematic approach, including the ability to classify, categorize, and memorize (26). Technical vocabulary must be mastered, formulas must be learned, and theory must be understood.

Directions become very important. The success of an experiment depends on the student's ability to follow directions. Reading in science, as in mathematics, is usually careful, analytical, and slow. It puts a premium on inductive reasoning and on detail. Every formula, chart, and graph is important. It demands a problem-solving approach similar to the steps of the scientific method. The student must learn to follow the scientist as he states the problem, enumerates the facts, formulates his hunch or hypothesis, investigates the facts to test the hypothesis, works toward his conclusion, and makes his verification. He must observe the facts, keep them in mind, relate them to each other, and determine whether or not they support a theory.

Science reading is even more difficult because (15):

1. There is a tremendous growth of new vocabulary and an accelerated obsolescence of other vocabulary each year.
2. Science teaching suffers from lack of sequence, with great overlap between grade levels, and thus is not conducive to developing a sequence in reading skills from grade level to grade level.

* See Don H. Parker, "Developing Reading in a Science Program," *Challenge and Experiment in Reading,* International Reading Association Conference Proceedings, 7 (1962), 88–90.

3. Scientific ideas are becoming increasingly complex, and it is difficult to utilize a one-syllable word for a ten-syllable science concept.
4. Writers of science materials do not agree on what the readability level of books should be.
5. Many of the terms are mathematical.
6. Many common words are used in a special sense (force, body).
7. Statements are concise (laws, definitions, formulas).
8. Students must learn to deal with equations, formulas, scales, cross-section and longitudinal models, and flow charts.

The teacher can help by:

1. Simplifying the vocabulary for most students—a *meteorologist* is simply a *weatherman*. The student needs to be taught how to comprehend technical symbols, graphs, maps, charts, diagrams, formulas, scales, and equations.
   a. Having students compile a science dictionary or develop a word-card file of science words and symbols.
   b. Having students read the section in the textbook entitled "To the Student." These sections describe the way the technical vocabulary is handled and alert the student to boldface or italicized terms, to definitions, to key words, etc.
2. Having students read for the main idea—"The purpose of this experiment is . . ."
3. Having students organize the material by jotting down the steps in an experiment.
4. Using films to illustrate and develop concepts.
5. Helping students adjust reading speed to the difficulty of the material, the purposes for reading, and the student's own familiarity with it.
6. Helping students to evaluate the competency of the writer or the experimenter.
7. Teaching students to use the problem-solving technique: formulating the hypotheses, collating the evidence, evaluating and organizing the evidence, forming a conclusion, and testing the conclusion.
8. Teaching students to recognize the sequence of steps.
9. Conducting hunts for information requiring the use of bibliographies, encyclopedias, card catalog, glossaries, indexes, dictionaries.
10. Directing the students in developing summaries and outlines.
11. Having students express formulas in their own words.

12. Developing competency in reading scales and diagrams and in understanding formulas and equations.

The low-ability student in science has the following added difficulties (17):

1. The textbooks in science, which often are too difficult even for the average or above-average reader, are especially handicapping to the slow learner.
2. Textbooks written for the slow learner do not match the junior high-school reader's interest and maturity.
3. Since appropriate texts are not available, and since the extension of the reader's vocabulary is secondary to the acquisition of science concepts, the teacher may have to prepare materials. The following guidelines might be helpful:
   a. Use simple, concrete, and familiar vocabulary.
   b. Use fewer different words.
   c. Use only one difficult word for every two hundred running words.
   d. Use short sentences.
   e. Provide repetition of ideas.
   f. Provide more cues in the way of details, more illustrative material.
   g. Use a readability formula to check the readability level of the materials.

Vocational Subjects (14, 9)

There are few books that help the trade instructor with the problem of teaching students to read, and yet vocational students do need training in reading in trade subject areas. In general we would recommend that the language arts—listening, speaking, writing, and reading—all be intertwined in the study of a lesson. Only after a study and reading of the job sheet should the teacher move the student back to the text.

The student in vocational courses should be able to do the following:

1. Read job and instruction sheets
2. Deal with the new vocabulary: *splice, junction, tap, tee, pigtail,* Western Union, *modulator, tailstock, keratin, lunula, pledget, sebum, bias wave, reverse roll, mortise, cat whisker, headstock, offset, inside caliper*
3. Understand the directions, but also *act* them out—apply his knowledge
4. Understand prints, charts, graphs
5. Read the selection orally

6. Understand the concepts shared
7. Associate symbol with concrete referend
8. Visualize the steps read about

SUMMARY

The key to this chapter lies in the clear understanding of Chapters 7–9. These chapters deal with the basic vocabulary, comprehension study, and rate skills that are transferable to content-area reading. The student needs to learn to apply these skills to each of the content areas. In addition, each of the content areas requires specific skills. These are the subject matter of Chapter 10.

QUESTIONS FOR DISCUSSION

1. What comprehension skills seem amenable to training?
2. How does the teacher develop meaning for paragraphs?
3. What is critical reading?
4. Discuss Robinson's SQ3R method and its applicability on the high school level.
5. Identify the different types of graphs and describe the problems they present for the reader.
6. Why is organization of what is being read positively related to comprehension?
7. What are the difficulties associated with map reading?

BIBLIOGRAPHY

1. AARON, I. E., "Reading in Mathematics," *Journal of Reading,* 8 (May 1965), 391–95, 401.
2. AUSUBEL, D., "The Use of Advance Organizers in the Learning and Retention of Meaningful Verbal Material," *Journal of Educational Psychology,* 51 (1960), 267–72.
3. BALOW, IRVING H., "Reading and Computation Ability as Determinants of Problem Solving," *The Arithmetic Teacher,* 11 (January 1964), 18–22.
4. BOND, G. L., and E. B. WAGNER, *Teaching the Child to Read* (rev. ed.). New York: The Macmillan Company, 1950.

5. CALL, R. J., and N. A. WIGGIN, "Reading and Mathematics," *The Mathematics Teacher*, 59 (1966), 149–57.

6. CHRIST, ALEX, "Reading Skills and Methods of Teaching Them," *Kansas Studies in Education*, 10 (February 1960), 12.

7. EARLY, MARGARET J., "What Does Research in Reading Reveal about Successful Reading Programs?" *What We Know about High School Reading*, pp. 40–53. National Council of Teachers of English, 1969.

8. FAY, LEO C., "The Relationship between Specific Reading Skills and Selected Areas of Sixth-Grade Achievement," *Journal of Educational Research*, 43 (March 1950), 544–47.

9. FERRERIO, A. J., "Use of the Industrial Arts in the Remedial Reading Program," *High Points*, 40 (May 1958), 58–61.

10. HANSEN, C. W., "Factors Associated with Superior and Inferior Achievement in Problem Solving in Sixth-Grade Achievement." Unpublished doctoral dissertation, University of Minnesota, 1943.

11. HERBER, HAROLD L., "Study Skills: Reading to Develop, Remember, and Use Ideas," *Reading in the Content Area*, pp. 13–21. Syracuse, N.Y.: Syracuse University, 1969.

12. HYNES, SISTER NANCY, "Learning to Read Short Stories," *Journal of Reading*, 13 (March 1970), 429–32.

13. LESSENGER, W. E., "Reading Difficulties in Arithmetical Computations," *Journal of Educational Research*, 11 (April 1925), 287–91.

14. LEVINE, ISIDORE N., "Solving Reading Problems in Vocational Subjects," *High Points*, 43 (April 1960), 10–27.

15. MALLINSON, GEORGE G., "Methods and Materials for Teaching Reading in Science." Reprinted from *Sequential Development of Reading Abilities*, Helen M. Robinson, editor, Supplementary Educational Monographs, No. 90, pp. 145–49, by permission of The University of Chicago Press. © 1960 by the University of Chicago Press.

16. MALONEY, MARTIN, "The Writer's Itch (III): How to Write Obvious Lies," *Etc.: A Review of General Semantics*, 17 (Winter 1959–60), 209–16.

17. MOORE, ARNOLD J., "Science Instructional Materials for the Low-Ability Junior High-School Student," *School Science and Mathematics*, 62 (November 1962), 556–63.

18. PETITT, DOROTHY, "Reading Literature: An Act of Creation," *Vistas in Reading*, pp. 176–81. International Reading Association, Newark, N.J., 1967.

19. PINGRY, ROBERT E., "Critical Thinking—What Is It?" *The Mathematics Teacher*, November 1951, 466–67.

20. RUSSELL, DAVID H., "Arithmetic Power through Reading," *Instruction in Arithmetic*, Twenty-fifth Yearbook, Chap. 9, pp. 211–12. Washington: National Council of Teachers of Mathematics, 1960.

21. SHAPIRO, PHYLLIS P., "The Language of Poetry," *Elementary School Journal*, 70 (December 1969), 130–34.

22. SIMMONS, JOHN S., "Reasoning through Reading," *Journal of Reading*, 8 (April 1965), 311–14.

23. SIMMONS, JOHN S., "Teaching Levels of Literal Understanding," *English Journal,* 54 (February 1965), 101–2, 107, 129.

24. SMITH, NILA B., "Patterns of Writing in Different Subject Areas," Part I, *Journal of Reading,* 8 (1964), 31–37; Part II, *Journal of Reading,* 8 (1964), 97–102.

25. STRANG, RUTH, CONSTANCE M. McCULLOUGH, and ARTHUR E. TRAXLER, *The Improvement of Reading.* New York: McGraw-Hill Book Company, 1961.

26. TREMONTI, JOSEPH B., and CELESTINE ALGERO, "Reading and Study Habits in Content Areas," *Reading Improvement,* 4 (Spring 1967), 54–57.

Teaching Rate
of Comprehension

CHAPTER **10**

WE SINGLE OUT RATE SKILLS FOR DETAILED DISCUSSION in this chapter because of the significance that is attached to them in the secondary school and because of the considerable public and professional attention focused on rate improvement.

In a previous article (4) we pointed out that rate of reading has frequently been described as rate of comprehension. Perhaps it is better described as speed in grasping the meanings intended by the writer. To read is to comprehend, but one may comprehend at a slow rate or at a relatively more rapid rate.

RELATIONSHIP BETWEEN RATE AND COMPREHENSION

The correlations between rate of reading and comprehension, especially on the secondary and on the college level, are positive but quite low (circa .30). Among bright students, fast readers tend to comprehend better than slow readers; among slow readers, slow reading tends to be accompanied by better comprehension.

These relationships between rate and comprehension are important to the teacher because he must decide when to stress rate improvement and when to emphasize comprehension skills. A reader who is low in both comprehension and rate will generally not benefit from an emphasis on speed. He needs training in basic comprehension skills. One who reads rapidly but with low comprehension likewise needs comprehension training. One who reads all materials slowly but with good comprehension, however, may well profit from training in speed. Perhaps this is because rapid reading requires his full attention, whereas when he plods along, his attention wanders. On the other hand, the slow learner's rate is limited by his comprehending or thinking rate.

In mathematics and science the correlations between comprehension and rate of reading tend to be low and negative. In general, the faster the student reads in these areas, the less he tends to understand.

In summary, the degree of correlation between rate and comprehension depends on the age of the reader, the intelligence of the reader, the kinds of materials employed, the methods used in measuring the two characteristics, and the purpose for the reading.

THE VALUE OF SPEED READING

Despite some of the ambivalent research and the uncertainty of the conclusions that one can deduce therefrom, rapidity in reading seems to have an economy value in its own right and should be investigated as a separate skill. Harris (7) suggests that rate training should be included in developmental reading programs and should begin at or above the sixth grade. Most readers cease improving in rate, if no attempts are made to increase it, by about the sixth grade. Ordinarily they read from two hundred to three hundred words per minute at that time.

There are fast readers, average readers, and slow readers, and on an average it seems more desirable to be a fast reader than a slow reader. Pauk (18), however, believes that speed reading has little if any positive effect on success with college assignments. He notes that he has never encountered a single case in which academic failure was the result of a student's inability to read fast enough. Rather, it was a lack of understanding of what was read. He adds that he has cases where speed reading was responsible for academic difficulties.

FLEXIBILITY IN READING

The superior reader supposedly pushes his eyes across the page as rapidly as his comprehension permits. This may or may not be good. No one can work at top efficiency all the time, and there is no great neceessity in even wanting to. There really is little advantage in rushing through a newspaper if, after the reader has finished, he does not know what to do with his time. We must constantly ask: What is speed for? What purpose does it serve? A lot of speeding has no reasonable justification (12). If the proofreader reads carefully and is completely accurate the first time he gets better results than if, because of too much speed, he has to reread the materials. Mortimer J. Adler notes: "In the case of good books, the point is not to see how many of them you can get through, but rather how many can get through you."

Thus slow reading is not necessarily poor reading. It affords the reader an opportunity to evaluate, to linger, to enjoy the beauty of the description (much as the traveler who stops to see points of scenic interest), and to read between the lines. At times, slowness is beauty. To read slowly, to think critically, and to feel deeply may be true enrichment.

That many readers read much more slowly than they could is obvious. That others read as rapidly as their comprehension abilities allow may also be true. And for these, rate improvement training is of little value.

Fast readers and slow readers may or may not comprehend well, but sometimes the fast reader comprehends better than the slow reader. This happens when the fast reader is reading approximately as rapidly as his comprehension abilities allow and when the slow reader is reading more slowly than his comprehension permits, thus allowing time for the mind to wander from the task.

Rate of reading, obviously is not the ultimate goal in reading. The ultimate aim is comprehension according to one's abilities and needs. This means that the good reader is a flexible reader.* Just as cars have in them the power to go slowly or to go rapidly as the occasion demands, so also the good reader can slow down or speed up as the nature of the material and his own needs change. He can shift gears in reading.

Flexibility appears to point to a critical difference between good and poor readers. The good reader sets comprehension as his goal and adjusts his rate rather automatically. The poor reader mechanically plods from word to word, and such comprehension as he obtains seems to be a by-product of the process rather than the central goal of his reading. Since children in the upper grades and those with higher intelligence generally are more mature in their reading, one expects to find them better able to vary their rate with the demands of the material.

Research (8) unfortunately indicates that most readers are rigid rather than flexible in rate of reading. Most readers tend to maintain a characteristic approach and use a relatively invariant rate with all types of material. This relatively invariant rate of reading may be constitutional or learned, or it may simply be the result of lack of appropriate training (13).

Efficiency in reading means simply this: With some purposes and some materials one should read slowly; with others, one should read more

---

* The *Reading Versatility Test,* by Arthur S. McDonald, measures flexibility of reading. It is designed for pupils in the fifth through ninth grades.

rapidly. This means that the reader should read as rapidly as possible, always meeting the comprehension specifications that he has set for himself or that the task has set for him (21).

It makes little sense to prod along at a snail's pace if one can read rapidly and still understand the materials. If the reader cannot understand what he is reading, then a slower rate is called for. The good driver slows down his car in snow, on ice, around curves, in city traffic, and whenever he is not sure of the conditions of the road. He thus transmits more power to the wheels while at the same time going slowly enough so that he can view the entire situation carefully. The good reader slows down whenever he needs to do so to understand what he is reading. When he does not understand, he is in as much trouble as is the driver whose car is stuck in mud. It may be necessary to slow down to a crawl so that he can use more of his thinking power.

Braam (2), in a study with high school seniors, demonstrated that flexibility could be taught in a six-week summer session. The mean difference between highest rate and lowest rate was only 19 words per minute before training; after training it was 159 words.

IMPROVING RATE OF READING

Rate of comprehension can undoubtedly be improved. Students on the high school level who have undertaken some form of rate improvement training do increase their speed and will generally read faster than those who have not had such training. Excessive rate of reading, however, is not desirable. Liddle's study (10) indicates that it may be injurious to comprehension when concentration is put on achieving extremely high reading rates.

Rate of reading, because the emphasis should be on flexibility, should always be dependent on the purposes, intelligence, and experience and knowledge of the reader and upon the difficulty level of the material. The rate is always dependent on the reader's motivation and his psychological and physical state, his mastery of the basic reading skills, and the format of the materials. More specifically, factors that affect speed and comprehension are the following (21): size of type, type style, blackness and sharpness of print, quality and tone of the paper, size of the page, organization of the material, amount of white space, kind and placement of illustrations, headings and subheadings, clarity of the writing, the field of knowledge from which the writing is drawn, the complexity of the ideas, the author's style, the kind of writing (poetry, narrative, or descriptive), the reader's personality, the way the reader feels (sleepy, alert, calm, nervous), the reader's mental ability, reading skill, and his likes and dislikes, the environment in which reading occurs, the reader's background of experience, his purpose, and his interest in the field or area in which he is reading, and his familiarity with the peculiarities of style and phraseology of the author.

The reader gets into trouble in reading and must proceed more slowly when the writer's style is too difficult; when the ideas are too abstract; when he is trying to learn and to remember what he is reading; when he is following directions such as the carrying out of an experiment; when he is reading poetry; when he is reading critically—trying to evaluate what he reads; and when he reads such specialized materials as science.

It is interesting to note that when the good reader reduces his speed, he does so for a purpose. It does not create a gap between his reading rate and his thinking rate. He reduces his speed because the materials require him to think more slowly. The good reader seeks to increase his understanding without sacrificing speed unnecessarily, or he may want to increase his speed without sacrificing his understanding. In short, he is a flexible reader. The flexible reader gears his reading rate to his thinking rate.

Rate improvement cannot be built on inadequate word-identification and word-recognition skills. It cannot be built on an experimental background that keeps the reader from understanding what he is reading. It cannot be built upon immaturity in intellectual development.

Advocates of rate improvement programs claim that such programs may also lead to more accurate perception, more accurate and more rapid visual discrimination, wider span of apprehension and of perception, better attention and concentration, shorter reaction time, fewer regressions, decrease in the number and duration of fixations, reduction of vocalization, better comprehension, and general improvement in perceptual skills.

Morton (17) found that readers shortened reading time or increased speed by using greater contextual constraint. Fast readers tend to use contextual clues more efficiently. In effect, they see fewer words when reading. If this is so, then instruction in key-word or key-phrase reading should be encouraged (19).

Research shows that it is desirable to say the word subvocally while reading. The fade-out of the visually acquired stimulus seems rapid if it is not recoded in acoustic form (19). An acoustic factor seems to be involved in immediate memory and recall. And, if this is so, it seems that instruction in fast reading should not do away with inner speech. Amble (1), reviewing the research on reading by phrases, concludes that perceptual span, reading comprehension, and reading rate can all be increased by phrase-reading training. He adds that reading by phrases is a unique reading skill, that it can be developed through training, and that it is a durable skill.

GADGETRY FOR RATE IMPROVEMENT

Let us take a look at the vast array of gadgetry available today that is intended to help the student develop rate skills. These gadgets might be grouped into tachistoscopes, accelerating devices, and other reading-related instruments.

Tachistoscopes

Tachistoscopes expose numbers, letters, words, phrases, or other images for short periods of time, usually ranging from 1/100 to 1½ seconds. Most training on these machines is at the higher speeds.

The tachistoscope, whether individual or group, primarily develops the person's perceptual intake skills. By forcing the student to cope with intake speeds of 1/10 of a second or less, the tachistoscope requires the student to see more rapidly, more accurately, and more orderly; to pay more attention to what was seen; and to organize what he has seen. He also has to develop better directional attack.

Since the tachistoscopic span is greater than the span in normal reading, researchers have asked: What are the effects of tachistoscopic training, and is there any value in increasing the tachistoscopic span?

A tachistoscopic exposure is followed by a period of "nonreading" in which the person can assimilate and integrate what he saw; in reading, there is continuous perceptual activity, the images overlap each other, and there is relatively little time to assimilate and interpret. Obviously, increasing the tachistoscopic span further seems to be of little value in reading. The training should be directed toward developing the intake aspect of perception and toward improving the seeing skills as a basis for better reading rather than toward developing reading skills per se (5).

"Seeing" can be improved, and tachistoscopic training is one of the better ways of doing this. It has been used in the armed services, in remedial reading, in orthoptics, in teaching spelling and arithmetic, in art and business education, and even in physical education. In each instance the emphasis has been on the development of general accuracy in seeing and remembering. This is of value in all learning situations in which the student must come to understanding through the use of vision (26, p. 6).

There are many by-products of tachistoscopic training. The student learns self-discipline, better habits of work, and better eye-hand coordination and improves his focusing ability.

Tachistoscopic training has greatest value in the elementary years when the pupil is learning to "see." Since much of the material is designed to develop accuracy of seeing and the retention of the particular placement of certain elements (for example, the pupil needs to see and remember 24571 in a definite order), it may have value in a word-attack program.

A list of tachistoscopes follows:

1. *All-Purpose Electric Tachistoscope* [Lafayette Instrument Company, Box 1279, Lafayette, Ind. 47902]. This is usable for individual or group presentation with any projector. Exposure times are from 1/125 to 1 second.

2. *Attachable Lens Barrel Tachistoscope* [Lafayette Instrument Company]. This is adaptable to any projector having a lens barrel size of 1⅞ to 2½ inches and is mounted directly to the lens barrel of the projector. Shutter exposure times range from 1/125 to 1 second.

3. *AVR Eye-Span Trainer* (AVR E-S-T 10) [Audio-Visual Research, 1509 Eighth St. S.E., Waseca, Minn. 56093]. This plastic mechanism offers a simple hand-operated shutter device for training in rapid recognition of numbers, words, money amounts, phrases, etc. Slides are available for the elementary, junior high, senior high, college, and adult levels.

4. *AVR Flash-Tachment* [Audio-Visual Research]. This is a simple attachment that converts any filmstrip projector into a tachistoscope. Speeds range from 1/25 to 1/100 of a second.

5. *EDL Flash-X* [Educational Development Laboratories, 74 Prospect St., Huntington, N.Y.]. In this device the student flicks the tab opening the shutter device for 1/25 of a second. The student records what he saw and then checks his answer. Discs are provided covering such areas as readiness, primary recognition, numbers, sight vocabulary, arithmetic, and spelling.

6. *EDL Tach-X Tachistoscope* [Educational Development Laboratories]. Images (numbers, pictures, letters, or words) can be projected on a screen for as long as 1½ seconds or as briefly as 1/100 of a second. The Tach-X is designed to develop visual discrimination and memory. Filmstrips range from the readiness to the adult level. Exercises such as the following are very effective: "Watch the screen. Ready?" The Tach-X flashes *yjjjj*. "Which letter was different?" The letters are shown again so the student can check for accuracy. Constant illumination is maintained, and the words flash in and out of focus.

7. *Electro-Tach* [Lafayette Instrument Company]. This is a near-point tachistoscopic training instrument for use at all age levels. The exposures are electronically controlled and range from 1/100 to 1 second. Training cards available cover digits, jumbled letters, words, phrases, sentences, and familiar objects.

8. *Flashmeter* [Keystone View Company, Meadville, Pa. 16335]. This device used with overhead projector forms a tachistoscope. The flashmeter is multibladed and has the following times: 1/2, 1/5, 1/10, 1/25, 1/50, and 1/100 of a second.

9. *The New T-Matic 150 Tachistoscope* [Psychotechnics, 1900 Pickwick Ave., Glenview, Ill. 60025]. This tachistoscope can be used for both small group and individual training. It has shutter speeds from 1/100 to 4 seconds.

10. *Phrase Flasher* [Reading Laboratory, Inc., 55 Day St., S. Norwalk, Conn. 06854]. This tachistoscope device is accompanied by a 940-card set of simple digits, words, and paragraphs.

11. *Rapid Reading Kit* [Better Reading Program, Inc., 232 East Ohio St., Chicago, Ill. 60611]. This is a self-help program designed to develop speed in comprehension. It includes the *Visualizer*, practice slides, *Reading Skill Book, Progress Records and Improvement Guide,* and two Reading Raters. Phrases are up to five words long and exposure is up to 1/100 of a second.

12. *Rheem T-Scope* [Califone, Los Angeles, Calif.]. This tachistoscopic projector comes with its own screenette.

13. *Selector-Tach* [Lafayette Instrument Company]. This is an individual near-point training tachistoscope. Exposure times are 1/100 to 1 second plus continuous. Also available are a *Film Strip or Slide Tachistoscope*, a *High-Speed Subliminal Tachistoscope,* and a *Constant Illumination Tachistoscope.*

14. *Speed-I-O-Scope* [Society for Visual Education, Diversey, Chicago, Illinois 60614]. This flash mechanism with shutterlike device mounts on a standard still projector. Speeds range from 1/100 to 1 second.

15. *Tachistoscope* [Lafayette Instrument Company). This all-purpose group tachistoscope permits exposures of 1, ½, 1/10, 1/25, 1/50, and 1/100 seconds. It is usable with any make of projector. The tachistoscopic attachment is adaptable to all makes of projectors.

16. *Tachisto-Flasher* [Learning Through Seeing, Inc., P.O. Box 368, Sunland, California]. This shutter mechanism, when set in front of the lens of a filmstrip projector, converts it into a tachistoscope. Exposure time can be teacher controlled up to 1/40 of a second.

17. *Tachisto-Viewer* [Learning Through Seeing, Inc.]. This tachistoscope filmstrip viewer has speeds of 1/5 to 1/40 of a second. Filmstrips are provided to develop word-recognition skills, spelling skills, and speed of visual perception.

18. *T-P Mark I Tachist-O-Flash Projector* [Learning Through Seeing, Inc.]. This filmstrip projector allows for speeds of 1–1½ seconds to 1/50 of a second.

Accelerating Devices

The accelerating devices provide rate training for the competent readers. The *Controlled Reader,* for example, presents materials in a left-to-right direction at a predetermined rate. A moving slot travels across the screen in a left-to-right direction, covering and uncovering the materials as it moves along (25).

Such devices lead to a reduction in fixations and regressions, better attention and concentration, more rapid thinking, and improved organization of what is read.

Once the student has attained a speed of 450 to 500 words, the words may be more satisfactorily uncovered a line at a time.

Accelerating devices are most useful in the upper elementary years and in junior high school.

Much group training with accelerators is at far-point. This is undesirable for students with myopic vision and for those who have difficulties with fusion because they are required to improve rate while handicapped visually. At far-point the person can also "read" more words than in normal reading. It is possible that this explains the relatively little transfer that occurs from machine programs to normal book reading.

A list of some accelerators follows:

1. *AVR Reading Rateometer* [Audio-Visual Research]. Three models of this machine are available. The standard model (model A) has a range of 70 to 2500 words per minute, model B has a range of 35 to 1000 words per minute, and model C has a range of 140 to 5000 words per minute. Each model is equipped with a pacing T-bar that moves down the page at a constant rate.

2. *Cenco Pacer* [Cenco Center, 2600 South Kostner Avenue, Chicago, Illinois 60623]. A reading pacer with fourteen sequential lesson rolls and a student workbook form the materials for this program usable with the slow learner.

3. *Controlled Reader* [Educational Developmental Laboratories]. A moving slot (picture) travels from left to right across the screen, or a full line may be uncovered at a time. It permits speeds of 60 to 1000 words per minute. Filmstrips are available from the kindergarten to the adult level, and question books and story books accompany each level.

4. *Craig Reader* [Craig Reader Division, 3410 So. La Crenage Blvd., Los Angeles, Calif.]. The *Craig Reader* adjusts to permit reading speeds of 75 to 1600 words per minute. The machine uses slide units rather than film. The slides contain twelve film frames in each slide. Twelve programs from elementary to university level are available.

5. *EDL Controlled Reader Jr.* This machine is similar to the Controlled Reader but is more economical for individual use.

6. *Keystone Reading Pacer* [Keystone View Company]. This device has a pointer which moves at speeds from 50 to 1000 words per minute. The pacer shuts itself off when the bottom of the page is reached and begins as it is moved to the top of the next page.

7. *NRI Speed-Reading Machine* [National Reading Institute, 24 Rope Ferry Road, Waterford, Conn.]. The automated speed-reading program includes the above machine, equipped with a self-timing device that enables an automatic increase in speed. This machine comes with programmed reading rolls that are fed through the machine.

8. *PDL Perceptoscope* [Perceptual Development Laboratories, P.O. Box 1911, Big Spring, Tex. 79720]. This projector serves as accelerator, projector, tachistoscope, or timer. Speeds may be varied on ten films from 120 to 4300 words per minute.

9. *Readamatic Pacer* [Americana Interstate Corporation, Mundelein, Illinois]. This pacer, quite similar in design to the Reading Rateometer, can vary speeds from 100 to 1000 words per minute.

10. *Shadowscope Reading Pacer* [Psychotechnics, Inc., 105 West Adams Street, Chicago, Illinois 60603]. The Shadowscope is designed for junior high level and up. The reading speeds may be varied from 105 to 2000 words per minute.

11. *SRA Reading Accelerator* [Science Research Associates, 259 E. Erie St., Chicago, Ill. 60611]. Model III offers rate adjustments of from less than 30 to more than 3000 words per minute. Model IV is a plastic portable.

12. *Tachomatic* [Psychotechnics, Inc.]. The Tachomatic film projector is designed for reading training at all levels, including that of adults. It utilizes a special film and highspeed mechanism to project series of words in a narrow band across a screen. The rate may be varied from very slow to motion picture speeds from 100 to 1200 words per minute, and the fixations may be one, two, or three per line.

Reading-related Machines

The reading teacher might also have use for one of the following machines in his reading program.

1. *Aud-X* [Educational Developmental Laboratories]. As students listen to interesting stories, they watch the screen to learn new words. Each time the narrator pronounces one of the several words being taught in a lesson, it appears on the screen in exact synchronization with its pronunciation. In follow-up word study lessons, students discover the graphic and sound

qualities of words through the unique sight-sound synchronization afforded by the Aud-X. Though the students may be part of a small group during Aud-X sessions, each one listens, looks, and responds in an individual manner. Through its autoinstructional capability, the Aud-X makes an important contribution to truly individualized learning.

2. *Delacato Stereo-Reading Service* [Keystone View Company]. This service with stereo reader is designed for remedial use with students who suffer from laterality confusions. It develops binocular reading. The Zweig-Bruno Stereo-Tracing Exercises, to be used with the Stereo-Reader, are effective in the correction of letter reversals, letter substitutions, in-word reversals, and poor hand-eye coordination.

3. *Language Master Machine* [Hoover Brothers, Kansas City, Missouri]. This machine comes with cards designed to teach vocabulary, sounds of English, phonics, etc.

4. *Leavell Language Development Service* [Keystone View Company]. This service with instrument develops eye control and hand-eye coordination. It is useful with mirror writers and children who reverse.

Skimming and Scanning

The only machine available today that is designed to develop the skimming skill is the *EDL Skimmer*. This machine is equipped with a bead of light that travels down the center fold of the book at the rate of one-half minute per page, or about eight hundred to one thousand words per minute. This informs the reader how rapidly he should proceed and keeps him perceptually alert. The device is useful also in developing scanning skills.

Skimming is selective reading. In skimming the reader chooses what he wants to read. He selects those sentences, clauses, and phrases that best serve his purposes. He gets a general impression of the selection and decides on the basis of his examination whether to read the selection more intensively. He takes a quick glance at the table of contents, the index, the chapter titles, the paragraph headings, the topic sentences, and the summary. These provide valuable clues to the main idea.

In scanning, the reader runs his eyes down the page with the purpose of finding an answer to a specific question.

We scan a crowd to find a certain person; we scan a bowl of candy for the right piece; and we scan a box of tools for a pliers. In reading, we scan to find an answer to a particular question, to locate a specific date or number, or to locate a reference, a name, a city, or a quotation.

Skimming and scanning are not accelerated reading. In them the reader switches from looking to reading to looking and so on. In fact, there may be less reading than looking, and when the person reads he reads in the usual way.

Schale (20) discusses three techniques, all involving skimming, for increasing rate of reading by learning to read vertically: the vertical skimming method, the square span method, and the narrow column method. In the vertical skimming method, the reader may glide his eyes over the irrelevant content until he lands on what he is looking for (exclusive skimming); he may survey material, identifying main ideas and inferring less important details (inclusive skimming); or he may, using nondirected skimming, move his eyes down the page in a narrow span. The square span method and the narrow column method both involve moving the eye over a small span—either the eye focuses on the center of a page or all the words are placed in narrow columns. Less skimming is involved in the latter two approaches.

Research tends to indicate that reading rates above eight hundred words per minute are in the nature of skimming and scanning. The reader characteristically omits part of the content and reads with considerably less comprehension (24, p. 6).

Skimming usually takes the form of preview, overview, or review (23, pp. 34–37). Skimming for preview purposes has already been described. In skimming for overview purposes the reader gets a general impression of the content. He reads more of the material than when doing preview skimming. He looks for the writer's organization, thinks along with the writer, and notes the transitions. Skimming for review is a useful technique in preparing for tests or to increase retention generally.

When the student should be taught to skim is difficult to say. Taylor and Frackenpohl (24, pp. 9–12) have identified the *type* of student who is ready for selective reading. The student must be a flexible reader. He needs visual coordination. He must have developed a proper directional attack, and he must be able to organize a series of data. He must be able to identify words rapidly, must retain them, and must relate them to each other. He must develop attention and concentration, while maintaining his composure. He must be relaxed and willing to settle for less than complete comprehension.

To skim, the student must develop a new perceptual skill. In selective reading "looking" is as important as is reading. The person must look back and forth and down the page in a "floating" manner as it were (24, p. 11). He learns to take in words, ideas, and organization at a subliminal level.

Teaching the student to skim may advance through many stages. Perhaps the first is the changing of the student's attitude (23, p. 36). The student must realize that partial comprehension meets certain needs. He should be taught that the title of an article by itself gives a general overview. Each student has read stories with a title and has probably been told what the title tells him. Generally, the title identifies the content or subject matter.

The table of contents describes the book. It is like a grocery advertisement in a newspaper. The advertisement gives a glimpse of the stock inside the store. It tries to interest the perceiver enough to get him to visit the store and to examine the contents more closely.

Scanning requires similar but also different skills. Much of a scanner's skill lies in knowing what he is looking for and in predicting how the specific point that he is trying to find is stated. For example, distances are usually stated in terms of miles, feet, minutes, or hours.

Let us give an example of how scanning might be taught.

Use the scanning technique as *you* try to find the answer to the following question: "How many children suffer from the condition known as retinoblastoma?"

Retinoblastoma is a cancer found in the eyes of infants and young children. It is somewhat like a tumor. The Retinoblastoma Clinic in the Institute of Ophthalmology of the Columbia-Presbyterian Medical Center in New York specializes in its treatment. Approximately one of every 23,000 children is affected by it. Children are born with it, and hence the condition is congenital.

The first symptoms consist of a yellowish-white reflection in the pupil of the eye. When the tumors are small, radiation treatment is frequently successful. At more advanced stages, the eye has to be removed. If this is not done, the cancer spreads and death ultimately occurs.

Evaluation of Machine Programs

No one would suggest that reading instruments make a total program. On the other hand, few would deny that they have a legitimate role in a balanced reading program. In evaluating their effectiveness one must always be cautious in generalizing from one instrument to all others. Each has its own strength and weakness and must be separately evaluated.

Certain principles, however, guide all evaluations. It is not enough to simply look for rate gains. The reader's relative efficiency is more than rate; it is also a function of the fixations and regressions

$$(RE) = \frac{Rate}{Fixations + Regressions}.$$

An increase in rate is significant only when it is accompanied by a reduction in fixations and regressions.

Mechanical devices are motivating. They may even increase comprehension achievement; however, they cannot increase comprehension potential. They merely help the mind to operate on a level approximating its potential.

Persons working with mechanical devices repeatedly have noticed among students an increase in interest in reading and in a desire to improve their reading skills. For some of these a successful experience in a machine program may develop a new attitude toward reading generally which may lead to improved performance in a number of areas including rate of comprehension.

It thus frequently is impossible to attribute rate improvements to machines alone. Increased motivation and increased teacher effectiveness may be as significant. No one would suggest that because no gains were made that the machine was necessarily useless. Nor could one infer that because gains were made in a machine program that these were the sole result of the machine. The effectiveness of any mechanical device depends on the user.

How good then are these gadgets? Tinker (27) makes the following observations:

1. Reading speed can be improved, but it is not at all certain that the gains are lasting.
2. Improved rate is not automatically transferred to other types of material.
3. There is evidence to indicate that pacers and accelerating devices are more effective developers of reading rate than are tachistoscopes. Tinker adds, "The tachistoscope is without value for increasing speed of reading."
4. The improvement through mechanical devices is no greater than that resulting from motivated reading alone. However, Maxwell and Mueller (13), in a study involving forty college students, found that those students who were given specific techniques for improving their speed showed significantly greater gains than either the control group or the group that was simply "motivated" to increase rate.
5. Pacing devices often are emphasized more than the processes of perception, apprehension, and assimilation, with a resultant decrease in flexibility.
6. There is perhaps too much of an emphasis upon "oculomotor mechanics."

Horn (9, pp. 201–2) notes that the classroom teacher needs to be concerned with movements of the eyes about as much as with the movements of the bones of the inner ear.

We would add the following generalizations:

1. The visual span or the perception span can be increased both vertically and horizontally.
2. Gains in rate tend to have an adequate degree of permanency.
3. Mechanical devices may destroy some flexibility in reading.

4. The tachistoscopic span (visual span) is already much larger than the recognition span of the average reader.

5. The mind, not vision, is generally the limiting element in reading. Fast and slow readers are differentiated on the basis of the central processes. Reading is primarily a perceptual function. Those who excel in rate of thinking tend to be high in rate of comprehension.

6. The more significant the material is to the individual, the wider will be his recognition span.

7. The machine and the purr of the motor have a psychological and motivational effect on students, especially boys. They do not stretch the visual span but rather spur the mind (3, p. 6).

8. Rather than speed training, with some students it might be better to improve the poor vocabulary and the word-recognition and word-analysis skills of the learner. Weaknesses in basic reading skills should be diagnosed and corrected before any consideration is given to rate of reading.

9. If, in fact, the good reader reacts to ever decreasing or minimal cues, then mechanical training may at times be successful simply because it teaches the student to read with fewer cues, to guess better what he sees peripherally, and to be more confident in dealing with indistinct portions of words.

10. Perhaps those traits that lead a student to seek reading improvement are the same traits that cluster to produce higher grades.

11. Marvel (11), working with high school sophomores, found that motivational factors, verbal set or mind set, without tachistoscopic training were most significant in improving both rate and permanency of rate.

12. The best use of mechanical devices may be with average and better-than-average readers having specific problems in rate of reading.

13. The amount of transfer of rate gains from machine-oriented programs to more typical reading is quite variable and unpredictable.

IMPLICATIONS OF RATE IMPROVEMENT PROGRAMS

There are still other concerns that constantly perplex the practitioner. For example: What is optimal reading speed on specific materials and how can it be determined? Which rate skills should receive most reinforcement? What are the side effects of speed programs? In some programs the student is taught rhythmic phraseology. Yet, the good reader is a flexible reader. Normal reading is continuous textual and nonrhythmic reading.

Finally, what is the student learning in rate improvement programs using tachistoscopic or other mechanical devices? Fletcher (6) found that when three equivalent forms were used in testing the student's perform-ance, at the end of the first, second, and last tachistoscopic training session, most of the gains occurred between the first and second session. The technique of rapid performance on a tachistoscope seems to be acquired rather quickly.

There seems to be little justification for emphasis on speed of reading in the primary school years. The intermediate pupil and the high school student, on the other hand, must be taught to adjust their reading speed to the materials and purposes for reading. They must be taught, either through book or machine programs, facility and speed in perceiving words and relating them to their meaning. They must be taught to read in thought units. They must be helped to overcome such faulty habits as moving the lips, pointing to words, or moving the head while reading.

The student must be encouraged to move his eyes as rapidly across the line of print as is possible. Too frequently, the student can read faster, but he has developed the habit of moving slowly. To overcome this habit the student should time himself on passages of a particular length. In the beginning the passages should be simple and interesting. If the print is in narrow columns, as in newspapers, the student should be encouraged to make only one fixation per line, forcing himself to move the eyes down the page.

The student is constantly tempted to regress so that he can read more accurately. Normally this may be good procedure, but it does not lead to increased speed. The student must fight against this. He can be helped to overcome excessive caution by cutting a slot out of a piece of paper and moving the paper down the page. This forces him to move ahead and keeps him from looking back or too far ahead. Another device consists simply of a sheet of paper which he may move down the page, covering a line at a time.

The student must learn that there is no best rate of reading. The good reader uses a flexible approach in reading. He uses a greater variety of approaches when reading, even though he may have learned this skill on his own (22). His reading varies in speed from very slow to moderate to very fast; from detailed analysis of what he reads to skimming and scanning; from rapid reading, skimming, and recreational reading to in-tensive reading. Even his comprehension tends to be flexible. Some ma-terials need to be understood thoroughly; others, only generally. Certain parts of a textbook must be read intensively; others may be skimmed. The flexible reader may read very rapidly or even skip those parts that are trivial, are already known, or are unrelated to his goals and purposes.

The flexible reader knows what he wants from the material. He has asked himself: Need I understand only the main idea, the supporting facts, or a combination of these? Am I reading for pleasure or for infor-mation? What is my purpose?

The flexible reader has also developed a flexible attitude toward reading. He adjusts his speed to the purpose for which he is reading and to the difficulty of the reading matter. He realizes that different reading situations call for different ways of reading. He reads differently when reading newspapers, magazines, advertisements, encyclopedias, textbooks, novels, how-to-do-it books, and editorials.

It is not enough to know what a flexible reader does. High school students need to be taught the ability to behave flexibly when reading. Exercises like the following teach what flexibility in reading means.

> This lesson is on flexibility in reading. How should you read the following? Which would you read most rapidly? Most slowly? Try to arrange the exercises in an order of increasing speed.
>
> 1. *Changing a mixed number to an improper fraction*
>   To change a mixed number (3½) to an improper fraction (value is one or more than one) multiply the whole number by the denominator of the fraction and add the numerator of the fraction to this product. The sum of the product and the numerator is then written over the denominator.
>
> 2. *Johannson-Patterson Fight*
>   With barely a minute gone the challenger Ingemar Johannson unleashed a right that sent Patterson helplessly toward the floor. Patterson recovered quickly but in another twenty seconds he again was sprawled on the canvas. Again Patterson rose. Suddenly, Patterson's left landed on the jaw of the challenger. Down went Johannson with a thud. History had been made in the first round of the fight. Three knockdowns and still no knockout.

The speed of reading these short paragraphs will obviously change depending on one's purposes and one's familiarity with the material. One would read them more slowly if it was necessary to know every little detail; one would read them more rapidly if one needed only general information. Thus, knowing why one is reading them is of first importance.

Similar exercises on the student's level can be developed to teach the various rate skills. The following are examples of such exercises:

1. Have the student read simple materials as rapidly as he can.
2. Have students time their reading of an article whose number of words they know.
3. Have the student skim a page in a textbook to find the answer to a question, to locate a new word, or to identify a quotation.
4. Have the student skim an encyclopedia article for a specific fact.
5. Have students determine purposes for reading and then discuss appropriateness of various rates for various reading purposes.

The aim of these exercises is not the development of an absolute reading rate. The student should develop an attitude favorable to reading at the rate that his comprehension and the nature of the materials allow. He should become unfavorably disposed to needlessly slow reading.

It is by recognizing poor habits in reading that we will be able to deal with them. The following habits hinder speed reading:

1. Excessive vocalizing
2. Word-by-word reading
3. Stopping to work out each strange word with meticulous care
4. Letting numbers or other symbols slow one down
5. Following a line of print with one's finger
6. Backtracking, refocusing, or rereading
7. Daydreaming
8. Reading all materials at the same pace

A good reader, of course, is one who has more than just ample rate skills.

1. He has an adequate vocabulary.
2. He engages in phrase reading rather than word-by-word reading.
3. His reading is purposeful and directed.
4. He uses a flexible approach in reading.
5. He reads critically.
6. He has the experience of wide, extensive reading.
7. He can apply various techniques to make his reading smooth and effective.
8. He has an adequate level of understanding.

The most difficult task for the teacher is often one not of identifying the symptoms, but of hooking symptoms with their proper cause. Here are four symptoms related to speed of reading, with suggested causes and recommendations.*

1. Continued low reading rates with low comprehension

Probable Cause or Condition	Recommendations
serious motor-vocalization	extensive mumbo-jumbo
a possible remedial or corrective problem—serious visual disorders	refer to proper specialist
material is too difficult	adjust material to level of student
poor concentration	pre-reading, questioning
poor motivation	adjust material to the interests of student

* *Administrator's Guide,* Developmental Reading Program (New York: The Reading Laboratory, Inc., 1966), pp. 61–62.

2. Continued low reading rates with high comprehension

Probable Cause or Condition	*Recommendations*
lack of confidence in help or technique	give easier material and focus on the development of speed, check application of phrase reading, space reading, indenting
overestimates the difficulty of the material	give additional phrase-marking
motor vocalization	stress additional mumbo-jumbo

3. High reading rates with continued low comprehension

Probable Cause or Condition	*Recommendations*
superficial attitude	give short readings and require detailed reports
skipping and skimming (trying to keep up without practicing)	check application of all reading techniques
does not organize his thought	require written results of pre-reading, questioning and summarizing done outside of class
underestimates the material	stress sentence jumble exercises

4. Eye strain

Probable Cause or Condition	*Recommendations*
uncorrected eye condition	recommend specialist
poor reading conditions	correct faults, make recommendations
overworks eyes	check reading habits
physical or psychological tension	interview and recommend suitable conditions and materials for reading

SUMMARY

In Chapter 9 we focused on the development of rate skills. We examined the relationship between rate and comprehension, the value of speed reading, and the goal of all reading programs: flexibility in reading. We found that both rate and flexibility can and should be taught as separate skills.

The chapter also evaluated machine programs, concentrating on such gadgets as tachistoscopes and accelerating devices and such specific devices as the EDL Skimmer. Skimming and scanning were described, and the pros and cons of machine programs were enumerated.

QUESTIONS FOR DISCUSSION

1. Enumerate key factors that are positively related to speed of reading.
2. What are the claims usually made for speed-reading programs?
3. Give the pros and cons of machine and book-centered programs.
4. Describe the values of tachistoscopes and accelerators.
5. Differentiate between *skimming* and *scanning*.
6. Discuss:
   a. The mind, not vision, is generally the limiting factor in reading.
   b. The good reader reacts to ever-decreasing cues.
7. How would you teach a student to become a flexible reader?
8. What are some poor habits in reading that hinder speed reading?
9. Relate readability of materials to comprehension and rate of comprehension.
10. Describe the cloze procedure and discuss its purposes.

BIBLIOGRAPHY

1. AMBLE, BRUCE R., "Reading by Phrases," *California Journal of Educational Research,* 18 (May 1967), 116–24.
2. BRAAM, LEONARD, "Developing and Measuring Flexibility in Reading," *The Reading Teacher,* 16 (January 1963), 247–54.
3. DEARBORN, WALTER F., "Motivation versus 'Control' in Remedial Reading," *Education,* 59 (September 1938), 1–6.
4. DECHANT, EMERALD, "Rate of Comprehension—Needed Research," *Changing Concepts of Reading Instruction,* ed. J. Allen Figurel, International Reading Association Conference Proceedings, 6, 223–25. New York: Scholastic Magazines, 1961.
5. EDL, *Report on Reading Instrument Usage,* EDL Newsletter No. 19. Huntington, N.Y.: Educational Developmental Laboratories.
6. FLETCHER, J. EUGENE, "Rapid Reading Perception, and the Tachistoscope," *College of Education Record,* University of Washington, 25 (May 1959), 52–55.
7. HARRIS, ALBERT J., *How to Increase Reading Ability* (3rd ed.). New York: Longmans, Green and Company, 1956.
8. HARRIS, ALBERT J., "Research on Some Aspects of Comprehension: Rate Flexibility and Study Skills," *Journal of Reading,* 1 (December 1968), 205–10, 258–60.

9. HORN, ERNEST, *Methods of Instruction in the Social Studies.* New York: Charles Scribner's Sons, 1937.

10. LIDDLE, WILLIAM, "An Initial Investigation of the Word Reading Dynamics Method." Unpublished doctoral dissertation, School of Education, University of Delaware, 1965.

11. MARVEL, JOHN, "Acquisition and Retention of Reading Performance on Two Response Dimensions as Related to Set and Tachistoscopic Training," *Journal of Educational Research,* 52 (February 1959), 232–37.

12. MATHEWS, JOHN W., "Some Sour Notes on Speed Reading," *Journal of Reading,* 9 (January 1966), 179–81, 185.

13. MAXWELL, MARTHA J., and ARTHUR C. MUELLER, "Relative Effectiveness of Techniques and Placebo Conditions in Changing Reading Rates," *Journal of Reading,* 11 (December 1967), 184–91.

14. MCCRACKEN, ROBERT A., "Internal versus External Flexibility of Reading Rate," *Journal of Reading,* 8 (January 1965), 208–9.

15. MCDONALD, ARTHUR S., "Flexibility in Reading," in *Reading as an Intellectual Activity,* ed. J. ALLEN FIGUREL. International Reading Association Conference Proceedings, 8 (1963), 81–84.

16. MCDONALD, ARTHUR S., "Research for the Classroom: Rate and Flexibility," *Journal of Reading,* 8 (January 1965), 187–91.

17. MORTON, JOHN, "The Effects of Context upon Speed Reading, Eye Movement and Eye-Voice Span," *Quarterly Journal of Experimental Psychology,* 16 (1964), 340–54.

18. PAUK, WALTER, "On Scholarship: Advice to High School Students," *The Reading Teacher,* November 1963, 73–78.

19. ROSE, LYNDON, "The Reading Process and Some Research Implications," *Journal of Reading,* 13 (October 1969), 25–28.

20. SCHALE, FLORENCE, "Vertical Methods of Increasing Rates of Comprehension," *Journal of Reading,* 8 (April 1965), 296–300.

21. SHORES, J. HARLAN, "Dimensions of Reading Speed and Comprehension," *Elementary English,* 45 (January 1968), 23–28, 43.

22. SMITH, HELEN K., "The Development of Effective, Flexible Readers," *Proceedings of the Annual Reading Conference,* pp 159–68. Chicago: University of Chicago Press, 1965.

23. TAYLOR, STANFORD E., *Speed Reading . . .vs. Improved Reading Efficiency.* Huntington, N.Y.: Educational Developmental Laboratories, 1962.

24. TAYLOR, STANFORD, E., and HELEN FRACKENPOHL, *EDL Skimmer.* Huntington, N.Y.: Educational Developmental Laboratories, 1961.

25. TAYLOR, STANFORD E., and HELEN FRACKENPOHL, *Teacher's Guide: Controlled Reader.* Huntington, N.Y.: Educational Developmental Laboratories, 1960.

26. TAYLOR, STANFORD E., and HELEN FRACKENPOHL, *Teacher's Guide: Tach-X Flash-X.* Huntington, N.Y.: Educational Developmental Laboratories, 1960.

27. TINKER, MILES A., "Devices to Improve Speed of Reading," *The Reading Teacher,* 20 (April 1967), 605–9.

Corrective and Remedial Reading in the Secondary School

CHAPTER **11**

BEFORE WE GET INTO THE MORE TECHNICAL ASPECTS of diagnosis and remediation, let us make a few general observations about the prevention of reading disabilities.

Many educators today are concerned that we may be overemphasizing remediation and ignoring prevention. Their fears are not entirely groundless. In too many instances the best teachers are removed from regular classroom teaching and put into the role of special or remedial reading teacher. This may lead to poorer instruction in the classroom and increased numbers of children with reading problems. It may well be that we are thus producing retarded readers at a rate much faster than we will ever be able to remediate.

Although we have done a better job of remediation than of prevention, it is far better to prevent than to remediate; it is far better that we deal with the problem in the classroom rather than wait until the student acquires a reading disability.

Prevention is not an easy task. No one has found the appropriate preventions, or we would not have the number of reading disabilities that we do have. Perhaps we have not looked for ways of preventing reading disability but have merely been satisfied with cures.

Reading failures can be prevented only if every lesson is a diagnostic and, in a sense, a remedial lesson. Perhaps even then many failures cannot be prevented, but the teacher must operate on the assumption that failures can be prevented, and it is only through accurate and continuous diagnosis of the student's needs and difficulties, of his assets and strengths, that the teacher can modify instruction to meet these needs.

Continuous diagnosis is a must in the reading classroom; prevention is its end product. Diagnosis identifies minor difficulties before they become disabilities and thus occasions adjustments in instruction that might remove these difficulties.

It is not uncommon for the teacher to observe within the classroom students who fit the following descriptions.

Some have developed habits of word-by-word reading, of vocalizing, of backtracking, of daydreaming while reading, of rereading, of plodding along at a snail's pace, or of word blocking. Others follow words with their fingers or move their heads from side to side rather than move their eyes across the page.

Serious problems? No, but these innocuous difficulties tend to snowball. Most remedial cases are probably instances of "an accumulation of unmet reading needs." Reading deficiency begins with simple inadequacies. Despite the good work of the classroom teacher, some students lose increasingly more ground with each year of school attendance. Retardation is cumulative.

To detect and diagnose the incipient reading problems, then, is a prime responsibility of the teacher. Prevention of reading difficulties should begin before the child starts formal reading instruction and should continue throughout his entire school career. Prevention is best brought about by diagnosis of and constant alertness to any incipient or existing difficulty.

The student with a reading disability must have the benefits of recognition (25). His problem needs to be identified early, or he will grow up with the disability intact. Beyond a certain point he no longer may be interested in or be able to benefit from educational recognition (25).

DEFINITION OF DIAGNOSIS

Diagnosis is defined in *Webster's New Collegiate Dictionary* as "the art or act of identifying a disease from its signs and symptoms." Brueckner (10, p. 2) notes that educational diagnosis refers to the techniques by which one discovers and evaluates the strengths and weaknesses of an individual. The diagnostician gathers data and then on the basis of the analysis and interpretation of these data suggests developmental or remedial measures.

Diagnosis is an identification of weakness or strength from an observation of symptoms. It is an inference from performance. It must include assessment of both level of performance (reading retardation) and manner of performance (inability to integrate visual stimuli). It is concerned with determining the nature of the problem, identifying the constellation of factors that produced it, and finding a point of attack.

PRINCIPLES OF DIAGNOSIS

As one scans the literature on diagnosis, a few general principles emerge:

1. Diagnosis begins with each student's unique instructional needs:
   a. What can he do?
   b. What are his difficulties?
   c. What are the causes of his difficulties?
   d. What can be done to remedy his difficulties?
2. Diagnosis is a continuous process.
3. Diagnosis should be directed toward formulating methods of remediation. Educational diagnosis is productive only if it is translated into specific educational strategies.
4. Diagnosis and remediation are no longer the special privileges of the slow or retarded learner—they are extended to the gifted and the average as well.
5. Diagnosis may be concerned merely with the symptomatology, but genuine diagnosis looks toward the causes of the symptoms. The diagnostic viewpoint is that behavior is caused. The teacher thus needs to understand the causes of inadequate performance rather than to blame the student for it. The student should not be labeled dumb or lazy, even though each may be a cause once in a while.
6. The causes of student inadequacy are usually multiple rather than single or unitary.
7. The teacher needs more than simply skill in diagnosing the causes of the student's difficulty. He needs ability to modify instruction to meet the need identified by diagnosis.
8. Decisions based on diagnosis should flow from a pattern of test scores and a variety of other data.
9. The analysis of reading difficulties is primarily an *educational-analysis* task; it is best done by an experienced teacher who knows the essential elements of reading instruction (23, 354–55).

STEPS IN DIAGNOSIS

Diagnosis leads to an ever more detailed study of the problem. It begins in reading with simple observation and possibly a survey test and ends up with a hypothesis for remediation. It involves the identification and description of the problem, discovery of the causes, and projection of remediation required. More specifically, the steps of the diagnostic procedure may be the following: *

1. The Overall Screening Process—Compare expected functioning level as determined by IQ and other test and personal data with actual functioning level as determined by the reading survey test or by other less formal procedures. This is the level of *survey diagnosis* and consists chiefly of classroom screening.

2. Diagnostic Testing—Describe the condition more specifically, checking on such specifics as knowledge of vocabulary, inability to associate sound with the beginning consonant, inability to phrase correctly, or reversal problems. Informal observations of the student's reading and diagnostic testing will help to identify the difficulties. This is the level of *specific diagnosis* and is identified with individual diagnosis.

3. Detailed Investigation of Causality—Make an analysis of the disability, looking for the correlates of disability. If the test results in step 2 show a weakness in phonic skills, the student's auditory discrimination might be checked. This is the level of *intensive diagnosis* and is associated with identifying the underlying causes of the reading disability.

4. Remediation—Finally, draw up a program of remediation. Diagnosis is complete only when remediation occurs. The diagnostic-remedial process is a single process.

Step 1: The Screening Process

Let us assume that we have a typical high school with about five hundred students and that the administration and staff want to begin a special reading program for those students who are more or less retarded in reading. The immediate aim will be to reduce the number of students for this special education to something under five hundred.

Screening separates those persons who are most likely to need special attention from those who are not likely to need it. It is commonly applied to large groups of students by classroom teachers. This first step tends to be more comprehensive in *breadth;* the later steps in diagnosis are more comprehensive in *depth.* Screening procedures should be simple, fairly quick, inexpensive, valid, reliable, and productive.

Many students do not need a detailed diagnosis. A more general diagnosis is sufficient. It is enough in most instances that we acquire sufficient knowledge about the five hundred students or the thirty students in a given classroom so that instruction may be adjusted to the group. This

* Barbara Bateman, "Learning Disabilities—Yesterday, Today, and Tomorrow," *Exceptional Children,* 31 (December 1965), 167–76.

overall screening process should identify the overall reading proficiency of the group or class, help to adjust instruction to individual differences within the group, and locate those students who are in need of further analysis of their disability.

There needs to be adequate provision for remediation of most reading disability cases in the regular classroom. One factor that operates against remediation in the regular classroom is the high student-teacher ratio. It is difficult to provide individual remediation when there are thirty students all clamoring for the teacher's time and attention.

THE NATURE OF RETARDATION   Perhaps the first prerequisite for anyone associated with the reading program, and indeed the educational program, is to have a clear conception of the meaning of retardation. There is a difference between slow learners, reluctant readers, disadvantaged readers, and retarded readers. Table 11-1 delineates some of these differences.

TABLE 11-1   CHARACTERISTICS OF VARIOUS POOR READERS

Slow Learner	Reluctant Reader	Disadvantaged Reader	Retarded Reader
ability level below 90 IQ ↓ generally reads on ability level ↓ generally reads below grade level ↓ instruction needs to be adapted to his limited ability—the pace of instruction and teacher expectations must be realistic	can read but will not ↓ the root of the reading difficulties is the mental attitude of the student ↓ solution to the reading problem begins with a change of attitude	potential often far exceeds performance ↓ generally can learn and wants to learn ↓ lacks adequate oral language because of inadequate experience ↓ does not look upon reading as life-related ↓ often feels alienated from the larger social structure ↓ often is deficient in auditory attention ↓ needs to learn how to learn	is usually of average or above-average intelligence, although a retarded reader could also be a slow learner ↓ does not read on ability level ↓ may or may not be reading below grade level ↓ may show blocks to learning, especially emotional or neurological, which keep him from learning to read

Retardation is usually defined in relation to level of general development, with perhaps the greater emphasis being on mental development. Retardation is associated with slower progress than is expected. A retarded reader is one whose reading capacity is considerably greater than his reading achievement. Wilson (54) suggests that on the high school level the retarded or problem reader is one who cannot read his textbooks effectively. He is a reader who benefits little from regular classroom instruction in the various content areas (2). Bryant (11) notes that disability is always dependent upon the material and methods used in instruction.

Retardation is also a matter of degree. The retarded reader of fifty years ago was more likely to be a student who could not read. Today, he is often a student who is not reading as well as he might. Durrell (22, p. 270) notes that a retardation of six months at the first-grade level is more serious than is a retardation of six months at the sixth-grade level. To be significant the difference between performance and potential must be at least nine months for children in grades four and five and about twelve months in grades six and above.

READING POTENTIAL   The first diagnostic step involves an analysis of (1) reading potential or reading expectancy level and (2) reading achievement. This presents the teacher with a knowledge of what the student's present level of achievement is and to what level he might progress. Without knowing a student's potential, education is target practice in the dark. No one can know where he is going if he does not know where he is at.

Various ways of assessing reading potential have been tried. The tests most frequently used to assess reading potential are intelligence or scholastic aptitude tests, which often provide IQ or mental age scores.

Since the idea is to obtain intelligence or scholastic aptitude test scores on all five hundred students in our sample school, or perhaps on a class of thirty, it is recommended that the first test be a group paper-and-pencil test. Tests useful for this purpose are the following:

1. *California Test of Mental Maturity,* California Test Bureau, Monterey, Calif.
2. *Kuhlmann-Anderson IQ Test,* Personnel Press, Inc., Princeton, N.J.
3. *Kuhlmann-Finch IQ Test,* American Guidance Service, Inc., Minneapolis.
4. *Lorge-Thorndike Intelligence Tests,* Houghton Mifflin Company, Boston.
5. *Otis-Lennon Mental Ability Test,* Harcourt, Brace & World, Inc., Chicago.

Most tests for fourth grade and above usually require reading. Some of these, however, provide nonverbal scores, and these scores can give clues for diagnosis. When the verbal score is substantially lower than the nonverbal score, the teacher may suspect that the student's performance on the verbal sections is limited by the lack of reading ability. The test is thus an unfair test for him. It often places the poor reader in the dull-normal category, thus underestimating his real ability.

Every student whose IQ score falls below 90 or below the twenty-fifth percentile on a test requiring reading should probably be given another intelligence or scholastic aptitude test. Another IQ test should also be given when the student's reading level score as determined by a reading achievement test is significantly below his grade level. This means that perhaps 25 percent, or 125 students of the original group of 500, need retesting. It may mean that from 6 to 8 students in a given classroom need to be retested. Their abilities need to be measured by a test that does not require reading to get the correct answer. The following tests are specifically designed to deal with this problem. Some of them may be given to a group of students and others must be given individually. Some of the latter require special training for their administration.

GROUP

IPAT Culture Fair Intelligence Tests, Institute for Personality and Ability Testing, Champaign, Ill.

INDIVIDUAL

1. *Chicago Non-Verbal Examination,* Psychological Corporation, New York.
2. *Columbia Mental Maturity Scale,* Harcourt, Brace & World, Inc., Chicago.
3. *Full Range Picture Vocabulary Test,* Psychological Test Specialists, Missoula, Mont.
4. *Peabody Picture Vocabulary Test,* American Guidance Service, Inc., Minneapolis.
5. *Quick Test,* Psychological Test Specialists, Missoula, Mont.
6. *Slosson Intelligence Test for Children and Adults,* Slosson Educational Publications, East Aurora, N.Y.
7. *Stanford-Binet Intelligence Scales,* Houghton Mifflin Company, Boston.
8. *Wechsler Intelligence Scale for Children,* Psychological Corporation, New York.

The IQ score should not be used as an absolute measure. A mechanical formula cannot decide for us when a student *is* a retarded reader, and it cannot tell us when he is no longer a disabled reader (36). Nevertheless, the IQ, though perhaps too simple an estimate of the student's present academic potential, is the best that we have. It is indicative of the minimum that we may expect from the student; it is certainly not indicative of the maximum of which he is capable. Blaming tests for group differences merely attacks the symptoms.

There is a second way of estimating the student's potential. The student's listening ability is a good indicator of the level on which he could be reading. Reading might be defined as listening through print. The following tests provide a measure of the student's listening comprehension:

1. *Botel Reading Inventory,* Follett Publishing Company, Chicago. This inventory for grades 1–12 has a section entitled "Word Opposites Listening Test." There are ten multiple-choice items at each level. Each item consists of four or five words, and the student must find a word in each line that is the opposite of the first word.

2. *Brown-Carlson Listening Comprehension Test,* Harcourt, Brace & World, Inc., New York. This test for grades 9–adult measures five important listening skills—immediate recall, following directions, recognizing transitions, recognizing word meanings, and lecture comprehension.

3. *Durell Listening–Reading Series,* Harcourt, Brace & World, Inc., New York. This test provides a comparison of children's listening and reading abilities in order to identify those who are in need of special help. The series consists of a Reading Test and a parallel Listening Test. The test is available for grades 7–9.

4. *Sequential Tests of Educational Progress: Listening,* Cooperative Test Division, Educational Testing Service, Princeton. This listening test is part of a large battery of tests usable on grade levels 4–14.

READING ACHIEVEMENT   The survey test is concerned with general achievement and typically is the first reading achievement test that the teacher will use. It emphasizes vocabulary knowledge, comprehension of sentences or paragraphs, and perhaps speed of comprehension. It gives a general picture by identifying broad areas in which the student excels or is weak. Some common survey tests are the following:

1. *American School Reading Tests,* Public School Publishing Company, Cincinnati, grades 10–13.

2. *Burnett Reading Series,* Scholastic Testing Service, Bensenville, Ill. grades 7–9.

3. *California Reading Test,* Jr. High Level, California Test Bureau, Monterey, Calif., grades 7–9.

4. *California Reading Test,* Advanced, California Test Bureau, Monterey, Calif., grades 9–14.

5. *Chapman Reading Comprehension Test,* Educational Test Bureau, Circle Pines, Minn., grades 5–12.

6. *Davis Reading Test,* Psychological Corporation, New York, grades 8–13.

7. *Gates-MacGinitie Reading Test—Survey E.,* Teachers College Press, Columbia University, grades K–12.

8. *High School Reading Test: National Achievement Tests,* Acorn Publishing Company, Brockport, Ill., grades 7–12.

9. *Iowa Every-Pupil Test of Basic Skills,* Houghton Mifflin Company, Boston, grades 3–9.

10. *Iowa Silent Reading Tests,* Harcourt, Brace & World, Inc., New York, grades 4–14.

11. *Iowa Tests of Basic Skills,* Houghton Mifflin Company, Boston, grades 3–9.

12. *Iowa Tests of Educational Development,* Science Research Associates, Chicago, grades 9–12.

13. *Kelley-Greene Reading Comprehension Test,* Harcourt, Brace & World, Inc., New York, grades 9–13.

14. *Metropolitan Achievement Test,* Harcourt, Brace & World, Inc., New York, grades 2–9.

15. *Minnesota Reading Examination for College Students,* University of Minnesota Press, Minneapolis, grades 9–16.

16. *Nelson-Denny Reading Test,* Houghton Mifflin Company, Boston, grades 9–16.

17. *Purdue Reading Test,* Purdue Research Foundation, Purdue University, grades 7–12.

18. *Reading Comprehension: Cooperative English Tests,* Cooperative Test Division, Educational Testing Service, Princeton, grades 9–14.

19. *Schrammel-Gray High School and College Reading Test,* Public School Publishing Company, Cincinnati, grades 7–16.

20. *S-R-A Reading Record,* Science Research Associates, Chicago, grades 6–12.

21. *Survey of Reading Achievement,* California Test Bureau, grades 9–12.

22. *Stanford Reading Tests,* Harcourt, Brace & World, Inc., New York, grades 3–9.

23. *Traxler High School Reading Test,* Public School Publishing Company, Cincinnati, grades 10–12.

24. *Wide Range Achievement Test,* Guidance Testing Associates, Austin, Tex., ages 12–adult.

After having obtained the intelligence test score and the survey reading test scores, it is possible to identify the number of students whose reading scores are significantly below their intelligence or scholastic aptitude test scores.

To determine degree of retardation, proceed as follows. Group the reading and scholastic aptitude scores into two columns.

Student	Reading Score (Grade Level)	IQ score
1	11.6	122
2	6.1	113

Then compare each student's reading performance with his mental age. The purpose of this procedure is to determine whether the reading score (reading age score) is substantially below the mental age score. You may also want to check whether it is below his listening comprehension score. To carry out this manipulation, it is necessary to know the student's age and IQ. Begin by converting the reading grade score into a reading age score. This is done by adding 5 to the grade score. In our sample below, the test itself furnished the reading age score. Then find the mental age. This may be done (as shown) by multiplying the age by the IQ, being careful to put a decimal point at the proper place in the IQ score.

Student	Grade-Level Reading Score	Reading Age Score (RA)	Chronological Age	IQ Score	Mental Age	Difference Between MA and RA
1	11.6	16.9	14.0	122	17.0 (14 × 1.22)	— .1
2	6.1	11.3	14.2	113	16.0 (14.2 × 1.13)	—4.7

In the two samples given, student 1 is retarded only .1 of a year; student 2 is retarded 4.7 years. Student 2 ought to be performing like the average youngster of sixteen (high school sophomore or junior level), but he is performing on the sixth-grade level.

Student 2 obviously calls for more thorough analysis. It is with this type of student that we need to follow through with steps 2, 3, and 4 of diagnosis.

By completing Step 1, we should have greatly reduced the number of students who need special attention. We should have differentiated students who are genuinely retarded (e.g., student 2) from those who simply need adapted instruction.

Step 2: Diagnostic Testing

Diagnostic testing continues the diagnostic process begun in step 1 and is the beginning of detailed diagnosis. It is directed toward defining the actual nature of the individual's reading difficulties and toward identifying the conditions causing them. It is a detailed investigation of the symptoms of reading disability, leading to a clinical diagnosis. Here the teacher is not satisfied to know that the student is reading on a seventh-grade level when in fact he might be able to read on a ninth-grade level. The teacher wants to know the specific reasons for the overall low performance. Is it the inability to attack words? Is it the limited vocabulary? Is it the failure to use context? Is it the lack of ability in auditory blending? Is it an orientational difficulty? Or is it a combination of factors?

Smith and Carrigan (49, p. 91) note that diagnosis must be based on a careful investigation of the symptoms, on psychological test behavior, and often on intensive clinical case studies. They note that such dead-end diagnosis as "he isn't trying" or "he needs more disciplining" must be replaced with a clinical diagnosis.

Step 2 thus is a specific, an individual, and a clinical diagnosis. It is a detailed analysis of the reading problems of students identified in step 1 as retarded readers. Let us assume that about 20 percent of the students studied in step 1 are actually retarded in reading. It is now necessary to determine what their specific difficulties are and where, whether in the regular classroom or in the remedial room, their difficulties might best be taken care of.

In many schools, the classroom teacher is still the person primarily responsible for the diagnosis and remediation of reading problems. In others, the teacher is assisted by a remedial teacher or a reading specialist. This special reading teacher might then direct the diagnostic process or actually do the diagnosing himself.

Step 2 should include, if possible, the personal data sheet, a learning and behavior checklist, and a formal or an informal inventory, an oral reading test, or a diagnostic test. Let us begin with the personal data sheet.

PERSONAL DATA SHEET   The first report on each student who was revealed in step 1 to be reading significantly below his ability should summarize personal data on the student. This report might be used as the referral form from the classroom teacher to the special teacher if this becomes necessary. It might also be sent to the student's new teacher when the student moves from one grade to another. In this way, the new teacher would have some knowledge of the student's needs and could then adjust his instruction to the student.

The personal data sheet includes such data as student's name, age, grade level, address, his previous grades, his attendance record, statements about his health, standardized test results, a compilation of the anecdotal reports by other teachers, and most of all the reason for the referral. The reason may be that the student is not reading up to ability level. The statement might simply read: "The test results indicate that he is reading about one grade level below his ability"; "He has a mental age of fourteen but is reading like the average ten-year-old"; or "His reading level is substantially below his listening comprehension level."

Whether the student is referred or kept in the regular classroom, it is imperative that the teacher know at least in a general sense what the problem is. The remaining instruments discussed in this chapter delve more deeply into the student's more specific problems and symptoms.

A form similar to Figure 11-1 might be used to compile basic information.

LEARNING AND BEHAVIOR CHECKLIST   There is also a need for another report, detailing the student's behavior and learning problems in the classroom. It is designed to summarize information about the student's usual scholastic performance and interaction in classroom affairs. A checklist, such as the one in Chapter 2 in *Diagnosis and Remediation of Reading Disability* (20, pp. 29–32), might be completed by the teacher on each student who is significantly retarded in reading.

FORMAL OR INFORMAL INVENTORY   A teacher's prime task (or the special teacher's) with the retarded may be to identify the student's frustration, instructional, and independent reading levels. To do this, he may administer additional individual intelligence tests, such as the *Wechsler Intelligence Scale for Children* (WISC) or the *Revised Stanford-Binet Scale* and additional achievement tests, but he certainly makes use of informal and formal reading inventories.

Informal Inventories   The classroom teacher has probably already used informal procedures in gauging the reader's achievement as well as his frustration, instructional, or independent level. He frequently determines the level of the student's performance through an informal analysis of the student's oral reading.

Betts (5) considers a student to be reading on a frustration level if he reads with less than 75 percent comprehension and less than 90 percent accuracy. He reads on an instructional level if he reads with 75 percent comprehension and 95 percent accuracy in word recognition. He reads on an independent level if he reads with 90 percent comprehension and 99 percent accuracy in word recognition.

Generally, the teacher will select a passage for the student to read orally. The teacher ought to have picked out the passages, made a readability check on each, and have some questions prepared to measure student competency before he uses a given book to make an informal check on a student's reading. The reading by the student tells something of the student's background of experience, of his vocabulary knowledge, of his

FIGURE 11-1   **PERSONAL DATA SHEET**

Student's Name _____Date of Birth _____

                                                                    Mo.   Day   Year

Parent's Name_____ Age _____ Grade _____

Address _____Phone _____

Academic Progress
   Report last year's grade(s)

Attendance Record
   Number of days absent for each grade: 9_____10_____11_____12_____

Health
   (List physical infirmities, accidents, and severe illnesses as listed in school record.)

Standardized Tests

   (Include all test results available—intelligence tests, achievement tests, etc.)
Date Given   *Name of Test*   *Score by*
                                                 Grade Level   *Percentile*

Reason for Referral

Anecdotal Reports or Comments of Former Teachers (Report on back of this page)

                                  Signed _____

                                  Position _____

Date of report _____ 19____

---

reading habits (slowness in reading, lip movements, or finger pointing), of his comprehension, and of his specific difficulties.

As the student reads, the teacher looks for student interest in materials, student concentration or apathy, the speed with which he completes his work, the willingness to read orally, and the ability to follow directions. The first sign indicative of poor reading is often the student's attitude toward reading. A student who does not read well generally is not willing to read aloud. He would rather hear others.

The teacher notes whether the student's oral reading indicates deficiencies in sight reading, in vocabulary, in structural or phonetic analysis, in comprehension, in eye-voice span, in phrasing, or in inflection. He checks whether in his silent reading the student follows instructions, reads for meaning, and uses the context to determine the meaning of the story. He is interested in whether the learner hears and sees likenesses and differences in letters and words. He evaluates the student's expressive and receptive abilities in the oral language area.

Inventories help the teacher to determine changes in instructional, frustration, and independent reading levels and to detect improvements or continuing inadequacies in dealing with individual reading skills. They provide a good measure of the student's true growth.

Powell (41) notes that the student does not really have an instructional level; he has only a performance level. He sees instructional modifications as being a teacher task. Perhaps we are talking of a situation where there is enough of a match and yet enough of a challenge in the materials (hence, a mismatch to a degree) so that the student has something to learn and, conversely, where he can be taught or instructed. The student's performance level is not at 100 percent efficiency or does not meet certain criteria, but the student's experience with similar materials is such that he can use it to advance in learning. We need experience to learn.

Formal Inventories   Many classroom teachers use formal or standardized inventories to gauge a student's reading level. These are usually compilations of graded reading selections with questions prepared in advance to test the reader's comprehension.

Frequently, the formal inventory is administered by the special or remedial reading teacher to students identified as retarded readers. He is especially interested in a more detailed diagnosis of the student's reading deficiencies. He is not satisfied with an overall estimate of the student's reading ability but wants to know specific strengths and weaknesses.

Two good standardized inventories are the *Botel Reading Inventory* and the *Classroom Reading Inventory.** The *Botel Reading Inventory,* designed for grades one through twelve and published by Follett Publishing Company, obtains an estimate of the student's instructional, independent, and frustration reading levels. It is useful only when the reading level is

---

* The *Standard Reading Inventory,* by Robert A. McCracken, is available through Klamath Printing Company, 320 Lowell Street, Klamath Falls, Oregon 97601. It is usable on the preprimer through seventh-grade levels.

below fourth grade. The inventory consists of two tests: the *Phonics Mastery Test* and the *Reading Placement Test.*

Standardized tests often overestimate the student's reading ability and thus greater reliance needs to be placed upon the results of formal and informal reading inventories. Betts (5, pp. 450–51) thinks that tests place students at their frustration level; Harris (28, p. 180) thinks that they identify the instructional level rather than the independent level. Sipay (48) found that standardized tests overestimate the pupil's instructional level of fourth graders by about one grade level and underestimate the frustration by about one grade level, leading him to conclude that it is impossible to generalize as to whether standardized tests indicate the frustration or instructional level.

Another inventory, *The Classroom Reading Inventory,* developed by Nicholas Silvaroli, is published by Wm. C. Brown Company, 135 South Locust Street, Dubuque, Iowa. It is designed specifically for teachers who have not had prior experience with individual diagnostic reading measures. The chief purpose of the inventory is to identify the frustration, instructional, and independent reading levels of the pupil. It is useful in grades two through eight.

The Classroom Reading Inventory is composed of two main parts: Part I, Graded Word Lists, and Part II, Graded Oral Paragraphs. Part III, A Graded Spelling Survey, may also be administered. Parts I and II must be administered individually; Part III may be administered to groups. The inventory may be administered quite easily in about fifteen minutes.

Inventories have an advantage in that they provide some clues as to why a student pronounced the word in a peculiar way, why he reversed letters, or why he skipped a word. They make it possible to evaluate reading behavior in depth and to study the behavior of the learner in an actual reading situation (41). In diagnosing, we are especially interested in the causes of errors. Our interest does not cease with a yes or a no answer; we want to know why and how the student got his answer.

In using inventories we are generally trying to determine what books a student can read independently and how difficult an assigned reading can be and still be used as instructional material. Although, unfortunately, grade-level designations furnished by the publishers of many books are far from accurate, experienced teachers can select a suitable set of books and other materials for use in informal determinations of students' reading abilities.

The classroom teacher should forward to the remedial teacher or to the reading clinic the results of any informal or formal inventories that he administered to the retarded reader while he was in the regular classroom.

ORAL READING TESTS   Oral reading tests are helpful both in measuring student reading achievement (especially in oral reading) and in making diagnostic evaluations. They possess many of the same advantages as the reading inventories in that they permit the teacher to detect the errors made by the student and to identify the reasons why the error was made.

Some common oral reading tests are the following:

1. *Gilmore Oral Reading Test,* Harcourt, Brace & World, New York, grades 1–8.
2. *Gray Standardized Oral Reading Paragraphs,* The Bobbs-Merrill Co., Inc., Indianapolis, grades 1–8.
3. *Leavell Analytical Oral Reading Test,* American Guidance Service, Inc., 720 Washington Avenue S.E., Minneapolis, Minn., grades 1–10.
4. *Slosson Oral Reading Test,* Slosson Educational Publications, East Aurora, N.Y., grades 1–12.
5. *New Gray Oral Reading Test,* The Bobbs-Merrill Co., Inc., Indianapolis, grades 1–16 and adult.

Oral reading tests are very useful in the diagnosis of reading difficulties. There is strong evidence to suggest that the oral reading errors of a student tend to be carried over to silent reading. The oral reading test thus reveals student strengths and weaknesses and suggests the kinds and types of reading experiences that should be provided. Analysis of student errors should help to identify areas where most of the mistakes occur and toward which remedial teaching ought to be directed.

DIAGNOSTIC READING TESTS   The diagnostic reading test, like some of the instruments already described, seeks to discover specific strengths and weaknesses. It is especially useful in planning remedial procedures. It is no doubt possible to make a successful diagnosis without using any objective test measures, just as it is possible for a physician to diagnose a disease correctly without x-ray analysis. For the most part, however, diagnostic tests prove helpful.

The survey test, the type given in step 1, tells us, for example, that a boy or a girl who is in ninth grade is reading at a level typical for fifth graders. The diagnostic test, on the other hand, identifies the student's specific deficiencies, his inability to work out unfamiliar words, his inability to blend sounds, or his tendency to reverse. It helps to locate those areas of deficiencies that need to be investigated further. It may also indicate which instructional adjustments are needed. It provides the basis for planning remedial teaching of such specifics as word analysis or phonic skills.

Unfortunately, there is no unanimity of purpose among the diagnostic tests. They attempt to measure such diverse areas as potential reading level, silent and oral reading performance, or independent, instructional, or frustration reading levels, and they claim to be able to identify inhibitory factors in reading, areas of skill deficiency, or inadequacies in word identification (56). At present, no instrument assesses even all the word-recognition skills, much less the total spectrum of reading performance. Diagnostic tests do not diagnose; *they can help the diagnostician* to identify strengths and weaknesses in reading performance.

The following diagnostic tests have demonstrated their usefulness:

1. *Diagnostic Reading Scales,* California Test Bureau, New Cumberland, Pa., grades 1–8 and retarded 9–12.
2. *Diagnostic Reading Tests,* Committee on Diagnostic Reading Tests, Mountain Home, N. C., grades 1–13.
3. *Diagnostic Reading Tests,* Science Research Associates, Chicago, grades 7–13.
4. *Digest-Diagnostic Inventory Group Evaluation Tests,* Science Research Associates, Chicago, grades 4–9.
5. *Group Diagnostic Aptitude and Achievement Tests,* Nevins Printing Company, Bradenton, Fla., grades 3–9.
6. *Pressy Diagnostic Reading Tests,* Public School Publishing Company, Cincinnati, grades 3–9.
7. *Reading Diagnostic Record for High School and College Students,* Bureau of Publications, Teachers College, Columbia University, New York, high school and college.
8. *Scholastic Diagnostic Reading Test,* Scholastic Testing Service, Bensenville, Ill., grades 4–9.
9. *Silent Reading Diagnostic Tests* (Bond, Clymer, Holt), Lyons and Carnahan, Chicago, grades 3–8.
10. *Doren Diagnostic Reading Test,* American Guidance Service, Inc., Circle Pines, Minn., grades 1–9.
11. *Gates-McKillop Reading Diagnostic Tests,* Bureau of Publications, Columbia University, New York, grades 1–8.

The teacher may want to give tests such as the following to evaluate a student's problem even more closely:

1. *Auditory Discrimination Test,* Language Research Associates, Chicago.
2. *Bennett Use of Library Test,* Bureau of Educational Measurements, Kansas State Teachers College, Emporia, high school and college.

3. *California Phonics Survey,* California Test Bureau, Monterey, Calif., grades 7–college.

4. *Illinois Test of Psycholinguistic Abilities,* Institute for Research on Exceptional Children, University of Illinois, Urbana.

5. *Leavell Hand-Eye Coordination Test,* Keystone View Company, Meadville, Pa.

6. *Marianne Frostig Developmental Test of Visual Perception,* Consulting Psychologists Press, Palo Alto, Calif.

7. *McCullough Word Analysis Tests,* Ginn and Company, Boston, grades 5 and up.

8. *McKee Inventory of Phonetic Skills,* Houghton Mifflin Company, Boston.

9. *Michigan Vocabulary Profile Test,* Harcourt, Brace & World, Inc., New York, grades 9–16.

10. *Mills Learning Methods Test,* Mills Center, Fort Lauderdale, Fla.

11. *Modality Assessment Profile* by Richard L. Carner, University of Miami Reading Center, Coral Gables, Fla.

12. *Perceptual Forms Test,* Winter Haven Lions Publication Committee, P.O. Box 1045, Winter Haven, Fla.

13. *Phonics Knowledge Survey,* Columbia University, New York.

14. *Phonics Mastery Test,* Follett Publishing Company, Chicago.

15. *Reading Versatility Test,* Educational Developmental Laboratories, Huntington, New York, grades 6–16 and adult.

16. *Road Map Test of Direction Sense,* Johns Hopkins Press, Baltimore, ages 7–18.

17. *Robbins Speech Sound Discrimination and Verbal Imagery Type Tests,* Expression Company, Magnolia, Mass.

18. *Roswell-Chall Auditory Blending Test,* Essay Press, P.O. Box 5, Planetarium Station, New York, N.Y.

19. *Screening Test for Identifying Children with Specific Language Disability,* Educators Publishing Service, Cambrdge, Mass.

20. *Specific Language Disability Test,* Educators Publishing Service, Cambridge, Mass., grades 6–8.

21. *Spitzer Study Skills Test,* Harcourt, Brace & World, Inc., New York, grades 9–13.

22. *Survey of Study Habits and Attitudes,* Psychological Corporation, New York, grades 7–14.

23. *Test of Auditory Discrimination,* American Guidance Service, Inc., Circle Pines, Minn., 56014.

24. *Tinker Speed of Reading Test,* University of Minnesota Press, Minneapolis, grades 7–16 and adult.

25. *Watson-Glasser Critical Thinking Appraisal,* Harcourt, Brace & World, Inc., New York, grades 9–16.

The Symptomatology of Reading Disability (Levels of Retardation)

What is the significance of step 2? It is an intensive study of the symptoms of reading disability. At this level we are still concerned primarily with identifying the areas of difficulty—with an intensive study of the symptoms. We are dealing with symptomatology. We study the symptoms to identify levels of retardation.

Many reading disabilities become disabilities because teachers are not familiar with some of the symptoms of disability. The result is that some reading needs are not met, leading to disability cases. A clear identification of the symptoms of reading disability is obviously needed.

Symptoms are observable characteristics which help the teacher to make some educated guesses about the student's reading problems. Symptoms rarely appear singly. There usually is a pattern of symptoms, a syndrome that characterizes the individual reading disability case. The teacher needs to know the pattern, must attempt to understand it, and must have the educational know-how to deal with the syndrome. The diagnostic responsibility of the classroom teacher or the reading specialist is to identify the pattern of symptoms, relate it to the appropriate skill area or areas, and plan a program to correct the deficiency. The interpretation of the syndrome pattern is much more significant than are the data themselves.

THE DEVELOPMENTAL READING PROGRAM   Let us again look at students found to be retarded. Our concern is to decide the type of help the student needs and where he can best receive help. Perhaps at this time we should take a look at various phases of the total reading program. Authorities in the field speak of the developmental reading program, the corrective reading program, and the remedial reading program.

The developmental program emphasizes reading instruction that is designed to develop systematically the skills and abilities considered essential at each level of reading advancement. It thus encompasses also the corrective and remedial programs. Perhaps we should then speak of developmental, corrective, and remedial instruction. Developmental instruction is the type of instruction that is given to the majority of children in the regular classroom.

Corrective instruction consists of remedial activities usually carried on by the regular classroom teacher within the framework of regular classroom instruction. Corrective instruction is provided when the entire class or a small group of students is deficient in a particular skill. Corrective reading deals with the problems of the partial disability case, that type of student who can identify words and comprehend what he reads, but only after great difficulty. The student may not have been ready for initial reading experiences, instruction may have consistently been above or below his level of ability, or classroom stimulation may have been inadequate.

Remedial instruction consists of remedial activities taking place outside the framework of regular class instruction and is usually conducted by a special teacher of reading. Remedial instruction should thus be restricted to a small clinical group with severe symptoms of reading retardation—those having difficulty mastering even the simplest mechanics of reading. Such students are often identified as word blind, alexiac, or dyslexiac learners. They have difficulty in remembering whole word patterns, do not learn easily by the sight method, and show orientational difficulties. The total reading program might schematically be portrayed as follows:

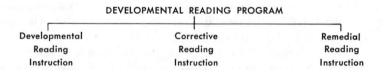

If the student has a reading problem and if he is not a slow learner, a reluctant reader, or a disadvantaged reader, he needs corrective or remedial instruction and should be able to be classified as either a general retardation or a specific retardation case or as a remedial disability case. It is on the basis of the symptoms that reading disability cases are divided into corrective and remedial readers.

This is another way of saying that there are six basic types of retardation or combinations of the same. Some of these call for corrective instruction and some call for remedial instruction. Figure 11-2 summarizes the various types.

FIGURE 11-2   TYPES OR LEVELS OF RETARDATION

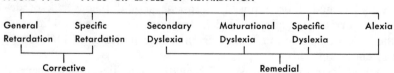

From a causal frame of reference, reading disability can be classified as follows:

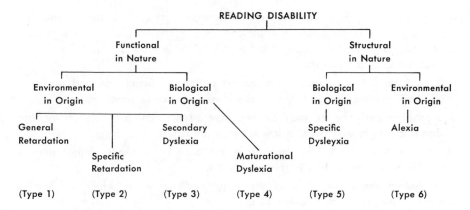

READING DISABILITY

Functional in Nature / Structural in Nature

Environmental in Origin / Biological in Origin / Biological in Origin / Environmental in Origin

General Retardation / Secondary Dyslexia / Specific Dysleyxia / Alexia

Specific Retardation / Maturational Dyslexia

(Type 1)   (Type 2)   (Type 3)   (Type 4)   (Type 5)   (Type 6)

CHARACTERISTICS OF THE CORRECTIVE READER

Type 1:   Case of General Retardation

The reading level is substantially lower than the mental age, but no other specific problem exists. He is a case of partial disability.

He is a student who learns only after undue and laborious effort; he is like the underweight child whose eating habits are not conducive to gaining weight but who, if he follows the proper diet, will gain. He learns after inhibiting factors have been removed.

He may not have been ready for initial reading experiences and thus fell further behind as his schooling continued.

Instruction and reading materials generally have been above the student's level of ability and above his level of achievement in word-recognition and comprehension skills.

He perhaps was absent from school at critical periods.

He perhaps was not stimulated to learn because instruction was below his ability level.

The reading profile of the generally retarded student is relatively uniform.

He needs more experience in reading, including systematic instruction at his level of ability. Usually a visual auditory technique or method is adequate. He does not need a VAKT method of teaching, such as the Fernald or the Gillingham method. There is a need for major adjustment in materials and instruction and for a reading program that motivates the student to learn.

Type 2:   Case of Specific Retardation

There is a definite weakness in a given area. This is usually a skill weakness. This is a case of reading retardation not complicated by neurological difficulties.

Learning capacity is adaquate, but deficiencies in regard to certain specifics in word analysis or comprehension indicate that he has not profited from regular classwork as well as he might. He has missed or has not profited from basic instruction in a given area.

Although each learner presents a distinct pattern of acquisition and remediation, there will usually be others in the class with similar problems.

His reading performance may be high overall in relation to his ability, but diagnostic testing will reveal a low subscore on a test.

There is usually a need for training in the area of weakness rather than a need for total remediation in the basic skills.

The student should be kept in the regular classroom in which reading is taught to subgroups of three to five.

CHARACTERISTICS OF THE REMEDIAL READER

Type 3: Secondary Dyslexia

Secondary dyslexia is often termed a secondary reading disability.* It is by far the most common form of disability seen in remedial readers. This syndrome is characterized by the following:

1. The learner's problems are more severe than those of the corrective reader and include inability to use contextual clues, poor comprehension, wild guessing at words, inability to deal with individual letter sounds, reversal tendency, and difficulty in structural analysis.

2. There usually is no single identifiable cause of the disability. Multiple causality is indicated, with the reading disability closely related to intellectual, emotional, environmental, psychological, or educational factors. It is probable that some factor is the precipitating cause; other factors are contributing causes.

3. The major cause is not attributable to dysfunction or delayed development of the brain. The capacity to read is intact. The causative factors are exogenous, that is, the disability is not innate or the result of a deficit in structure or functioning of the brain. There is usually no familial history of reading disability. This learner reads poorly, but he has a normal reading potential. His reading differs from the normal in quantity but not in quality.

4. A therapeutic diagnosis is adequate. This concerns itself with the conditions that are now present in the learner in order to give direction to a program of reeducation. The diagnostician is concerned with the reading strengths and limitations of the learner and any characteristics within the environment

* See Janet W. Lerner, "A Thorn by Any Other Name: Dyslexia or Reading Disability," *Elementary English*, 48 (January 1971), 75–80.

that need to be corrected before remedial instruction can be successful or with conditions that need to be adjusted to before he can be expected to make maximum progress.

5. This learner should be taught in small groups in a remedial setting.

Type 4: Maturational Dyslexia

Maturational dyslexia indicates the presence of some brain pathology, but it is not aphasic in nature. There is no structural defect, deficiency, or loss. It is more like aplasia in that the neural tissues have failed to develop. There is an absence of function rather than a loss of function. The condition flows from cerebral immaturity or a maturational lag or slowness in certain specialized aspects of neurological development. There is delayed or irregular neurological development. The potential is there, but it has not yet been realized. He is a late bloomer. He is not yet matured, but he is capable of maturing.

The characteristics that identify this reader are very much like those of type five, specific dyslexia.

Generalized language disturbances frequently run in families and are associated with disturbances in body image, poor motor and visuo-motor patterning, inadequate figure-ground discriminations and hyperactivity. Clumsiness in manipulation of small muscle groups (such as in writing) is rather common. The execution in writing is jerky and arrhythmic. The jerkiness in writing is accompanied by jerky, stumbling, and explosive speech (cluttering). The writing looks as the speech sounds. Drawings of the human form are immature and distorted. The limbs are out of proportion, incorrectly placed, or perhaps omitted. Finally, because of inadequate figure-ground discrimination, children with general language disabilities hear speech as an undifferentiated noise and see words on the printed page as an undifferentiated design. On more advanced levels (ten–fourteen years) these children will usually have difficulty in organizing what they read or study. In explaining the language-disturbance syndrome, the underlying cause is often delayed or disorganized maturation of the neural system.

Delacato's description of reading disability, with its emphasis on neurological maturity, neurological organization, and hemispheric dominance, fits here.

Type 5: Specific Dyslexia

Specific dyslexia goes by various names: primary reading disability, specific reading disability, congenital reading disability, constitutonal reading disability, developmental dyslexia, and congenital wordblindness. It is difficult to describe because there is no single clinical feature that can be accepted as pathognomic (17). There is no invariable common core of symptoms. It is a massive unreadiness for reading (38). It is a defect in the visual interpretation of verbal symbols and in the association of sounds with symbols. It is a failure to learn to read even though the child has had appropriate instruction, comes from a culturally adequate home, is properly motivated, has adequate sensory equipment, has normal intelligence, and shows no gross neurological defect or brain pathology (24, p. 19). Retardation nevertheless is based on some organic incapacity (42). The neurological signs are minimal.

Reading ability is a function of the brain, and from a neurological standpoint reading is translating graphic symbols into sound according to a recognized system (19).

The student is deficient in even the most fundamental basic reading skills. It is almost as though he had never been in school. Remedial instruction often seems to have little effect, and where it is effective, it may well be that the learner is a type 4 rather than a genuine case of specific dyslexia.

The dyslexic reader, on the basis of symptoms, can usually be identified as one of three types (7):

1. *Auditory dyslexics:* They may show deficits in symbol-sound integration, cannot develop phonic skills, or cannot auditorize. They have difficulty differentiating between the sounds that they hear. Their ability to visualize may be quite normal. They are visual learners and may best be taught initially through a whole-word configuration or sight method. They remember the shapes of the letters but cannot associate the proper phoneme with the proper shape. They need to be taught to do this.

2. *Visual dyslexics:* They cannot develop gestalts for letters or words, and they show little ability in distinguishing between shapes and patterns. They are weak in visual imagery, have poor visual memory, and have poor visual discrimination skill. Initial remedial teaching might begin with tactile-kinesthetic techniques (the Fernald method) if the learners have not yet acquired visual recognition for letters. Remedial phonics, such as the Orton-Gillingham approach, might be used if letter recognition has occurred.

3. *Auditory-visual dyslexics:* This group represents a combination of groups one and two. The pupil cannot read by sight or by ear. Jastak (33) speaks of "intrasensory transcoding difficulties." He notes that learning to transcode messages by intersensory cooperation is a difficult and complex task for many children. Visual and auditory stimuli are received in the reception areas in the brain, but the meanings are not correctly decoded and encoded.

Additional identifying characteristics of dyslexics are the following:

1. The dyslexic reader is usually a boy, although girls can also be dyslexic. Delacato suggests that boys have bigger heads, and so the incidence of difficult birth is greater among boys. This does not mean that the disability is inherited. It simply means that predisposing conditions are present in certain families. It may be that reading disability is related to the body structure of the woman which in some instances causes difficulty of birth (35).

2. His IQ is usually in the normal range, but the verbal IQ tends to be significantly below the performance IQ. Belmont and Birch (4) found that retarded readers are generally inadequate in language functioning rather than in perceptual and manipulative skills.

3. There is more persistent and frequent left-right confusion.

   a. There is a reversal of concepts (*floor* for *ceiling, go* for *stop, east* for *west*). The dyslexic frequently makes kinetic reversals. He reads entire words backward (*saw-was*); he reverses letters (*flim* for *film*); and he confuses sounds (*graduate* for *gratitude*). He may perform as well if the book is held upside down.

   b. He comes from a family in which there is left-handedness or language disorders or both.

   c. He shows evidence of delayed or incomplete establishment of one-sided motor preferences. He tends to be left-handed or ambidextrous, or he shows mixed dominance. These orientational problems may not be present in the older dyslexic.

4. Penmanship is characterized by poorly formed and irregular characters, untidiness, malalignment, omissions, linkages that are too short or too long, and fusion of letters. Drawing and copying are poor.

5. He often has speech difficulties and poor auditory discrimination. Stuttering, lisping, stammering, and cluttering often are quite noticeable.

6. He is more likely to have been premature or to have survived some complication of pregancy.

7. He is hyperactive, distractive, distractable, and impulsive, shows poor motor coordination, has a short attention span, and perseverates excessively. *The Purdue Perceptual-Motor Survey* is a diagnostic remediation instrument useful in assessing the perceptual motor abilities of children.*

8. He has difficulty in spatial relationships and in figure-ground perception.

The basic difficulty, however, is one of three: (1) deficiency in visual identification of symbols; (2) inability to associate sound with graphic

* E. G. Roach, and N. D. Kephart, *The Purdue Perceptual-Motor Survey.* (Columbus, Ohio: Charles E. Merrill Books, Inc., 1966).

symbols—he cannot deal with the phoneme-grapheme correspondences; or (3) inability to associate meaning with symbols.

Let us look at each of these.

1. Deficiency in visual identification

This deficiency reveals itself in many ways and can be described in many ways. The learner has a letter or a word-naming difficulty (anomia). He cannot deal with letters or words as symbols, with resultant diminished ability to integrate the meaningfulness of written materials (43). He has great difficulty with visual recognition and recall of familiar words.

The following observations relating to deficiencies in visual identification are common when one deals with a severe disability:

a. The student does not experience the "flash," global identification of a word as a whole, and cannot synthesize the word out of its component letter units. He does not see the word as an entity.

b. The letter standing alone has no language identity. S may be described as traffic sign.

c. Spelling of words may be peculiar and odd. This is because the student ignores many details in words.

d. His reading is arrhythmical and replete with word-recognition errors. He demonstrates more vowel, consonant, reversal, omission, addition, substitution, perseveration, and repetition errors.

e. He will ask again and again for help with the same word.

f. The student cannot pronounce unfamiliar words. He has a tendency to guess wildly at words. He pays attention to specific letters and guesses wildly at the rest (horse becomes house). His rendition of a word is often phonetically unrelated to the desired response (dog becomes chay).

g. He has difficulty blending sounds so as to constitute a word. He can spell b-a-n-a-n-a but cannot pronounce it.

h. He confuses similar-appearing words: e.g., bed-fed.

i. He frequently loses his place in reading and does not move easily from the end of one line to the beginning of another line.

j. He vocalizes excessively while reading silently.

k. The reading behavior of the dyslexic is extremely variable. On a given day he may reverse; the following day no reversal problem occurs.

2. Deficiency in associating phoneme and grapheme

The basic deficiency here is one of inability to relate symbols. Sometimes this happens because the auditory symbols fail to achieve identity.

There are numerous examples of the phoneme-to-grapheme mixup in the English language: The phoneme /f/, for example, can be written as *f* (scarf), *ff* (chaff), *gh* (laugh), and *ph* (graph). Another term for the mixup is *irregular orthography,* and it is the mismatching of phoneme and grapheme that is the heart of the problem for many dyslexic children. Dyslexia is nothing more than an oral/written disorder.*

3. Deficiency in associating meaning with symbols

The student will also have meaning and comprehension problems. He frequently exhibits an associative learning disability, making it impossible for him to associate experiences and meanings with symbols. Comprehension is poor, and rate of comprehension is significantly below the norm.

Type 6: Alexia

Alexia is the loss of the ability to read as a result of damage, injury, or lesion to the association and connection areas in and around the angular gyrus of the dominant cerebral hemisphere. For most of us this is the left hemisphere. There is clear brain pathology which prevents the learner from becoming a reader. He may see black marks on paper, but he does not recognize that they represent words. The past history of such an individual often reveals normal speech development initially. There may be no family history of reading difficulty. Instructional techniques alone cannot come directly to grips with the reading problem. This is a reader who is neurologically unable to read. The reading disability is actually a symptom of an earlier lesion to the nervous system (42). The symptoms of reading disability are much like those that are seen in type 5.

The aphasic or brain-injured child (39) is hyperactive. He flits from one activity to another without apparent purpose or meaning. His behavior is compulsive, and the condition may be associated with difficulties in perception, memory, attention, and social control. Frequently, he is destructive.

A mild brain damage (39), frequently undetected, is associated with difficulties in reading (alexia), writing, and arithmetic. The child finds abstract thinking difficult and has poor coordination and concentration. His speech is rapid and mumbled and hence unintelligible. He can count to twenty or recite the alphabet, but he cannot tell what number comes after eight or what letter comes after *c*. He reverses the letters in writing, omits letters, and spells as though English were a completely phonetic language. The writing is cramped and angular. The letters vary in size and slant.

The brain-injured child has often not developed dominance. He

* Alex Bannatyne, "Spelling and Sound Blending," *Academic Therapy,* 7 (Fall 1971), 73–77.

switches from one hand to the other and confuses left with right. He perseverates, repeating activities again and again.

Harris (29) notes that in reading disability cases exhibiting neurological defects, the whole-part relationship is inadequate. Parts (letters) are seen as discrete units rather than as parts of a whole, and wholes (words) are seen as undifferentiated wholes. He also points out that frequently there is a figure-ground disturbance. The figure (word) does not have clear boundaries. The problem seems to become more acute when the figure is discontinuous or when the contrast with the ground is minimal. Harris raises the question whether word perception might be improved if the letters were continuous or if they were in a different color, perhaps red.

Hinshelwood (32, p. 53) points out that any condition that reduces the number of cortical cells within the angular area (area 39) and supra-marginal (area 40) gyri of the left side of the cortex or that interferes with the supply of the blood to that area lowers the functional activity of that part of the brain and will be accompanied by a diminished retention of the visual images of letters and words. He (32, p. 102) believes that treatment for structural wordblindness consists in developing (1) a visual memory for the letters of the alphabet; (2) an auditory memory for words by having the child spell aloud the word letter by letter; and (3) a visual memory for words.

The teacher may suspect neurological injury when:

1. The student does not stick with any task over a long period of time.
2. The student never sits still. He is hyperactive, flitting from one activity to another without apparent purpose or meaning.
3. The student's behavior is complusive.
4. There are difficulties in perception, memory, and attention and in social control, motor coordination, and concentration.
5. The speech is often rapid and mumbled.
6. The student reverses and omits letters.
7. The writing is cramped and angular.
8. The student perseverates—he repeats activities again and again.
9. He can read but often does not comprehend.
10. He exhibits difficulties in arithmetic.

THE TEACHER'S TASK   As the teacher works with the symptomatology in a given case, he should ask himself four questions (55):

1. Did the student make the same error on both easy and difficult material or were his errors chiefly the result of having to read material which for him was on a frustration level? Diagnostic conclusions and remediation should

not be based on errors made on material that is clearly too difficult for the student.

2. Were his slowness in reading and his constant need to regress while reading the result of poor reading skill or simply of his desire to read carefully? Diagnostic conclusions should not be based on comprehension errors made over material the student did not have time to read. Sometimes, the student's reading grade level is inaccurate because he answered questions incorrectly on a test that he did not have time to finish.

3. Was the student's performance reliable, or was it poorer than usual because he was nervous, upset, or distracted during the testing situations?

4. Was the student's poor reading performance basically in the area of comprehension skills, word-identification skills, rate skills, oral reading, or a combination of these?

Step 3: A Detailed Investigation of Causality

Step 3 of diagnostic procedure is a thorough analysis of the reading disability leading to an identification of the causal factors involved. It is the level of intensive diagnosis, a detailed study of the correlates of disability.

Chapters 3 and 4 looked at some of the major causes of reading disability. We discussed such areas as inadequate experiential background, inadequate language background, inadequate maturation, inadequacies in intellectual-social-emotional development, lack of motivation, instructional inadequacies, visual and auditory inadequacy, and deficiencies in other physical-physiological areas.

An important question is surely: So what? You know the causes of reading disability, but what can you do about it?

The teacher can do something about the causes of reading disability by:

1. Providing preparatory experiences necessary for learning.

2. Using and developing reading materials that capitalize on the student's preferred modes of learning.

3. Providing appropriate environmental stimulations so that maturational development may progress at an appropriate rate. Let instruction march slightly, but only slightly, ahead of the student's maturation process.

4. Using intelligence test scores and other data to gear the instructional program to the ability level of the student.

5. Checking the student for:

   a. Signs of illness or overall poor health.

b. Visual problems.

c. Hearing problems.

6. Looking for symptoms of neurological disturbances and referring the student to a specialist if this is indicated.

But even more important than the above is the need to develop competency in hooking symptoms to their proper cause. The special or remedial reading teacher is by definition an expert in tying together symptom and cause. The classroom teacher can become quite expert in doing the same thing.

It requires considerable skill and care to transfer the diagnostic data into an accurate prescription that can serve as the basis for remediation. In making the transfer we must recognize certain dangers. Sometimes the learner's symptoms may lead us to take faulty steps toward his remediation. What may appear to be the cause of his difficulty may be quite unrelated to it or may even be a result or symptom of his problems. But skill and experience in the translation of diagnostic data and an earnest desire to help each student attain the highest goals that his capabilities permit should serve as a firm foundation for remediation.

The two symptoms in Table 11-2 are common symptoms of reading disability. But what is their cause? We have suggested four possible ones for symptom 1 (there are others) and three for symptom 2 and have suggested remediation in each instance. This is the type of skill needed by the classroom teacher.

As one completes this third step, the chances are that the following has been done:

1. A case history has been compiled.

2. The student's capacity has been analyzed including, if possible, the results of hearing tests, visual screening tests, eye-movement data, hand and eye preference tests.

3. The level of oral and silent reading achievement has been determined.

4. The reading problem has been identified.

5. The factors that interfere with reading have been isolated.

6. The data have been collated and interpreted.

The written report of the diagnosis should include recommendations as to *how* the pupil should be taught and should suggest materials that may be used in teaching. It should outline specific weaknesses in word analysis and in comprehension. There might be statements about the ease or lack of it with which the pupil develops insight into phonic generaliza-

TABLE 11-2   TWO COMMON SYMPTOMS OF READING DISABILITY

Symptom	Possible Cause	Possible Remedy
1. Makes frequent substitutions of words.	a. Poor vision.	a. Check and remediate visual defect. Have student engage in exercises teaching discrimination of letters.
	b. Inability to tie letters together and remember them (c-a-t). Poor visual memory span.	b. Provide tracing exercises to develop a "feel" for the word; stress training in visual discrimination of words.
	c. Reverses letters and so cannot discriminate and remember them (b-d).	c. Check if he also reverses nonsense syllables. Have student engage in exercises designed to change the pattern.
	d. Inattention, not wanting to learn.	d. Use language-experience approach.
2. Inability to discriminate word sounds. For example, the teacher might say, "Now listen for the sound pig . . . *big, dig,* pig, pick."	a. Poor hearing—poor auditory acuity.	a. Check hearing and consult doctor.
	b. Speech defects: *father* becomes *fodder, shishter* for *sister, kool* for *school.*	b. Provide training in articulation.
	c. Poor auditory discrimination.	c. Check for high-tone deafness and watch for sounds *f, v, s, z, sh, zh, th, t, d, p, b, k,* and *g;* provide exercises in auditory discrimination.

tions; statements about the pupil's awareness or lack of awareness of phonetic differences in words; or statements about the reasons why the pupil substitutes words of similar meaning.

The teacher needs to become expert in reading the causes of reading disability. Smith and Carrigan (49) note:

> Clinicians are like a small group standing beside a river full of drowning people. The victims are being swept seaward by the current of time. The clinicians can pull out a few, but the rest are lost. Few of the group are willing to go upstream to find out how the victims get into the river in the first place.*

The teacher needs to know how the disabled reader gets into the river in the first place. To do this, he needs to be able to read the causes

* D. E. P. Smith and Patricia Carrigan, *The Nature of Reading Disability* (New York: Harcourt, Brace and Company, Inc., 1959), p. 6. Reprinted with permission.

of reading disability. It is not enough to know the symptoms. The symptom has to be hooked up with the proper cause. Only in this way is remediation of reading disability possible.

An important phase of diagnosis is the checking of one's own hypothesis about causality. For example, in step 2 on the basis of symptomatology you may have decided that you are dealing with a case of secondary dyslexia. In step 3 you have analyzed possible causes to explain the symptoms. Do your conclusions match with the causal structure in the categorization of causes of reading disability given in Figure 11-3?

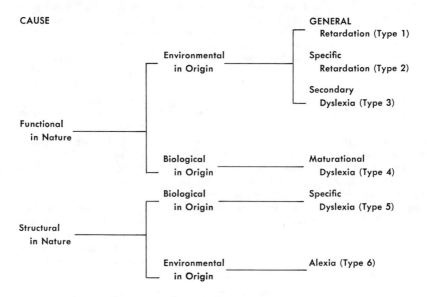

FIGURE 11-3   CAUSES OF READING DISABILITY

Step 4: Remediation

Step 4 of diagnostic procedure is actually the development of a plan for remediation. Identification of symptoms and causes is simply not enough. Diagnosis is meant to lead to remediation; it must serve as a blueprint from which remediation is structured. From a study of the diagnostic data, the teacher evolves a plan by and through which it is hoped the learner will improve in reading. The principles that we will discuss later in this section should help the teacher to formulate such a plan. They are basic procedures and principles that should guide all remedial instruction, irrespective of the type of reading disability.

This section thus deals with four questions: What decisions or what knowledge does the teacher of reading need before he can plan an effective remedial program? What principles should guide remedial instruction?

What are the skills that must be developed in all remedial programs? And how can a corrective or remedial program be organized? Let us consider the first of these.

DECISIONS REQUIRED OF THE TEACHER   Somehow, either on his own or with specially skilled help if it is available, the teacher must identify the student's problems and then plan and carry through the best possible corrective measures. This requires certain decisions based on particular information.

1. The teacher must decide whether the student actually is a retarded reader rather than a student of low ability. If he is a retarded reader, he must identify the nature of his retardation.
2. He must decide what type of teaching is needed. Teacher objectives must be translated into student tasks.
3. He must determine whether the needed remedial work can best be done in the classroom or in separate facilities, and if in the classroom, whether individually or in a subgroup.
4. He must make an estimate of the proper length of the instructional period. The length will depend upon the skill being taught and on the physical well-being and social-emotional maturity of the student.
5. He must determine the most efficient methods and materials that can be used. He needs to determine what the difficulty level of the materials should be and whether the materials are interesting to the student. Bond and Tinker (8, p. 454) emphasize ". . . there should be no compromise with difficulty even to get material of high interest."
6. He must be alert to and decide how to make adjustments for the student's special interests, for any emotional or physical defects, or for conditions in the student's home and community environment that may block his reading growth.
7. He must be alert to and decide how to deal with the environmental factors, institutional factors, that might be keeping the student from progressing in reading.
8. He must decide how to interpret to the student the progress he might make.
9. He must plan independent work activities for the student.

PRINCIPLES OF REMEDIATION   Remedial teachers have developed certain principles that should guide all remedial or corrective instruction. A general observation might be that the principles underlying remedial or corrective reading instruction are basically the same that govern developmental reading instruction. Of these principles, the following seem most significant.

1. Develop a plan of remediation, put it on paper, and refer to it frequently as remediation progresses. Incidental teaching is simply inadequate with the retarded reader. Write flexibility into the plan. There needs to be flexibility in materials, methods, and attitudes.

2. Discover the student's area and level of confidence. Start where the student knows something. Nothing succeeds quite like success. One of the most therapeutic experiences for reading disability cases is success. Thus remedial instruction should begin at the level at which the student can be successful, probably about one grade level below the student's ability. It must begin where the student is, not where the curriculum guide suggests that ninth-grade learners on the average are. It should begin with short assignments, inspire confidence, and restore status to the student in the eyes of his peers, his parents, and his teachers.

   In dealing with corrective or remedial cases it is necessary to remember that

   a. The student is generally anxious and fearful of discussing his problem with an adult.

   b. His anxiety and guilt are especially high when he has experienced disapproval from his parents. Reich (45) notes that over every remedial reading case hovers an anxious parent: a parent who is overprotective, is disappointed, and often feels guilty himself.

   c. The student's "don't care" attitude toward reading frequently is a "do care very much" attitude (8 p. 183). It is a safety valve that permits the student to save face. Both teacher and parent should permit the student to have this apparent attitude without developing a feeling of guilt on the part of the student.

3. The corrective or remedial methods are hardly distinct from developmental methods. One cannot "reteach" a student who never learned. One cannot remedy what was always lacking. Students receiving remedial education are distinct from normal readers in that they did not learn as a result of the educational procedures that were effective with most students. All the principles that apply to effective developmental instruction also apply to what is termed *remedial teaching*. The good teacher, whatever his title may be, starts at the student's present reading level, builds self-confidence in reading, and uses a variety of reading methods. Perhaps the remedial teacher is somewhat more permissive, delves more precisely into the causes of the reading problem, uses a greater variety of materials and motivational devices, and individualizes the program to a greater degree. The methods and principles of remedial teaching and developmental teaching are distinguishable, if at all, by the emphasis on individualization. Remedial reading is not a magic hocus-pocus of special methods, but a more intense and personal application of the techniques used with all

others. Consequently, it is the nature of the student rather than the nature of the teaching that distinguishes the two procedures. Remedial measures are not cure-alls. They do not correct and eliminate all reading difficulties.

4. Develop those skills and abilities that are most necessary for immediate successful reading.

5. Remediation should be based on and accompanied by continuous diagnosis. This identifies areas that need unteaching and helps to identify the student who is ready for regular classroom instruction.

6. No one symptom, error, or mistake of itself implies an ailment or a general deficiency. Even the best reader will err at times.

7. Perfect results on a test do not mean complete mastery. It is not uncommon to find students getting the correct answer through the use of an incorrect method.

8. The student's symptoms, if not correctly interpreted, may lead the teacher to provide the improper remediation. The so-called cause, upon careful analysis, is frequently found to be an effect of poor reading. The teacher thus expects from the expert psychological insight into why a given method is recommended. Too often, the expert comes up with a diagnosis such as "he is a dyslexic reader," without any recommendations as to the type of program to follow. The expert's diagnosis must be translated into "what to do" in the classroom. It is the going from the diagnostic hypothesis to the remedial method that is the difficult task.

9. The pattern of symptoms is usually more significant than the individual symptom.

10. Cures do not necessarily mean that the correct method of cure has been found. The intangibles of teacher-student motivations and teacher effectiveness generally play an important role. The good teacher may have good results regardless of method used. The poor teacher may experience only failure.

11. No remedial method has universal application. Methods of instruction should be selected that are in harmony with the best mode of learning for a given student.

12. The teacher's personality and his ability to enlist each student's active cooperation are often more important than the specific method used. Learning occurs in a relationship. Rapport is a subtle thing. The student needs to develop a desire to learn.

   In dealing with remedial cases, psychotherapeutic principles should be incorporated into the process. The teacher should:

   a. Develop a constructive relationship with the student (rapport). Drop the role of an authoritative teacher. Become an interested teacher.

   b. Be a genuine person.

    c. Give total and unequivocal acceptance of the student despite his frequent failures in school.

    d. Have complete faith in the student's improvableness and ability to read. If the significant adults in a student's life believe that he can succeed, his chances for success are appreciably improved.

    e. Develop a feeling of empathy, not sympathy. Objectivity must be maintained. If sympathy develops, the student feels that he has to please his teacher and that he cannot make mistakes. This often leads to tension (34, 47).

    f. Having a structured, well-defined program. The remedial program is more structured than the psychotherapeutic session.

    g. Arouse interest by judicious choice of materials.

    If the corrective or remedial teacher provides a relationship in which he is (a) genuine, internally consistent; (b) acceptant, prizing the learner as a person of worth; and (c) empathically understanding of the learner's private world of feelings and attitudes, then certain changes are likely to occur in the learner. For example, the learner becomes (a) more realistic in his self-perceptions; (b) more confident and self-directing; (c) more positively valued by himself; (d) less likely to repress elements of his experience; (e) more mature, and adaptive in his behavior; (f) less upset by stress and quicker to recover from it; (g) more like the healthy, integrated, well-functioning person in his personality structure; and (h) a better learner (46).

13. No two reading disability cases probably stem from the same source, have exactly the same pattern, or need the same instruction.

14. Select materials that the student can handle and in which he is interested. To do this, the teacher needs to know the student's instructional level. It is very important to remember that reading skills do not operate in a vacuum. The teacher needs proper materials, perhaps packets and kits; however, "packets and kits are fine for practice, tackling the dummy, but practice isn't to be confused with playing the game, of football or reading." It is often not what materials that are used with retarded readers that is most significant, but rather what the teacher does with the materials.

15. Instill in the student a feeling of responsibility for his own progress. It is important that the student not gain a false sense of security and that he realize that remediation is a result of his personal effort; it cannot be donated by the teacher (2). Not only must the teacher give, but the student must be able and willing to take and to utilize the help given (37). Progress charts should be developed. The units of improvement need to be small enough so that progress can be recorded at frequent intervals.

16. Some remedial approaches, if used flexibly, appear applicable to reading

disability cases almost irrespective of cause. Students in grades 9–12 rarely can handle sessions that are longer than one hour in duration.

17. Remedial sessions must be adapted to the student.

18. When we speak of remedial reading or reading disability, we often imply that there is a basic deficiency in the learner that impedes progress. It may be helpful to remind ourselves that the basic deficiency may be poor teaching.

Improvement in reading is not necessarily brought about by spending more money, by bringing in consultants, by buying more gadgets and mechanical devices, or by resorting to newer approaches. Outstanding instructional programs in reading will be achieved "only through outstanding instruction" (31).

This means, as Heilman notes, that our teaching practices ought to be in accord with what we know about student-learning and what we know about reading and its relation to all school learning.

Individualization of instruction is the chief identifying mark of good teaching and is totally dependent upon student diagnosis. The wise teacher identifies individual differences and teaches each student accordingly. The aim of remediation is to direct a student into that set of learning experiences most appropriate for him. The teacher thus must be extraordinarily sensitive to the needs of the learner.

But what if the diagnosis is incorrect? This would obviously result in wrong remediation; the greater the error in diagnosis, the greater might be the harm. We all realize that even the best diagnosis often is not totally reliable. The diagnostic information is fallible, but this does not make it worthless. It does mean that the degree of differentiation in remediation that should be attempted is directly proportional to the accuracy of the diagnosis. It would seem wise, then, to begin remediation by using those principles, methods, and procedures that are developmentally sound. Only gradually and with great care should the remediation depart from these.

The diagnostic-remediation process may be viewed as a matter of obtaining and transmitting information. Diagnosis brings forth information about the student. We have suggested in this chapter a positive and direct way of doing this by observation, questionnaire, inventory, and test. Another approach is to begin the remediation process with the problem as the student presents it and to help the student rather immediately in solving it. This latter approach consists of observing the student, working with him, and studying, analyzing, and remediating during actual instruction and practice in reading. This approach calls for the use of few tests.

One teacher might want to narrow the point where remediation might be applied. He is confident that he can and actually has identified the significant areas of difficulty. A second teacher believes that it is not possible to predict what areas will be significant in the case before him. He prefers to risk some loss of time in order to avoid the risk of overlook- a significant area. The first teacher would thus at once plunge into a reading diagnosis. The second teacher would fear that such a direct attack might actually cause the student to fail to mention the real reason why he hates reading.

Each teacher is gambling. It would appear that if the teacher strongly believes, because of his experience and knowledge, that the significant area is to be found in a limited area, he should study that area with maximum precision (18). It would appear that experienced teachers would be safer in doing this than inexperienced teachers.

REMEDIAL METHODS   This chapter would not be complete without a résumé of remedial methods. We have already indicated that there is no one best method for teaching reading, and there is no one best remedial or corrective method. There may be a best method for a given learner. There may be a best method for a special segment of the learner population. There may even be a best method for a given teacher because he is most comfortable with it. The teacher of reading thus has to look at many methods. Because he does not know whose brand of reading method is the best buy, he has to consider a variety of possibilities, each of which might have some merit and validity in a specific teaching situation.

It is not possible to survey all remedial methods, but the following are some key ones.*

Fernald Method (26)   The steps in the Fernald method vary from word tracing to word analysis and are determined somewhat by the ability and progress of the pupil. At the lower ranges of achievement, the pupil selects a word that he wishes to learn. The teacher writes the word on paper in large script or print. The child may even dictate a sentence, such as "I like my mother." The teacher records this on paper. There is little or no control of the vocabulary. The child then traces each word with the forefinger, saying each part of the word as he does the tracing. The process continues until the child can write the word without the bene- fit of the copy. The child's fingers must make contact with the paper as he traces. Words thus learned are later typewritten and then included in stories for the child to read. As new words are learned, they are collected by the pupil in an alphabetical file. As the child advances, tracing may cease entirely, but pronouncing the word while writing it is always an es- sential feature.

The kinesthetic method develops through four stages:

* For a more detailed discussion, see Emerald Dechant, *Diagnosis and Remedia- tion of Reading Disability* (New York: Parker Publishing Company, 1968).

1. Tracing, calling, and writing the word.
    a. The teacher writes the word for the pupil in large print, perhaps on the chalkboard.
    b. The pupil traces the word, pronouncing the world in syllables as he traces.
    c. The pupil tries to write the word, repeating steps one and two if he is unable to do so.
2. Writing without tracing. Gradually the pupil attempts to write new words without having to trace them.
3. Recognizing the word. The pupil gradually comes to recognize the word on sight. He learns the printed word by saying it to himself before writing.
4. Word analysis. The pupil is taught to break the word into smaller parts. He now recognizes words by their similarity to words that he already knows.

Niensted (40) adapted the Fernald method to group use with high school juniors. The method involves teacher-prepared duplicated manuscripts to be traced by the students as the graphemes are pronounced, followed by an underlining of the syllables and a reading of the passage, using meaningful phrasing.

The kinesthetic method is time-consuming, but it has many advantages. It teaches left-to-right orientation, and the sound of the word is associated with the visual stimulus. The pupil seems to acquire phonic skills without having formal training, and he develops skills in syllabication. The method is designed especially for clinical use and requires almost constant direction from the teacher.

The Hegge, Kirk, and Kirk Grapho-Vocal Method (30) requires the pupil to sound out and write each word. The pupil pronounces the word entirely phonetically (synthetic phonics) and later writes the word from dictation. The steps thus are the following:

1. Sound the words letter by letter.
2. Blend the sounds together.
3. Pronounce the words.
4. Write the words.

Fernald's method is a VAKT (visual, auditory, kinesthetic, and tactile) method. There are similar methods labeled only VAK. In these, the pupil does not do any tracing of the word.

Cooper (16) found that there were no distinct differences in modality preference between good and poor first graders, but that modality preference was more important for poor readers than for good readers. More surprising was the finding that poor readers tended not to learn best through the kinesthetic modality, whereas good readers did.

Color Phonics System   The Color Phonics System presents the letters in color in such a way that once the principle of coding has been mastered the pupil can immediately identify the sound.* The method is designed to be used with the dyslexic reader. It is not to be used with the color blind or with the brain injured suffering from color agnosia. The system is based, among others, on the following assumptions:

1. The most successful techniques for teaching dyslexics are founded on a phonetic basis.
2. Each letter should be taught separately or in given combinations which can be arranged and rearranged again and again in various orders. Bannatyne (3) believes that the fundamental neuropsychological deficit of the dyslexic pupil is the inability to sequence correctly, especially auditorily. The pupil must vocalize constantly, sounding out the successive phonemes which make up a word.
3. The dyslexic pupil has difficulty mastering the irregular orthography of the English language, but replacing the irregular phonetic structure of the language with a regular one requires the pupil to transfer to the traditional orthography at a later date. As the dyslexic reader finds it extremely difficult to memorize a set of sound-symbol associations, an additional set of symbols for the same sounds is scarcely likely to solve his problems (3, p. 196). Color coding permits the pupil to identify the sound in a direct way.
4. The pupil must overlearn sound-symbol associations through a variety of stimuli and sensory pathways.

Bannatyne (3) believes that the Color Phonics System can be used in conjunction with the Fernald method, the Gillingham method, or Daniel's and Diack's systems as developed through the Royal Road Readers. For teaching with this system the following points are emphasized by Bannatyne:

1. If the pupil suffers from severe dyslexia, the teacher usually begins with the phonetically regular words and short sentences, and initially short vowels. Consonants are introduced later.
2. The vowels are printed in red. The pupil learns that there must never be a word or syllable without a red letter (the letter y has a red band because it can be used as a vowel).

---

* Color Phonics System (Cambridge, Mass.: Educators Publishing Service, 301 Vassar Street).

3. At all times, words are broken up into syllables whenever the individual letters are used. One technique which helps the pupil with breaking a word into syllables, memorizing colors, and spelling generally is the use of rhymes and rhyming.

4. A problem frequently encountered is that of blending phonemes. Frequently, the inability to blend is a direct result of faulty teaching, inasmuch as the pupil has learned to voice unvoiced consonants by adding unwanted vowels. The word *lit* cannot be blended if the *l* is pronounced /luh/. More often than not, this inability to synthesize sounds into meaningful speech is an aspect of the primary inability of the dyslexic to sequence auditory material in the absence of auditory sounds. Clear vocalization and auditory sequencing of words are the most important requisites for successful remediation.

5. There are only two methods for facilitating blending. The first is to tell the pupil to form his mouth in preparation for saying the initial consonant of a syllable but then to say the following vowel instead. This technique is useful when the initial consonants are unvoiced ones anyway. The second technique consists of demonstrating a single syllable in two parts, namely, the initial consonant and the remainder of the syllable as a whole. Thus *cat* is taught not as *c a t, but as c at*. At the same time, the word *cat,* as a *gestalt,* is presented in both its written and spoken forms, and these are simultaneously analyzed into their component letters and phonemes.

6. The pupil is introduced to the twenty or so spelling rules one by one. He is given plenty of practice in applying the rules. In the long run, it is easier for a dyslexic, with his weak verbal memory, to remember a few set principles than thousands of those arbitrary letter-sound sequences called (printed) words.

7. Gradually, the black vowels replace the colored vowels.

Progressive Choice Reading Method   The Progressive Choice Reading Method is an outgrowth of studies by Myron Woolman.* Two programs based on Woolman's ideas are available today. The first of these, entitled *Lift Off to Reading,* is useful with the educable and trainable mental retardates, the culturally disadvantaged, the emotionally disturbed, the bilinguals, and the dyslexics.† *Reading in High Gear* is designed for older, underachieving, culturally disadvantaged readers at the adolescent level.‡ Woolman emphasizes elements in words. He begins with a "target

* M. Woolman, *The Progressive Choice Reading Program* (Washington, D.C.: Institute of Educational Research, Inc., 1962).

† M. Woolman, *Lift off to Reading* (Chicago: Science Research Associates, 1966).

‡ M. Woolman, *Reading in High Gear* (Chicago: Science Research Associates, 1965).

word" by discussing its meaning. The learner must then differentiate the linear and curvilinear components which compose the letters of the target word. These components are then combined into individual letters and discrimination of the letters is stressed. The student next writes the letter by tracing the letter, finally writing the letter without tracing. The third step consists of learning the sound that is most commonly associated with the letter. Woolman teaches the *g,* for example, as */guh/,* noting that this is a necessary crutch in the beginning and that the student quickly gets rid of it when he has mastered a "feeling" for the consonant. The learner must utter the sound when he sees the printed form of the letter and he must write the letter when he hears it pronounced for him. Fourth, the reader must learn to combine various vowels and consonants into single sounds. Finally, the student must read and write the "target words."

Gillingham Method   The Gillingham Method is a multisensory approach emphasizing the linguistic and graphic regularities of English words.* It is termed an alphaphonetic method and begins by teaching the learner a few short vowels and consonants that have only one sound. It does not use letters that, if reversed, become new letters. Thus initially it steers clear of letters like *b* and *d*. It is a combination method, using the auditory, visual, and kinesthetic sense avenues. It is a synthetic phonics system rather than an analytical phonics approach. The teaching processes that result in the association of the visual, auditory, and kinesthetic are called *linkages.* The method consists of eight such linkages.

Linkage 1.   The name of the letter is associated with the printed symbol; then the sound of the letter is associated with the symbol.

Linkage 2.   The teacher makes the letter and explains its form. The pupil traces it, copies it, and writes it from memory. The teacher directs the pupil to move in the right direction and to begin in the right place when making the letters.

Linkage 3.   The phonogram is shown to the pupil and he names it. The pupil learns to associate the letter with its "look" and its "feel." He learns to form the symbol without looking at the paper as he writes.

Linkage 4.   The teacher says the phoneme, and the pupil writes it.

Linkage 5.   The pupil is shown the letter and asked to sound it. The teacher moves the pupil's hand to form the letter, and the pupil sounds it.

---

* Anna Gillingham and Bessie W. Stillman, *Remedial Training for Children with Specific Disability in Reading, Spelling, and Penmanship* (Cambridge: Educators Publishing Service, 1966). Available also are *Phonetic Drill Cards, Phonetic Word Cards, Syllable Concept, Little Stories,* and *Introduction of Diphthongs.*

Linkage 6. The teacher gives the name of the phonogram, and the pupil gives the sound.

Linkage 7. The teacher makes the sound, and the pupil gives the name of the letter.

Linkage 8. The teacher makes the sound, and the pupil writes the phonogram. Sometimes the pupil writes without looking at the paper and also names the letter.

Using the multisensory approach, the Gillingham method introduces the linguistic and graphically regular words first. Only gradually is the pupil introduced to exceptions.

PRINCIPLES OF LEARNING

The teacher's prime task is to get students to learn, so he obviously needs to know how learning takes place. He needs to know how to provide the conditions for effective learning.

Through the years various schools of learning have emerged. If one wanted to do justice to even one of them, an entire book would have to be devoted to the task. In our book *Improving the Teaching of Reading* we described in detail the various theories and their implications for the teaching of reading.* The key principles of learning can be summarized as follows:

1. All learning involves a stimulus (S), a response (R), and a connection between the stimulus and the response. The student is stimulated by a book (S) and reads words, sentences, and paragraphs (R).

2. Learning proceeds best when the learner understands what he is doing. It is imperative that the teacher find out what students know and do not know before starting instruction.

   a. Teachers need to be aware that sometimes the student comes up with the correct response by accident or by guessing, *without understanding why his answer is correct.*

   b. The teacher needs to determine whether to reward the correct response, the correct process, or only the correct response when it is accompanied by the correct process.

3. The student learns by doing; learning occurs under conditions of practice, and overlearning is of crucial importance to poor readers. Practice or

* Emerald Dechant, *Improving the Teaching of Reading*, 2nd ed. (Englewood Cliffs, N.J.: Prentice-Hall, Inc., 1970).

repetition *per se,* however, does not cause learning. The student's practice must be both motivated and rewarded, and it should be slightly varied from session to session. The reconditioning should have a creative aspect and should not degenerate into drudgery (51).

4. The learner learns best when he is psychologically and physiologically ready to respond to the stimulus. The student should feel a need for improving his reading ability. The learner should have a proper attitude, should be ready to attend to the stimulus, and should have a felt need to learn. He should also have adequate maturity for learning. The learner will not respond unless he is motivated, and he cannot learn unless he responds. The reader's performance will improve only if he is interested in his work, if he is interested in improving himself, if the material to be learned has special significance for him, and if he is attentive to the situation. The student must recognize his reading problem as one he wants to solve (51). Reduce motivations to zero and there is no performance and, hence, no learning.

5. The learner cannot learn without doing, but he will not do anything without being rewarded. The task should relate to the student's interest. The best rewards in the reading setting are often pleasant student-teacher relationships and a sense of success and progress. The teacher must divide the gross learning skills into numerous small steps and must reward the learning of each discrete step.

6. Learning is often a matter of present organization and reorganization, not simply past accretion. Perhaps no individual is ever completely free to behave on the basis of the present situation. Previous experiences have developed a set or pattern of behavior that is difficult to change. The retarded reader, even if he now sincerely wants to be a good reader, must live with his previous inapplications. But, each new situation has within it the potentiality for change. The student can usually make positive advances toward new goals and achievements. He has the potentiality for growth.

7. Letters might best be taught to most children as parts of a whole word, but the perceptual whole for the retarded reader often is the single letter. The size of the unit of instruction depends on the nature of the pupil, and many retarded readers benefit greatly from a synthetic-phonetic approach.

8. Reading involves response selection. A pupil who can read *the* and *there* may not be too sure of *their.* He makes provisional tries at the word, and when he comes up with the correct pronunciational response, the teacher reinforces this response, thus gradually stamping it in. Thus, from a series of possible responses the pupil gradually learns to select the correct response.

9. Each activity (reading of a sentence, for example) consists of a complex of individual movements, and improvement and learning are not neces-

sarily attained by *much* reading but rather by increasing the number of correct movements in reading (moving from left to right, proper identification of the word, association of the proper meaning with the word, development of proper eye movements) and by reducing the number of incorrect movements (excessive regressions, improper word attack, etc.) in the total complex of movements comprising the total capacity. Improvement occurs because the learner gradually replaces the erroneous movements that he is still making with correct ones. Thus additional practice gives more opportunity to master the myriad of movements comprising a complex total performance.

This view of the learning of a skill certainly emphasizes the need for the teaching of specific habits. Telling a retarded reader "to read" is not specific enough. We need to teach specific habits in specific situations. This requires careful job analysis, leading to an identification of all specific movements. The curriculum, methods, and materials must be so specific that they will serve as proper stimuli to call forth appropriate responses. It is not enough to identify large, all-embracing abilities, such as "gaining a sight vocabulary." It is necessary to break the broad area into basic subskills, such as the ability to discriminate between sounds, to see elements within a word, and to blend the elements into the total word.

10. When a stimulus is followed by a response, there is a tendency for the same response to occur when the stimulus recurs. The pupil who responds to **was** with **saw** on the next presentation of the stimulus **was** tends to respond again with **saw**. In the classroom, much teaching follows this contiguity principle.

It is important, especially when learning is a one-shot or a one-trial affair, that the teacher not permit the learner to leave a learning situation without performing the response correctly. A learner should read the word correctly before going on to another word. Bugelski (14, p. 104) notes that teachers should also see the folly of allowing youngsters to do homework without having the answers supplied. He adds that such homework is not training or practice, it is a *test*.

The reader should not "get by" with approximations of the correct answer (14, p. 103). The student should not be permitted simply to get a "general idea." Teachers frequently give partial credit for partially correct answers. Partially correct answers, such as reading *their* for *them*, are in fact totally wrong. Bugelski (14, p. 103) notes that too many students are rated as "knowing what to do" without being able to do.

11. If the learner tends to repeat the response that was made most recently in the presence of the stimulus, the teacher should exercise great care, especially with the retarded reader, in not permitting extraneous materials to come between the stimulus and the response. The teacher must see to it that

when the response is made, it is made to the proper stimulus and not to any of many other possible stimuli that may have intervened. Too frequently in teaching, by the time the proper response occurs, the original stimulus situation has disappeared. The teacher must take great care that the necessary stimuli are so distinct for the student that he cannot help but see the connection between a given stimulus and the objective of teaching.

12. The teacher will make fewer mistakes in teaching if he analyzes all the variables in behavior. There are multiple causes of behavior.

13. Whenever a stimulus is presented to an organism, the organism is generally capable of responding in one or more ways. All the responses possible in the situation may be thought of as comprising a hierarchy of responses, each of which has a certain probability of occurring. Education thus might be a "changing of relative positions in a hierarchy" (14, pp. 74–75).

Learning requires the elimination of faulty habits or competitive responses or of those members in the hierarchy that have higher probability. If these constantly intrude, learning cannot occur. As all teachers have seen, sometimes it is more difficult to undo a wrong habit or to unlearn what has been learned faultily than to teach the correct procedure from scratch. A "correct" baseball stance is easier to assume by the beginning player than by one in whom an incorrect procedure has become ingrained.

Bugelski (14, p. 80) notes the great value in teaching a variety of methods for reaching a goal. The student needs to learn to switch approaches to solve problems when necessary.

14. Recognition of a word is not reading. The student must react with meaning, and this frequently requires the organization of previous experiences.

15. The meanings taken to a word usually are many more than one, but also far fewer than they could be. The greater the number of meanings that are associable with a word, the more difficult it is to understand such a word and the less reliable the individual learner's meaning for such a word tends to be. This is why students have difficulty with multiple meanings of words.

16. The meaning comes from the learner rather than from the word and is determined primarily by the learner's previous experiences but also by his own constitutional makeup, by the number, quality, and organization of his experiences, by his ability to reconstruct his own experiences, by his affective state, and by his culture. The learner reacts as an organized whole.

17. The central process that controls the learner's particular reaction to printed materials or that modifies the stimulus materials is termed *cognition* and depends on adequate neural functioning.

18. The learner's differentiations of meaning are prevented or inhibited by such factors as visual or auditory inadequacies, brain injuries, lack of in-

telligence, and lack of experience. Learning retardation frequently results because the learner cannot make the proper differentiations required for mastery of the learning task.

Differentiations take time, and the teacher must constantly make adjustments for this. Thus the application of white paint at the choice points in an otherwise completely black maze leads to quicker and more accurate learning by the rat. In classroom learning, the method of teaching can be simplified or made unnecessarily difficult. The teacher can arrange the learning situation in such a way that the differentiations comes easily or are more difficult. Teaching machines essentially strive to make each step to be learned so simple and small that it can be taken with great confidence and success. With the retarded reader in particular, the learning task needs to be presented in structured, carefully planned steps.

The manner in which a problem is presented determines at least in some way whether past experiences can be used appropriately or not. Some classroom arrangements are more conducive than others to the elicitation of insightful solutions. The evidence indicates that with retarded readers, who are often weak in the visual association-memory area, materials should be presented through the auditory and kinesthetic channels. Learning is chiefly under the influence of the learner's perceptual field at the moment of action. Students learn best by surveying the situation and grasping relationships by perceiving meaningful relationships among the elements of the goal toward which they are striving.

19. Learning to read requires an association between a stimulus (the word) and a response (the meaning) and is most easily brought about when the printed symbol is associated with a spoken word for which the learner has previously learned a meaning under conditions of spaced and varied practice.

20. Learning proceeds best when the task is challenging but still within the potentiality of the learner. The student must have sufficient interest in the task to use the responses of which he is capable. The student needs experience in setting realistic goals, goals neither so low as to elicit little effort nor so high as to discourage him from trying altogether or that in his opinion foredoom him to failure.

21. Transfer of learning to new tasks is best promoted by the perception of the interrelationships within the situation and by actual experience in applying the principles to new situations. The student should see, for example, the interrelationships between letters in words and applying this knowledge to new words.

22. *A commonly accepted principle in remedial teaching is that remedial approaches, if used flexibly, are applicable to reading disability cases almost irrespective of cause.*

The normal sequence for the teaching of reading might be the following:

1. Picture reading (associating meaning with a picture)
2. Associating the sound with the *whole* word
3. Learning the names of the letters
4. Writing or printing the letter
5. Associating the sound with the beginning consonant and medial vowel letter

If this procedure does not work with a given learner, the teacher has two basic options: (1) He can use a fully developed method, such as Gillingham's alphaphonetic method, or (2) he can develop a system of his own incorporating a combination of the following testing techniques.

1. *Focus on the simplest, most basic perceptual-associational element within a total word or gestalt (map-nap). Teach the name of the letter.* Hinshelwood stresses the need to develop visual memory of the letter first. Initial remedial teaching might begin with tactile-kinesthetic techniques (the Fernald method) if the pupil has not yet acquired visual recognition for letters. Remedial phonics, such as the Orton-Gillingham approach, might be used if letter recognition has occurred.

2. *Associate sound with this element.* This element may be a letter or syllable or word. Monroe put pictures on a card and the pupil learned first to *hear* the consonant sound. Others show the letter and associate the sound with it.

3. *If the pupil begins with distinct sounds, he must learn to blend.*
   a. Have the student form his mouth in preparation for saying the initial consonant but then say the following vowel instead: *b-y*.
   b. Have the student learn *cat*, not /c-a-t/, but /c-at/. The beginning consonant is joined to the ending phonogram and the vowel is joined to the consonant that follows.

4. *Write or trace the letter or the word, form it in clay, write letters in wet sand, etc.*
   a. Monroe has pupils use a pencil to trace the word.
   b. Fernald has pupils trace each word with the forefinger.

5. *Use all senses.* Hear, say, see, and write the word. Have him get the main idea of a paragraph from hearing it read aloud to him, from reading silently, and from expressing ideas both orally and in writing. A good example of this multisensory approach is the Gillingham method. Fernald's method is a VAKT method (the *T* implies tracing of the word). Blau suggests use of AKT in which the visual modality is blocked. The eyes are blindfolded, with the learner saying the letters as he traces them.

6. *Use a spelling-writing approach.* Sooner or later the learner must be able to write the letter or the word from memory. After the learner has developed a visual memory for the letter, Hinshelwood has him develop an auditory memory for words by spelling aloud the word letter by letter.

7. *Teach the phonograms by having students say the sounds in unison, have them write them, etc.* (In the Unified Phonics method, phonograms include all the letters, such as *b, c, d* plus such phonograms as *eigh, igh, ug, ed*).

8. *Use color to regularize the phoneme-grapheme correspondences, as in Words in Color and in the Color Phonics System.*

9. *Always make sure that the pupil associates sound with the whole word,* which is the smallest linguistic unit that can represent meaning.

10. *Use the oral neurological-impress method.* This is a system of unison reading whereby the student and the teacher read aloud simultaneously at a rapid rate. This approach is especially effective with those who are phonics-bound, who have had intensive phonics training but still are not reading fluently.

EVALUATING REMEDIAL INSTRUCTION

The reading teacher, whether in or out of the regular classroom, must constantly evaluate his instruction. He needs to determine the effectiveness of various procedures in terms of the gains in reading achievement. Over the course of years many quite different procedures have been suggested for evaluating remedial teaching, but too few data are available concerning their relative effectiveness. And for that matter, some writers actually challenge the effectiveness of special methods of remediation. Young (57), for example, suggests that the personality of the teacher and his ability to enlist each learner's active cooperation are more important than the specific method used. On the other hand, numerous studies on remedial and diagnostic methods indicate that reading difficulties can be either entirely or at least largely eliminated.

Balow (1) found that remedial instruction was effective in dealing with the problems of the disabled reader, but he also notes that severe reading disability is not corrected by short-term intensive treatment and that it should be considered a relatively chronic illness needing long-term treatment rather than the short course typically organized in current programs. Buerger (13) also reports that pupils who received remedial instruction demonstrated significant reading gains, but they did not make greater long-term educational progress than other pupils who did not receive remedial instruction.

Rankin and Tracy (44, 52) list three methods of measuring and evaluating individual differences in reading improvement.

1. *Crude gain.* In this situation comparable tests are given before (the pretest) and after (the posttest) a remedial program. The score at the start of the program is subtracted from the score at the end of the program, and the difference is considered as improvement. Students will naturally show improvement if a difficult test is given in the beginning and if an easier test is administered after the completion of the program.

2. *Percentage gain.* In this approach the gain between the pretest and the posttest is expressed as a percentage of the initial score. The formula then is

$$\text{percent of gain} = \frac{\text{pretest}-\text{posttest}}{\text{posttest}}$$

3. *Residual gain.* This is the difference between the actual posttest score and the score that was predictable from the pretest score. (For a discussion of this third procedure the reader may want to consult the articles by Rankin and Tracy in the *Journal of Reading,* March 1965 and March 1967. Another good survey of various evaluative procedures is by George H. Maginnis, "Evaluating Remedial Reading Gains," *Journal of Reading,* 13 (April 1970), 523–28).

Many faulty conclusions have apparently been drawn from reading research because residual gain was not considered. As Sommerfield (50) points out, there is a natural tendency for those people who score at the extremes of a distribution on the first test to score closer to the mean of the distribution on the second test. The scores tend to regress toward the mean.

Although the research worker can use control groups or make statistical corrections to eliminate regression effects, this frequently is not done.

Dolch (21, p. 80) has cautioned that research can come up with the wrong answer unless it is carefully planned and watched. He recommends vigilance in these areas:

1. Compare equal teachers working equally hard.
2. Compare pupils of equal ability and equal home influences.
3. Compare equal school time and emphasis.
4. Watch carefully size of class.
5. Beware of misleading averages.
6. Watch for unmeasured results.

In discussing these points, Dolch emphasizes that the teacher using the method frequently is far more important than the method used. Numerous variables enter into any experiment. Sommerfield (50, p. 56) indicates that the reported results of experimental reading programs may be influenced by the subjects involved, the techniques and materials used, the conditions under which the study was done, the tests that were employed, the statistical devices used, and perhaps the bias or misinterpretations of the investigator.

Studies often do not make allowance for the differences in both skill and motivation among teachers. Control groups are taught by the "regular" teachers; experimental groups are taught by teachers who have a special interest in the project and can give more time to their students. Studies do not control for the Hawthorne effect (15), which is the learning that results simply because the program is new and presents for students and teachers alike an opportunity for recognition. Brownell (9) notes that the critical determinant of achievement is teaching competency rather than the system of instruction. He also notes that results are frequently evaluated by means of test scores, but this is not necessarily what is educationally significant. The measurable is not necessarily the significant, and the significant is not necessarily measurable. There are no published tests available that measure how well students read to gain information in specific courses. In this area general reading tests are of limited value. In many instances achievement at the moment is evaluated; the transfer value of what has been learned is rarely evaluated. There may also be differences in motivation between the students in a control group using the regular methods and the experimental group using a new method.

There also is a difference between educational significance and statistical significance. Sometimes a difference of one-tenth of a year is significant at the .05 level of confidence, but it may have no practical significance.

Weiner (53) notes that to evaluate changes in reading behavior we must consider all relevant functions: perceptual, integrative, and motivational. We need to evaluate processes rather than simply end products, measurable and nonmeasurable changes, and changes in self-concept and attitudes as a result of remedial programs. We need to find ways of analyzing the process that produced the outcome and of determining cause-and-effect relationships. Hardy (27) found that early referral for help was related to superior achievement in a remedial program. When assessing process, we encounter such difficult-to-evaluate variables as student-teacher interaction, attitudes, interests, and enthusiasm. Weiner notes that evidence of improvement is greater accuracy in responses to printed material, greater dependability, greater retention of and confidence in one's responses, and greater speed.

In advancing a clinical concept of assessment Weiner (53) stresses the qualitative aspects of assessment and suggests that gains must be measured from the point of actual departure and not from an arbitrary zero point on a grade-level scale. Students in need of remedial services start not from scratch, but from behind scratch.

SUMMARY

This chapter outlines the diagnostic remedial process. It draws a distinction between developmental, corrective, and remedial instruction. It takes a look at various remedial methods, and it offers ideas on evaluating remedial methods.

QUESTIONS FOR DISCUSSION

1. Discuss prevention of reading disability as an important principle in the teaching of reading.
2. What does a comprehensive individual diagnosis consist of?
3. What are the criteria for estimating a student's independent reading level?
4. Compare the advantages and disadvantages of the informal and the formal reading inventory.
5. Which diagnostic test would you recommend for grade levels nine through twelve?
6. Identify basic symptoms of reading disability and suggest possible causes for each. How would you go about identifying the specific cause?
7. Suggest four possible classroom organizations that make allowance for corrective instruction.
8. Differentiate between the needs of the slow learner and the needs of the disadvantaged student.
9. List the factors to be considered when evaluating the effectiveness of remedial instruction.

BIBLIOGRAPHY

1. BALOW, BRUCE, "The Long-Term Effect of Remedial Reading Instruction," *The Reading Teacher,* 18 (April 1965), 581–86.
2. BAMMAN, HENRY A., "Organizing the Remedial Program in the Secondary School," *Journal of Reading,* 8 (November 1964), 103–8.
3. BANNATYNE, ALEX D.,"The Color Phonics System," *The Disabled Readers,* ed. John Money, pp. 193–214. Baltimore: Johns Hopkins Press, 1966.

4. BELMONT, LILLIAN, and HERBERT G. BIRCH, "The Intellectual Profile of Retarded Readers," *Perceptual and Motor Skills,* 22 (1966), 787–816.

5. BETTS, EMMETT A., *Foundations of Reading Instruction.* New York: American Book Company, 1957.

6. BLAU, H., and HARRIET BLAU, "A Theory of Learning to Read," *The Reading Teacher,* 22 (1968), 126.

7. BODER, ELENA, "Developmental Dyslexia: A Diagnostic Screening Procedure Based on Three Characteristic Patterns of Reading and Spelling," *Claremont Reading Conference,* 1968, pp. 173–87.

8. BOND, GUY L., and MILES A. TINKER, *Reading Difficulties: Their Diagnosis and Correction.* New York: Appleton-Century-Crofts, 1967.

9. BROWNELL, W. A., "The Evaluation of Learning under Dissimilar Systems of Instruction," *California Journal of Educational Research,* 17 (March 1966), 80–90.

10. BRUECKNER, LEO J., "Introduction," *Educational Diagnosis,* Thirty-fourth Yearbook of the National Society for the Study of Education, pp. 1–14. Bloomington: Public School Publishing Company, 1935.

11. BRYANT, N. DALE, "Learning Disabilities in Reading," *Reading as Intellectual Activity.* International Reading Association Conference Proceedings, pp. 142–46. New York: Scholastic Magazines, 1963.

12. BRYANT, N. DALE, "Some Principles of Remedial Instruction for Dyslexia," *The Reading Teacher,* 18 (April 1965), 567–72.

13. BUERGER, THEODORE A., "A Follow-up of Remedial Reading Instruction," *The Reading Teacher,* 21 (January 1968), 329–34.

14. BUGELSKI, B. R., *The Psychology of Learning Applied to Teaching.* Indianapolis: The Bobbs-Merrill Co., Inc., 1964.

15. CONGREVE, WILLARD J., "Implementing and Evaluating the Use of Innovations," *Innovation and Change in Reading Instruction,* 67 Yearbook of the National Society for the Study of Education, pp. 291–319. Chicago: University of Chicago Press, 1968.

16. COOPER, J. DAVID, "A Study of the Learning Modalities of Good and Poor First Grade Readers," *Reading Methods and Teacher Improvement,* pp. 87–97. International Reading Association, Newark, N.J., 1971.

17. CRITCHLEY, MACDONALD, *Developmental Dyslexia,* pp. 81–89. London: William Heinemann Medical Books, Ltd., White Friars Press, 1964.

18. CRONBACH, LEE J., "The Counselor's Problems from the Perspective of Communication Theory," *New Perspectives in Counseling.* Minneapolis: University of Minnesota Press, 1955.

19. CROSBY, R. M. N., and ROBERT A. LISTON, *The Waysiders,* p. 38. New York: Delacorte Press, 1968.

20. DECHANT, EMERALD, *Diagnosis and Remediation of Reading Disability.* West Nyack, N.Y.: Parker Publishing Company, 1968.

21. DOLCH, E. W., "School Research in Reading," *Elementary English,* 33 (February 1956), 76–80.

22. DURRELL, DONALD D., *The Improvement of Basic Reading Abilities.* Yonkers, N.Y.: World Book Company, 1940.

23. DURRELL, DONALD D., *Improving Reading Instruction.* New York: World Book Company, 1956.

24. EISENBERG, LEON, "Epidemiology of Reading Retardation," in *The Disabled Reader,* ed. John Money, p. 19. Baltimore: Johns Hopkins Press, 1966.

25. ELLINGSON, C. D., "The Obsolescent Child," *Journal of Learning Disabilities,* 1 (February 1968), 34–37.

26. FERNALD, GRACE M., *Remedial Techniques in Basic School Subjects.* New York: McGraw-Hill Book Company, 1966.

27. HARDY, MADELINE I., "Disabled Readers: What Happens to Them After Elementary School?" *Canadian Education and Research Digest,* 8 (December 1968), 338–46.

28. HARRIS, ALBERT J., *How to Increase Reading Ability* (3rd ed.). New York: David McKay Co., Inc., 1961.

29. HARRIS, ALBERT J., "Perceptual Difficulties in Reading Disability," *Changing Concepts of Reading Instruction,* International Reading Association Conference Proceedings, pp. 282–90. New York: Scholastic Magazines, 1961.

30. HEGGE, T., SAMUEL KIRK and WINIFRED KIRK, *Remedial Reading Drills.* Ann Arbor: George Wahr, Publishers, 1955.

31. HEILMAN, ARTHUR W., "Moving Faster toward Outstanding Instructional Programs," *Vistas in Reading,* Proceedings of the Eleventh Annual Convention, pp. 273–76. International Reading Association, Newark, N.J., 1967.

32. HINSHELWOOD, JAMES, *Congenital Word-Blindness.* London: H. K. Lewis and Company, Ltd., 1917.

33. JASTAK, J. D., and S. R. JASTAK, *The Wide Range Achievement Test Manual.* Wilmington: Guidance Associates, 1965.

34. KLAUSNER, DOROTHY C., "Screening and Development of the Remedial Reading Teacher," *Journal of Reading,* 10 (May 1967), 552–59.

35. KOLSON, CLIFFORD J., and GEORGE KALUGER, *Clinical Aspects of Remedial Reading,* p. 27. Springfield, Ill.: Charles C Thomas, Publisher, 1963.

36. McLEOD, JOHN, "Reading Expectancy from Disabled Learners," *Journal of Learning Disabilities,* 1 (February 1968), 7–15.

37. MILLS, DONNA M., "Corrective and Remedial Reading Instruction in the Secondary School," *Reading as an Intellectual Activity,* 8 (1963), 56–59, International Reading Association.

38. MONEY, JOHN, ed., *Reading Disability.* Baltimore: Johns Hopkins Press, 1962.

39. NELSON, C. DONALD, "Subtle Brain Damage: Its Influences on Learning and Language," *The Elementary School Journal,* 61 (March 1961), 317–21.

40. NIENSTED, SERENA, "A Group Use of the Fernald Technique," *Journal of Reading,* 11 (March 1968), 435–37, 440.

41. POWELL, WILLIAM R., "The Validity of the Instructional Reading Level," *Diagnostic Viewpoints in Reading,* pp. 121–33. International Reading Association, Newark, N.J., 1971.

42. QUADFASSEL, F. A., and H. GOODGLASS, "Specific Reading Disability and Other Specific Disabilities," *Journal of Learning Disabilities,* 1 (October 1968), 590–600.

43. RABINOVICH, R. D., and WINIFRED INGRAM, "Neuropsychiatric Considerations in Reading Retardation," *The Reading Teacher,* 15 (1962), 433–38.

44. RANKIN, EARL F., JR., and ROBERT J. TRACY, "Residual Gain as a Measure of Individual Differences in Reading Improvement," *Journal of Reading,* 8 (March 1965), 224–33.

45. REICH, RIVA R., "More Than Remedial Reading," *Elementary English,* 39 (March 1962), 216.

46. ROGERS, CARL R., "The Place of the Person in the New World of the Behavioral Sciences," *Personnel and Guidance Journal,* 39 (February 1961), 442–51.

47. ROSWELL, FLORENCE, "Psychotherapeutic Principles Applied to Remedial Reading," *Improvement of Reading through Classroom Practice,* pp. 145–47. International Reading Association Conference Proceedings, Newark, N.J., 1964.

48. SIPAY, E. A., "A Comparison of Standardized Reading Scores and Functional Reading Levels," *The Reading Teacher,* 17 (January 1964), 265–68.

49. SMITH, D. E. P., and PATRICIA M. CARRIGAN, *The Nature of Reading Disability.* New York: Harcourt, Brace and Company, Inc., 1959.

50. SOMMERFIELD, ROY E., "Some Recent Research in College Reading." *Techniques and Procedures in College and Adult Reading Programs,* Sixth Yearbook of the Southwest Reading Conference, p. 24. Fort Worth, Texas: Christian University Press, 1957.

51. STEINKELLNER, ROBERT H., "Reading Improvement Needs in High School," *Reading Improvement,* 4 (Summer 1967), 77–79.

52. TRACY, ROBERT J., and EARL F. RANKIN, "Methods of Computing and Evaluating Residual Gain Scores in the Reading Program," *Journal of Reading,* 10 (March 1967), 363–71.

53. WEINER, BLUMA B., "Dimensions of Assessment," *Exceptional Children,* 28 (September 1961), 483–86.

54. WILSON, ROBERT M., "Diagnosing High-School Students' Reading Problems," *Junior College and Adult Reading,* pp. 263–67. National Reading Conference, 1967.

55. WILSON, ROBERT M., *Diagnostic and Remedial Reading.* Columbus, Ohio: Charles E. Merrill Books, Inc., 1967.

56. WINKLEY, CAROL K., "What Do Diagnostic Reading Tests Really Diagnose?" *Diagnostic Viewpoints in Reading,* pp. 64–80. International Reading Association, Newark, N.J., 1971.

57. YOUNG, ROBERT A., "Case Studies in Reading Disability," *American Journal of Orthopsychiatry,* 8 (April 1938), 230–54.

Materials for the Teaching of Reading

THE MATERIALS SURVEYED in this chapter include those for both developmental and remedial instruction. Materials are an important variable in learning, and the reading teacher needs to know *what* materials to use, *when* to use them, and *with whom* to use them. It would obviously be desirable if we could offer an evaluation of all the materials listed. Perhaps this might be possible if we were talking about five to ten items of material and if we were recommending for a given student. It is clearly impossible when dealing with the numerous materials on the market today.

To provide for the specific needs of slow learners, disadvantaged readers, reluctant readers, and retarded readers, a great variety of remedial and special help programs has been developed. There is no panacea for reading problems, but the newer media can help. Materials are a basic component of a good reading program. The resources available to the teacher determine whether he can provide a systematic and enriched program, and they determine whether he can provide for individual differences.

It is most important that the materials used with a given student be suited to his needs. Incorrect materials or the incorrect use of appropriate materials can actually cause or intensify reading problems. In selecting materials, the teacher should make sure that they are on the appropriate difficulty level and interest level and that they take into account the student's deficiencies and problems. The student should be able to manage the materials without becoming frustrated. It makes sense to vary materials from time to time.

Every specialist in reading today has a host of materials and techniques available to him for correcting reading problems. Some of these materials emphasize such ideas as stimulus bombardment or modality isolation. Their greatest benefit may be that they allow the teacher to use learning activities that not only are appropriate to the student's strengths and weaknesses but are novel and exciting and not aversive. They facilitate an increase in approach and a decrease in avoidance tendencies on the part of the student.*

One of the real dangers today is the tendency to turn to "canned" instructional programs and materials with the hope that these will solve all problems. Too many schools, particularly high schools, rely almost completely upon commercially prepared materials, and yet these packaged mixes do not remedy all weaknesses.

A school must get an effective return for every dollar spent on materials. To do this the teacher must be familiar with the wide range of materials that are available, must acquaint himself with the research findings, and must learn how to use the materials wisely.

The following additional guidelines may help the teacher to make appropriate choices of materials:

1. The materials should contribute to the attainment of the objectives of the program.

2. The materials should provide for continuous and sequential development of the basic skills.

3. The program should provide a multiple approach to learning.

4. The program should give guidance in developing the thinking skills of the student.

5. The materials should elicit active responses on the part of the student.

6. The program should provide for diagnostic teaching, extensive diagnostic measures for assessing student needs, and activities designed to meet individual differences.

7. The program should provide guidance and materials for structuring flexible instructional groups.

8. The program should be easy to use, should be appropriate, should be keyed to specific objectives, and should have been tested prior to public distribution. It should actually instruct, allow for independent learning, and pace learning to individual differences. It should be suitable for use in reviewing instruction given by the teacher, thus facilitating the teacher's efforts.

* Howard S. Adelman, "Learning Problems," *Academic Therapy*, 6 (Spring 1971), 287–92.

GENERAL SOURCES

It is impossible to catalog all materials in one short chapter. The teacher of reading on the junior high–high school level should first familiarize himself with general compilations of reading materials such as the following:

CAPUZZI, DAVID T., *Sources for Teaching Developmental Reading,* College Skills Center, New York, 1969. Valuable source for reading teachers on high school and college level.

CARLSON, G. ROBERT, *Books and the Teen-Age Reader.* New York: Bantam Books, 1967.

DEVINE, THOMAS G., "About Materials for Teaching Reading," *What We Know about High School Reading,* National Council of Teachers of English, 1969, 85–90.

DIMITROFF, LILLIAN, *An Annotated Bibliography of Audiovisual Materials Related to Understanding and Teaching Culturally Disadvantaged.* Washington, D.C.: National Education Association, 1969.

DUNN, ANITA E., and MABEL E. JACKMAN, *Fare for the Reluctant Reader* (3rd ed.). Albany, N.Y.: Capital Area School Development Association, 1964.

EMERY, RAYMOND C., and MARGARET B. HOUSHOWER, *High Interest–Easy Reading for Junior and Senior High School Reluctant Readers.* Champaign, Ill.: National Council of Teachers of English, 1965.

SMALL, MARY P., "Materials for the Retarded Reader in the Junior High School: An Annotated Bibliography," *Reading Horizons,* 9 (Spring 1969), 142–48.

SPACHE, GEORGE D., *Good Reading for the Disadvantaged Reader. Champaign,* Ill.: Garrard Publishing Co., 1970.

SPACHE, GEORGE D., *Good Reading for Poor Readers* (rev. ed.). Champaign, Ill.: Garrard Publishing Co., 1964.

STENSLAND, ANNA LEE, "American Indian Culture and the Reading Program: A Bibliography," *Journal of Reading,* 15 (October 1971), 22–26.

STRANG, RUTH, *et al., Gateways to Readable Books* (4th ed.). New York: H. W. Wilson Co., 1966.

U.S. Office of Education, *Book Selection Aids for Children and Teachers in Elementary and Secondary Schools*. Washington, D.C.: Government Printing Office, 1966.

U.S. Office of Education, *Literature for Disadvantaged Children: A Bibliography*. Washington, D.C.: Government Printing Office, 1968.

SPECIFIC MATERIALS

The listing of materials that follows contains developmental, corrective, and remedial materials. It includes readers, workbooks and skillbooks, periodicals, laboratories, filmstrips, records, and programmed materials. The teacher must decide which materials best meet the needs of a given student. The greatest obligation is to motivate students to like books. It is better for a student to read a poor book that he finds interesting and rewarding than to read a great book that he finds dull and purposeless.

We have organized the materials by publisher.

ALLYN & BACON, INC., Rockleigh, N.J. 07647

High Trails, reader, grade 7, all skills.

Widening Views, reader, grade 8, all skills.

A Cavalcade of Life in Writing, reader, grade 9, word recognition and comprehension.

A Cavalcade of World Writing, reader, grade 10, all skills.

A Cavalcade of American Writing, reader, grade 11, word recognition and comprehension.

A Cavalcade of British Writing, reader, grade 12, all skills.

Breakthrough Series, paperback books for the reading dropout, high-interest, low-readability level, for inner-city junior and senior high school students, two books on each reading level (2–6) with skills activities.

AMERICAN BOOK COMPANY, 55 Fifth Avenue, New York, N.Y. 10003

High School Reading Books 1 and 2, supplementary readers, grades 9–12, all skills.

Reading Skillbooks, grades 7–8.

AMERICAN EDUCATION PUBLICATIONS, Education Center, Columbus, Ohio 43216

Know Your World, weekly periodical, ages 11–15, reading level grades 2–3, all skills.

You and Your World, weekly periodical, ages 15 and up, reading level grades 3–5, all skills.

Read Magazine, published semimonthly, grades 7–9, emphasizes all communication skills.

Reading Success Books, basic skills books, ages 10–16, all skills. Score I or book 1 begins with grade 2 reading level; six books.

PAUL S. AMIDON & ASSOCIATES, INC., 1035 Plymouth Building, Minneapolis, Minn. 55400

Listen: Hear, a skill-improvement laboratory, grades 5–8.

AMSCO SCHOOL PUBLICATIONS, 315 Hudson Street, New York, N.Y. 10013.

Vocabulary for the High School Student, workbook.

APPLETON-CENTURY-CROFTS, 60 East Forty-second Street, New York, N.Y. 10017

Improving Reading Ability, spiral-bound soft-cover manual, designed to improve reading and increase reading speed, high school to adult level.

ASSOCIATED EDUCATIONAL SERVICES CORPORATION, 630 Fifth Avenue, New York, N.Y. 10020

Split Cherry Tree, supplementary reader, grades 5–8, word recognition and comprehension.

A Man Who Had No Eyes, enrichment reader, grades 5–10, word recognition and comprehension.

The Monkey's Paw, enrichment reader, grades 7–9, word recognition and comprehension.

A Slander, enrichment reader, grades 9–10, word recognition and comprehension.

The Freshest Boy, enrichment reader, grades 10–college, word recognition and comprehension.

The Birds, enrichment reader, grades 10–college, word recognition and comprehension.

The Form of the Sword, enrichment reader, grades 11–college, word recognition and comprehension.

The Short Story as a Literary Form, enrichment reader, grades 8–9.

BALDRIDGE READING INSTRUCTION MATERIALS, INC., 14 Grigg Street, Greenwich, Conn. 06830

Reading and Study Techniques for Academic Subjects, resource book on how to improve reading and study techniques at the junior high school and high school levels; specific suggestions are given for applying the techniques to the student's own history, mathematics, science, language, and literature texts.

Introductory Technique Application Sheet, work sheet used by the student, in conjunction with his own books, for applying the techniques of surveying for central theme and main points, summarizing after reading, and relating to other readings and experiences, grades 7–college.

Technique Application Sheet, more detailed work sheet used by the student, in conjunction with his own books, for applying the techniques of surveying, establishing a purpose, questioning, structuring, summarizing, relating and evaluating, grades 7–college.

BENEFIC PRESS, 10300 West Roosevelt Road, Westchester, Ill. 60153

World of Adventure Series, supplementary remedial readers, grades 4–9, difficulty level grades 2–6.

BETTER READING PROGRAM, INC,. 232 East Ohio Street, Chicago, Ill. 60611

Rapid Reading Kit, includes visualizer; practice slides in graded sets, from grade 1 through adult level; progress record booklet; a *Reading Skills* lesson book; *Reader Rater* test booklets; and an improvement guide booklet.

BOOK-LAB, INC., Dept. Ac, 1449 Thirty-seventh Street, Brooklyn, N.Y. 11218

Hip-Reader, designed for teaching reading to nonreaders, grades 4–12, and to adult nonreaders.

Young Adult Sequential Reading Lab, designed for teen-agers who experience unusual difficulty in learning to read.

WM. C. BROWN COMPANY, 135 South Locust Street, Dubuque, Iowa 52001

Reading Improvement Program, workbook, teaches comprehension, vocabulary, and study skills.

BURGESS PUBLISHING COMPANY, 426 South Sixth Street, Minneapolis, Minn. 55415

Developing Reading Efficiency, workbook, difficulty level grade 11, teaches word recognition, word meaning, phrase meaning, sentence meaning, ideas reading, exploratory reading, and study reading.

Maintaining Reading Efficiency, workbook, junior high to college level, includes timed exercises.

CLIFF'S NOTES, INC., Dept. CEOIO, Bethany Station, Lincoln, Nebr. 68505

How to Take an Essay Examination, enrichment reader, grades 9–12, study skills.

Secrets of Studying, enrichment reader, grades 9–12, study skills.

COLLEGE SKILLS CENTER, 101 West Thirty-first Street, New York, N.Y. 10001

88 Passages to Develop Reading Comprehension, designed for developmental programs in junior high and for remedial programs in high school and college.

100 Passages to Develop Reading Comprehension, workbook, somewhat more difficult than the above, is accompanied by a separate question book.

Sack-Yourman Developmental Speed Reading Course, designed for grades 10 through adult level, program for the improvement of reading fluency, comprehension, and retention, includes reading selections, test booklet, and teacher's manual.

Notebook and Study Guide for Reading Improvement, includes flexibility chart, progress chart, SQ4R, what to do about forgetting, five ways to attack words, forms of organization, outlining and critical reading.

Variable Speed Cassettes for 88 Passages, 88 passages have been recorded on cassettes to be played at speeds of from 150–400 words per minute and three sets are available: for students learning English as a second language, for urban and ghetto groups, slow readers, or disadvantaged, and for general use.

CURRICULUM RESEARCH ASSOCIATES, 330 New York Avenue, Box 848, Huntington, N.Y. 11743

Reading as Thinking Series—Paragraph Comprehension, 1970, two books designed to upgrade reading potential of college-bound students.

DEVELOPMENTAL READING DISTRIBUTORS, 1944 Sheridan, Laramie, Wyo.

Developing Reading Efficiency, grades 6–12.

Maintaining Reading Efficiency, grades 7 to adult.

EDUCATIONAL DEVELOPMENT LABORATORIES, 74 Prospect Street, Huntington, N.Y. 11746.

Fluency-Building Filmstrips, grade levels 1–14, accompanied by *Study Guides* and study cards.

Comprehension Power Development, series of filmstrips, grade levels 3–8, provides perceptual training and recall, association, interpretation, and evaluation.

EDL Study Skills Library, series of kits, grade levels 3–9, teaches interpretation, evaluation, organization, and reference; self-directed; deals with reading in the content areas: science, social studies, and reference skills.

Listen and Read, laboratory, series of tapes and accompanying workbooks, grade levels 7–12 and college, teaches listening, reading, and study skills.

Skimming and Scanning Program, teaches skimming and scanning skills, senior high and college level, thirty lessons in workbook form.

Reading 300, laboratory approach to developmental reading for junior and senior high schools, combines Tach-X training, Controlled Reading, Study Skills Library, EDL's Listening Programs, Word Clues, Skimming and Scanning; programmed for self-instruction and self-correction.

Reading 100, laboratory program for the retarded, provides instruction in reading, writing, listening, speaking.

Word Clues, grades 7–13.

EDUCATIONAL RECORD SALES, 157 Chambers Street, New York, N.Y. 10007

> *Building Verbal Power in the Upper Grades,* five records, grades 5–9, teaches vocabulary and word usage, listening, ability to think, oral comprehension, etc.
>
> *Sound Skills for Upper Grades,* three records, grades 5–9, teaches consonants, vowels, and word analysis skills—syllabication, accentuation, roots, word endings, and compounds.

EDUCATORS PUBLISHING SERVICE, 301 Vassar Street, Cambridge, Mass. 02139

> *The Structure of Words,* workbook, grades 7–10, word recognition and vocabulary.
>
> *A Vocabulary Builder Series,* Books 1–7, workbooks, grades 6–12, word recognition, vocabulary, and comprehension.
>
> *Word Attack Manual,* grades 7–8, word recognition and vocabulary.
>
> *Methods and Habits: A Study Manual,* workbook, grades 9–12, study skills, comprehension, and reading in the content fields.
>
> *Efficient Study Skills,* workbook, grades 7–12, all study skills.
>
> *Wordly Wise,* Books 1 and 2, vocabulary workbooks.

ELDORADO PRESS, Dayton, Va. 22821

> *Aids for the Slow Reader,* difficulty level grades 2–3, stories for older students and adults.

EYE GATE HOUSE, INC., 146–01 Archer Avenue, Jamaica, N.Y. 11435

> *Fundamentals of Vocabulary Building,* series of nine filmstrips, teaches vocabulary skills, junior high level.
>
> *Advanced Reading Skills,* ten filmstrips, develops reading skills (origin and meaning of words, associating facts and ideas, creativity, Shakespeare, oral and written composition), junior high level.

FEARON PUBLISHERS, INC., 2165 Park Boulevard, Palo Alto, Calif. 94306

> *Pacemaker Series,* supplementary readers, difficulty level grade 2, junior high interest level, word recognition and comprehension, includes *The Last of the Mohicans, The Moonstone, Robinson Crusoe,* and *The Jungle Book.*
>
> *Jerry Works in a Service,* supplementary reader, difficulty level grade 2, junior high to senior high interest level. Workbooks with low difficulty but high interest level that develop word-recognition and comprehension skills are *Eddie in School, You and Your World, Time and Telling Time, Measure Up, Plans for Living, Money Makes Sense, Getting a Job, Using Dollars and Sense, To Be a Good American in Your Family, To Be a Good American in Your Community, To Be a Good American in Your State,* and *To Be a Good American in Your Country.*

FIELD EDUCATIONAL PUBLICATIONS, INC., 609 Mission Street, San Francisco, Calif. 94105

Happenings, series of readers, interest level grades 7–12, difficulty level 4.2–4.6.

The Checkered Flag Series, series of readers, interest level grades 6–12, difficulty level 2.4–4.5.

The Americans All Series, series of readers, interest level grades 3–8, difficulty level 4.4.

The Reading-Motivated Series, series of readers, interest level grades 4–10, difficulty level 4.5–5.3.

The Morgan Bay Mysteries, series of readers, interest level grades 4–10, difficulty level 2.3–4.1.

The Deep-Sea Adventure Series, series of readers, interest level grades 3–10, difficulty level 1.8–5.

The Kaleidoscope Readers, interest level grades 7–12, difficulty level 2–9, all skills.

Cyclo-Teacher Learning Aid School Kit, uses programmed instruction; covers language arts, word attack, vocabulary, syntax, pronunciation, spelling, study skills, reference materials, reading and understanding maps; includes two Cyclo-teacher machines, study wheels, instruction and index card, and teacher's manual.

Checkered Flag Classroom Audio-Visual Kits, series of sound filmstrips, records, magnetic tapes, and teacher's guide.

FOLLETT PUBLISHING COMPANY, 1010 West Washington Boulevard, Chicago, Ill. 60607

Success in Language A, workbook, difficulty level grades 4–6 with junior-senior high interest level, all skills.

High-Interest, Easy-to-Read Books, grades 7–12.

Turner-Livingstone Communication Series, grades 9–12, six low-reading-level text-workbooks, useful with disadvantaged or unmotivated teen-age students.

Learning Your Language, One and Two, grades 7–8, six booklets at each level, for slow learners, all skills.

GARRARD PUBLISHING CO., 1607 North Market Street, Champaign, Ill. 61820

Group Sounding Game, grades 3–8, proceeds from the recognition of initial consonants to the syllabication of three-syllable words.

Read and Say Verb Game, grades 3 through high school, improves reading skills and develops habits of correct speech.

Folklore of the World Series, grades 7–8, remedial.

Pleasure Reading Series, grades 7–8, remedial.

GINN AND COMPANY, Statler Building, Boston, Mass. 02117

Reading 360, grades 1–13, basal reading series, teaches all skills.

Ginn Basic Reading Program, grades K–9, teaches all skills.

GLOBE BOOK COMPANY, 175 Fifth Avenue, New York, N.Y. 10010

Adventuring in the City, reader, difficulty level grade 4, junior-senior high interest level, all skills. Other readers with similar characteristics with difficulty level to grade 7 are *American Folklore and Legends, Myths and Folk Tales Around the World, Stories for Teenagers, Successful Reading, 20,000 Leagues Under the Sea, Programmed Reading, Vocational English, Better Reading, Effective Reading, The Odyssey of Homer, Achieving Reading Skills, Journeys in Reading, Journeys in English, Stories for Today's Youth, From Earth to Moon, Word Study for Improved Reading, Pathways in Science, Exploring the Non-Western World,* and *Exploring American History.*

GOOD READING COMMUNICATIONS, INC., 505 Eighth Avenue, New York, N.Y. 10018

Fire Safety Begins at Home, supplementary reader, difficulty level grade 6, adult interest level, teaches comprehension skills. Other readers in the series are *Make Politics Your Business, How to Be More Creative,* and *Act on Fact.*

GROLIER EDUCATIONAL CORPORATION, 845 Third Avenue, New York, N.Y. 10022

Reading Attainment System, series of 120 four-page pamphlets, 3–4 grade reading level, high school-adult interest level, useful for remedial reading, includes reading selections, skill cards, record books, answer keys, and instructor's manual.

C. S. HAMMOND & CO., Maplewood, N.J. 07040

Words Are Important, directed toward word study and vocabulary improvement, series designed for grade levels 7–college.
Building Reading Confidence, workbook, step-by-step developmental reading text for grades 5–7.

HARCOURT, BRACE & WORLD, INC., 757 Third Avenue, New York, N.Y. 15017

Adventures in Literature Series, difficulty level grades 7–12, all skills.
The New World Series, difficulty level grades, 7–10, all skills.
Design for Good Reading, workbooks, levels A, B, C, D, grades 7–9, all skills.
The New Companion Series: Adventures in Literature, grades 7–12, all skills.
Word-Attack: A Way to Better Reading, grades 9–12, remedial.

HARPER & ROW, PUBLISHERS, 2500 Crawford Avenue, Evanston, Ill. 60201

Word Clues, workbook, grades 9–12, all skills.
Language Arts Program, grades 7–8, includes two strands: developmental reading and reading in the subject-matter areas.
Scope/Reading, grades 7–12.

D. C. HEATH & COMPANY, 285 Columbus Avenue, Boston, Mass. 02116

> *Guide to Effective Reading,* workbook, self-teaching, skill development in such areas as flexibility, speed, decoding skills, meaning, vocabulary, dictionary usage, skimming, study skills, organization skills, etc.; college level.
>
> *Toward Reading Comprehension,* workbook, basic reading and study skills, stresses vocabulary, organization, and reading speed; remedial, for college students.
>
> *Reading Caravan Series,* grades 7–8, remedial.
>
> *Teenage Tales,* grades 7–12, remedial.

HOFFMAN INFORMATION SYSTEMS, INC., 2626 South Peck Road, Monrovia, Calif. 91016

> *Hoffman Gold Series,* laboratory, grades 3–9.

HOLT, RINEHART & WINSTON, INC., 383 Madison Avenue, New York, N.Y. 10017

> *Word Wealth Junior,* grades 7–8, word recognition and vocabulary.
>
> *Increasing Reading Efficiency,* workbook, college, word recognition, vocabulary, and comprehension.
>
> *Let's Read Series,* grades, 7–12.
>
> *Holt's Impact Series,* Level 1, junior high, four paperbound anthologies, with recording.
>
> *Realizing Reading Potential,* for unprepared college students, students with a foreign language background, and disadvantaged students, work text, all skills.
>
> *Successful Reading,* for students seeking to expand their reading skills.

HOUGHTON MIFFLIN COMPANY, 110 Tremont Street, Boston, Mass. 02107

> *Riverside Reading Series,* enrichment reader, grades 7–12, all skills.

LAIDLAW BROTHERS, Thatcher and Madison, River Forest, Ill. 60305

> *New Horizons through Reading and Literature,* three books, grades 7–9.
>
> *Study Exercises for Developing Reading Skills,* four books.
>
> *Gateways to Reading Treasures,* grades 7–8, remedial.

LEARN INCORPORATED, 21 East Euclid Avenue, Haddonfield, N.J. 08033

> *Rapid Comprehension through Effective Reading,* teacher's guide, student packs, all skills, developmental, permits each student to progress at his own rate.
>
> *Communication through Effective Reading,* grades 7–9, study books or workbooks and four paperbacks, emphasizes how to learn through efficient reading.

LEARNING MATERIALS, INC., 100 East Ohio Street, Chicago, Ill. 60611

Literature Sampler, laboratory, grades 4–9.

J. B. LIPPINCOTT COMPANY, East Washington Square, Philadelphia, Pa. 19105

Reading for Meaning Series, grades 4–12.

RAND - MᶜNALLY

~~LYONS AND CARNAHAN~~, 407 East Twenty-fifth Street, Chicago, Ill. 60616

A Call to Adventure and *Deeds of Men,* basal readers, grades 7–8, with workbooks.
Phonics We Use, grades 1–8.

THE MACMILLAN COMPANY, 866 Third Avenue, New York, N.Y. 10022

The Macmillan Reading Program: Advanced Skills in Reading, three books, grade 7 and above, all skills.
Decoding for Reading, grade 4 and above, audio-instructional program, two readalong books and sixteen LP records.
Audio-Lingual English: A Self-instructional Language Laboratory Program, six workbooks, teacher's guide, and 230 tapes, beginning through intermediate level.
Macmillan Reading Spectrum, laboratory, grades 2–8.

CHARLES E. MERRILL BOOKS, INC., 1300 Alum Creek Drive, Columbus, Ohio 43216

New Modern Reading Skilltext Series, workbook, grades 7–9, all skills.
Improve Your Reading Ability, workbook, grades 11–12, all skills.

NEW DIMENSIONS IN EDUCATION, INC., 131 Jericho Turnpike, Jericho, N.Y. 11753

The Name of the Game, program for urban secondary students who are reluctant learners, includes anthologies, film, records, activity book, game, and teacher's manual.

NOBLE & NOBLE, PUBLISHERS, INC., 750 Third Avenue, New York, N.Y. 10017

Crossroads, grades 7–10, for slow learners, includes anthologies and records, student activity book.
Operation Alphabet, for illiterate adults, includes films, handwriting book, and such reading materials as *Live and Learn, How We Live, Your Family and Your Job, Write Your Own Letters,* etc.

OXFORD BOOK COMPANY, 387 Park Avenue South, New York, N.Y. 10016

Vocabulary Workshop, workbook, grades 7–12, word recognition and comprehension.
Enriching Your Vocabulary, workbook, grade 9 through college, word recognition and comprehension.
New Building Word Power, workbook for high school students.

Program for Vocabulary Growth, systematic development of vocabulary skills.

Reading Comprehension Workshop, four workbooks for junior-senior high school youngsters.

PERCEPTUAL DEVELOPMENT LABORATORIES, P.O. Box 1911, Big Spring, Tex. 79720; 6767 Southwest Avenue, St. Louis, Mo. 63143

Word Power Development, difficulty level grade 6, junior high-senior high interest level, word recognition, includes films, loops, and manual.

Comprehension Skill Development, workbook, difficulty level grade 6, junior-senior high interest level, all skills, includes films.

Vocabulary Book, workbook, difficulty level grade 8, word recognition and vocabulary, includes films.

Reading and Writing with Phonics, program includes films, loops, tapes, and instructor's manual, useful for remedial work with nonreading young people or adults.

Intermediate Reading, for corrective use on junior-senior high level, includes visual perception, vocabulary development, and controlled reading; comes with films, loops, and instructor's manual; specifics taught are reading in thought units, reading with a purpose, surveying, skimming, scanning, critical reading, reading to speak and listen, and reading for pleasure.

Developmental Reading, junior high level, includes controlled reading, tachistoscopic exercises, and practice reading, covers basically the same areas as the *Intermediate Reading* program.

Advanced Reading, for average readers on the senior high level, developmental, ten filmed lessons of twenty-six articles with tachistoscopic materials.

Reading Improvement, reading series of ten modules, includes filmed articles with tachistoscopic practice materials, junior high level, emphasizes word and comprehension skills.

POLASKI COMPANY, Box 7466, Philadelphia, Pa. 19101

The Reading Line, multidisciplinary reading improvement program for grades 7–12, six books and the Reading Line Lab, emphasizes content-area reading: literature, science, social studies, mathematics, business, vocational-technical.

PRENTICE-HALL, INC., Englewood Cliffs, N.J. 07632

Be a Better Reader Series, grades 4–12, six text-workbooks, developmental.

Be a Better Reader: Foundations, three books, useful for upper elementary grades or in a remedial reading program in junior high or high school, emphasize reading in the content areas.

READER'S DIGEST SERVICES, INC., Pleasantville, N.Y. 10570

Grow in Word Power, workbook, difficulty level grade 9, word recognition and vocabulary.

Help Yourself to Improve Your Reading, grades 7–10, emphasizes rate of comprehension, consists of self-help readers.

New Reading Skill Builder Kits, grades 4–10, forty-six books plus practice pads, all skills, includes eight audio lessons (cassettes, tapes, and records) which cover reading for a purpose, understanding main ideas, making comparisons, skimming, awareness of sequence, understanding humor, understanding author's purpose, interpreting fact versus opinion.

THE READING LABORATORY, INC., 55 Day Street, South Norwalk, Conn. 06854

Skill File, laboratory, grades 6–13.

ST. MARTIN'S PRESS, INC., 175 Fifth Avenue, New York, N.Y. 10010

Passport to Reading Series, five developmental reading anthologies, grades 7–10, difficulty level grades 2–10, for slow and reluctant readers.

SCHOLASTIC MAGAZINES, INC., 904 Sylvan Avenue, Englewood Cliffs, N.J. 07632

The Action Kit, includes three unit books, twenty stories, twelve plays, and record, grade level 2–3.1, emphasizes word attack skills and comprehension skills, for reluctant junior high and senior high school students.

Scoposters and Scope Visuals, for reluctant learners, difficulty level grades 4–6, junior-senior high interest level, deal with reading skills, vocabulary, observation skills, determining sequence, and reasoning skills.

Scholastic Literature Units, each unit consists of three paperback books, grades 6–11.

Scope Skills, exercise books, for disadvantaged, undermotivated, and slow learners, deal with word attack and comprehension.

Reluctant Reader Libraries, supplemental readers, grades 6–12, difficulty level grades 2–7.

Poetry, forty paperback anthologies, a recording, six wall charts, and a teaching guide, grades 7–9.

SCIENCE RESEARCH ASSOCIATES, INC., 259 East Erie Street, Chicago, Ill. 60611

Better Reading Books, supplementary readers, grades 4–12, all skills, difficulty level 5–10.9.

You Can Read Better, supplementary reader, grades 6–10, all skills.

How to Become a Better Reader, supplementary reader, grades 8–12, all skills.

Streamline Your Reading, supplementary reader, grades 9–12, all skills.

Developing Your Vocabulary, workbook, grades 9–12, vocabulary skills.

Words, workbook, grades 7–8, word recognition and vocabulary.

Reading Laboratory, grades 7–12, includes *Power Builders, Listening Skill Builders, Listening-Notetaking Skill Builders, Rate Builders,* and *Student Record Book,* difficulty level 3–14, all skills.

Synchroteach, recorded system in cassettes or reel-to-reel tapes for use with the SRA *Reading Laboratory,* tells students how to use the library.

Reading in High Gear, five workbooks, grades 7–12, for culturally disadvantaged and virtual nonreaders, programmed, all skills.

Reading for Understanding, grades 5–12, three units with four hundred lesson cards each, comprehension skills.

New Rochester Occupational Reading Series, grades 9–12, difficulty level grades 2–5, three books.

How to Improve Your Reading, helps student to adjust rate to the purpose and nature of the material and develops vocabulary skill, grades 7–12.

Studying a Textbook, grades 9–12.

Cracking the Code, intermediate students, designed to develop independence in word attack, includes a reader, a work text, and a teacher's guide.

SCOTT, FORESMAN & COMPANY, 1900 East Lake Avenue, Glenview, Ill. 60025

Sounds of Spoken English, grades 9–10, audio aid.

Reading Skills and Test Book, workbook, grade 8, all skills.

Vocabulary Development Program, four records, grades 9–12, word recognition and vocabulary.

Better Work Habits, emphasizes how to study.

Tactics in Reading I & II, grades 9–11, emphasize reading for understanding and word perception; workbooks, also available as exercise cards.

Basic Reading Skills for Junior High, grades 9–12.

ACE 401, includes paperback books, activity cardboards, skill booklets; covers listening, writing, and English language skills.

SILVER BURDETT COMPANY, Morristown, N.J. 07960

Building Your Language Power, self-directed basic reading program of six books for adults.

STECK-VAUGHN COMPANY, P.O. Box 2028, Austin, Tex. 78767

Reading Essentials Series, includes *Progress in Reading* (grade 7), *Mastery in Reading* (grade 8), and *New Goals in Reading* (remedial for intermediate grades, all skills).

TEACHERS COLLEGE PRESS, 1234 Amsterdam Avenue, New York, N.Y. 10027

Gates-Peardon Reading Exercises, graded reading exercises for grades 1–7.

McCall-Crabbs Standard Test Lessons in Reading, Book E, grades 7–12.

J. WESTON WALCH, PUBLISHER, Portland, Maine 04104

Keys to Your Reading Improvement, junior and senior high, deals with vowels, consonants, syllables, prefixes, suffixes, dictionary, reading speed, skimming, vocabulary development, comprehension of main idea and details, reading in the content areas, etc.

Propaganda, student work-text, teaches recognition of propaganda techniques in writing.

Harr Wagner Publishing Co.

The Reading-Motivated Series, grades 6–9.

Webster Division, McGraw-Hill Book Company, Manchester Road, Manchester, Mo. 63011

Conquests in Reading, grades 4–9, remedial workbook, emphasizes phonetic and structural analysis.

Reading Incentive Series, five books, grades 5–12, difficulty level grades 3–7.

Everyreader Series, supplementary readers for slow learners, low difficulty level (below grade 4), interest level ages 10–18.

Webster Classroom Reading Clinic, kit, useful for corrective and remedial work, grades 4–9, includes ten to twenty copies of *Conquests in Reading, Reading Skill Cards, New Webster Word Wheels, The Everyreader Series, Basic Sight Vocabulary Cards,* and *The Magic World of Dr. Spello.*

New Practice Readers, emphasize comprehension skills, up to grade 8 reading level.

Programmed Reading for Adults, designed to bring individual up to grade 6 level, eight programmed books.

Step Up Your Reading Power, five graded practice readers for young adults, teaches basic comprehension skills.

Vocabulary Improvement, work text.

Reading Shelf I and II, supplementary readers, grades 7–12, difficulty level grades 4–6.

Vocab-70, six-book vocabulary improvement series, grades 9–12.

Reading for Concepts, grades 2–10,, eight books for students with reading difficulties or for reluctant readers.

Word Games, P.O. Box 305, Healdsburg, Calif. 95448

Word Games—Book II, grades 6–8, teaches word and vocabulary skills.

Multiple Spellings
of Certain Consonant Sounds

APPENDIX

/B/: The *b* sound may be spelled as *b* (bad) or as *bb* (rabbit).

/Ch/: The *ch* sound may be spelled as *ch* (church), as *tch* (watch), as *te* (righteous), as *ti* (question), or as *tu* (nature, actual, future).

/D/: The *d* sound in verbs is frequently spelled *ed* (begged, bragged, canned, crammed). Usually the sound is simply spelled by *d* (bed, fed, red) or *dd* (add).

/F/: The *f* sound may be spelled as *f, ff, ph,* or *gh*. In *fad, fan, fat, fed,* and *for,* the /f/ is spelled as *f*. In *effort,* it is a double *ff*. In *cough, draught, laugh, rough, trough, tough,* and *enough,* the /f/ is spelled as *gh*. In *phase, phew, phlegm, phone,* and *phrase,* the /f/ is spelled as *ph*. The *ph* spelling is common in scientific and medical terms of Greek origin (morphine, lymphatic, diaphragm, diphtheria).

/G/: The *g* sound is spelled as *g* (go), *gg* (egg), *gh* (ghost), *gu* (guest), or *gue* (dialogue).

/H/: The *h* sound is spelled as *h* (he) or as *wh* (who).

/J/: The *j* sound is spelled as *g* (magic), *ge* (page), *dg* (judgment), *dge* (judge), *ch* (Greenwich), *di* (soldier), *du* (verdure), and *gg* (exaggerate). The most common spellings are *j, g, ge,* and *dge*. The *j* sound is spelled as *j* in *jam, jet, Jim, job;* it is spelled as *g* in *gem, gene, germ, gist;* it is spelled as *ge* in *age, barge, gauge, hinge;* and it is spelled as *dge* in *badge, bridge, budge, dodge*. The common spellings for /j/ at the ends of words are *ge* and *dge*.

/K/: The *k* sound is spelled as *c* (call), *cc* (account), *ch* (choir), *ck* (back), *cu* (biscuit), *cq* (acquire), *cque* (sacque), *lk* (folk), *k* (rank), *qu* (liquor), and *que* (clique). The *c* spelling of *k* is most common (cat, can, come, came). Before *e* and *i,* the initial *k* sound is spelled with a *k* (keg, kept, kick, kid, kill, kin, king.) *K* is also used in *khaki* and *kangaroo.*

A final *k* sound preceded by a consonant is usually spelled as *k* (ark, ask, balk, bark, bask). When the final *k* sound is preceded by a short vowel sound (back, beck, black, buck, click), it is spelled as *ck.* A final *k* sound preceded by a long vowel has two options—*eke* or *eak, oak* or *oke.* In a medial position, when the *k* sound begins a new syllable it is usually spelled *c.* There are many exceptions: *yokel, market, basket, trinket, blanket, tinkle, twinkle, wrinkle, lambkin,* and *manikin.*

The student should become familiar with the various combinations of *act, ect, ict, oct, uct,* and *inct,* as in the words *fact, compact, elect, reject, depict, evict, concoct, conduct, instruct,* and *instinct.*

In words ending in *et* and *le* (ticket, jacket, pocket, rocket, bucket, tackle, sickle, trickle), the first syllable usually ends in *ck.* The *k* sound is spelled as *ch* in many Greek words (chasm, choir, Christ, chrism, chrome, scheme). It appears also, for example, in *ache, archive, chaos, chorus, school, character, chronology, echo, epoch, lichen, orchid, drachma,* and *troche.*

Finally, the *k* sound may be spelled as *que* (clique, unique, antique, mosque).

/Ks/: The *ks* sound is spelled as *ks, cks, cs, ks,* and *x.* Nouns ending in *k* form their plural by adding an *s;* the third person singular of verbs also ends in s. Usually, the *ks* sound at the end of words is an *x* (fix, mix, six). The *ks* sound may be spelled as *cc* or *cs* before *e* or *i* (access, success, tocsin.)

/L/: The *l* sound is spelled as *l* (land) or *ll* (tell).

/M/: The m sound is spelled as *chm* (drachm), *gm* (paradigm), *lm* (calm), *m* (me), *mb* (climb), *mm* (common), and *mn* (solemn).

/N/: The *n* sound is spelled as *gn* (gnaw), *kn* (knife), *mn* (mnemonic), *n* (no), *nn* (manner), and *pn* (pneumonia).

/Ng/: The *ng* sound is spelled as *nk* (ink), *ng* (long), and ngue (tongue).

/P/: The *p* sound is spelled as *p* (cup) or *pp* (happy).

/R/: The *r* sound is spelled as *r* (run), *rh* (rhythm), *rr* (carry), and *wr* (wrong).

/S/: The *s* sound may be spelled as *c, s, ps* (psychology), *sch* (schism), *ss* (miss), or *sc.* Generally, the *c* or *sc* spelling occurs before *e, i, y.* The most common exceptions to this are *self, silk, system, sell, sent, site.* The final *s* sound may be spelled as *s, se,* or *ce.* Although most words end in *ence* or *ance,* some (dense, sense, expense, dispense, condense, intense, nonsense, defense, pretense, immense, and recompense) end in *ense*.

/Sh/: The *sh* sound may be spelled as *sh* (ship), *ch* (machine), *sch* (schmo), *ce* (ocean), *s* (sure), *ss* (issue), *ti* or *si* (mission), *sci* (conscience), *ci* (special), *psh* (pshaw), *sci* (conscience), and *se* (nauseous). The *ch* spelling occurs commonly in words of French origin (cache, chef, gauche, chute, chandelier, Chicago, champagne, moustache, parachute, chiffon, stanchion, luncheon). The *sh* sound of *ci* is evident in *ferocious, ancient, glacial, spacious*. The *sh* sound of *s* or *ss* occurs in fissure, issue, pressure, sure, sugar, and tissue.

Students should learn the *sh* sound of *ti* and *si*. Numerous words in English are examples of this (compulsion, expulsion, impulsion, propulsion, immersion, submersion, aversion, diversion, ascension, comprehension, controversial, transient, vexatious, contentious, negotiate, partial, venetian, spatial, condition, expedition, ignition, ingratiate).

/T/: The *t* sound is commonly spelled as *t;* in past particles, such as *clapped, dipped,* and *dripped,* it is often spelled *ed*. It also is *ght* (bought), *pt* (ptomaine), *th* (Thomas), and *tt* (button).

/Th/: The *th* sound is spelled as *th* (think) or *the* (breathe).

/V/: The *v* sound is spelled as *f* (of), *ph* (Stephen), *v* (very) or *vv* flivver).

/W/: The *w* sound is spelled as *o* (choir), *u* (quick), or *w* (will).

/Y/: The *y* sound is spelled as *i* (opinion), *j* (hallelujah), or *y* (yes).

/Z/: the *z* sound is spelled as *s, sc* (discern), *ss* (scissors), *z* (zero), *zz* (buzz), and *x*. The students need to become especially familiar with the suffixes, *ize, lyze, ism*. The *z* sound is spelled as *s* in many common words (is, his, was, has, rise, pose, wise, those, poise, these, tease, close, chose, prose, noise, cause, ease, lose, easel, use, cheese, abuse, amuse, propose, please, praise, confuse, dispose, infuse, busy, advise, advertise, exercise, surprise, blouse, accuse, rose, nose, hose).

/Zh/: The *zh* sound often is spelled as *s* or *z* (treasure, pleasure, collision, casual, azure, and seizure). It is also spelled *g* (garage), *si* (division), or *zi* (brazier).

Index